CHILD GUIDANCE

CHILD GUIDANCE

Counsels to Seventh-day Adventist
Parents as Set Forth in the Writings
of Ellen G. White

——— *by* ———
ELLEN G. WHITE

REVIEW AND HERALD® PUBLISHING ASSOCIATION
HAGERSTOWN, MD 21740

Cover design copyright © 2002 by
Review and Herald® Publishing Association
Cover designed by Willie Duke
Paperback cover by Stanborough Press Limited
Cover illustration by Lee Christiansen
Type: 12.5/13.5 Bembo

PRINTED IN U.S.A.

ISBN 0-8280-1569-4 CHL
ISBN 0-8280-1582-1 White
ISBN 1-904685-07-2 Paper

Foreword

As marriage unites two hearts and lives in love, and a new home is created, an early concern of its founders is that the children which grace this new home shall be properly reared. The question of Manoah of old, "How shall we order the child?" is thoughtfully pondered by parents today as they look into the face of the precious and helpless gift entrusted to their care.

The significance of instruction on child guidance is best understood as we note the important place it takes in the Word of God and the frequent and detailed references to the subject in the Spirit of prophecy writings. In her several books, but more particularly in the articles on practical Christian living which appeared from week to week in the various journals of the denomination, Mrs. White set forth a wealth of counsel to parents. In addition to this, she addressed to various families hundreds of personal testimonies in which she dealt specifically with the problems they faced. In these articles and personal testimonies she described the principles which should guide parents, and the procedures they should follow as they were kept before her in vision.

In her later years Mrs. White expressed a desire to bring out a book for Christian parents that would make clear "the mother's duty and influence over her children." In the recently issued *The Adventist Home* and this companion work, that desire is now fulfilled. Only the thoughtful and prayerful perusal of the significant counsels of this volume can reveal the tremendous and far-reaching influence of training the child properly as God has placed the responsibility with parents. The fact that Ellen White was the mother of four boys enabled her to set forth in an understanding and sympathetic manner the instruction imparted to her. Her experience in the practical application of the principles she has set before others begets confidence in the heart of the reader.

All the E. G. White sources, published and unpublished, have been drawn upon in preparing *Child Guidance*. Because the content of this volume has been brought together from a number of sources written over a period of seventy years, there occasionally occurs an unavoidable break in thought and manner of address as the several statements are linked together in their natural subject sequence. The compilers were limited in their work to the selecting and arranging of the various statements and to the supplying of headings.

Child Guidance was prepared under the direction of the Board of Trustees of the Ellen G. White Publications in their offices in Washington, D.C. The work was done in harmony with Mrs. White's instruction to her trustees that they should provide for the printing of compilations from her manuscript and published sources.

The need for this volume is great. Eternal interests are at stake. The detailed counsels on discipline, character building, and physical and spiritual education will be treasured by every thoughtful parent. That this volume, standing by the side of *The Adventist Home, Messages to Young People,* and other of the E. G. White books of counsel to parents and youth, may serve to guide fathers and mothers in their most important work is the sincere wish of the publishers and

The Trustees of the
Ellen G. White Publications

Contents

Section 5
Other Basic Lessons

Section 6
Lessons in Practical Virtues

Section 7
Developing Christian Qualities

To the Reader

It is the privilege of parents to take their children with them to the gates of the City of God, saying, "I have tried to instruct my children to love the Lord, to do His will, and to glorify Him." To such the gate will be thrown open, and parents and children will enter in. But all cannot enter. Some are left outside with their children, whose characters have not been transformed by submission to the will of God. A hand is raised, and the words are spoken, "You have neglected home duties. You have failed to do the work that would have fitted the soul for a home in heaven. You cannot enter." The gates are closed to the children because they have not learned to do the will of God, and to parents because they have neglected the responsibilities resting upon them. Manuscript 31, 1909.

Light has been shining from the Word of God and the testimonies of His Spirit so that none need err in regard to their duty. God requires parents to bring up their children to know Him and to respect His claims; they are to train their little ones, as the younger members of the Lord's family, to have beautiful characters and lovely tempers, that they may be fitted to shine in the heavenly courts. By neglecting their duty and indulging their children in wrong, parents close to them the gates of the city of God. These facts must be pressed home upon parents; they must arouse and take up their long-neglected work. *Testimonies for the Church*, vol. 5, pp. 325, 326.

Ellen G. White

HOME, THE FIRST SCHOOL

CHAPTER 1

Importance of
the Home School

Education Begins at Home. It is in the home that the education of the child is to begin. Here is his first school. Here, with his parents as instructors, he is to learn the lessons that are to guide him throughout life—lessons of respect, obedience, reverence, self-control. The educational influences of the home are a decided power for good or for evil. They are in many respects silent and gradual, but if exerted on the right side, they become a far-reaching power for truth and righteousness. If the child is not instructed aright here, Satan will educate him through agencies of his choosing. How important, then, is the school in the home! *Counsels to Parents, Teachers, and Students*, p. 107.

Here the Foundations Are Laid. Upon all parents there rests the obligation of giving physical, mental, and spiritual instruction. It should be the object of every parent to secure to his child a well-balanced, symmetrical character. This is a work of no small magnitude and importance—a work requiring earnest thought and prayer no less than patient, persevering effort. A right foundation must be laid, a framework, strong and firm, erected; and then day by day the work of building, polishing, perfecting, must go forward. *Ibid.*, pp. 107, 108.

Deny the Child Anything but This Right. Parents, remember that your home is a training school, in which your children are to be prepared for the home above. Deny them anything rather than the education that they should receive in their earliest years. Allow no word of pettishness. Teach your child to be kind and patient.

Teach them to be thoughtful of others. Thus you are preparing them for higher ministry in religious things. Manuscript 102, 1903.

The home should be a preparatory school, where children and youth may be fitted to do service for the Master, preparatory to joining the higher school in the kingdom of God. Manuscript 7, 1899.

Not a Secondary Matter. Let not home education be regarded as a secondary matter. It occupies the first place in all true education. Fathers and mothers have entrusted to them the molding of their children's minds. *Review and Herald,* June 6, 1899.

How startling is the proverb, "As the twig is bent, the tree is inclined." This is to be applied to the training of our children. Parents, will you remember that the education of your children from their earliest years is committed to you as a sacred trust? These young trees are to be tenderly trained, that they may be transplanted to the garden of the Lord. Home education is not by any means to be neglected. Those who neglect it neglect a religious duty. Manuscript 84, 1897.

The Great Scope of Home Education. Home education means much. It is a matter of great scope. Abraham was called the father of the faithful. Among the things that made him a remarkable example of godliness was the strict regard that in his home he paid to the commands of God. He cultivated home religion. He who sees the education given in every home, and who measures the influence of this education, said, "I know him that he will command his children and his household after him, and they shall keep the way of the Lord, to do justice and judgment." Letter 9, 1904.

God commanded the Hebrews to teach their children His requirements, and to make them acquainted with all

His dealings with their people. The home and the school were one. In the place of stranger lips, the loving hearts of the father and mother were to give instruction to their children. Thoughts of God were associated with all the events of daily life in the home dwelling. The mighty works of God in the deliverance of His people were recounted with eloquence and reverential awe. The great truths of God's providence and of the future life were impressed on the young mind. It became acquainted with the true, the good, the beautiful.

By the use of figures and symbols the lessons given were illustrated, and thus more firmly fixed in the memory. Through this animated imagery the child was, almost from infancy, initiated into the mysteries, the wisdom, and the hopes of his fathers, and guided in a way of thinking and feeling and anticipating, that reached beyond things seen and transitory, to the unseen and eternal. *Fundamentals of Christian Education,* p. 95.

It Precedes and Prepares for the Day School. The work of parents precedes that of the teacher. They have a home school—the first grade. If they seek carefully and prayerfully to know and to do their duty, they will prepare their children to enter the second grade—to receive instructions from the teacher. *Review and Herald,* June 13, 1882.

It Fashions Character. The home may be a school where the children are indeed fashioned in character after the similitude of a palace. Manuscript 136, 1898.

Education in the Nazareth Home. Jesus secured His education in the home. His mother was His first human teacher. From her lips, and from the scrolls of the prophets, He learned of heavenly things. He lived in a peasant's home and faithfully and cheerfully acted His part in bearing the household burdens. He who had been the commander of heaven was a willing servant, a loving, obedient son. He learned a trade, and with His own hands worked in the carpenter's shop with Joseph. *The Ministry of Healing,* p. 399.

CHAPTER 2

The First Teachers

Parents to Understand Their Responsibility. The father and the mother should be the first teachers of their children. Manuscript 67, 1903.

Fathers and mothers need to understand their responsibility. The world is full of snares for the feet of the young. Multitudes are attracted by a life of selfish and sensual pleasure. They cannot discern the hidden dangers or the fearful ending of the path that seems to them the way of happiness. Through the indulgence of appetite and passion, their energies are wasted, and millions are ruined for this world and for the world to come. Parents should remember that their children must encounter these temptations. Even before the birth of the child, the preparation should begin that will enable it to fight successfully the battle against evil. *The Ministry of Healing,* p. 371.

More than human wisdom is needed by parents at every step, that they may understand how best to educate their children for a useful, happy life here, and for higher service and greater joy hereafter. *Review and Herald,* Sept. 13, 1881.

Child Training an Important Part of God's Plan. The training of children constitutes an important part of God's plan for demonstrating the power of Christianity. A solemn responsibility rests upon parents so to train their children that when they go forth into the world, they will do good and not evil to those with whom they associate. *Signs of the Times,* Sept. 25, 1901.

Parents should not lightly regard the work of training their children, nor neglect it upon any account. They should employ much time in careful study of the laws which regulate our being. They should make it their first object to become intelligent in regard to the proper manner of dealing with their children, that they may secure to them sound minds in sound bodies. . . .

Many who profess to be followers of Christ are sadly neglectful of home duties; they do not perceive the sacred importance of the trust which God has placed in their hands, to so mold the characters of their children that they will have the moral stamina to resist the many temptations that ensnare the feet of youth. *Pacific Health Journal,* April 1890.

Cooperation With God Is Necessary. Christ did not ask His Father to take the disciples out of the world, but to keep them from the evil in the world, to keep them from yielding to the temptations which they would meet on every hand. This prayer fathers and mothers should offer for their children. But shall they plead with God, and then leave their children to do as they please? God cannot keep children from evil if the parents do not cooperate with Him. Bravely and cheerfully parents should take up their work, carrying it forward with unwearying endeavor. *Review and Herald,* July 9, 1901.

If parents would feel that they are never released from their burden of educating and training their children for God, if they would do their work in faith, cooperating with God by earnest prayer and work, they would be successful in bringing their children to the Saviour. *Signs of the Times,* Apr. 9, 1896.

How One Couple Met Their Responsibilities. An angel from heaven came to instruct Zacharias and Elizabeth as to how they should train and educate their child, so as to work in harmony with God in preparing a messenger to announce the coming of Christ. As parents they were to faithfully cooperate with God in forming such a character in John as would fit him to perform the part God had assigned him as a competent worker.

John was the son of their old age, he was a child of miracle, and the parents might have reasoned that he had a special work to do for the Lord and the Lord would take care of him. But the parents did not thus reason; they moved to a retired place in the country, where their son would not be exposed to the temptations of city life, or induced to depart from the counsel and instruction which they as parents would give him. They acted their part in developing a character in the child that would in every way meet the purpose for which God had designed his life. . . . They sacredly fulfilled their obligation. *Signs of the Times,* Apr. 16, 1896.

Regard Children as a Trust. Parents are to look upon their children as entrusted to them of God to be educated for the family above. Train them in the fear and love of God; for "the fear of the Lord is the beginning of wisdom." *Ibid.*

Those who are loyal to God will represent Him in the home life. They will look upon the training of their children as a sacred work, entrusted to them by the Most High. Manuscript 103, 1902.

Parents to Qualify as Christian Teachers. The work of parents, which means so much, is greatly neglected. Awake, parents, from your spiritual slumber and understand that the very first teaching the child receives is to be given to him by you. You are to teach your little ones to know Christ. This work you must do before Satan sows his seeds in their hearts. Christ calls the children, and they are to be led to Him, educated in habits of industry, neatness, and order. This is the discipline Christ desires them to receive. *Review and Herald,* Oct. 9, 1900.

Sin will lie at the door of parents unless they take themselves in hand and qualify themselves to become wise, safe, Christian teachers. Manuscript 38, 1895.

Unity Between Parents Is Necessary. Husband and wife are to be closely united in their work in the home school. They are to be very tender and very guarded in their speech, lest they open a door of temptation through which Satan will enter to obtain victory after victory. They are to be kind and courteous to each other, acting in such a way that they can respect one another. Each is to help the other to bring into the home a pleasant, wholesome atmosphere. They should not differ in the presence of their children. Christian dignity is ever to be preserved. Letter 272, 1903.

The Special Instructor Given for Every Child. The mother must ever stand preeminent in this work of training the children; while grave and important duties rest upon the father, the mother, by almost constant association with her children, especially during their tender years, must always be their special instructor and companion. *Pacific Health Journal,* January 1890.

An Education Broader Than Mere Instruction. Parents must learn the lesson of implicit obedience to God's voice, which speaks to them out of His Word; and as they learn this lesson, they can teach their children respect and obedience in word and action. This is the work that should be carried on in the home. Those who do it will reach upward themselves, realizing that they must elevate their children. This education means much more than mere instruction. Manuscript 84, 1897.

Haphazard Work Not Acceptable. Haphazard work in the home will not pass the review in the judgment. Faith and works are to be combined by Christian parents. As Abraham commanded his household after him, so they are to command their households after them. The standard which every parent must raise is given: "They shall keep the way of the Lord." Every other way is a path which leads, not to the city of God, but to the ranks of the destroyer. *Review and Herald,* Mar. 30, 1897.

Let Parents Review Work. Will parents review their work in the educating and training of their children, and consider whether they have done their whole duty in hope and faith that these children may be a crown of rejoicing in the day of the Lord Jesus? Have they so labored for the welfare of their children that Jesus can look down from heaven and by the gift of His Spirit sanctify their efforts? Parents, it may be yours to prepare your children for the highest usefulness in this life and to share at last the glory of that which is to come. *Good Health,* January 1880.

CHAPTER 3

When to Begin
the Child's Training

Education Begins With the Infant. The word "education" means more than a course of study at college. Education begins with the infant in its mother's arms. While the mother is molding and fashioning the character of her children, she is educating them. *Good Health,* July 1880.

Parents send their children to school; and when they have done this, they think they have educated them. But education is a matter of greater breadth than many realize: it comprises the whole process by which the child is instructed from babyhood to childhood, from childhood to youth, and from youth to manhood. As soon as a child is capable of forming an idea, his education should begin. *Review and Herald,* June 27, 1899.

Start When the Mind Is Most Impressible. The work of education and training should commence with the babyhood of the child; for then the mind is the most impressible, and the lessons given are remembered. Letter 1, 1877.

Children should virtually be trained in a home school from the cradle to maturity. And, as in the case of any well-regulated school, the teachers themselves gain important knowledge; the mother especially, who is the principal teacher in the home, should there learn the most valuable lessons of her life. *Pacific Health Journal,* May 1890.

It is a parent's duty to speak right words. . . . Day by day parents should learn in the school of Christ lessons from One that loves them. Then the story of God's everlasting love will be repeated in the home school to the tender flock. Thus, before reason is fully developed, children may catch a right spirit from their parents. Manuscript 84, 1897.

Give Study to the Early Training. The early training of children is a subject that all should carefully study. We need to make the education of our children a business, for their salvation depends largely upon the education given them in childhood. Parents and guardians must themselves maintain purity of heart and life, if they desire their children to be pure. As fathers and mothers, we should train and discipline ourselves. Then as teachers in the home, we can train our children, preparing them for the immortal inheritance. *Review and Herald,* Sept. 8, 1904.

Make a Right Beginning. Your children are God's property, bought with a price. Be very particular, O fathers and mothers, to treat them in a Christlike manner. Manuscript 126, 1897.

The youth should be carefully and judiciously trained, for the wrong habits formed in childhood and youth often cling to the entire life experience. May God help us to see the necessity of beginning right. *The Gospel Herald,* Dec. 24, 1902.

Importance of Training the First Child. The first child especially should be trained with great care, for he will educate the rest. Children grow according to the influence of those who surround them. If they are handled by those who are noisy and boisterous, they become noisy and almost unbearable. Manuscript 64, 1899.

The Plant—An Object Lesson in Child Training. The gradual development of the plant from the seed is an object lesson in child training. There is "first the blade, then the ear, after that the full corn in the ear" (Mark

4:28). He who gave this parable created the tiny seed, gave it its vital properties, and ordained the laws that govern its growth. And the truths taught by the parable were made a reality in His own life. He, the Majesty of heaven, the King of glory, became a babe in Bethlehem, and for a time represented the helpless infant in its mother's care. In childhood He spoke and acted as a child, honoring His parents, and carrying out their wishes in helpful ways. But from the first dawning of intelligence He was constantly growing in grace and in a knowledge of truth. *Education,* pp. 106, 107.

SECTION 2

METHODS AND TEXTBOOKS

CHAPTER 4

Methods of Teaching

Parental Government to Be a Study. The work of the parent is seldom done as it should be. . . . Parents, have you studied parental government that you may wisely train the will and impulse of your children? Teach the young tendrils to entwine about God for support. It is not enough that you say, Do this, or, Do that, and then become utterly regardless and forgetful of what you have required, and the children are not careful to do your commands. Prepare the way for your child to obey your commands cheerfully; teach the tendrils to cling to Jesus. . . . Teach them to ask the Lord to help them in the little things of life; to be wide awake to see the small duties which need to be done; to be helpful in the home. If you do not educate them, there is one who will, for Satan is watching his opportunity to sow the seeds of tares in the heart. Manuscript 5, 1896.

Approach Task With Restful Spirit and Loving Heart. My sister, has God entrusted you with the responsibilities of a mother? . . . You need to learn right methods and acquire tact for the training of your little ones, that they may keep the way of the Lord. You need to seek constantly the highest culture of mind and soul, that you may bring to the education and training of your children a restful spirit, a loving heart; that you may imbue them with pure aspirations, and cultivate in them a love for things honest and pure and holy. As a humble child of God, learn in the school of Christ; seek constantly to improve your powers, that you may do the most perfect, thorough work at home, by both precept and example. *Review and Herald,* Sept. 15, 1891.

The Effect of a Quiet, Gentle Manner. Few realize the effect of a mild, firm manner, even in the care of an infant. The fretful, impatient mother or nurse creates peevishness in the child in her arms, whereas a gentle manner tends to quiet the nerves of the little ones. *Pacific Health Journal,* January 1890.

Theories Are to Be Tested. The study of books will be of little benefit, unless the ideas gained can be carried out in practical life. And yet the most valuable suggestions of others should not be adopted without thought and discrimination. They may not be equally adapted to the circumstances of every mother, or to the peculiar disposition or temperament of each child in the family. Let the mother study with care the experience of others, note the difference between their methods and her own, and carefully test those that appear to be of real value. *Signs of the Times,* Feb. 9, 1882.

Methods Employed in Ancient Times. From the earliest times the faithful in Israel had given much attention to the matter of education. The Lord had directed that the children, even from babyhood, should be taught of His goodness and His greatness, especially as revealed in His law and shown in the history of Israel. Through song and prayer, and lessons from the Scriptures, adapted to the opening mind, fathers and mothers were to instruct their children that the law of God is an expression of His character, and that as they received the principles of the law into the heart, the image of God was traced on mind and soul. In both the school and the home, much of the teaching was oral, but the youth also learned to read the Hebrew writings; and the parchment rolls of the Old Testament Scriptures were open to their study. *Fundamentals of Christian Education,* p. 442.

Teach With Kindliness and Affection. It is the special work of fathers and mothers to teach their children with kindliness and affection. They are to show that as parents they are the ones to hold the lines, to govern, and not to be governed by their children. They are to teach that obedience is required of them. Letter 104, 1897.

The restless spirit naturally inclines to mischief; the active mind, if left unoccupied with better things, will give heed to that which Satan may suggest. The children need . . . to be instructed, to be guided in safe paths, to be kept from vice, to be won by kindness, and be confirmed in well-doing. Letter 28, 1890.

Fathers and mothers, you have a solemn work to do. The eternal salvation of your children depends upon your course of action. How will you successfully educate your children? Not by scolding, for it will do no good. Talk to your children as if you had confidence in their intelligence. Deal with them kindly, tenderly, lovingly. Tell them what God would have them do. Tell them that God would have them educated and trained to be laborers together with Him. When you act your part, you can trust the Lord to act His part. Manuscript 33, 1909.

Take Time to Reason. Every mother should take time to reason with her children, to correct their errors, and patiently teach them the right way. *Testimonies for the Church,* vol. 1, p. 390.

Vary the Manner of Instruction. The greatest care should be taken in the education of youth, to vary the manner of instruction so as to call forth the high and noble powers of the mind. . . . There are very few who realize the most essential wants of the mind, and how to direct the developing intellect, the growing thoughts and feelings of youth. *Counsels to Parents, Teachers, and Students,* p. 73.

Teach the First Lessons in the Out-of-doors. Mothers, let the little ones play in the open air; let them listen to the songs of the birds and learn the love of God as expressed in His beautiful works. Teach them simple lessons from the book of nature and the things about them; and as their minds expand, lessons from books may be added and firmly fixed in their memory. *Ibid.,* p. 146.

The cultivation of the soil is good work for children and youth. It brings them into direct contact with nature and nature's God. And that they may have this advantage, there should be, as far as possible, in connection with our schools, large flower gardens and extensive lands for cultivation.

An education amid such surroundings is in accordance with the directions which God has given for the instruction of youth. . . .

To the nervous child or youth, who finds lessons from books exhausting and hard to remember, it will be especially valuable. There is health and happiness for him in the study of nature; and the impressions made will not fade out of his mind, for they will be associated with objects that are continually before his eyes. *Ibid.,* pp. 186, 187.

Make Lessons Short and Interesting. When parents thoroughly act their part, giving them line upon line, and precept upon precept, making their lessons short and interesting, and teaching them not only by precept but by example, the Lord will work with their efforts and make them efficient teachers. *Signs of the Times,* Aug. 13, 1896.

"Say It Simply; Say It Often." Those who instruct children should avoid tedious remarks. Short remarks and to the point will have a happy influence. If much is to be said, make up for briefness by frequency. A few words of interest, now and then, will be more beneficial than to have it all at once. Long speeches burden the small minds of children. Too much talk will lead them to loathe even spiritual instruction, just as overeating burdens the stomach and lessens the appetite, leading even to a loathing of food. The minds of the people may be glutted with too much speechifying. *Testimonies for the Church,* vol. 2, p. 420.

Encourage Independent Thinking. While the children and youth gain a knowledge of facts from teachers and textbooks, let them learn to draw lessons and discern truth for themselves. In their gardening, question them as to what they learn from the care of their plants. As they look on a beautiful landscape, ask them why God clothed the fields and woods with such lovely and varied hues. Why was not all colored a somber brown? When they gather the flowers, lead them to think why He spared us the beauty of these wanderers from Eden. Teach them to notice the evidences everywhere manifest in nature of God's thought for us, the wonderful adaptation of all things to our need and happiness. *Education,* p. 119.

Direct Childhood Activity. Parents need not feel that it is necessary to repress the activity of their children, but they are to understand that it is essential to guide and train them in right and proper directions. These active impulses are like the vines, that, if untrained, will run over every stump and brush, and fasten their tendrils upon low supports. If the vines are not trained about some proper support, they waste their energies to no purpose. So it is with children. Their activities must be trained in the right direction. Give their hands and minds something to do that will advance them in physical and mental attainments. *Signs of the Times,* Aug. 13, 1896.

Teach Helpfulness at an Early Age. Very early the lesson of helpfulness should be taught the child. As soon as strength and reasoning power are sufficiently developed, he should be given duties to perform in the home. He should be encouraged in trying to help father and mother, encouraged to deny and to control himself, to put others' happiness and convenience before his own, to watch for opportunities to cheer and assist brothers and sisters and playmates, and to show kindness to the aged, the sick, and the unfortunate. The more fully the spirit of true ministry pervades the home, the more fully it will be developed in the lives of the children. They will learn to find joy in service and sacrifice for the good of others. *The Ministry of Healing,* p. 401.

Parents, help your children to do the will of God by being faithful in the performance of the duties which really belong to them as members of the family. This will give them a most valuable experience. It will teach them that they are not to center their thoughts upon themselves, to do their own pleasure, or to amuse themselves. Patiently educate them to act their part in the family circle. *Review and Herald,* Nov. 17, 1896.

Fashion Character by Little Attentions, Often Repeated. Parents, in the training of your children, study the lessons that God has given in nature. If you would train a pink, or rose, or lily, how would you do it? Ask the gardener by what process he makes every branch and leaf to flourish so beautifully, and to develop in symmetry and loveliness. He will tell you that it was by no rude touch, no violent effort; for this would only break the delicate stems. It was by little attentions, often repeated. He moistened the soil and protected the growing plants from the fierce blasts and from the scorching sun, and God caused them to flourish and to blossom into loveliness. In dealing with your children, follow the method of the gardener. By gentle touches, by loving ministrations, seek to fashion their characters after the pattern of the character of Christ. *The Desire of Ages,* p. 516.

Give Attention to Little Things. What a great mistake is made in the education of children and youth, in favoring, indulging, and petting them! They become selfish and inefficient, and lack energy in the little things of life. They are not trained to acquire strength of character by the performance of everyday duties, lowly though they may be. . . .

No one is qualified for great and important work, unless he has been faithful in the performance of little duties. It is by degrees that the character is formed, and that the soul is trained to put forth effort and energy proportionate to the task which is to be accomplished. *Testimonies for the Church,* vol. 3, pp. 46, 47.

Talented Children Require Greater Care. We should imprint upon our children's minds that they are not their own, to go, and to come, and dress, and act, as they please. . . . If they possess personal attractions and rare natural abilities, greater care should be taken in their education, lest these endowments be turned to a curse, and are so used as to disqualify them for the sober realities of this life, and, through flattery and vanity and love of display, unfit them for the better life. *Signs of the Times,* Dec. 9, 1875.

Refrain From Undue Notice or Flattery. Give children but little notice. Let them learn to amuse themselves. Do not put them on exhibition before visitors as prodigies of wit or wisdom, but leave them as far as possible to the simplicity of their childhood. One great reason why so many children are forward, bold, and impertinent is they are noticed and praised too much, and their smart, sharp sayings repeated in their hearing. Endeavor not to censure unduly, nor to overwhelm with praise and flattery. Satan will all too soon sow evil seed in their young hearts, and you should not aid him in his work. *Signs of the Times,* Feb. 9, 1882.

Read to Your Children. Fathers and Mothers, obtain all the help you can from the study of our books and publications. Take time to read to your children. . . . Form a home reading circle, in which very member of the family shall lay aside the busy cares of the day, and unite in study. Especially will the youth who have been accustomed to reading novels and cheap storybooks receive benefit from joining in the evening family study. *Counsels to Parents, Teachers, and Students,* p. 138.

"Train," Not "Tell." To parents is committed the great work of educating and training their children for the future, immortal life. Many fathers and mothers seem to think that if they feed and clothe their little ones, and educate them according to the standard of the world, they have done their duty. They are too much occupied with business or pleasure to make the education of their children the study of their lives. They do not seek to train them so that they will employ their talents for the honor of their Redeemer. Solomon did not say, "Tell a child the way he should go, and when he is old, he will not depart from it." But *"Train* up a child in the way he should go, and when he is old, he will not depart from it." *Review and Herald,* June 24, 1890.

Educate for Self-control. No work ever undertaken by man requires greater care and skill than the proper training and education of youth and children. There are no influences so potent as those which surround us in our early years. . . . The nature of man is threefold, and the training enjoined by Solomon comprehends the right development of the physical, intellectual, and moral powers. To perform this work aright, parents and teachers must themselves understand "the way the child should go." This embraces more than a knowledge of books or the learning of the schools. It comprehends the practice of temperance, brotherly kindness, and godliness; the discharge of our duty to ourselves, to our neighbors, and to God.

The training of children must be conducted on a different principle from that which governs the training of irrational animals. The brute has only to be accustomed to submit to its master, but the child must be taught to control himself. The will must be trained to obey the dictates of reason and conscience. A child may be so disciplined as to have, like the beast, no will of its own, his individuality being lost in that of his teacher. Such training is unwise, and its effect disastrous. Children thus educated will be deficient in firmness and decision. They are not taught to act from principle; the reasoning powers are not strengthened by exercise. So far as possible, every child should be trained to self-reliance. By calling into exercise the various faculties, he will learn where he is strongest, and in what he is deficient. A wise instructor will give special attention to the development of the weaker traits, that the child may form a well-balanced harmonious character. *Fundamentals of Christian Education,* p. 57.

CHAPTER 5

The Bible as a Textbook

The Child's First Textbook. The Bible should be the child's first textbook. From this book, parents are to give wise instruction. The Word of God is to be made the rule of the life. From it the children are to learn that God is their father, and from the beautiful lessons of His Word they are to gain a knowledge of His character. Through the inculcation of its principles, they are to learn to do justice and judgment. *Counsels to Parents, Teachers, and Students,* pp. 108, 109.

A Book of Promises, Blessings, and Reproofs. The mother must keep her mind refreshed and stored with the promises and blessings of God's Word, and also the forbidden things, that when her children do wrong she may present as a reproof the words of God, and show them how they are grieving the Spirit of God. Teach them that the approbation and smiles of Jesus are of greater value than the praise or flattery or approval of the most wealthy, the most exalted, the most learned of the earth. Lead them to Jesus Christ day by day, lovingly, tenderly, earnestly. You must not allow anything to come between you and this great work. *Review and Herald,* Apr. 14, 1885.

Its Study Builds Character. The lessons of the Bible have a moral and religious influence on the character, as they are brought into the practical life. Timothy learned and practiced these lessons. The great apostle often drew him out and questioned him in regard to Scripture history. He showed him the necessity of shunning every evil way and told him that blessing would surely attend all who are faithful and true, giving them a faithful, noble

41

manhood. A noble, all-round manhood does not come by chance. It is the result of the molding process of character building in the early years of youth, and a practice of the law of God in the home. God will bless the faithful efforts of all who teach their children as He has directed. Letter 33, 1897.

It Presents God's Love as a Pleasant Theme. The children in every family are to be brought up in the nurture and admonition of the Lord. Evil propensities are to be controlled, evil tempers subdued; and the children are to be instructed that they are the Lord's property, bought with His own precious blood, and that they cannot live a life of pleasure and vanity, have their own will and carry out their own ideas, and yet be numbered among the children of God. The children are to be instructed with kindness and patience. . . . Let the parents teach them of the love of God in such a way that it will be a pleasant theme in the family circle, and let the church take upon them the responsibility of feeding the lambs as well as the sheep of the flock. *Review and Herald,* Oct. 25, 1892.

Its Stories Bring Assurance to the Timid Child. Only the sense of God's presence can banish the fear that, for the timid child, would make life a burden. Let him fix in his memory the promise, "The angel of the Lord encampeth round about them that fear him, and delivereth them." Psalm 34:7. Let him read that wonderful story of Elisha in the mountain city, and, between him and the hosts of armed foemen, a mighty encircling band of heavenly angels. Let him read how to Peter, in prison and condemned to death, God's angel appeared; how, past the armed guards, the massive doors and great iron gateway with their bolts and bars, the angel led God's servant forth in safety. Let him read of that scene on the sea, when to the tempest-tossed soldiers and seamen, worn with labor and watching and long fasting, Paul the prisoner, on his way to trial and execution, spoke those grand words of courage and hope: "Be of good cheer: for there shall be no loss of any man's life among you. . . . For there stood by me this night the angel of God, whose I am, and whom I serve, saying, Fear not, Paul; thou must be brought before Caesar: and, lo, God hath given thee all them that sail with thee." In the faith of this promise Paul assured his companions, "There shall not an hair fall from the head of any of you." So it came to pass. Because there was in that ship one man through whom God could work, the whole shipload of heathen soldiers and sailors was preserved. "They escaped all safe to land." Acts 27:22-24, 34, 44.

These things were not written merely that we might read and wonder, but that the same faith which wrought in God's servants of old might work in us. In no less marked a manner than He wrought then will He work now wherever there are hearts of faith to be channels of His power. *Education,* pp. 255, 256.

Be strong in faith, and teach your children that we are all dependent upon God. Read to them the story of the four Hebrew children, and impress their minds with a realization of the influence for good that was exerted in Daniel's time because of strict adherence to principle. Manuscript 33, 1909.

Make the Bible Lessons Simple. The parents are to teach their children lessons from the Bible, making them so simple that they can readily be understood. Letter 189, 1903.

Teach your children that the commandments of God must become the rule of their life. Circumstances may occur to separate them from the parents and from their homes, but the lessons of instruction given in childhood and youth will be a blessing to them throughout their lifetime. Manuscript 57, 1897.

CHAPTER 6

The Book of Nature

An Unfailing Source of Instruction. Next to the Bible, nature is to be our great lesson book. *Testimonies for the Church,* vol. 6, p. 185.

To the little child, not yet capable of learning from the printed page or of being introduced to the routine of the schoolroom, nature presents an unfailing source of instruction and delight. The heart not yet hardened by contact with evil is quick to recognize the Presence that pervades all created things. The ear as yet undulled by the world's clamor is attentive to the Voice that speaks through nature's utterances. And for those of older years, needing continually its silent reminders of the spiritual and eternal, nature's teaching will be no less a source of pleasure and of instruction. *Education,* p. 100.

Used as a Textbook in Eden. The whole natural world is designed to be an interpreter of the things of God. To Adam and Eve in their Eden home, nature was full of the knowledge of God, teeming with divine instruction. To their attentive ears it was vocal with the voice of wisdom. Wisdom spoke to the eye and was received into the heart, for they communed with God in His created works. *Counsels to Parents, Teachers, and Students,* p. 186.

The book of nature, which spread its living lessons before them, afforded an exhaustless source of instruction and delight. On every leaf of the forest and stone of the mountains, in ever shining star, in earth and sea and sky, God's name was written. With both the animate and the inanimate creation—with leaf and flower and tree, and with every living creature, from the leviathan of the waters to the mote in the sunbeam—the dwellers in Eden held converse, gathering from each the secrets of its life. God's glory in the heavens, the innumerable worlds in their orderly revolutions, "the balancings of the clouds" (Job 37:16), the mysteries of light and sound, of day and night— all were objects of study by the pupils of earth's first school. *Education,* p. 21.

Added Lessons Since the Fall. Although the earth was blighted with the curse, nature was still to be man's lesson book. It could not now represent goodness only; for evil was everywhere present, marring earth and sea and air with its defiling touch. Where once was written only the character of God, the knowledge of good, was now written also the character of Satan, the knowledge of evil. From nature, which now revealed the knowledge of good and evil, man was continually to receive warning as to the result of sin. *Ibid.,* p. 26.

Nature Illustrates Bible Lessons. Many illustrations from nature are used by the Bible writers; and as we observe the things of the natural world, we shall be enabled, under the guiding of the Holy Spirit, more fully to understand the lessons of God's Word. *Ibid.,* p. 120.

In the natural world God has placed in the hands of the children of men the key to unlock the treasure house of His Word. The unseen is illustrated by the seen; divine wisdom, eternal truth, infinite grace, are understood by the things that God has made. *Counsels to Parents, Teachers, and Students,* pp. 187, 188.

Children should be encouraged to search out in nature the objects that illustrate Bible teachings, and to trace in the Bible the similitudes drawn from nature. They should search out, both in nature and in Holy Writ, every object representing Christ, and those also that He employed in illustrating truth. Thus may they learn to see Him in tree and vine, in lily and rose, in sun and star. They may learn to hear His voice in the song of birds, in the sighing of the trees, in the rolling thunder, and in the music of the sea. And every object in nature will repeat to them His precious lessons.

To those who thus acquaint themselves with Christ the earth will nevermore be a lonely and desolate place. It will be their Father's house, filled with the presence of Him who once dwelt among men. *Education,* p. 120.

The Bible Interprets Nature's Mysteries. The child, as he comes in contact with nature, will see cause for perplexity. He cannot but recognize the working of antagonistic forces. It is here that nature needs an interpreter. Looking upon the evil manifest even in the natural world, all have the same sorrowful lesson to learn—"An enemy hath done this." Matthew 13:28.

Only to the light that shines from Calvary can nature's teaching be read aright. Through the story of Bethlehem and the cross let it be shown how good is to conquer evil, and how every blessing that comes to us is a gift of redemption.

In brier and thorn, in thistle and tare, is represented the evil that blights and mars. In singing bird and opening blossom, in rain and sunshine, in summer breeze and gentle dew, in ten thousand objects in nature, from the oak of the forest to the violet that blossoms at its root, is seen the love that restores. And nature still speaks to us of God's goodness. *Ibid.,* p. 101.

Lessons in the Ideal Schoolroom. As the dwellers in Eden learned from nature's pages, as Moses discerned God's handwriting on the Arabian plains and mountains, and the Child Jesus on the hillsides of Nazareth, so the children of today may learn of Him. The unseen is illustrated by the seen. *Ibid., p.* 100.

Cultivate a Love of Nature. Let the mother . . . find time to cultivate in herself and her children a love for the beautiful things of nature. Let her point them to the glories spread out in the heavens, to the thousand forms of beauty that adorn the earth, and then tell them of Him who made them all. Thus she can lead their young minds up to the Creator, and awaken in their hearts reverence and love for the Giver of every blessing. The fields and hills—nature's audience chamber—should be the schoolroom for little children. Here treasures should be their textbook. The lessons thus imprinted upon their minds will not be soon forgotten. *Review and Herald,* January 10, 1882.

Parents may do much to connect their children with God by encouraging them to love the things of nature which He has given them, and to recognize the hand of the Giver in all they receive. The soil of the heart may thus early be prepared for casting in the precious seeds of truth, which in due time will spring up and bear a rich harvest. *Signs of the Times,* Dec. 6, 1877.

Join Birds in Songs of Praise. The little children should come especially close to nature. Instead of putting fashion's shackles upon them, let them be free like the lambs, to play in the sweet, fresh sunlight. Point them to shrubs and flowers, the lowly grass and the lofty trees, and let them become familiar with their beautiful, varied, and delicate forms. Teach them to see the wisdom and love of God in His created works; and as their hearts swell with joy and grateful love, let them join the birds in their songs of praise.

Educate the children and youth to consider the works

of the great Master Artist, and to imitate the attractive graces of nature in their character building. As the love of God wins their hearts, let them bring into their lives the beauty of holiness. So shall they use their capabilities to bless others and to honor God. *Counsels to Parents, Teachers, and Students,* p. 188.

Point From Nature to Nature's God. The children need to be given lessons that will nurture in them courage to resist evil. Point them from nature to nature's God, and they will thus become acquainted with the Creator. How can I best teach my children to serve and glorify God? should be the question occupying the minds of parents. If all heaven is interested in the welfare of the human race, should not we be diligent to do all in our power for the welfare of our children? Manuscript 29, 1886.

Nature Study Strengthens the Mind. The glory of God is displayed in His handiwork. Here are mysteries that the mind will become strong in searching out. Minds that have been amused and abused by reading fiction may in nature have an open book, and read truth in the works of God around them. All may find themes for study in the simple leaf of the forest tree, the spires of grass covering the earth with their green velvet carpet, the plants and flowers, the stately trees of the forest, the lofty mountains, the granite rocks, the restless ocean, the precious gems of light studding the heavens to make the night beautiful, the exhaustless riches of the sunlight, the solemn glories of the moon, the winter's cold, the summer's heat, the changing, recurring seasons, in perfect order and harmony, controlled by infinite power; here are subjects which call for deep thought, for the stretch of the imagination.

If the frivolous and pleasure-seeking will allow their minds to dwell upon the real and true, the heart cannot but be filled with reverence, and they will adore the God of nature. The contemplation and study of God's character as revealed in His created works will open a field of thought that will draw the mind away from low, debasing, enervating amusements. The knowledge of God's works and ways we can only begin to obtain in this world; the study will be continued throughout eternity. God has provided for man subjects of thought which will bring into activity every faculty of the mind. We may read the character of the Creator in the heavens above and the earth beneath, filling the heart with gratitude and thanksgiving. Every nerve and sense will respond to the expressions of God's love in His marvelous works. *Testimonies for the Church,* vol. 4, p. 581.

Nature and the Bible Were Jesus' Textbooks. His [Jesus'] education was gained from Heaven-appointed sources, from useful work, from the study of the Scriptures, from nature, and from the experiences of life—God's lesson books, full of instruction to all who bring to them the willing hand, the seeing eye, and the understanding heart. *The Ministry of Healing,* p. 400.

His intimate acquaintance with the Scriptures shows how diligently His early years were given to the study of God's Word. And spread out before Him was the great library of God's created works. He who had made all things studied the lessons which His own hand had written in earth and sea and sky. Apart from the unholy ways of the world, He gathered stores of scientific knowledge from nature. He studied the life of plants and animals, and the life of man. From His earliest years He was possessed of one purpose; He lived to bless others. For this He found resources in nature; new ideas of ways and means flashed into His mind as He studied plant life and animal life. . . .

Thus to Jesus the significance of the Word and the works of God was unfolded, as He was trying to understand the reason of things. Heavenly beings were His attendants, and the culture of holy thoughts and communings was His. From the first dawning of intelligence He was constantly growing in spiritual grace and knowledge of truth.

Every child may gain knowledge as Jesus did. As we try to become acquainted with our heavenly Father through His Word, angels will draw near, our minds will be strengthened, our characters will be elevated and refined. *The Desire of Ages,* pp. 70, 71.

Later Used by Him in His Teaching. The great Teacher brought His hearers in contact with nature, that they might listen to the voice which speaks in all created things; and as their hearts became tender and their minds receptive, He helped them to interpret the spiritual teaching of the scenes upon which their eyes rested. The parables, by means of which He loved to teach lessons of truth, show how open His spirit was to the influences of nature, and how He delighted to gather the spiritual teaching from the surroundings of daily life.

The birds of the air, the lilies of the field, the sower and the seed, the shepherd and the sheep—with these Christ illustrated immortal truth. He drew illustrations also from the events of life, facts of experience familiar to the hearers—the leaven, the hid treasure, the pearl, the fishing net, the lost coin, the prodigal son, the houses on the rock and the sand. In His lessons there was something to interest every mind, to appeal to every heart. Thus the daily task, instead of being a mere round of toil, bereft of higher thoughts, was brightened and uplifted by constant reminders of the spiritual and the unseen.

So we should teach. Let the children learn to see in nature an expression of the love and the wisdom of God; let the thought of Him be linked with bird and flower and tree; let all things seen become to them the interpreters of the unseen, and all the events of life be a means of divine teaching.

As they learn thus to study the lessons in all created things, and in all life's experiences, show that the same laws which govern the things of nature and the events of life are to control us; that they are given for our good; and that only in obedience to them can we find true happiness and success. *Education,* pp. 102, 103.

CHAPTER 7

Practical Lessons From Nature's Book

God's Voice in His Handiwork. Wherever we turn, we hear the voice of God and behold His handiwork. From the solemn roll of the deep-toned thunder and old ocean's cease-less roar, to the glad songs that make the forests vocal with melody, nature's ten thousand voices speak His praise. In earth and sea and sky, with their marvelous tint and color, varying in gorgeous contrast or blended in harmony, we behold His glory. The everlasting hills tell of His power. The trees that wave their green banners in the sunlight, and the flowers in their delicate beauty, point to their Creator. The living green that carpets the brown earth tells of God's care for the humblest of His creatures. The caves of the sea and the depths of the earth reveal His treasures. He who placed the pearls in the ocean and the amethyst and chrysolite among the rocks is a lover of the beautiful. The sun rising in the heavens is a representative of Him who is the life and light of all that He has made. All the brightness and beauty that adorn the earth and light up the heavens speak of God.

Shall we, then, in the enjoyment of His gifts, forget the Giver? Let them rather lead us to contemplate His goodness and His love. Let all that is beautiful in our earthly home remind us of the crystal river and green fields, the waving trees and living fountains, the shining city and the and the white-robed singers, of our heavenly home—that world of beauty which no artist can picture, no mortal tongue describe. "Eye hath not seen, nor ear heard, neither have entered into the heart of man, the things which God hath prepared for them that love him." 1 Corinthians 2:9. *Counsels to Parents, Teachers, and Students,* pp. 54, 55.

Of God's Love and Character. Mothers . . . should not be so engrossed with the artificial and burdened with care that they cannot have time to educate their children from God's great book of nature, impressing their young minds with the beauties of opening buds and flowers. The lofty trees, the lovely birds caroling forth their happy songs to their Creator, speak to their senses of the goodness, mercy, and benevolence of God. Every leaf and flower with their varied tints, perfuming the air, teach them that God is love. All that is good and lovely and beautiful in this world speaks to them of the love of our heavenly Father. The character of God they may discern in His created works. *Signs of the Times,* Aug. 5, 1875.

Of God's Perfection. As the things of nature show their appreciation of the Master Worker by doing their best to beautify the earth and to represent God's perfection, so human beings should strive in their sphere to represent God's perfection, allowing Him to work out through them His purposes of justice, mercy, and goodness. Letter 47, 1903.

Of the Creator and the Sabbath. Who gives us the sunshine which makes the earth bring forth and bear? and who the fruitful showers? Who has given us the heavens above the sun and stars in the heavens? Who gave you your reason, and who keeps watch over you from day to day? . . . Every time we look at the world, we are reminded of the mighty hand of God which called it into existence. The canopy over our head, and the earth beneath covered with a carpet of green, call to remembrance the power of God and also His loving-kindness. He might have made the grass brown or black, but God is a lover of the beautiful, and therefore He has given us beautiful things upon which to look. Who could paint upon the flowers the delicate tint with which God has clothed them? . . .

We can have no better lesson book than nature. "Consider the lilies of the field; . . . they toil not, neither do they spin: and yet I say unto you, That even Solomon in all his glory was not arrayed like one of these." Let the minds of our children be carried up to God. It is for this that He has given us the seventh day and left it as a memorial of His created works. Manuscript 16, 1895.

Obedience to Law. The same power that upholds nature is working also in man. The same great laws that guide alike the star and the atom control human life. The laws that govern the heart's action, regulating the flow of the current of life to the body, are the laws of the mighty Intelligence that has the jurisdiction of the soul. From Him all life proceeds. Only in harmony with Him can be found its true sphere of action. For all the objects of His creation the condition is the same— a life sustained by receiving the life of God, a life exercised in harmony with the Creator's will. To transgress His law— physical, mental, or moral—is to place one's self out of harmony with the universe, to introduce discord, anarchy, ruin.

To him who learns thus to interpret its teachings, all nature becomes illuminated; the world is a lesson book, life a school. The unity of man with nature and with God, the universal dominion of law, the results of transgression, cannot fail of impressing the mind and molding the character. These are lessons that our children need to learn. *Education,* pp. 99, 100.

Other Lessons From Nature's Laws. In the cultivation of the soil the thoughtful worker will find that treasures little dreamed of are opening up before him. No one can succeed in agriculture or gardening without attention to the laws involved. The special needs of every variety of plant must be studied. Different varieties require different soil and cultivation, and compliance with the laws governing each is the condition of success.

The attention required in transplanting, that not even a root fiber shall be crowded or misplaced, the care of the young plants, the pruning and watering, the shielding from frost at night and sun by day, keeping out weeds, disease, and insect pests, the training and arranging, not only teach important lessons concerning the development of character, but the work itself is a means of development. In cultivating carefulness, patience, attention to detail, obedience to law, it imparts a most essential training.

The constant contact with the mystery of life and the loveliness of nature, as well as the tenderness called forth in ministering to these beautiful objects of God's creation, tends to quicken the mind and refine and elevate the character; and the lessons taught prepare the worker to deal more successfully with other minds. *Ibid.,* pp. 111, 112.

Lessons From Seed Sowing. The parable of the sower and the seed conveys a deep spiritual lesson. The seed represents the principles sown in the heart, and its growth the development of character. Make the teaching on this point practical. The children can prepare the soil and sow the seed; and as they work, the parent or teacher can explain to them the garden of the heart, with the good or bad seed sown there; and that as the garden must be prepared for the natural seed, so the heart must be prepared for the seed of truth. As the plant grows, the correspondence between the natural and the spiritual sowing can be continued. *Counsels to Parents, Teachers, and Students,* p. 142.

As the seed is cast into the ground, they can teach the lesson of Christ's death; and as the blade springs up, the truth of the resurrection. *Education,* p. 111.

The Garden of the Heart Needs Cultivating. From the tilling of the soil, lessons may constantly be learned. No one settles upon a raw piece of land with the expectation that it will at once yield a harvest. Diligent, persevering labor must be put forth in the preparation of the soil, the sowing of the seed, and the culture of the crop. So it must be in the spiritual sowing. The garden of the heart must be cultivated. The soil must be broken up by repentance. The evil growths that choke the good grain must be uprooted. As soil once overgrown with thorns can be reclaimed only by diligent labor, so the evil tendencies of the heart can be overcome only by earnest effort in the name and strength of Christ. *Ibid.*

Growth in Grace. Tell your children about the miracle-working power of God. As they study the great lesson book of nature, God will impress their minds. The farmer plows his land and sows his seed, but he cannot make the seed grow. He must depend on God to do that which no human power can do. The Lord puts His vital power into the seed, causing it to spring forth into life. Under His care the germ of life breaks through the hard crust encasing it, and springs up to bear fruit. First appears the blade, then the ear, then the full corn in the ear. As the children are told of the work that God does for the seed, they learn the secret of growth in grace. *Counsels to Parents, Teachers, and Students,* pp. 124, 125.

Rising Above Surroundings. In America we have the fresh water lilies. These beautiful lilies come up pure, spotless, perfect, without a single mar. They come up through a mass of debris. I said to my son, "I want you to make an effort to get me the stem of that lily as near the root as possible. I want you to understand something about it."

He drew up a handful of lilies, and I looked at them. They were all full of open channels, and the stems were gathering the properties from the pure sands beneath, and these were being developed into the pure and spotless lily. It refused all the debris. It refused every unsightly thing, but there it was developed in its purity.

Now this is exactly the way that we are to educate our youth in this world. Let their minds and hearts be instructed who God is, who Jesus Christ is, and the sacrifice that He has made in our behalf. Let them draw the purity, the virtue, the grace, the courtesy, the love, the forbearance; let them draw it from the Source of all power. Manuscript 43a, 1894.

Lessons in Trust and Perseverance. "Ask now the beasts, and they shall teach thee; and the fowls of the air, and they shall tell thee: . . . and the fishes of the sea shall declare unto thee." "Go to the ant; . . . consider her ways." "Behold the birds." "Consider the ravens." Job 12:7, 8; Proverbs 6:6; Matthew 6:26, American Standard Version; Luke 12:24.

We are not merely to tell the child about these creatures of God's. The animals themselves are to be his teachers. The ants teach lessons of patient industry, of perseverance in surmounting obstacles, of providence for the future. And the birds are teachers of the sweet lesson of trust. Our heavenly Father provides for them; but they must gather the food, they must build their nests and rear their young. Every moment they are exposed to enemies that seek to destroy them. Yet how cheerily they go about their work! How full of joy are their little songs!

How beautiful the psalmist's description of God's care for the creatures of the wood—

"The high hills are a refuge for the wild goats;
And the rocks for the conies." Psalm 104:18.

He sends the springs to run among the hills, where the birds have their habitation and "sing among the branches" Psalm 104:12. All the creatures of the woods and hills are a part of His great household. He opens His hand and satisfies "the desire of every living thing" [Psalm 145:16.] *Education,* pp. 117, 118.

The Insects Teach Industry. The industrious bee gives to men of intelligence an example that they would do well to imitate. These insects observe perfect order, and no idler is allowed in the hive. They execute their appointed work with an intelligence and activity that are beyond our comprehension. . . . The wise man calls our attention to the small things of the earth: "Go to the ant, thou sluggard; consider her ways, and be wise; which having no guile, overseer, or ruler, provideth her meat in the summer, and gathereth her food in the harvest." "The ants are a people not strong, yet they prepare their meat in the summer." We may learn from these little teachers a lesson of faithfulness. Should we improve with the same diligence the faculties which an all-wise Creator has bestowed upon us, how greatly would our capacities for usefulness be increased. God's eye is upon the smallest of His creatures; does He not, then, regard man formed in His image, and require of him corresponding returns for all the advantages He has given him? *Testimonies for the Church,* vol. 4, pp. 455, 456.

SECTION 3

TEACHERS ADEQUATELY TRAINED

CHAPTER 8

Preparation Is Needed

The Mother's Preparation Strangely Neglected. The child's first teacher is the mother. During the period of greatest susceptibility and most rapid development his education is to a great degree in her hands. To her first is given opportunity to mold the character for good or for evil. She should understand the value of her opportunity and, above every other teacher, should be qualified to use it to the best account. Yet there is no other to whose training so little thought is given. The one whose influence in education is most potent and far-reaching is the one for whose assistance there is the least systematic effort. *Education,* p. 275.

Careful, Thorough Preparation Urgent. Those to whom the care of the little child is committed are too often ignorant of its physical needs; they know little of the laws of health or the principles of development. Nor are they better fitted to care for its mental and spiritual growth. They may be qualified to conduct business or to shine in society; they may have made creditable attainments in literature and science; but of the training of a child they have little knowledge. . . .

Upon fathers as well as mothers rests a responsibility for the child's earlier as well as its later training, and for both parents the demand for careful and thorough preparation is most urgent. Before taking upon themselves the possibilities of fatherhood and motherhood, men and women should become acquainted with the laws of physical development—with physiology and hygiene, with the bearing of prenatal influences, with the laws of heredity, sanitation, dress, exercise, and the treatment of disease; they should also understand the laws of mental development and moral training. . . .

Never will education accomplish all that it might and should accomplish until the importance of the parents' work is fully recognized, and they receive a training for its sacred responsibilities. *Ibid.*, pp. 275, 276.

Parents should study the laws of nature. They should become acquainted with the organism of the human body. They need to understand the functions of the various organs, and their relation and dependence. They should study the relation of the mental to the physical powers, and the conditions required for the healthy action of each. To assume the responsibilities of parenthood without such preparation is a sin. *The Ministry of Healing,* p. 380.

"Who Is Sufficient?" Parents may well inquire, "Who is sufficient for these things?" God alone is their sufficiency, and if they leave Him out of the question, seeking not His aid and counsel, hopeless indeed is their task. But by prayer, by study of the Bible, and by earnest zeal on their part, they may succeed nobly in this important duty, and be repaid a hundredfold for all their time and care. . . . The source of wisdom is open, from which they may draw all necessary knowledge in this direction. *Testimonies for the Church,* vol. 4, p. 198.

At times the heart may be ready to faint; but a living sense of the dangers threatening the present and future happiness of their loved ones should lead Christian parents to seek more earnestly for help from the source of strength and wisdom. It should make them more circumspect, more decided, more calm yet firm, while they watch for these souls, as they that must give account. *Review and Herald,* p. Aug. 30, 1881.

Child Training Calls for Understanding God's Will. Parents are without excuse if they fail to obtain a clear understanding of God's will, that they may obey the laws of His kingdom. Only thus can they lead their children to heaven. My brethren and sisters, it is your duty to understand God's requirements. How can you educate your children in the things of God unless you first know yourselves what is right and what is wrong, unless you realize that obedience means eternal life and disobedience eternal death?

We must make it our lifework to understand the will of God. Only as we do this can we train our children aright. Manuscript 103, 1902.

God's Manual With Full Instructions. Parents cannot properly fulfill their responsibilities unless they take the Word of God as the rule of their life, unless they realize that they are to so educate and fashion the character of each dear human treasure that it may at last lay hold of eternal life. Manuscript 84, 1897.

The Bible, a volume rich in instruction, should be their textbook. If they train their children according to its precepts, they not only set their young feet in the right path, but they educate themselves in their most holy duties. *Testimonies for the Church,* vol. 4, p. 198.

The work of parents is an important, a solemn, work; the duties devolving upon them are great. But if they will study the Word of God carefully, they will find in it full instructions and many precious promises made to them on condition that they perform their work faithfully and well. *Signs of the Times,* Apr. 8, 1886.

Rules for Parents and Children. God has given rules for the guidance of parents and children. These rules are to be strictly obeyed. The children are not to be indulged and allowed to think that they can follow their own desires without asking the advice of their parents. . . .

From the rules that God has given for the guidance of parents and children, there can be no sinless swerving. God expects parents to give their children a training that is in accordance with the principles of His Word. Faith and works are to be combined. Everything that is done in the home life and in the school life must be done decently and in order. Letter 9, 1904.

To the Law and the Testimony. The work of education in the home, if it is to accomplish all that God designs it shall, demands that parents be diligent students of the Scriptures. They must be learners of the great Teacher. Day by day the law of love and kindness must be upon their lips. Their lives must reveal the grace and truth that was seen in the life of their Example. Then a sanctified love will bind the hearts of parents and children together, and the youth will grow up established in the faith and rooted and grounded in the love of God.

When the will and ways of God become the will and ways of Seventh-day Adventist parents, their children will grow up to love and honor and obey God. Satan will not be able to gain control of their minds, for they have been educated to regard the Word of the Lord as supreme, and they will test every experience that comes to them by the law and the testimony. Letter 356, 1907.

If Negligent, Redeem the Time. Parents should be studying the Word of God for themselves and for their families. But instead of this, many children are left to grow up untaught, unmanaged, unrestrained. Parents should now do everything in their power to redeem their neglect and place their children where they will be under the very best influences. Manuscript 76, 1905.

Then search the Scriptures, parents. Be not only hearers; be doers of the Word. Meet God's standard in the education of your children. Manuscript 57, 1897.

The Guiding Rule: What Saith the Lord? The work of all parents is to train their children in the way of the Lord. This is not a matter that can be trifled with, or set aside, without incurring the displeasure of God. We are not called upon to decide what course others shall pursue, or how we may get on the most easily, but, What saith the Lord? Neither parents nor children can have peace or happiness or rest of spirit in any false path. But when the fear of God reigns in the heart, combined with love for Jesus, peace and joy will be felt.

Parents, spread out the Word of God before Him who reads your heart and every secret thing, and inquire, What saith the Scripture? This must be the rule of your life. Those who have a love for souls will not be silent when they see their danger. We are assured that nothing but the truth of God can make parents savingly wise in dealing with human minds, and keep them so. *Review and Herald,* Mar. 30, 1897.

Individual Preparation. If there is any post of duty above another which requires a cultivation of the mind, where the intellectual and physical powers require healthy tone and vigor, it is the training of children. *Pacific Health Journal,* June 1890.

In view of the individual responsibility of mothers, every woman should develop a well-balanced mind and pure character, reflecting only the true, the good, and the beautiful. The wife and mother may bind her husband and children to her heart by an unremitting love, shown in gentle words and courteous deportment, which, as a rule, will be copied by her children. *Pacific Health Journal,* September 1890.

Mother, This Is Your Sacred Work. My sister, Christ has committed to you the sacred work of teaching His commandments to your children. In order to be fitted for this work, you must yourself live in obedience to all His precepts. Cultivate a watchful observance of every word and action. Guard most diligently your words. Overcome all hastiness of temper; for impatience, if manifested, will help the adversary to make the home life disagreeable and unpleasant for your children. Letter 47a, 1902.

Work in Partnership With the Divine. Mothers, let your hearts be open to receive the instruction of God, ever bearing in mind the fact that you must act your part in conforming to the will of God. You must place yourself in the light and seek from God wisdom, that you may know how to act, that you may acknowledge God as the chief worker, and realize that you are a laborer together with Him. Let your heart be drawn out in contemplation of heavenly things. Exercise your God-given talents in doing the duties which God has enjoined upon you as a mother, and work in partnership with divine agencies. Labor intelligently, and, "whether therefore ye eat, or drink, or whatsoever ye do, do all to the glory of God." *Signs of the Times,* Apr. 9, 1896.

The mother should surrender herself and her children to the care of the compassionate Redeemer. Earnestly, patiently, courageously, she should seek to improve her own abilities, that she may use aright the highest powers of the mind in the training of her children. She should make it her highest aim to give her child an education which will receive the approval of God. As she takes up her work understandingly, she will receive power to perform her part. *Signs of the Times,* Apr. 3, 1901.

The mother should feel her need of the Holy Spirit's guidance, that she may herself have a genuine experience in submission to the way and will of the Lord. Then, through the grace of Christ, she can be a wise, gentle, loving teacher of her children. *Review and Herald,* May 10, 1898.

If You Have Begun Wrong. To parents who have begun their training wrong, I would say, Do not despair. You need to be soundly converted to God. You need the true spirit of obedience to the Word of God. You must make decided reforms in your own customs and practices, conforming your life to the saving principles of the law of God. When you do this, you will have the righteousness of Christ which pervades that law, because you love God and recognize His law as a transcript of His character. True faith in the merits of Christ is not fancy. It is of the highest importance that you bring the attributes of Christ into your own life and character, and educate and train your children with persevering effort to be obedient to the commandments of God. A "Thus saith the Lord" should guide you in all your plans of education. . . .

Let there be a deep and thorough repentance before God. Commence the year . . . by earnestly seeking God for grace, for spiritual discernment to discover the defects in the work of the past. Repent before God for your neglected work as home missionaries. Manuscript 12, 1898.

This is your day of trust, your day of responsibility and opportunity. Soon will come your day of reckoning. Take up your work with earnest prayer and faithful endeavor. Teach your children that it is their privilege to receive every day the baptism of the Holy Spirit. Let Christ find you His helping hand to carry out His purposes. By prayer you may gain an experience that will make your ministry for your children a perfect success. *Counsels to Parents, Teachers, and Students,* p. 131.

CHAPTER 9

A Call for Self-improvement

Continual Advancement Necessary. The mother's work is such that it demands continual advancement in her own life, in order that she may lead her children to higher and still higher attainments. But Satan lays his plans to secure the souls of both parents and children. Mothers are drawn away from the duties of home and the careful training of their little ones, to the service of self and the world. *Christian Temperance and Bible Hygiene,* p. 60.

For the sake of their children, if for no other reason, mothers should cultivate their intellects, for they bear a greater responsibility in their work than does the king upon his throne. Few mothers feel the weight of the trust that is given them, or realize the efficiency they can attain for their peculiar work through patient, thorough effort in self-culture.

And first, the mother needs to strictly discipline and cultivate all the faculties and affections of the mind and heart, that she may not have a distorted or one-sided character and leave the marks of her deficiency or eccentricity upon her offspring. Many mothers need [to] be roused to see the positive necessity of a change in their purposes and characters in order to perform acceptably the duties they have voluntarily assumed by entering upon the married life. The channel of woman's usefulness can be widened and her influence extended to an almost unlimited degree if she will give proper attention to these matters, which affect the destiny of the human race. *Pacific Health Journal,* May 1890.

Constantly Increase in Wisdom and Efficiency. Mothers, above all others, should accustom themselves to thought and investigation if they would increase in wisdom and efficiency. Those who persevere in this course will soon perceive that they are acquiring the faculty in which they thought themselves deficient; they are learning to form aright the characters of their children. The result of the labor and thought given to this work will be seen in their obedience, their simplicity, their modesty and purity. This result will richly repay all the effort made.

God would have mothers seek constantly to improve both the mind and the heart. They should feel that they have a work to do for Him in the education and training of their children, and the more perfectly they can improve their own powers, the more efficient will they become in their work as parents. *Signs of the Times,* Feb. 9, 1882.

Parents Should Grow Intellectually and Morally. It is the duty of mothers to cultivate their minds and keep their hearts pure. They should improve every means within their reach for their intellectual and moral improvement, that they may be qualified to improve the minds of their children. *Testimonies for the Church,* vol. 3, p. 147.

Parents should be constant learners in the school of Christ. They need freshness and power, that with the simplicity of Christ they may teach the younger members of God's family the knowledge of His will. *Signs of the Times,* Sept. 25, 1901.

The Amazing Power of Christian Culture. Parents have not yet aroused to understand the amazing power of Christian culture. There are mines of truth to be worked that have been strangely neglected. This careless indifference does not meet the approval of God. Parents, God calls upon you to look at this matter with anointed eyes. You have as yet only skimmed the surface. Take up your long-neglected work, and God will cooperate with you. Do your work with wholeheartedness, and God will help you to make improvement. Begin by bringing the gospel into the home life. *Signs of the Times,* Apr. 3, 1901.

We are now in God's workshop. Many of us are rough stones from the quarry. But as the truth of God is brought to bear upon us, every imperfection is removed and we are prepared to shine as lively stones in the heavenly temple, where we shall be brought into association, not only with the holy angels, but with the King of heaven Himself. *Christian Temperance and Bible Hygiene,* p. 161.

The Aim—Perfection. Mothers, will you not dispense with useless, unimportant labor for that which must perish with the using? Will you not seek to draw near to God, that His wisdom may guide and His grace assist you, in a work which will be as enduring as eternity? Aim to make your children perfect in character. Remember that such only can see God. . . .

Many parents are neglecting their God-given work. They are themselves far from purity and holiness, and they do not see the defects of their children as they would if their own eyes were beholding and admiring the perfection of Christ's character. *Signs of the Times,* July 1, 1886.

How to Become an Ideal Mother. Instead of sinking into a mere household drudge, let the wife and mother take time to read, to keep herself well informed, to be a companion to her husband, and to keep in touch with the developing minds of her children. Let her use wisely the opportunities now hers to influence her dear ones for the higher life. Let her take time to make the dear Saviour a daily companion and familiar friend. Let her take time for the study of His Word, take time to go with the children into the fields and learn of God through the beauty of His works.

Let her keep cheerful and buoyant. Instead of spending every moment in endless sewing, make the evening a pleasant social season, a family reunion after the day's duties. Many a man would thus be led to choose the society of his home before that of the clubhouse or the saloon. Many a boy would be kept from the street or the corner grocery. Many a girl would be saved from frivolous, misleading associations. The influence of the home would be to parents and children what God designed it should be, a lifelong blessing. *The Ministry of Healing,* p. 294.

Make a Success of Domestic Life—Counsel to a Mother. You should not follow your own inclinations. You should be very careful to set a right example in all things. Do not be inactive. Arouse your dormant energies. Make yourself a necessity to your husband by being attentive and helpful. Be a blessing to him in everything. Take up the duties essential to be done. Study how to perform with alacrity the plain, uninteresting, homely, but most needful duties which relate to domestic life. . . .

Try to make a success of your domestic life. It means more to fill the position of wife and mother than you have thought. . . . You need the culture and experience of domestic life. You need the variety, the stir, the earnest effort, the cultivation of the willpower, that this life brings. Letter 5, 1884.

Parents Who Are Too Busy. Many parents plead that they have so much to do that they have no time to improve their minds, to educate their children for practical life, or to teach them how they may become lambs of Christ's fold. *Testimonies for the Church,* vol. 3, p. 145.

Parents must not neglect to arm their own minds against sin, to guard against that which will not only ruin themselves, but transmit pain and every kind of misery and evil to their offspring. By correctly educating themselves, parents are to teach their children that the heavens do rule. Letter 86, 1899.

Parents Should Welcome Counsel. While they sleep in godless indifference, Satan is sowing in the hearts of their children seeds which will spring up to bear a harvest of death. Yet often such parents resent counsel as to their mistakes. They act as though they would like to ask those who offer advice, What right have you to meddle with my children? But are their children not God's children also? How does He regard their wicked neglect of duty? What excuse will they offer when He asks them why they brought children into the world, and then left them to be the sport of Satan's temptations? *Signs of the Times,* Apr. 3, 1901.

Be prepared to listen to counsel from others. Do not feel that it is no business of your brethren or sisters how you treat your children, or how your children conduct themselves. Manuscript 27, 1911.

Benefits of Meetings for Mutual Counsel.★ God has committed to our hands a most sacred work, and we need to meet together to receive instruction, that we may be fitted to perform this work. . . . We need to meet together and receive the divine touch that we may understand our work in the home. Parents need to understand how they may send forth from the sanctuary of the home their sons and daughters so trained and educated that they will be fitted to shine as lights in the world. *Testimonies for the Church,* vol. 6, pp. 32, 33.

From the camp meeting we may take with us a better understanding of our home duties. There are lessons to be learned here regarding the work the Lord would have our sisters do in their homes. They are to learn to cultivate politeness of speech when speaking to husband and children. They are to study how they may help to bring every member of the family under discipline to God. Let fathers and mothers realize that they are under obligation to make home pleasant and attractive, and that obedience is not to be obtained by scolding and threats. Many parents have yet to learn that no good is accomplished by outbursts of scolding. Many do not consider the need of speaking kindly to the children. They do not remember that these little ones are bought with a price and are the purchased possession of the Lord Jesus. Manuscript 65, 1908.

---

 * Note: Reference is here made to group study as in camp meeting.

SECTION 4

OBEDIENCE, THE
MOST IMPORTANT LESSON

CHAPTER 10

The Key to Happiness and Success

Happiness Dependent on Obedience. Let fathers, mothers, and the educators in our schools remember that it is a higher branch of education to teach children obedience. Altogether too little importance is attached to this line of education. Manuscript 92, 1899.

Children will be happier, far happier, under proper discipline than if left to do as their untrained impulses suggest. Manuscript 49, 1901.

Prompt and continual obedience to wise parental rule will promote the happiness of the children themselves, as well as the honor of God and the good of society. Children should learn that in submission to the laws of the household is their perfect liberty. Christians will learn the same lesson— that in their obedience to God's law is their perfect freedom. *Review and Herald,* Aug. 30, 1881.

The will of God is the law of heaven. As long as that law was the rule of life, all the family of God were holy and happy. But when the divine law was disobeyed, then envy, jealousy, and strife were introduced, and a part of the inhabitants of heaven fell. As long as God's law is revered in our earthly homes, the family will be happy. *Ibid.*

Disobedience Caused Loss of Eden. The history of Adam and Eve's disobedience in the very beginning of this earth's history is fully given. By that one act of disobedience our first parents lost their beautiful Eden home. And it was such a little thing! We have reason to be thankful that it was not a larger matter, because if it had been, little disregards in disobedience would have been multiplied. It was the least test that God could give the holy pair in Eden.

Disobedience and transgression are ever a great offense to God. Unfaithfulness in that which is least will soon, if uncorrected, lead to transgression in that which is great. It is not the greatness of the disobedience, but the disobedience itself which is the crime. Manuscript 92, 1899.

The Foundation of Temporal and Spiritual Prosperity. Temporal and spiritual prosperity are made conditional upon obedience to the law of God. But we do not read God's Word, and thus become familiar with the terms of the blessing that is to be given to all who hearken diligently to God's law and teach it diligently in their families. Obedience to God's Word is our life, our happiness. We look upon the world and see it groaning under the wickedness and violence of men who have degraded the law of God. He has withdrawn His blessing from orchard and vineyard. Were it not for His commandment-keeping people who live upon the earth, He would not stay His judgments. He extends His mercy because of the righteous, who love and fear Him. Manuscript 64, 1899.

Guide the Children Into Paths of Obedience. A sacred duty rests upon parents to guide their children into paths of strict obedience. True happiness in this life and in the future life depends upon obedience to a "Thus saith the Lord." Parents, let Christ's life be the pattern. Satan will devise every possible means to break down this high standard of piety as one altogether too strict. It is your work to impress upon your children in their early years the thought that they are formed in the image of

God. Christ came to this world to give them a living example of what they all must be, and parents who claim to believe the truth for this time are to teach their children to love God and to obey His law. This is the greatest and most important work that fathers and mothers can do. . . . It is God's design that even the children and youth shall understand intelligently what God requires, that they may distinguish between righteousness and sin, between obedience and disobedience. Manuscript 67, 1909.

Obedience to Become a Delight. Parents should educate their children line upon line, precept upon precept, here a little and there a little, not allowing any disregard of God's holy law. They should rely upon divine power, asking the Lord to help them to keep their children true to Him who gave His only-begotten Son to bring the disloyal and disobedient back to their allegiance. God longs to pour upon men and women the rich current of His love. He longs to see them delighting to do His will, using every jot of their entrusted powers in His service, teaching all who come within the sphere of their influence that the way to be treated as righteous for Christ's sake is to obey the law. Manuscript 36, 1900.

CHAPTER 11

To Be Taught
From Babyhood

Begin the Teaching Early. Obedience to parental authority should be inculcated in babyhood and cultivated in youth. *Review and Herald,* Mar. 13, 1894.

Some parents think that they can let their little ones have their own way in their babyhood, and then when they get older, they will reason with them; but this is a mistake. Begin in the baby life to teach obedience. . . . Require obedience in your home school. Letter 75, 1898.

From their earliest life children should be taught to obey their parents, to respect their word, and to reverence their authority. *Review and Herald,* July 16, 1895.

Before Reason Is Developed. One of the first lessons a child needs to learn is the lesson of obedience. Before he is old enough to reason, he may be taught to obey. *Education,* p. 287.

The mother's work should commence with the infant. She should subdue the will and temper of the child and bring its disposition into subjection. Teach it to obey, and as the child grows older, relax not the hand. *Signs of the Times,* Feb. 26, 1880.

Before Self-will Grows Strong. Few parents begin early enough to teach their children obedience. The child is usually allowed to get two or three years the start of its parents, who forbear to discipline it, thinking it is too young to learn to obey. But all this time self is growing strong in the little being, and every day makes it a harder task for the parent to gain control of the child.

At a very early age children can comprehend what is plainly and simply told them, and, by kind and judicious management, can be taught to obey. . . . The mother should not allow her child to gain an advantage over her in a single instance; and, in order to maintain this authority, it is not necessary to resort to harsh measures; a firm, steady hand and a kindness which convinces the child of your love will accomplish the purpose. But let selfishness, anger, and self-will have their course for the first three years of a child's life, and it will be hard to bring it to submit to wholesome discipline. Its disposition has become soured; it delights in having its own way; parental control is distasteful. These evil tendencies grow with its growth, until, in manhood, supreme selfishness and a lack of self-control place him at the mercy of the evils that run riot in our land. *Pacific Health Journal,* April 1890.

Never should they [the children] be allowed to show their parents disrespect. Self-will should never be permitted to go unrebuked. The future well-being of the child requires kindly, loving, but firm discipline. *Counsels to Parents, Teachers, and Students,* p. 112.

Obedience to Parents Leads to Obedience to God. The youth and children who have praying parents have been greatly privileged, for such have an opportunity to know and love God. In respecting and rendering obedience to their parents, they may learn how to respect and obey their heavenly Father. If they walk as children of the light, they will be kind and courteous, loving and respectful, to their parents, whom they have seen, and thus be better qualified to love God, whom they have not seen. If they are faithful representatives of their parents, practicing the truth through the help given them of God, then by precept and example they acknowledge the ownership of God and honor Him by a well-ordered life and godly conversation. *Youth's Instructor,* June 15, 1893.

Only the Obedient Enter Heaven. Let parents and teachers impress upon the minds of the children that the Lord is proving them in this life, to see if they will render obedience to Him with love and reverence. Those who would not be obedient to Christ here would not obey Him in the eternal world. *Counsels on Sabbath School Work,* p. 79.

If parents or children are ever welcomed into the mansions above, it will be because they have in this world learned to obey the commands of God. Manuscript 60, 1903.

CHAPTER 12

Obedience Must Become a Habit

Use Gentle but Persistent Effort. Children are to be taught that their capabilities were given them for the honor and glory of God. To this end they must learn the lesson of obedience. . . . By gentle, persistent effort the habit should be established. Thus to a great degree may be prevented those later conflicts between will and authority that do so much to arouse in the minds of the youth alienation and bitterness toward parents and teachers, and too often resistance of all authority, human and divine. *Counsels to Parents, Teachers, and Students,* pp. 110, 111.

Allow No Arguments or Evasions. The first care of the parents should be to establish good government in the family. The word of the parents should be law, precluding all arguments or evasions. Children should be taught from infancy to implicitly obey their parents. *Pacific Health Journal,* January 1890.

Strict discipline may at times cause dissatisfaction, and children will want their own way; yet where they have learned the lesson of obedience to their parents, they are better prepared to submit to the requirements of God. Thus the training received in childhood influences the religious experience and molds the character of the man. *Signs of the Times,* Feb. 26, 1880.

Permit No Exceptions. As teachers in their own family, parents are to see that the rules are not disobeyed. . . . By allowing their children to go on in disobedience, they fail to exercise proper discipline. Children must be brought to the point of submission and obedience. Disobedience must not be allowed. Sin lies at the door of the parents who allow their children to disobey. . . . Children are to understand that they are to obey. Manuscript 82, 1901.

Require Prompt, Perfect Obedience. When parents fail to require prompt and perfect obedience in their children, they fail to lay the right foundation of character in their little ones. They prepare their children to dishonor them when they are old, and bring sorrow to their hearts when they are nearing the grave. Manuscript 18, 1891.

Requirements Should Be Reasonable. The requirements of the parents should always be reasonable; kindness should be expressed, not by foolish indulgence, but by wise direction. Parents are to teach their children pleasantly, without scolding or faultfinding, seeking to bind the hearts of the little ones to them by silken cords of love. Let all, fathers and mothers, teachers, elder brothers and sisters, become an educating force to strengthen every spiritual interest, and to bring into the home and the school life a wholesome atmosphere, which will help the younger children to grow up in the nurture and admonition of the Lord. *Counsels to Parents, Teachers, and Students,* pp. 158, 159.

In our own training of children, and in the training of children of others, we have proved that they never love parents and guardians less for restraining them from doing evil. *Review and Herald,* May 10, 1898.

Reasons for Obedience Should Be Given. Children are to learn to obey in the family government. They are to form a symmetrical character that God can approve, maintaining law in the home life. Christian parents are to educate their children to obey the law of God. . . . The reasons for this obedience and respect for the law of God may be impressed upon the children as soon as they can understand its nature, so that they will know what they should do, and what they should abstain from doing. Manuscript 126, 1897.

The Parent's Word Should Be Law. Your children, that are under your control, should be made to mind you. Your word should be their law. *Review and Herald,* Sept. 19, 1854.

Many Christian parents fail to *command* their children after them, and then wonder that their children are perverse, disobedient, unthankful, and unholy. Such parents are under the rebuke of God. They have neglected to bring their children up in the nurture and admonition of the Lord. They have failed to teach them the first lesson of Christianity: "The fear of the Lord is the beginning of wisdom." "Foolishness," says the wise man, "is bound in the heart of a child." The love of folly, the desire to do evil, the hatred of holy things, are some of the difficulties that parents must meet in the home mission field. . . .

In the strength of God, parents must arise and command their households after them. They must learn to repress wrong with a firm hand, yet without impatience or passion. They should not leave the children to guess at what is right, but should point out the way in unmistakable terms and teach them to walk therein. *Review and Herald,* May 4, 1886.

Influence of One Disobedient Child. One disobedient child will do great harm to those with whom he associates, for he will fashion other children after his own pattern. *Review and Herald,* Mar. 13, 1894.

Winking at Sin. Teach your children to honor you, because the law of God lays this duty upon children. If you allow your children to lightly esteem your wishes and pay no regard to the laws of the household, you are winking at sin; you are permitting the devil to work as he will; and the same insubordination, want of reverence, and love of self will be carried with them even into the religious life and into the church. And the beginning of all this evil is charged in the books of heaven to the neglect of the parents. *Review and Herald,* Apr. 14, 1885.

Habit of Obedience Established by Repetition. Lessons on obedience, on respect for authority, need to be often repeated. This kind of work done in the family will be a power for good, and not only will the children be restrained from evil and constrained to love truth and righteousness, but parents will be equally benefited. This kind of work which the Lord requires cannot be done without much serious contemplation on their part, and much study of the Word of God, in order that they may instruct according to His directions. Manuscript 24b, 1894.

SECTION 5

OTHER BASIC LESSONS

CHAPTER 13

Self-control

Prepare Children for Life and Its Duties. Well may the mother inquire with deep anxiety, as she looks upon the children given to her care, What is the great aim and object of their education? Is it to fit them for life and its duties, to qualify them to take an honorable position in the world, to do good, to benefit their fellow-beings, to gain eventually the reward of the righteous? If so, then the first lesson to be taught them is self-control; for no undisciplined, headstrong person can hope for success in this world or reward in the next. *Pacific Health Journal,* May 1890.

Train the Child to Yield. The little ones, before they are a year old, hear and understand what is spoken in reference to themselves, and know to what extent they are to be indulged. Mothers, you should train your children to yield to your wishes. This point must be gained if you would hold the control over your children, and preserve your dignity as a mother. Your children quickly learn just what you expect of them, they know when their will conquers yours, and will make the most of their victory. *Signs of the Times,* Mar. 16, 1891.

It is the veriest cruelty to allow wrong habits to be developed, to give the law into the hands of the child and let him rule. Manuscript 32, 1899.

Do Not Gratify Selfish Wishes. If parents are not careful, they will treat their children in such a way as will lead the children to demand attention and privileges that will call for the parents to deprive themselves in order to indulge their little ones. The children will call

91

upon the parents to do things for them, to gratify their wishes, and the parents will concede to their wishes, regardless of the fact that it is inculcating selfishness in their children. But in doing this work parents are wronging their children, and will find out afterwards how difficult a thing it is to counteract the influence of the education of the first few years in a child's life. Children need to learn early that they cannot be gratified when selfishness prompts their wishes. *Signs of the Times,* Aug. 13, 1896.

Give Nothing for Which Children Cry. One precious lesson which the mother will need to repeat again and again is that the child is not to rule; he is not the master, but her will and her wishes are to be supreme. Thus she is teaching them self-control. Give them nothing for which they cry, even if your tender heart desires ever so much to do this; for if they gain the victory once by crying they will expect to do it again. The second time the battle will be more vehement. Manuscript 43, 1900.

Never Permit Display of Angry Passions. Among the first tasks of the mother is the restraining of passion in her little ones. Children should not be allowed to manifest anger; they should not be permitted to throw themselves upon the floor, striking and crying because something has been denied them which was not for their best good. I have been distressed as I have seen how many parents indulge their children in the display of angry passions. Mothers seem to look upon these outbursts of anger as something that must be endured, and appear indifferent to the child's behavior. But if an evil is permitted once, it will be repeated, and its repetition will result in habit, and so the child's character will receive an evil mold. *Signs of the Times,* Mar. 16, 1891.

When to Rebuke the Evil Spirit. I have often seen the little one throw itself and scream if its will was crossed in any way. This is the time to rebuke the evil spirit. The enemy will try to control the minds of our children, but shall we allow him to mold them according to his will? These little ones cannot discern what spirit is influencing them, and it is the duty of parents to exercise judgment and discretion for them. Their habits must be carefully watched. Evil tendencies are to be restrained, and the mind stimulated in favor of the right. The child should be encouraged in every effort to govern itself. *Christian Temperance and Bible Hygiene,* p. 61.

Begin With the "Songs of Bethlehem." Mothers should educate their babies in their arms after correct principles and habits. They should not allow them to pound their heads on the floor. . . . Let the mothers educate them in their infancy. Commence with the songs of Bethlehem. These soft tunes will have a quieting influence. Sing them these subdued tunes in regard to Christ and His love. Manuscript 9, 1893.

No Wavering or Indecision. Perverse temper should be checked in the child as soon as possible; for the longer this duty is delayed, the more difficult it is to accomplish. Children of quick, passionate disposition need the special care of their parents. They should be dealt with in a particularly kind but firm manner; there should be no wavering or indecision on the part of the parents in their case. The traits of character which would naturally check the growth of their peculiar faults should be carefully nourished and strengthened. Indulgence of the child of passionate and perverse disposition will result in his ruin. His faults will strengthen with his years, retard the development of his mind, and overbalance all the good and noble traits of his character. *Pacific Health Journal,* January 1890.

An Example of Parental Self-control Is Vital. Some parents have no control over themselves. They do not control their own morbid appetites or their passionate temper; therefore they cannot educate their children in regard to the denial of their appetite, and teach them self-control. *Pacific Health Journal,* October 1897.

If parents desire to teach their children self-control, they must first form the habit themselves. The scolding and fault-finding of parents encourages a hasty, passionate temper in their children. *Signs of the Times,* Nov. 24, 1881.

Weary Not in Well-doing. Parents are too fond of ease and pleasure to do the work appointed them of God in their home life. We should not see the terrible state of evil that exists among the youth of today if they had been properly trained at home. If parents would take up their God-given work and would teach self-restraint, self-denial, and self-control to their children, both by precept and example, they would find that while they were seeking to do their duty, so as to meet the approval of God, they would be learning precious lessons in the school of Christ. They would be learning patience, forbearance, love, and meekness; and these are the very lessons that they must teach to their children.

After the moral sensibilities of the parents are aroused, and they take up their neglected work with renewed energy, they should not become discouraged or allow themselves to be hindered in the work. Too many become weary in well-doing. When they find that it requires taxing effort, and constant self-control, and increased grace, as well as knowledge, to meet the unexpected emergencies that arise, they become disheartened, and give up the struggle, and let the enemy of souls have his own way. Day after day, month after month, year after year, the work is to go on, till the character of your child is formed, and the habits established in the right way. You should not give up and leave your families to drift along in a loose, ungoverned manner. *Review and Herald,* July 10, 1888.

Never Lose Control of Yourselves. Never should we lose control of ourselves. Let us ever keep before us the perfect Pattern. It is a sin to speak impatiently and fretfully or to feel angry—even though we do not speak. We are to walk worthy, giving a right representation of Christ. The speaking of an angry word is like flint striking flint: it at once kindles wrathful feelings.

Never be like a chestnut bur. In the home do not allow yourself to use harsh, rasping words. You should invite the heavenly Guest to come into your home, at the same time making it possible for Him and the heavenly angels to abide with you. You should receive the righteousness of Christ, the sanctification of the Spirit of God, the beauty of holiness, that you may reveal to those around you the Light of life. Manuscript 102, 1901.

"He that is slow to anger," says the wise man, "is better than the mighty; and he that ruleth his spirit, than he that taketh a city." The man or woman who preserves the balance of the mind when tempted to indulge passion stands higher in the sight of God and heavenly angels than the most renowned general that ever led an army to battle and to victory. Said a celebrated emperor when on his dying bed, "Among all my conquests there is but one which affords me any consolation now, and that is the conquest I have gained over my own turbulent temper."

Alexander and Caesar found it easier to subdue a world than to subdue themselves. After conquering nation after nation, they fell—one of them "the victim of intemperance, the other of mad ambition." *Good Health,* November 1880.

CHAPTER 14

Quietness, Respect, and Reverence

Repress Undue Noise and Turbulence. Let not a mother allow her mind to be occupied with too many things. . . . With the greatest diligence and the closest watchfulness she must care for the little ones who, if allowed, will follow every impulse springing out of the fullness of their unpracticed, ignorant hearts. In their exuberance of spirit they will give utterance to noise and turbulence in the home. This should be checked. Children will be just as happy if they are educated not to do these things. They are to be taught that when visitors come, they are to be quiet and respectful. Manuscript 64, 1899.

Let Quietness Reign in the Home. Fathers and mothers, . . . teach your children that they must be subordinate to law. Do not allow them to think that because they are children, it is their privilege to make all the noise they wish in the house. Wise rules and regulations must be made and enforced, that the beauty of the home life may not be spoiled. *Signs of the Times,* Sept. 25, 1901.

Parents do their children great wrong when they allow them to scream and cry. They should not be allowed to be careless and boisterous. If these objectionable traits of character are not checked in their early years, the children will take them with them, strengthened and developed, into religious and business life. Children will be just as happy if they are taught to be quiet in the house. *Ibid.*

Teach Respect for Experienced Judgment. Children should be taught to respect experienced judgment. They should be so educated that their minds will be united with the minds of their parents and teachers, and so instructed that they can see the propriety of heeding their counsel. Then when they go forth from the guiding hand, their characters will not be like the reed trembling in the wind. *Counsels to Parents, Teachers, and Students,* p. 75.

Parental Laxness Encourages Disrespect. If in their own homes children are allowed to be disrespectful, disobedient, unthankful, and peevish, their sins lie at the door of their parents. Letter 104, 1897.

The mother . . . is to rule her household wisely, in the dignity of her motherhood. Her influence in the home is to be paramount; her word, law. If she is a Christian, under God's control, she will command the respect of her children. Tell your children exactly what you require of them. *Counsels to Parents, Teachers, and Students,* p. 111.

When parents do not maintain their authority, when the children go to school, they have no particular respect for the teachers or principal of the school. The reverence and respect that they should have, they were never taught to have at home. Father and mother were on the same level with the children. Manuscript 14, 1894.

Results of Unchecked Impertinence. Show respect for your children, and do not allow them to speak one disrespectful word to you. Manuscript 114, 1903.

A Wise Youthful Attitude. Wise is that young man and highly blest who feels it to be his duty, if he has parents, to look up to them, and if he has not, who regards his guardian, or those with whom he lives, as counselors, as comforters, and in some respects as his rulers, and who allows the restraints of his home to abide upon him. *Testimonies for the Church,* vol. 2, p. 308.

Reverence to Be Carefully Cherished. ⋆ Reverence . . . is a grace that should be carefully cherished. Every child should be taught to show true reverence for God. *Prophets and Kings,* p. 236.

The Lord desires us to understand that we must place our children in right relation to the world, the church, and the family. Their relation to the family is the first point to be considered. Let us teach them to be polite to one another, and polite to God. "What do you mean," you may inquire, "by saying that we should teach them to be polite to God?" I mean that they are to be taught to reverence our heavenly Father and to appreciate the great and infinite sacrifice that Christ has made in our behalf. . . . Parents and children are to sustain so close a relation to God that the heavenly angels can communicate with them. These messengers are shut out from many a home where iniquity and impoliteness to God abound. Let us catch from His Word the spirit of heaven and bring it into our life here below. Manuscript 100, 1902.

How to Teach Reverence. Parents can and should interest their children in the varied knowledge found in the sacred pages. But if they would interest their sons and daughters in the Word of God, they must be interested in it themselves. They must be familiar with its teachings and, as God commanded Israel, speak of it "when thou sittest in thine house, and when thou walkest by the way, when thou liest down, and when thou risest up."

Deuteronomy 11:19. Those who desire their children to love and reverence God must talk of His goodness, His majesty, and His power, as revealed in His Word and in the works of creation. *Patriarch and Prophets*, p. 504.

Reverence Is Revealed by Obedience. Let children be shown that true reverence is revealed by obedience. God has commanded nothing that is unessential, and there is no other way of manifesting reverence so pleasing to Him as by obedience to that which He has spoken. *Counsels to Parents, Teachers, and Students*, p. 111.

---

* Note: For a fuller treatment of this subject, see Chapter 80, "Reverence for That Which Is Holy."

CHAPTER 15

Care in Handling Property

Repress Destructive Tendencies. Education must be all-round and uniform. Every mother needs to be diligent. She must allow nothing to divert her mind. She must not allow her children to follow their uneducated will in handling things in the home. They should be taught that they are not to keep the house in perpetual disorder by handling things for their own amusement. Mothers, teach your children from their earliest years that they are not to look upon everything in the home as playthings for them. By these little things order is taught. No matter what fuss the children may make, let not the organ of destruction, which is large in babyhood and childhood, be strengthened and cultivated. "Thou shalt," and "Thou shalt not," God says. Without loss of temper, but decidedly, parents are to say to their children, No, and mean it.

With firmness they are to refuse to allow everything in the home to be handled freely and thrown about on the floor or in the dirt. Those who allow a child to pursue such a course are doing him a great wrong. He may not be a bad child, but his education is making him very troublesome and destructive. Manuscript 64, 1899.

Teach Respect for Others' Property. Some parents allow their children to be destructive, to use as playthings things which they have no right to touch. Children should be taught that they must not handle the property of other people. For the comfort and happiness of the family, they must learn to observe the rules of propriety.

Children are no happier when they are allowed to handle everything they see. If they are not educated to be caretaking, they will grow up with unlovely, destructive traits of character. *Signs of the Times,* Sept. 25, 1901.

Strong and Durable Playthings. Do not give the children playthings that are easily broken. To do this is to teach lessons in destructiveness. Let them have a few playthings, and let these be strong and durable. Such suggestions, small though they may seem, mean much in the education of the child. *Counsels to Parents, Teachers, and Students,* p. 123.

CHAPTER 16

Health Principles

Begin Health Education Early. The Creator of man has arranged the living machinery of our bodies. Every function is wonderfully and wisely made. And God has pledged Himself to keep this human machinery in healthful action if the human agent will obey His laws and cooperate with God. . . . We may behold and admire the work of God in the natural world, but the human habitation is the most wonderful.

From the first dawn of reason, the human mind should become intelligent in regard to the physical structure. Here Jehovah has given a specimen of Himself, for man was made in the image of God. *Medical Ministry*, p. 221.

The first study of the young should be to know themselves and how to keep their bodies in health. *Testimonies for the Church*, vol. 3, p. 142.

Lessons of Primary Importance. In the early education of children, many parents and teachers fail to understand that the greatest attention needs to be given to the physical constitution, that a healthy condition of body and brain can be secured. *Health Reformer*, December 1872.

The future happiness of your families and the welfare of society depend largely upon the physical and moral education which your children receive in the first years of their life. *Fundamentals of Christian Education*, p. 156.

Parents to Understand and Teach Physiology. If parents themselves would obtain knowledge and feel the importance of putting it to a practical use in the education of their dear children, we should see a different order of things among youth and children. The children need to be instructed in regard to their own bodies. There are but few youth who have any definite knowledge of the mysteries of human life. They know but little about the living machinery. Says David, "I will praise thee, for I am fearfully and wonderfully made."

Teach your children to study from cause to effect; show them that if they violate the laws of their being, they must pay the penalty by suffering disease. If in your effort you can see no special improvement, be not discouraged; patiently instruct, line upon line, precept upon precept, here a little and there a little. . . . Press on until the victory is gained. Continue to teach your children in regard to their own bodies, and how to take care of them. Recklessness in regard to bodily health tends to recklessness in moral character. *Testimonies for the Church,* vol. 2, pp. 536, 537.

Healthful Living Should Be a Family Matter. Healthful living must be made a family matter. Parents should awake to their God-given responsibilities. Let them study the principles of health reform and teach their children that the path of self-denial is the only path of safety. The mass of the inhabitants of the world by their disregard of physical law are destroying their power of self-control and unfitting themselves to appreciate eternal realities. Willingly ignorant of their own structure, they lead their children in the path of self-indulgence, thus preparing the way for them to suffer the penalty of the transgression of nature's laws. *Ibid.,* vol. 6, p. 370.

Physical Training Should Be Given. Physical training, the development of the body, is far more easily given than spiritual training. The nursery, the playground, the workshop; the sowing of the seed, and the gathering of the harvest—all these give physical training.

Under ordinarily favorable circumstances a child naturally gains healthful vigor and a proper development of the bodily organs. Yet even in physical lines the child should be carefully trained. *Counsels to Parents, Teachers, and Students,* p. 108.

Obedience to Nature's Laws Brings Health and Happiness. Our children should be instructed that they may be intelligent in regard to their own physical organism. They can at an early age, by patient instruction, be made to understand that they should be made to obey the laws of their being if they would be free from pain and disease. They should understand that their lives cannot be useful if they are crippled by disease. Neither can they please God if they bring sickness upon themselves by the disregard of nature's laws. *Health Reformer,* August 1871.

CHAPTER 17

Cleanliness

God Is Particular. The Lord commanded the children of Israel to wash their clothes and put away all impurity from their encampment, lest in passing by He should see their uncleanness. God is passing by our homes today, and He looks upon the unsanitary conditions of families and the lax habits. Had we not better reform, and that without delay?

Parents, God has made you His agents, that you may instill right principles in the minds of your children. You have in trust the Lord's little ones, and that God who was so particular that the children of Israel should grow up with habits of cleanliness will not sanction any impurity in the home today. God has given you the work of educating your children in these lines, and in training your children in habits of cleanliness, you teach them spiritual lessons. They will see that God would have them clean in heart as well as in body, and will be led to an understanding of the pure principles which God designs should prompt every act of their lives. Manuscript 32, 1899.

If God was so particular to enjoin cleanliness upon those journeying in the wilderness, who were in the open air nearly all the time, He requires no less of us who live in ceiled houses, where impurities are more observable and have a more unhealthful influence. *Counsels on Health,* p. 82.

Cleanliness Should Become Second Nature. Uncleanness in the home is a great mistake, for it is educating in its effects and casts its influence abroad. Even in babyhood a right direction should be given to the minds and habits of children. . . . Show them that uncleanness, whether in body or dress, is objectionable to God. Teach them to eat in a clean manner. Constant vigilance must be exercised that these habits may become second nature to them. . . . Impurity will be despised as it should be. . . .

Oh, that all would understand that these small duties are not to be neglected. The whole of their future life will be shaped by the habits and practices of their childhood. Children are peculiarly susceptible to impressions, and sanitary knowledge may be imparted to them by not permitting disorder. Manuscript 32, 1899.

Teach Love for Cleanliness and Hatred for Dirt. You should cultivate a love for neatness and strict cleanliness. *Testimonies for the Church,* vol. 2, p. 66.

Dress your children simply and plainly. Let their clothes be made of durable material. Keep them sweet and clean. Teach them to hate anything like dirt and filth. Manuscript 79, 1901.

Let the strength which is now given to the unnecessary planning of what you shall eat and drink, and wherewithal you shall be clothed, be directed to keeping their persons clean and their clothes neat. Do not misunderstand me in this. I do not say that you must keep them indoors, like dolls. There is nothing impure in clean sand and dry earth; it is the emanations from the body that defile, requiring the clothing to be changed and the body washed. *Christian Temperance and Bible Hygiene,* p. 141.

Keep Premises Clean. Whole families might be helped and blessed if parents would find something for their children to do. Why are not ministers and teachers more explicit on this subject that means so much to physical health and spiritual soundness? The boys and girls of the family should feel that they are a part of the home firm. They should strive to keep the premises cleansed from every unpleasant sight. Instruction in these lines should be given. Letter 108, 1898.

Every form of uncleanliness tends to disease. Death-producing germs abound in dark, neglected corners, in decaying refuse, in dampness and mold and must. No waste vegetables or heaps of fallen leaves should be allowed to remain near the house to decay and poison the air. Nothing unclean or decaying should be tolerated within the home. In towns or cities regarded perfectly healthful, many an epidemic of fever has been traced to decaying matter about the dwelling of some careless householder. Perfect cleanliness, plenty of sunlight, careful attention to sanitation in every detail of the home life, are essential to freedom from disease and to the cheerfulness and vigor of the inmates of the home. *The Ministry of Healing,* p. 276.

Personal Cleanliness Essential to Health. Scrupulous cleanliness is essential to both physical and mental health. Impurities are constantly thrown off from the body through the skin. Its millions of pores are quickly clogged unless kept clean by frequent bathing, and the impurities which should pass off through the skin become an additional burden to the other eliminating organs.

Most persons would receive benefit from a cool or tepid bath every day, morning or evening. Instead of increasing the liability to take cold, a bath, properly taken, fortifies against cold because it improves the circulation; the blood is brought to the surface, and a more easy and regular flow is obtained. The mind and the body are alike invigorated. The muscles become more flexible; the intellect is made brighter. The bath is a soother of the nerves. Bathing helps the bowels, the stomach, and the liver, giving health and energy to each, and it promotes digestion.

It is important also that the clothing be kept clean. The garments worn absorb the waste matter that passes off through the pores; if they are not frequently changed and washed, the impurities will be reabsorbed. *Ibid.*

Clean Surroundings Are an Aid to Purity. I have often seen children's beds in such a condition that the foul, poisonous odor constantly rising from them was to me unendurable. Keep everything the eyes of the children rest upon and that comes in contact with the body, night or day, clean and wholesome. This will be one means of educating them to choose the cleanly and the pure. Let the sleeping room of your children be neat, however destitute it may be of expensive furniture. *Christian Temperance and Bible Hygiene,* p. 142.

Maintain a Proper Balance. Cleanliness and order are Christian duties, yet even these may be carried too far and made the one essential, while matters of greater importance are neglected. Those who neglect the interests of the children for these considerations are tithing the mint and cumin, while they neglect the weightier matters of the law—justice, mercy, and the love of God. *Ibid.,* p. 68.

CHAPTER 18

Neatness, Order, and Regularity

Cultivate Order and Taste. The cultivation of order and taste is an important part of the education of children. . . .

As the guardian and teacher of your children, you are in duty bound to do every little thing in the home with nicety and in order. Teach your children the invaluable lesson of keeping their clothing tidy. Keep your own clothing clean and sweet and respectable. . . .

You are under obligation to God always to be patterns of propriety in your home. . . . Remember that in heaven there is no disorder, and that your home should be a heaven here below. Remember that in doing faithfully from day to day the little things to be done in the home, you are a laborer together with God, perfecting a Christian character. Letter 47a, 1902.

Bear in mind, parents, that you are working for the salvation of your children. If your habits are correct, if you reveal neatness and order, virtue and righteousness, sanctification of soul, body, and spirit, you respond to the words of the Redeemer, "Ye are the light of the world." Manuscript 79, 1901.

Train in Habits of Neatness. Every family is required to be trained in habits of neatness, cleanliness, and thoroughness. We who profess to believe the truth must make manifest to the world that the principles of truth and righteousness do not make people coarse, rough, untidy, and disorderly . . .

110

Love for God will be expressed in the family by love for our children. Genuine love will not let them drift into slackness and untidiness, because this is the easiest way; but from the pure example set before them by the parents, by the loving but inflexible firmness in cultivating industrious habits, they will educate their children after the same order. Manuscript 24, 1894.

Teach Children to Care for Clothing. Begin early to teach the little ones to take care of their clothing. Let them have a place to lay their things away and be taught to fold every article neatly and put it in its place. If you cannot afford even a cheap bureau, use a dry-goods box, fitting it with shelves and covering it with some bright, pretty-figured cloth. This work of teaching neatness and order will take a little time each day, but it will pay in the future of your children, and in the end will save you much time and care. *Christian Temperance and Bible Hygiene,* p. 142.

To Keep Own Room Tidy. If the children have a room which they know is their own, and if they are taught how to keep it tidy and make it pleasant, they will have a sense of ownership—they will feel that they have within the home a home of their own, and will have a satisfaction in keeping it neat and nice. The mother will necessarily have to inspect their work and make suggestions and give instruction. This is the mother's work. *Ibid.,* p. 142.

To Have Regular Hours for Sleep. How prevalent is the habit of turning day into night, and night into day. Many youth sleep soundly in the morning, when they should be up with the early singing birds and be stirring when all nature is awake. *Youth's Instructor,* Sept. 7, 1893.

Some youth are much opposed to order and discipline. They do not respect the rules of the home by rising at a regular hour. They lie in bed some hours after daylight, when everyone should be astir. They burn the midnight oil, depending upon artificial light to supply the place of the light that nature has provided at seasonable hours. In so doing they not only waste precious opportunities, but cause additional expense. But in almost every case the plea is made, "I cannot get through my work; I have something to do; I cannot retire early." . . . The precious habits of order are broken, and the moments thus idled away in the early morning set things out of course for the whole day.

Our God is a God of order, and He desires that His children shall *will* to bring themselves into order and under His discipline. Would it not be better, therefore, to break up this habit of turning night into day, and the fresh hours of the morning into night? If the youth would form habits of regularity and order, they would improve in health, in spirits, in memory, and in disposition.

It is the duty of all to observe strict rules in their habits of life. This is for your own good, dear youth, both physically and morally. When you rise in the morning, take into consideration, as far as possible, the work you must accomplish during the day. If necessary, have a small book in which to jot down the things that need to be done, and set yourself a time in which to do your work. *Youth's Instructor,* Jan. 28, 1897.

CHAPTER 19

Purity

Give Instruction in the Principles of Purity. Christian mothers, be entreated by a mother to realize the responsibility resting upon you. Teach your children from the cradle to practice self-denial and self-control. Bring them up to have sound constitutions and good morals. Impress upon their tender minds the truth that God does not design that we shall live for present gratification merely, but for our ultimate good. These lessons will be as seed sown in fertile soil, and they will bear fruit that will make your hearts glad. Manuscript 44, 1900.

To shield their children from contaminating influences, parents should instruct them in the principles of purity. Those children who in the home form habits of obedience and self-control will have little difficulty in their school life and will escape many of the temptations that beset the youth. Parents should train their children to be true to God under all circumstances and in all places. They should surround them with influences that tend to strengthen character. With such a training, children, when sent away to school, will not be a cause of disturbance or anxiety. They will be a support to their teachers and an example and encouragement to their fellow pupils. *Counsels to Parents, Teachers, and Students,* p. 150.

Exercise Unceasing Watchfulness. Parents and guardians must themselves maintain purity of heart and life if they would have their children pure. They must give the needed instruction, and in addition to this they must exercise unceasing watchfulness. Every day new thoughts are awakened in the minds of the young, new impressions made upon their hearts. The associations they form, the books they read, the habits they cherish—all must be guarded. *Signs of the Times,* May 25, 1882.

Keep the Home Pure and Attractive. The home must be kept pure and clean. Unclean, neglected corners in the house will tend to make impure, neglected corners in the soul. Mothers, you are the educators of your children, and you can do a great deal if you begin early to inculcate pure thoughts, by fitting up their rooms in a cleanly, tasteful, attractive manner. *Christian Temperance and Bible Hygiene,* pp. 142, 143.

Guard the Associations. If parents desire their children to be pure, they must surround them with pure associations such as God can approve. *Ibid.,* p. 142.

With what care parents should guard their children from careless, loose, demoralizing habits! Fathers and mothers, do you realize the importance of the responsibility resting on you? Do you allow your children to associate with other children without being present to know what kind of education they are receiving? Do not allow them to be alone with other children. Give them your special care. Every evening know where they are and what they are doing. Are they pure in all their habits? Have you instructed them in the principles of moral purity? If you have neglected to teach them line upon line, precept upon precept, here a little and there a little, let not another day pass without confessing to them your neglect to do this. Then tell them that you mean now to do your God-appointed work. Ask them to take hold with you in the reform. Manuscript 119, 1901.

Neighbors may permit their children to come to your house to spend the evening and the night with your children. Here is a trial and a choice for you, to run the risk of offending your neighbors by sending their children to their own home, or gratify them, and let them lodge with your children, and thus expose them to be instructed in that knowledge which would be a lifelong curse to them. To save my children from becoming corrupted, I have not allowed them to sleep in the same bed, or in the same room, with other boys, and have, as occasion has required, when traveling, made a scanty bed upon the floor for them, rather than have them lodge with others. I have tried to keep them from associating with rough, rude boys and have presented inducements before them to make their employment at home cheerful and happy. By keeping their minds and hands occupied, they have had but little time, or disposition, to play in the street with other boys and obtain a street education. *Solemn Appeal,* p. 56.

Erect Barriers Against Sensuality. Those who have charge of God's property in the souls and bodies of the children formed in His image should erect barriers against the sensual indulgence of the age, which is ruining the physical and moral health of thousands. If many of the crimes of this time were traced to their true cause, it would be seen that they are chargeable to the ignorance of fathers and mothers who are indifferent on this subject. Health and life itself are being sacrificed to this lamentable ignorance.

Parents, if you fail to give your children the education which God has made it your duty to give them, you must answer to Him for the results. These results will not be confined merely to your children. As the one thistle permitted to grow in the field produces a harvest of its kind, so the sins resulting from your neglect will work to ruin all who come within the sphere of their influence. *Review and Herald,* June 27, 1899.

Fill the Mind With Images of Purity. The Christian life is one of constant self-denial and self-control. These are the lessons to be taught the children from their infancy. Teach them that they must practice temperance, purity in thought and heart and act, that they belong to God because they have been bought with a price, even the precious blood of His dear Son. *Christian Temperance and Bible Hygiene,* p. 145.

If in their tender years the minds of children are filled with pleasant images of truth, of purity and goodness, a taste will be formed for that which is pure and elevated, and their imagination will not become easily corrupted or defiled. While if the opposite course is pursued, if the minds of the parents are continually dwelling upon low scenes; if their conversation lingers over objectionable features of character; if they form a habit of speaking complainingly of the course others have pursued, the little ones will take lessons from the words and expressions of contempt and will follow the pernicious example. The evil impress, like the taint of the leprosy, will cleave to them in afterlife.

The seed sown in infancy by the careful, God-fearing mother will become trees of righteousness, which will blossom and bear fruit; and the lessons given by a God-fearing father by precept and example will, as in the case of Joseph, yield an abundant harvest by and by. *Good Health,* January 1880.

SECTION 6

LESSONS IN PRACTICAL VIRTUES

CHAPTER 20

Helpfulness

Teach the Children to Be Helpful. In the home school the children should be taught how to perform the practical duties of everyday life. While they are still young, the mother should give them some simple task to do each day. It will take longer for her to teach them how than it would to do it herself, but let her remember that she is to lay for their character building the foundation of helpfulness. Let her remember that the home is a school in which she is the head teacher. It is hers to teach her children how to perform the duties of the household quickly and skillfully. As early in life as possible they should be trained to share the burdens of the home. From childhood boys and girls should be taught to bear heavier and still heavier burdens, intelligently helping in the work of the family firm. *Counsels to Parents, Teachers, and Students*, p. 122.

Overlook Childish Mistakes. Thousands in their own homes are left almost uneducated. "It is so much trouble," says the mother. "I would rather do these things myself; it is such a trouble; you bother me."

Does not mother remember that she herself had to learn in jots and tittles before she could be helpful? It is a wrong to children to refuse to teach them little by little. Keep these children with you. Let them ask questions, and in patience answer them. Give your little children something to do, and let them have the happiness of supposing they help you.

There must be no repulsing of your children when trying to do proper things. If they make mistakes, if accidents happen and things break, do not blame them.

119

Their whole future life depends upon the education you give them in their childhood years. Teach them that all their faculties of body and mind were given to them to use, and that all are the Lord's, pledged to His service. To some of these children the Lord gives an early intimation of His will. Parents and teachers, begin early to teach the children to cultivate their God-given faculties. Letter 104, 1897.

Let Children Share Home Burdens. Make the life of your children pleasant, and at the same time teach them to be obedient and helpful, bearing small burdens as you bear larger ones. Educate them to habits of industry, so that the enemy will not make a workshop of their minds. Give your children something to think of, something to do, that they may be fitted for usefulness in this life and in the future life. Manuscript 62, 1901.

From their earliest years they should be trained to carry their share of the home burdens. They should be taught that obligations are mutual. They should also be taught to work quickly and neatly. This education will be of the greatest value to them in after years. *Signs of the Times,* Dec. 11, 1901.

Each member of the family should understand just the part he is expected to act in union with the others. All, from the child six years old and upward, should understand that it is required of them to bear their share of life's burdens. *Testimonies for the Church,* vol. 2, p. 700.

A Source of Experience and Pleasure. How important that fathers and mothers should give their children, from their very babyhood, the right instruction. They are to teach them to obey the command, "Honor thy father and thy mother: that thy days may be long upon the land which the Lord thy God giveth thee." And the children as they grow in years are to appreciate the care that their parents have given them. They are to find their greatest pleasure in helping father and mother. Manuscript 129, 1903.

A Charm May Surround the Humblest Employment. If children were taught to regard the humble round of every-day duties as the course marked out for them by the Lord, as a school in which they were to be trained to render faithful and efficient service, how much more pleasant and honorable would their work appear. To perform every duty as unto the Lord throws a charm around the humblest employment and links the workers on earth with the holy beings who do God's will in heaven. And in our appointed place we should discharge our duties with as much faithfulness as do the angels in their higher sphere. *Signs of the Times,* Oct. 11, 1910.

CHAPTER 21

Industry

A Safeguard for the Young. One of the surest safeguards of the young is useful occupation. Children who are trained to industrious habits, so that all their hours are usefully and pleasantly employed, have no inclination to repine at their lot and no time for idle daydreaming. They are in little danger of forming vicious habits or associations. *Counsels to Parents, Teachers, and Students,* p. 122.

There is untold value in industry. Let the children be taught to do something useful. More than human wisdom is needed that parents may understand how best to educate their children for a useful, happy life here and for higher service and greater joy hereafter. *Ibid.,* p. 125.

Assign Tasks Appropriate to Age and Ability. From infancy children should be trained to do those things which are appropriate for their age and ability. Parents should now encourage their children to become more independent. Serious troubles are soon to be seen upon the earth, and children should be trained in such a way as to be able to meet them. *Signs of the Times,* Aug. 13, 1896.

Teach your children to be useful, to bear burdens according to their years; then the habit of laboring will become second nature to them, and useful work will never seem like drudgery. *Review and Herald,* June 24, 1890.

The Fruitage of Idleness. Parents cannot commit a greater sin than to neglect their God-given responsibilities in leaving their children with nothing to do; for these children will soon learn to love idleness and grow up to be shiftless, useless men and women. When they become old enough to earn their living and are taken into employment, they will work in a lazy, droning way and will think they will be paid just the same if they idle away their time, as if they did faithful work. There is every difference between this class of worker and the one who realizes that he must be a faithful steward. In whatever line of work they engage, the youth should be "diligent in business, fervent in spirit, serving the Lord"; for he that is unfaithful in that which is least is unfaithful also in much. Manuscript 117, 1899.

If children have proper home training, they will not be found upon the streets, receiving the haphazard education that so many receive. Parents who love their children in a sensible way will not permit them to grow up with lazy habits and ignorant of how to do home duties. Ignorance is not acceptable to God and is unfavorable for the doing of His work. *Counsels to Parents, Teachers, and Students,* p. 149.

The Wise Use of Time. Where there is an abundance of idleness, Satan works with his temptations to spoil life and character. If youth are not trained to useful labor, whether they be rich or poor, they are in peril; for Satan will find employment for them after his own order. The youth who are not barricaded with principle do not regard time as a precious treasure, a trust from God, for which every human being must give an account. Manuscript 43, 1900.

Children should be educated to make the very best use of their time, to be helpful to father and mother, to be self-reliant. They should not be allowed to consider themselves above doing any kind of labor that is necessary. Letter 11, 1888.

The value of time is beyond computation. Time squandered can never be recovered. . . . The improvement of wasted moments is a treasure. Manuscript 117, 1899.

Overcome Every Indolent Habit. In His Word God has marked out a plan for the education of children, and this plan parents are to follow. They are to teach their children to overcome every indolent habit. Each child should be taught that he has a work to do in the world. Manuscript 98, 1901.

Laziness and indolence are not the fruit borne upon the Christian tree. Manuscript 24, 1894.

Indolence is a great curse. God has blessed human beings with nerves, organs, and muscles; and they are not to be allowed to deteriorate because of inaction, but are to be strengthened and kept in health by exercise. To have nothing to do is a great misfortune, for idleness ever has been and ever will be a curse to the human family. Manuscript 24, 1894.

Children, never prove unfaithful stewards in the home. Never shirk your duty. Good hard work makes firm sinews and muscles. In promoting the prosperity of the home, you will bring the richest blessing to yourselves. Manuscript 117, 1899.

Why Work Before Play? My mother taught me to work. I used to ask my mother, "Why must I always do so much work before I play?" "It is to educate and train your mind for useful labor, and another thing, to keep you out of mischief; and when you get older, you will thank me for it." When one of my little girls [a granddaughter] said to me, "Why must I knit? Grandmothers knit," I replied, "Will you tell me how grandmothers learned to knit?" "Why, they began when they were little girls." Manuscript 19, 1887.

Value of a Daily Program. As far as possible, it is well to consider what is to be accomplished through the day. Make a memorandum of the different duties that await your attention, and set apart a certain time for the doing of each duty. Let everything be done with thoroughness, neatness, and dispatch. If it falls to your lot to do the chamber work, then see that the rooms are well aired, and that the bed clothing is exposed to the sunlight. Give yourself a number of minutes to do the work, and do not stop to read papers and books that take your eye, but say to yourself, "No, I have just so many minutes in which to do my work, and I must accomplish my task in the given time." . . .

Let those who are naturally slow of movement seek to become active, quick, energetic, remembering the words of the apostle, "Not slothful in business; fervent in spirit; serving the Lord."

If it falls to your lot to prepare the meals, make careful calculations, and give yourself all the time necessary to prepare the food, and set it on the table in good order, and on exact time. To have the meal ready five minutes earlier than the time you have set is more commendable than to have it five minutes later. But if you are under the control of slow, dilatory movements, if your habits are of a lazy order, you will make a long job out of a short one; and it is the duty of those who are slow to reform and to become more expeditious. If they will, they can overcome their fussy, lingering habits. In washing dishes they may be careful and at the same time do quick work. Exercise the will to this end, and the hands will move with dispatch. *Youth's Instructor,* Sept. 7, 1893.

Blend the Physical With the Mental. When children were sent into my family to board, and they would say, "My mother does not want me to do my washing," I would say, "Well, shall we do it for you and charge you half a dollar more for your board?" "Oh, no! Mother doesn't want to pay any more for me." "Well, then," I would say, "you may get up in the morning and do it for yourself. God never designed that you should be waited upon by us. Instead of your mother getting up and getting breakfast in the morning while you lie in bed, you should be the one to say, 'Mother, don't you get up in the morning. We will take hold of these burdens and perform these duties.' You should let those whose hairs are growing gray take their rest in the morning."

Why is this not so? Where is the trouble? It is with the parents who let their children come up without bearing any burdens in the family. When these children go out to school, they say, "Ma says she doesn't want me to work." Such mothers are foolish. They spoil their children and then send them to the school to spoil it. . . . Work is the very best discipline they can have. It is no harder for them than for their mothers. Blend the physical labor with the mental, and the powers of the mind will develop far better. Manuscript 19, 1887.

Devise Ways. Parents should devise ways and means for keeping their children usefully busy. Let the children be given little pieces of land to cultivate, that they may have something to give as a freewill offering. Manuscript 67, 1901.

Allow them to help you in every way they can, and show them that you appreciate their help. Let them feel that they are a part of the family firm. Teach them to use their minds as much as possible, so to plan their work that they may do it quickly and thoroughly. Teach them to be prompt and energetic in their work, to economize time so that no minutes may be lost in their allotted hours of work. Manuscript 60, 1903.

Labor Is Noble. Let us teach the little ones to help us while their hands are small and their strength is slight. Let us impress upon their minds the fact that labor is noble, that it was ordained to man of heaven, that it was enjoined upon Adam in Eden, as an essential to the healthy development of mind and body. Let us teach them that innocent pleasure is never half so satisfying as when it follows active industry. *Pacific Health Journal,* May 1890.

CHAPTER 22

Diligence and Perseverance

Satisfaction in Tasks Completed. Children frequently begin a piece of work with enthusiasm; but, becoming perplexed or wearied with it, they wish to change and take hold of something new. Thus they may take hold of several things, meet with a little discouragement, and give them up; and so they pass from one thing to another, perfecting nothing. Parents should not allow the love of change to control their children. They should not be so much engaged with other things that they will have no time to patiently discipline the developing minds. A few words of encouragement, or a little help at the right time, may carry them over their trouble and discouragement; and the satisfaction they will derive from seeing the task completed that they undertook will stimulate them to greater exertion.

Many children, for want of words of encouragement and a little assistance in their efforts, become disheartened and change from one thing to another. And they carry this sad defect with them in mature life. They fail to make a success of anything they engage in, for they have not been taught to persevere under discouraging circumstances. Thus the entire lifetime of many proves a failure, because they did not have correct discipline when young. The education received in childhood and youth affects their entire business career in mature life, and their religious experience bears a corresponding stamp. *Testimonies for the Church,* vol. 3, pp. 147, 148.

Habits of Indolence Are Carried Into Later Life. Children who have been petted and waited upon always expect it; and if their expectations are not met, they are disappointed and discouraged. This same disposition will be seen through their whole lives; they will be helpless, leaning upon others for aid, expecting others to favor them and yield to them. And if they are opposed, even after they have grown to manhood and womanhood, they think themselves abused; and thus they worry their way through the world, hardly able to bear their own weight, often murmuring and fretting because everything does not suit them. *Ibid.,* vol. 1, pp. 392, 393.

Develop Habits of Thoroughness and Dispatch. From the mother the children are to learn habits of neatness, thoroughness, and dispatch. To allow a child to take an hour or two in doing a piece of work that could easily be done in half an hour is to allow it to form dilatory habits. Habits of industry and thoroughness will be an untold blessing to the youth in the larger school of life, upon which they must enter as they grow older. *Counsels to Parents, Teachers, and Students,* pp. 122, 123.

Counsel Especially for Girls. Another defect that has caused me much uneasiness and trouble is the habit some girls have of letting their tongues run, wasting precious time in talking of worthless things. While girls give their attention to talk, their work drags behind. These matters have been looked upon as little things, unworthy of notice. Many are deceived as to what constitutes a little thing. Little things have an important relation to the great whole. God does not disregard the infinitely little things that have to do with the welfare of the human family. *Youth's Instructor,* Sept. 7, 1893.

Importance of "Little Things." Never underrate the importance of little things. Little things supply the actual discipline of life. It is by them that the soul is trained that it may grow into the likeness of Christ, or bear the likeness of evil. God help us to cultivate habits of thought, word, look, and action that will testify to all about us that we have been with Jesus and learned of Him! *Youth's Instructor,* Mar. 9, 1893.

Make Mistakes a Stepping-stone. Let the child and the youth be taught that every mistake, every fault, every difficulty conquered becomes a stepping-stone to better and higher things. It is through such experiences that all who have ever made life worth the living have achieved success. *Counsels to Parents, Teachers, and Students,* p. 60.

CHAPTER 23

Self-denial, Unselfishness, and Thoughtfulness

Lessons That Are Needed in Every Home. In every home there should be taught lessons of self-denial. Fathers and mothers, teach your children to economize. Encourage them to save their pennies for missionary work. Christ is our example. For our sakes He became poor, that we through His poverty might be made rich. He taught that all should come together in love and unity, to work as He worked, to sacrifice as He sacrificed, to love as the children of God. *Testimonies for the Church,* vol. 9, pp. 130, 131.

Learn the lesson of self-denial, and teach it to your children. All that can be saved by self-denial is needed now in the work to be done. The suffering must be relieved, the naked clothed, the hungry fed; the truth for this time must be told to those who know it not. *Messages to Young People,* p. 314.

Sacrifice Should Become Habitual. By precept and example, teach self-denial, economy, largeheartedness, and self-reliance. Everyone who has a true character will be qualified to cope with difficulties and will be prompt in following a "Thus saith the Lord." Men are not prepared to understand their obligation to God until they have learned in Christ's school to wear His yoke of restraint and obedience. Sacrifice is the very beginning of our work in advancing the truth and in establishing institutions. It is an essential part of education. Sacrifice must become habitual in all our character building in this life, if we would have a building not made with hands, eternal in the heavens. *Testimonies for the Church,* vol. 6, p. 214.

A Self-denial Box. Children are to be educated to deny themselves. At one time, when I was speaking in Nashville, the Lord gave me light on this matter. It flashed upon me with great force that in every home there should be a self-denial box, and that into this box the children should be taught to put their pennies they would otherwise spend for candy and other unnecessary things. . . .

You will find that as the children place their pennies in these boxes, they will gain a great blessing. . . . Every member of the family, from the oldest to the youngest, should practice self-denial. *Review and Herald,* June 22, 1905.

Children Should Not Be the Center of Attraction. Children of two to four years of age should not be encouraged to think that they must have everything that they ask for. Parents should teach them lessons of self-denial and never treat them in such a way as to make them think they are the center, and that everything revolves about them.

Many children have inherited selfishness from their parents, but parents should seek to uproot every fiber of this evil tendency from their natures. Christ gave many reproofs to those who were covetous and selfish. Parents should seek, on the first exhibition of selfish traits of character, whether in their presence, or when in association with other children, to restrain and uproot these traits from the character of their children. *Signs of the Times,* Aug. 13, 1896.

Some parents give much time and attention to amusing their children, but children should be trained to amuse themselves, to exercise their own ingenuity and skill. Thus they will learn to be content with very simple pleasures. They should be taught to bear bravely their little disappointments and trials. Instead of calling attention to every trifling pain or hurt, divert their minds; teach them to pass lightly over little annoyances or discomforts. *The Ministry of Healing,* p. 389.

The Grace of Self-forgetfulness. One of the characteristics that should be especially cherished and cultivated in every child is that self-forgetfulness which imparts to the life such an unconscious grace. Of all excellences of character this is one of the most beautiful, and for every true lifework it is one of the qualifications most essential. *Education,* p. 237.

Study how to teach the children to be thoughtful of others. The youth should be early accustomed to submission, self-denial, and regard for others' happiness. They should be taught to subdue the hasty temper, to withhold the passionate word, to manifest unvarying kindness, courtesy, and self-control. *Counsels to Parents, Teachers, and Students,* pp. 123, 124.

How carefully should parents manage their children in order to counteract every inclination to selfishness! They should continually suggest ways by which their children may become thoughtful for others and learn to do things for their fathers and mothers, who are doing everything for them. *Signs of the Times,* Aug. 13, 1896.

CHAPTER 24

Economy and Thrift

Eliminate Extravagant Habits. Teach your children that God has a claim upon all they possess, and that nothing can ever cancel this claim; all they have is theirs only in trust, to prove whether they will be obedient. Money is a needed treasure; let it not be lavished upon those who do not need it. Someone needs your willing gifts. . . . If you have extravagant habits, cut them away from the life as soon as possible. Unless you do this, you will be bankrupt for eternity. And habits of economy, industry, and sobriety are, even in this world, a better portion for you and your children than a rich dowry. Manuscript 139, 1898.

Instruct the Children in Economy. The light given me now by the Lord is that we are to be careful not to spend our precious time and money unwisely. Many things may suit our fancy, but we are to guard against the expenditure of money for that which is not bread. We shall need much means to advance the work decidedly in our cities. Everyone is to have a part to act in the Lord's work. Parents are to instruct their children in lessons of economy, in order that the younger members of the flock may learn to share the responsibility of supporting the cause of God at this time. Letter 4, 1911.

Love Not Expressed by Extravagance. Practice economy in your homes. By many idols are cherished and worshiped. Put away your idols. Give up your selfish pleasure. Do not, I beg of you, absorb means in embellishing your houses; for it is God's money, and it will be required of you again. Parents, for Christ's sake do not use the Lord's money to please the fancies of your children. Do not teach them to seek after style and ostentation in order to obtain an influence in the world. . . .

Do not educate your children to think that your love for them must be expressed by indulging their pride, their extravagance, their love of display. There is no time now to invent ways of using money. Your inventive faculties are to be put to the stretch, to see how you can economize. Manuscript 139, 1898.

Christ's Lesson in Economy. There is a lesson for us in the feeding of the five thousand, a lesson that has a special application to those times when we are placed in trying circumstances and are compelled to practice close economy. Having worked the miracle and satisfied the hunger of the multitude, Christ was careful that the food that remained should not be wasted. Manuscript 3, 1912.

He said to the disciples, "Gather up the fragments that remain, that nothing be lost." Though He had all the resources of heaven at His command, He would not suffer even a morsel of bread to be wasted. Letter 20a, 1893.

Discard Nothing Useful. Nothing that can be utilized should be thrown away. This will require wisdom, and forethought, and constant care. It has been presented to me that the inability to save, in little things, is one reason why so many families suffer for lack of the necessities of life. Manuscript 3, 1912.

They Never Learned to Economize. There is much work to be done for the Master, and men who might today be occupying high positions in connection with the work of God have failed because they never learned to economize. They did not limit their wants to their incomes when they entered the work, and their spendthrift habits proved the ruin of their usefulness in the cause. Letter 48, 1888.

How to Teach the Right Use of Money. Let every youth and every child be taught, not merely to solve imaginary problems, but to keep an accurate account of his own income and outgoes. Let him learn the right use of money by using it. Whether supplied by their parents or by their own earnings, let boys and girls learn to select and purchase their own clothing, their books, and other necessities; and by keeping an account of their expenses, they will learn, as they could learn in no other way, the value and the use of money. *Counsels on Stewardship,* p. 294.

The Value of Keeping Accounts. When very young, children should be educated to read, to write, to understand figures, to keep their own accounts. They may go forward, advancing step by step in this knowledge. *Counsels to Parents, Teachers, and Students,* pp. 168, 169.

Let children be taught to keep an account. This will enable them to be accurate. The spendthrift boy will be the spendthrift man. The vain, selfish, self-caring girl will be the same kind of woman. We are to remember there are other youth for whom we are accountable. If we train our children to correct habits, through them we shall be able to influence others. Letter 11, 1888.

SECTION 7

DEVELOPING CHRISTIAN QUALITIES

CHAPTER 25

Simplicity

Educate in Natural Simplicity. The little ones should be educated in childlike simplicity. They should be trained to be content with the small, helpful duties and the pleasures and experiences natural to their years. Childhood answers to the blade in the parable, and the blade has a beauty peculiarly its own. Children should not be forced into a precocious maturity, but as long as possible should retain the freshness and grace of their early years. The more quiet and simple the life of the child—the more free from artificial excitement and the more in harmony with nature—the more favorable it is to physical and mental vigor and to spiritual strength. *Education,* p. 107.

Parents should by their example encourage the formation of habits of simplicity, and draw their children away from an artificial to a natural life. *Signs of the Times,* Oct. 2, 1884.

Unaffected Children Are Most Attractive. Those children are most attractive who are natural and unaffected. It is not wise to give children special notice. . . . Vanity should not be encouraged by praising their looks, their words, or their actions. Nor should they be dressed in an expensive and showy manner. This encourages pride in them and awakens envy in the hearts of their companions. Teach the children that the true adorning is not outward. "Whose adorning let it not be that outward adorning of plaiting the hair, and of wearing of gold, or of putting on of apparel; but let it be the hidden man of the heart, in that which is not corruptible, even the ornament of a meek and quiet spirit, which is in the sight of God of great price." 1 Peter 3:3, 4. *Counsels to Parents, Teachers, and Students,* pp. 141, 142.

The Secret of True Charm. Girls should be taught that the true charm of womanliness is not alone in beauty of form or feature, nor in the possession of accomplishments; but in a meek and quiet spirit, in patience, generosity, kindness, and a willingness to do and suffer for others. They should be taught to work, to study to some purpose, to live for some object, to trust in God and fear Him, and to respect their parents. Then as they advance in years, they will grow more pure-minded, self-reliant, and beloved. It will be impossible to degrade such a woman. She will escape the temptations and trials that have been the ruin of so many. *Health Reformer,* December 1877.

Seeds of Vanity. In many families the seeds of vanity and selfishness are sown in the hearts of the children almost during babyhood. Their cunning little sayings and doings are commented upon and praised in their presence, and repeated with exaggerations to others. The little ones take note of this and swell with self-importance; they presume to interrupt conversations and become forward and impudent. Flattery and indulgence foster their vanity and willfulness, until the youngest not unfrequently rules the whole family, father and mother included.

The disposition formed by this sort of training cannot be laid aside as the child matures to riper judgment. It grows with his growth, and what might have appeared cunning in the baby, becomes contemptible and wicked in the man or woman. They seek to rule over their associates; and if any refuse to yield to their wishes, they consider themselves aggrieved and insulted. This is because they have been indulged to their injury in youth, instead of being taught the self-denial necessary to bear the hardships and toils of life. *Testimonies for the Church,* vol. 4, pp. 200, 201.

Do Not Foster Love of Praise. Children need appreciation, sympathy, and encouragement; but care should be taken not to foster in them a love of praise. . . . The parent or teacher who keeps in view the true ideal of character and the possibilities of achievement cannot cherish or encourage self-sufficiency. He will not encourage in the youth the desire or effort to display their ability or proficiency. He who looks higher than himself will be humble, yet he will possess a dignity that is not abashed or disconcerted by outward display or human greatness. *Education,* p. 237.

Encourage Simplicity in Diet and Dress. Parents have a sacred duty to perform in teaching their children to help bear the burdens of the home, to be content with plain and simple food, and neat and inexpensive dress. *Counsels to Parents, Teachers, and Students,* p. 158.

Oh, that mothers and fathers would realize their responsibility and accountability before God! What a change would take place in society! Children would not be spoiled by being praised and petted, or made vain by indulgence in dress. *Review and Herald,* Apr. 13, 1897.

Teach Simplicity and Trust. We should teach our children lessons in simplicity and trust. We should teach them to love, and fear, and obey their Creator. In all the plans and purposes of life His glory should be held paramount; His love should be the mainspring of every action. *Review and Herald,* June 13, 1882.

Christ Our Example. Jesus, our Redeemer, walked the earth with the dignity of a king; yet He was meek and lowly of heart. He was a light and blessing in every home because He carried cheerfulness, hope, and courage with Him. Oh, that we could be satisfied with less heart-longings, less striving for things difficult to obtain wherewith to beautify our homes, while that which God values above jewels, the meek and quiet spirit, is not cherished. The grace of simplicity, meekness, and true affection would make a paradise of the humblest home. It is better to endure cheerfully every inconvenience than to part with peace and contentment. *Testimonies for the Church,* vol. 4, p. 622.

CHAPTER 26

Courtesy and Reserve

Courtesy Begins in the Home.★ Parents, teach your children . . . how to conduct themselves in the home with true politeness. Educate them to show kindness and tenderness to one another. Allow no selfishness to live in the heart or find room in the home. Manuscript 74, 1900.

The youth who grow up careless and rude in words and manners reveal the character of their home training. The parents have not realized the importance of their stewardship; and the harvest they have sown, they have also reaped. Manuscript 117, 1899.

Principles of Heaven to Pervade. The principles of heaven are to be brought into the government of the home. Every child is to be taught to be polite, compassionate, loving, pitiful, courteous, tenderhearted. Manuscript 100, 1902.

When all are members of the royal family, there will be true politeness in the home life. Each member of the family will seek to make it pleasant for every other member. Manuscript 60, 1903.

Teach It by Precept and Example. Children, as well as those of older years, are exposed to temptations; and the older members of the family should give them, by precept and example, lessons in courtesy, cheerfulness, affection, and in the faithful discharge of their daily duties. Manuscript 27, 1896.

Respect for Weary Feet Nearing Their Rest. And God
has especially enjoined tender respect toward the aged. He
says, "The hoary head is a crown of glory, if it be found in
the way of righteousness." Proverbs 16:31. It tells of battles
fought and victories gained, of burdens borne and temptations resisted. It tells of weary feet nearing their rest, of places
soon to be vacant. Help the children to think of this, and
they will smooth the path of the aged by their courtesy and
respect, and will bring grace and beauty into their young
lives as they heed the command to "rise up before the hoary
head, and honor the face of the old man." Leviticus 19:32.
Education, p. 244.

Teach Reserve and Modesty. Pride, self-esteem, and
boldness are marked characteristics of the children of this
day; and they are the curse of the age. . . . The most sacred
lessons of modesty and humility are to be taught to the children, both at home and in the Sabbath school. *Counsels on
Sabbath School Work*, p. 46.

Will you to whom I now address these words take heed
to the instruction given you? Let the youth take warning; let
them not be forward in conversation, but be modest and retiring. Let them be quick to hear things that will profit the
soul, and be slow to speak, unless it be to represent Jesus, and
to witness to the truth. Show humility of mind by modesty
of demeanor. *Youth's Instructor*, July 11, 1895.

A Guard to Virtue. Cherish the precious, priceless gem
of modesty. This will guard virtue. . . . I feel impelled by
the Spirit of the Lord to urge my sisters who profess
godliness to cherish modesty of deportment and a becoming reserve. . . . I have inquired, When will the youthful sisters act with propriety? I know there will be no
decided change for the better until parents feel the

importance of greater carefulness in educating their children correctly. Teach them to act with reserve and modesty. *Testimonies for the Church,* vol. 2, pp. 458, 459.

True Graces. A child's truest graces consist in modesty and obedience—in attentive ears to hear the words of direction, in willing feet and hands to walk and work in the path of duty. And a child's true goodness will bring its own reward, even in this life. *Review and Herald,* May 10, 1898.

---

* NOTE: See *The Adventist Home,* pp. 421-429, chapter entitled "Courtesy and Kindness."

CHAPTER 27

Cheerfulness
and Thankfulness

Let a Sweet Influence Pervade the Home. Above all things else, let parents surround their children with an atmosphere of cheerfulness, courtesy, and love. A home where love dwells, and where it is expressed in looks, in words, and in acts, is a place where angels delight to manifest their presence.

Parents, let the sunshine of love, cheerfulness, and happy contentment enter your own hearts; and let its sweet, cheering influence pervade your home. Manifest a kindly, forbearing spirit; and encourage the same in your children, cultivating all the graces that will brighten the home life. The atmosphere thus created will be to the children what air and sunshine are to the vegetable world, promoting health and vigor of mind and body. *The Ministry of Healing,* pp. 386, 387.

Let the Countenance Be Cheerful. There is nothing gloomy in the religion of Jesus. While all lightness, trifling, and jesting, which the apostle says are not convenient, are to be studiously avoided, there is a sweet rest and peace in Jesus that will be expressed in the countenance. Christians will not be mournful, depressed, and despairing. They will be sober-minded, yet they will show to the world a cheerfulness which only grace can impart. *Review and Herald,* Apr. 15, 1884.

Children are attracted by a cheerful, sunny demeanor. Show them kindness and courtesy, and they will manifest the same spirit toward you and toward one another. *Education,* p. 240.

Educate the soul to cheerfulness, to thankfulness, and

to the expression of gratitude to God for the great love wherewith He hath loved us. . . . Christian cheerfulness is the very beauty of holiness. *Youth's Instructor,* July 11, 1895.

Speak Pleasant, Cheery Words. Pleasant, cheery words cost no more than unpleasant, moody words. Do you dislike to have harsh words spoken to you? Remember that when you speak such words, others feel the sharp sting. . . . Parents, bring practical godliness into the home. Angels are not attracted to a home where discord reigns. Educate your children to speak words that will bring sunshine and joy. *Review and Herald,* Dec. 31, 1901.

Encourage a Happy Frame of Mind. If there is anyone who should be continually grateful, it is the Christian. If there is anyone who enjoys happiness, even in this life, it is the faithful follower of Jesus Christ. It is the duty of God's children to be cheerful. They should encourage a happy frame of mind. God cannot be glorified by His children living continually under a cloud and casting a shadow wherever they go. The Christian should cast sunshine instead of a shadow. . . . He will bear a cheerful countenance. *Review and Herald,* Apr. 28, 1859.

Children hate the gloom of clouds and sadness. Their hearts respond to brightness, to cheerfulness, to love. *Counsels on Sabbath School Work,* p. 98.

Smile, Parents, Smile. Some parents—and some teachers as well—seem to forget that they themselves were once children. They are dignified, cold, and unsympathetic. . . . Their faces habitually wear a solemn, reproving expression. Childish mirth or waywardness, the restless activity of the young life, finds no excuse in their eyes. Trifling misdemeanors are treated as grave sins. Such discipline is not Christlike. Children thus trained fear their parents or teachers, but do not love them; they do not confide to them their childish experiences. Some of the most valuable qualities of mind and heart are chilled to death, as a tender plant before the wintry blast.

Smile, parents; smile, teachers. If your heart is sad, let not your face reveal the fact. Let the sunshine from a loving, grateful heart light up the countenance. Unbend from your iron dignity, adapt yourselves to the children's needs, and make them love you. You must win their affection if you would impress religious truth upon their heart. *Review and Herald,* Mar. 21, 1882.

A Fitting Prayer. Make your work pleasant with songs of praise. If you would have a clean record in the books of heaven, never fret or scold. Let your daily prayer be, "Lord, teach me to do my best. Teach me how to do better work. Give me energy and cheerfulness." . . . Bring Christ into all that you do. Then your lives will be filled with brightness and thanksgiving. . . . Let us do our best, moving forward cheerfully in the service of the Lord, with our hearts filled with His joy. *Australasian Union Record,* Nov. 15, 1903.

Teach Children to Be Grateful. "Thou shalt rejoice in every good thing which the Lord thy God hath given thee." Thanksgiving and praise should be expressed to God for temporal blessings and for whatever comforts He bestows upon us. God would have every family that He is preparing to inhabit the eternal mansions above give glory to Him for the rich treasures of His grace. Were children, in the home life, educated and trained to be grateful to the Giver of all good things, we would see an element of heavenly grace manifest in our families. Cheerfulness would be seen in the home life, and coming from such homes, the youth would bring a spirit of respect and reverence with them into the schoolroom and into the church. There would be an attendance in the sanctuary where God meets with His people, a reverence for all the ordinances of His worship, and grateful praise and thanksgiving would be offered for all the gifts of His providence.

If the word of the Lord were now as strictly carried out as it was when enjoined upon ancient Israel, fathers and mothers would give to their children an example which would be of the highest value. . . . Every temporal blessing would be received with gratitude, and every spiritual blessing become doubly precious because the perception of each member of the household had become sanctified by the Word of truth. The Lord Jesus is very near to those who thus appreciate His gracious gifts, tracing all their good things back to the benevolent, loving, care-taking God, and recognizing Him as the great Fountain of all comfort and consolation, the inexhaustible Source of grace. Manuscript 67, 1907.

CHAPTER 28

Truthfulness

Let Parents Be Models of Truthfulness. Parents and teachers, be true to God. Let your life be free from deceitful practices. Let no guile be found in your lips. However, disagreeable it may be to you at the time, let your ways, your words, and your works show uprightness in the sight of a holy God. Oh, the effect of the first lesson in deceit is terrible! Shall any who claim to be sons and daughters of God give themselves up to deceitful practices and lying?

Never let your children have the semblance of an excuse for saying, Mother does not tell the truth. Father does not tell the truth. When you are tried in the heavenly courts, shall the record be made against your name, A deceiver? Shall your offspring be perverted by the example of those who ought to guide them in the way of truth? Instead of this, shall not the converting power of God enter the hearts of mothers and fathers? Shall not the Holy Spirit of God be allowed to make its mark upon their children?

It cannot be expected that children will be altogether guileless. But there is danger that through unwise management, parents will destroy the frankness which should characterize child experience. By word and action parents should do all in their power to preserve artless simplicity. As children advance in years, parents should not give the slightest occasion for the sowing of that seed which will develop into deceit and falsehood, and mature into untrustworthy habits. *Review and Herald,* Apr. 13, 1897.

Never Prevaricate. Parents should be models of truthfulness, for this is the daily lesson to be impressed upon the heart of the child. Undeviating principle should govern parents in all the affairs of life, especially in the education and training of their children. "Even a child is known by his doings, whether his work be pure, and whether it be right." *Good Health,* January 1889.

A mother who lacks discernment, and who does not follow the guidance of the Lord, may educate her children to be deceivers and hypocrites. The traits of character thus cherished may become so persistent that to lie will be as natural as to breathe. Pretense will be taken for sincerity and reality. *Review and Herald,* Apr. 13, 1897.

Parents, never prevaricate; never tell an untruth in precept or in example. If you want your child to be truthful, be truthful yourself. Be straight and undeviating. Even a slight prevarication should not be allowed. Because mothers are accustomed to prevaricate and be untruthful, the child follows her example. Manuscript 126, 1897.

Untruthfulness Is Encouraged by Harsh Words. Do not become impatient with your children when they err. When you correct them, do not speak abruptly and harshly. This confuses them, making them afraid to tell the truth. Manuscript 2, 1903.

CHAPTER 29

Honesty and Integrity

Honesty to Be Practiced and Taught. It is essential that honesty be practiced in all the details of the mother's life, and it is important in the training of children to teach the youthful girls as well as boys never to prevaricate or to deceive in the least. Letter 41, 1888.

The Standard God Requires. God wants men in His service, under His banner, to be strictly honest, unimpeachable in character, that their tongues shall not utter a semblance of untruth. The tongue must be true, the eyes must be true, the actions wholly and entirely such as God can commend. We are living in the sight of a holy God, who solemnly declares, "I know thy works." The divine eye is ever upon us. We cannot cover one act of unjust deal from God. The witness of God to our every action is a truth which but few realize. *Ibid.*

Those who realize their dependence upon God will feel that they must be honest with their fellowmen, and, above all, they must be honest with God, from whom come all the blessings of life. The evasion of the positive commands of God concerning tithes and offerings is registered in the books of heaven as robbery toward Him. *Counsels on Stewardship,* p. 77.

Honest Weights and Measures. An honest man, according to Christ's measurement, is one who will manifest unbending integrity. Deceitful weights and false balances, with which many seek to advance their interests in the world, are abomination in the sight of God. . . . Firm integrity shines forth as gold amid the dross and rubbish of the world. Deceit, falsehood, and unfaithfulness may be glossed over and hidden from the eyes of man, but not from the eyes of God. The angels of God, who watch the development of character and weigh moral worth, record in the books of heaven these minor transactions which reveal character. *Testimonies for the Church,* vol. 4, p. 310.

Honest With Time and Money. Men are wanted whose sense of justice, even in the smallest matters, will not allow them to make an entry of their time that is not minute and correct—men who will realize that they are handling means that belong to God, and who would not unjustly appropriate one cent to their own use; men who will be just as faithful and exact, careful and diligent, in their labor, in the absence of their employer as in his presence, proving by their faithfulness that they are not merely men-pleasers, eyeservants, but are conscientious, faithful, true workmen, doing right, not for human praise, but because they love and choose the right from a high sense of their obligation to God. *Ibid.,* vol. 3, p. 25.

Just What He Wants Others to Think He Is. In every business transaction a Christian will be just what he wants his brethren to think he is. His course of action is guided by underlying principles. He does not scheme; therefore he has nothing to conceal, nothing to gloss over. He may be criticized, he may be tested, but his unbending integrity will shine forth like pure gold. He is a blessing to all connected with him, for his word is trustworthy. He is a man who will not take advantage of his neighbor. He is a friend and benefactor to all, and his fellowmen put confidence in his counsel. . . . A truly honest man will never take advantage of weakness and incompetency in order to fill his own purse. Letter 3, 1878.

Allow No Deviation From Rigid Honesty. In every business transaction be rigidly honest. However tempted, never deceive or prevaricate in the least matter. At times a natural impulse may bring temptation to diverge from the straightforward path of honesty, but do not vary one hairs–breadth. If in any matter you make a statement as to what you will do, and afterward find that you have favored others to your own loss, do not vary a hairsbreadth from principle. Carry out your agreement. By seeking to change your plans you would show that you could not be depended on. And should you draw back in little transactions, you would draw back in larger ones. Under such circumstances some are tempted to deceive, saying, I was not understood. My words have been taken to mean more than I intended. The fact is, they meant just what they said, but lost the good impulse, and then wanted to draw back from their agreement, lest it prove a loss to them. The Lord requires us to do justice, to love mercy, and truth, and righteousness. Letter 103, 1900.

Maintain Strict Principles. In all the details of life the strictest principles of honesty are to be maintained. . . . Deviation from perfect fairness in business deal may appear as a small thing in the estimation of some, but our Saviour did not thus regard it. His words on this point are plain and explicit: "He that is faithful in that which is least is faithful also in much." A man who will overreach his neighbor on a small scale will overreach in a larger scale if the temptation is brought to bear upon him. A false representation in a small matter is as much dishonesty in the sight of God as falsity in a larger matter. Letter 3, 1878.

Honesty should stamp every action of our lives.

Heavenly angels examine the work that is put into our hands; and where there has been a departure from the principles of truth, "wanting" is written in the records. *Counsels on Stewardship,* p. 142.

CHAPTER 30

Self-reliance and Sense of Honor

Train Every Child to Be Self-reliant. So far as possible, every child should be trained to self-reliance. By calling into exercise the various faculties, he will learn where he is strongest, and in what he is deficient. A wise instructor will give special attention to the development of the weaker traits, that the child may form a well-balanced, harmonious character. *Fundamentals of Christian Education,* p. 57.

Too Much Ease Will Develop Weaklings. If parents, while they live, would assist their children to help themselves, it would be better than to leave them a large amount at death. Children who are left to rely principally upon their own exertions make better men and women and are better fitted for practical life than those children who have depended upon their father's estate. The children left to depend upon their own resources generally prize their abilities, improve their privileges, and cultivate and direct their faculties to accomplish a purpose in life. They frequently develop characters of industry, frugality, and moral worth, which lie at the foundation of success in the Christian life. Those children for whom parents do the most, frequently feel under the least obligation toward them. *Testimonies for the Church,* vol. 3, pp. 122, 123.

Obstacles Develop Strength. It is obstacles that make men strong. It is not helps, but difficulties, conflicts, rebuffs, that make men of moral sinew. Too much ease and avoiding responsibility have made weaklings and dwarfs of those who ought to be responsible men of moral power and strong spiritual muscle. *Ibid.,* p. 495.

From the earliest years it is necessary to weave into the character principles of stern integrity, that the youth may reach the highest standard of manhood and womanhood. They should ever keep the fact before their eyes that they have been bought with a price and should glorify God in their bodies and spirits, which are His. The youth should seriously consider what shall be their purpose and lifework, and lay the foundation in such a way that their habits shall be free from all taint of corruption. If they would stand in a position where they shall influence others, they must be self-reliant. *Youth's Instructor,* Jan. 5, 1893.

Prepare Children to Meet Problems Bravely. Beyond the discipline of the home and the school, all have to meet the stern discipline of life. How to meet this wisely is a lesson that should be made plain to every child and to every youth. It is true that God loves us, that He is working for our happiness, and that, if His law had always been obeyed, we should never have known suffering; and it is no less true that, in this world, as the result of sin, suffering, trouble, burdens, come to every life. We may do the children and the youth a lifelong good by teaching them to meet bravely these troubles and burdens. While we should give them sympathy, let it never be such as to foster self-pity. What they need is that which stimulates and strengthens rather than weakens.

They should be taught that this world is not a parade ground, but a battlefield. All are called to endure hardness, as good soldiers. They are to be strong and quit themselves like men. Let them be taught that the true test of character is found in the willingness to bear burdens, to take the hard place, to do the work that needs to be done, though it bring no earthly recognition or reward. *Education,* p. 295.

Strengthen the Sense of Honor. The wise educator, in dealing with his pupils, will seek to encourage confidence and to strengthen the sense of honor. Children and youth are benefited by being trusted. Many, even of the little children, have a high sense of honor; all desire to be treated with confidence and respect, and this is their right. They should not be led to feel that they cannot go out or come in without being watched. Suspicion demoralizes, producing the very evils it seeks to prevent. . . . Lead the youth to feel that they are trusted, and there are few who will not seek to prove themselves worthy of the trust. *Ibid.,* pp. 289, 290.

THE PARAMOUNT TASK—
CHARACTER DEVELOPMENT

CHAPTER 31

Importance of Character

The Only Treasure Taken From This World. A character formed according to the divine likeness is the only treasure that we can take from this world to the next. Those who are under the instruction of Christ in this world will take every divine attainment with them to the heavenly mansions. And in heaven we are continually to improve. How important, then, is the development of character in this life. *Christ's Object Lessons,* p. 332.

True Character a Quality of the Soul. Mental ability and genius are not character, for these are often possessed by those who have the very opposite of a good character. Reputation is not character. True character is a quality of the soul, revealing itself in the conduct. *Youth's Instructor,* Nov. 3, 1886.

A good character is a capital of more value than gold or silver. It is unaffected by panics or failures, and in that day when earthly possessions shall be swept away, it will bring rich returns. Integrity, firmness, and perseverance are qualities that all should seek earnestly to cultivate; for they clothe the possessor with a power which is irresistible—a power which makes him strong to do good, strong to resist evil, strong to bear adversity. *Counsels to Parents, Teachers, and Students,* pp. 225, 226.

Its Two Essential Elements. Strength of character consists of two things—power of will and power of self-control. Many youth mistake strong, uncontrolled passion for strength of character; but the truth is that he who is mastered by his passions is a weak man. The real greatness and nobility of the man is measured by his powers to subdue his feelings, not by the power of his feelings to subdue him. The strongest man is he who, while sensitive to abuse, will yet restrain passion and forgive his enemies. *Ibid.,* p. 222.

More Necessary Than Outward Show. If it were considered as important that the young possess a beautiful character and amiable disposition as it is that they imitate the fashions of the world in dress and deportment, we would see hundreds where there is one today coming upon the stage of active life prepared to exert an ennobling influence upon society. *Fundamentals of Christian Education,* p. 69.

Its Development Is the Work of a Lifetime. The formation of character is the work of a lifetime, and it is for eternity. If all could realize this, if they would awake to the thought that we are individually deciding our own destiny for eternal life or eternal ruin, what a change would take place! How differently would this probationary time be occupied, and what different characters would fill our world! *Youth's Instructor,* Feb. 19, 1903.

Development and Growth. The germination of the seed represents the beginning of spiritual life, and the development of the plant is a figure of the development of character. There can be no life without growth. The plant must either grow or die. As its growth is silent and imperceptible, but continuous, so is the growth of character. At every stage of development our life may be perfect; yet if God's purpose for us is fulfilled, there will be constant advancement. *Education,* pp. 105, 106.

It Is the Harvest of Life. The harvest of life is character, and it is this that determines destiny, both for this life and for the life to come. The harvest is a reproduction of the seed sown. Every seed yields fruit after its kind. So it is with the traits of character we cherish. Selfishness, self-love, self-esteem, self-indulgence, reproduce themselves; and the end is wretchedness and ruin. "He that soweth to his flesh shall of the flesh reap corruption; but he that soweth to the Spirit shall of the Spirit reap life everlasting." Galatians 6:8. Love, sympathy, and kindness yield fruitage of blessing, a harvest that is imperishable. *Ibid.,* p. 109.

The Greatest Evidence of Christianity. If Christian mothers will present to society children with integrity of character, with firm principles and sound morals, they will have performed the most important of all missionary labors. Their children, thoroughly educated to take their places in society, are the greatest evidence of Christianity that can be given to the world. *Pacific Health Journal,* June 1890.

The Influence of One Child Properly Trained. No higher work was ever committed to mortals than the shaping of character. Children are not only to be educated, but trained as well; and who can tell the future of a growing child, or youth? Let the greatest care be bestowed upon the culture of your children. One child, properly disciplined in the principles of truth, who has the love and fear of God woven through the character, will possess a power for good in the world that cannot be estimated. *Signs of the Times,* July 13, 1888.

CHAPTER 32

How Character Is Formed

Attained by Persevering, Untiring Effort. Character does not come by chance. It is not determined by one outburst of temper, one step in the wrong direction. It is the repetition of the act that causes it to become habit, and molds the character either for good or for evil. Right characters can be formed only by persevering, untiring effort, by improving every entrusted talent and capability to the glory of God. Instead of doing this, many allow themselves to drift wherever impulse or circumstances may carry them. This is not because they are lacking in good material, but because they do not realize that in their youth God wants them to do their very best. *Youth's Instructor,* July 27, 1899.

Our first duty to God and our fellow beings is in self-development. Every faculty with which the Creator has endowed us should be cultivated to the highest degree of perfection, that we may be able to do the greatest amount of good of which we are capable. In order to purify and refine our characters, we need the grace given us of Christ that will enable us to see and correct our deficiencies and improve that which is excellent in our characters. *Pacific Health Journal,* April 1890.

By Cultivating God-given Powers. To a great extent everyone is the architect of his own character. Every day the structure more nearly approaches completion. The Word of God warns us to take heed how we build, to see that our building is founded upon the Eternal Rock. The time is coming when our work will stand revealed just as it is. Now is the time for all to cultivate the powers that God has given them, that they may form characters for usefulness here and for a higher life hereafter.

Faith in Christ as a personal Saviour will give strength and solidity to the character. Those who have genuine faith in Christ will be sober-minded, remembering that God's eye is upon them, that the Judge of all men is weighing moral worth, that heavenly intelligences are watching to see what manner of character is being developed. *Counsels to Parents, Teachers, and Students,* pp. 222, 223.

It Is Influenced by Every Act. Every act of life, however unimportant, has its influence in forming the character. A good character is more precious than worldly possessions, and the work of forming it is the noblest in which men can engage.

Characters formed by circumstance are changeable and discordant—a mass of contraries. Their possessors have no high aim or purpose in life. They have no ennobling influence upon the characters of others. They are purposeless and powerless. *Testimonies for the Church,* vol. 4, p. 657.

Perfected by Following God's Pattern. God expects us to build characters in accordance with the pattern set before us. We are to lay brick by brick, adding grace to grace, finding our weak points and correcting them in accordance with the directions given. When a crack is seen in the walls of a mansion, we know that something about the building is wrong. In our character building, cracks are often seen. Unless these defects are remedied, the house will fall when the tempest of trial beats upon it. *Youth's Instructor,* Oct. 25, 1900.

God gives us strength, reasoning power, time, in order that we may build characters on which He can place His stamp of approval. He desires each child of His to build a noble character, by the doing of pure, noble deeds, that in the end he may present a symmetrical structure, a fair temple, honored by man and God.

In our character building we must build on Christ. He is the sure foundation—a foundation which can never be moved. The tempest of temptation and trial cannot move the building which is riveted to the Eternal Rock.

He who would grow into a beautiful building for the Lord must cultivate every power of the being. It is only by the right use of the talents that the character can develop harmoniously. Thus we bring to the foundation that which is represented in the Word as gold, silver, precious stones—material that will stand the test of God's purifying fires. In our character building Christ is our example. *Youth's Instructor,* May 16, 1901.

Temptation Must Be Resisted. The life of Daniel is an inspired illustration of what constitutes a sanctified character. It presents a lesson for all, and especially for the young. A strict compliance with the requirements of God is beneficial to the health of body and mind. *Fundamentals of Christian Education,* p. 80.

Daniel's parents had trained him in his childhood to habits of strict temperance. They had taught him that he must conform to nature's laws in all his habits; that his eating and drinking had a direct influence upon his physical, mental, and moral nature, and that he was accountable to God for his capabilities; for he held them all as a gift from God and must not, by any course of action, dwarf or cripple them. As the result of this teaching, the law of God was exalted in his mind and reverenced in his heart. During the early years of his captivity Daniel was passing through an ordeal which was to familiarize him with courtly grandeur, with hypocrisy, and with paganism. A strange school indeed to fit him for a life of sobriety, industry, and faithfulness! And yet he lived uncorrupted by the atmosphere of evil with which he was surrounded.

Daniel and his companions enjoyed the benefits of correct training and education in early life, but these advantages alone would not have made them what they were. The time came when they must act for themselves—when their future depended upon their own course. Then they decided to be true to the lessons given them in childhood. The fear of God, which is the beginning of wisdom, was the foundation of their greatness. His Spirit strengthened every true purpose, every noble resolution. Manuscript 132, 1901.

The Aim Must Be High. If the youth today would stand as Daniel stood, they must put to the stretch every spiritual nerve and muscle. The Lord does not desire that they shall remain novices. He wishes them to reach the highest round of the ladder, that they may step from it into the kingdom of God. *Youth's Instructor,* July 27, 1899.

If the youth rightly appreciate this important matter of character building, they will see the necessity of doing their work so that it will stand the test of investigation before God. The humblest and weakest, by persevering effort in resisting temptation and seeking wisdom from above, may reach heights that now seem impossible. These attainments cannot come without a determined purpose to be faithful in the fulfillment of little duties. It requires constant watchfulness that crooked traits shall not be left to strengthen. The young may have moral power, for Jesus came into the world that He might be our example and give to all youth and those of every age divine help. *Youth's Instructor,* Nov. 3, 1886.

Counsel and Reproof Must Be Heeded. Those who are defective in character, in conduct, in habits and practices, are to take heed to counsel and reproof. This world is God's workshop, and every stone that can be used in the heavenly temple must be hewed and polished, until it is a tried and precious stone, fitted for its place in the Lord's building. But if we refuse to be trained and disciplined, we shall be as stones that will not be hewed and polished, and that are cast aside at last as useless. *Youth's Instructor,* Aug. 31, 1893.

It may be that much work needs to be done in your character building, that you are a rough stone which must be squared and polished before it can fill a place in God's temple. You need not be surprised if with hammer and chisel God cuts away the sharp corners of your character, until you are prepared to fill the place He has for you. No human being can accomplish this work. Only by God can it be done. And be assured that He will not strike one useless blow. His every blow is struck in love, for your eternal happiness. He knows your infirmities, and works to restore, not to destroy. *Testimonies for the Church,* vol. 7, p. 264.

CHAPTER 33

Parental Responsibility in Character Formation

A Divine Commission to Parents. God has given parents their work, to form the characters of their children after the divine Pattern. By His grace they can accomplish the task; but it will require patient, painstaking effort, no less than firmness and decision, to guide the will and restrain the passions. A field left to itself produces only thorns and briers. He who would secure a harvest for usefulness or beauty must first prepare the soil and sow the seed, then dig about the young shoots, removing the weeds and softening the earth, and the precious plants will flourish and richly repay his care and labor. *Signs of the Times,* Nov. 24, 1881.

Character building is the most important work ever entrusted to human beings, and never before was its diligent study so important as now. Never was any previous generation called to meet issues so momentous; never before were young men and young women confronted by perils so great as confront them today. *Education,* p. 225.

Here is your work, parents, to develop the characters of your children in harmony with the precepts of the Word of God. This work should come first, for eternal interests are here involved. The character building of your children is of more importance than the cultivation of your farms, more essential than the building of houses to live in, or of prosecuting any manner of business or trade. *Signs of the Times,* Sept. 10, 1894.

Home, the Best Place for Character Building. Neither the church school nor the college affords the opportunities for establishing a child's character building upon the right foundation that are afforded in the home. *Counsels to Parents, Teachers, and Students,* p. 162.

Crooked Characters Must Be Straightened. Those who do not make the crooked character straight in this life can have no part in the future immortal life. Oh, how important it is for the youth to keep straight. Parents act an important part in this matter. On them rests the sacred responsibility of training their children for God. To them has been given the work of helping their little ones form characters which will gain for them entrance into the courts above. Letter 78, 1901.

Parents, Do Not Blunder Here. Parents, for Christ's sake do not blunder in your most important work, that of molding the characters of your children for time and for eternity. An error on your part in neglect of faithful instruction, or in the indulgence of that unwise affection which blinds your eyes to their defects and prevents you from giving them proper restraint, will prove their ruin. Your course may give a wrong direction to all their future career. You determine for them what they will be and what they will do for Christ, for men, and for their own souls.

Deal honestly and faithfully with your children. Work bravely and patiently. Fear no crosses, spare no time or labor, burden or suffering. The future of your children will testify the character of your work. Fidelity to Christ on your part can be better expressed in the symmetrical character of your children than in any other way. They are Christ's property, bought with His own blood. If their influence is wholly on the side of Christ, they are

His colaborers, helping others to find the path of life. If you neglect your God-given work, your unwise course of discipline places them among the class who scatter from Christ and strengthen the kingdom of darkness. *Testimonies for the Church,* vol. 5, pp. 39, 40.

A Clean House, but Children Untrained. I have seen a mother whose critical eye could discern anything imperfect in the matching of the woodwork of her house, and who was very particular to have her house cleaning thoroughly done at the precise time she had set, and would carry it through frequently at the expense of physical and spiritual health, while her children were left to run in the street and obtain a street education. These children were growing up coarse, selfish, rude, and disobedient. The mother, although she had hired help, was so much engaged in household cares that she could not afford time to properly train her children. She let them come up with deformity of character, undisciplined, and untrained. We could but feel that the fine taste of the mother was not exercised in the right direction, or she would have seen the necessity of molding the minds and manners of her children and educating them to have symmetrical characters and lovely tempers.

If the mother had let these things which she had allowed to claim her first attention come in secondarily, she would have regarded the physical, mental, and moral training of her children of almost infinite importance. Those who take upon themselves the responsibility of mothers should feel under the most solemn obligation to God and to their children to so educate them that they will have amiable and affectionate dispositions, and that they will be pure in morals, refined in taste, and lovely in character. *Signs of the Times,* Aug. 5, 1875.

Only by God's Spirit. Shall we consider that we are capable of fashioning our lives and characters to enter into the portals of glory? We cannot do it. We are dependent every moment upon the Spirit of God operating upon us and upon our children. Manuscript 12, 1895.

If parents would see a different state of things in their family, let them consecrate themselves wholly to God, and the Lord will devise ways and means whereby *a transformation may take place in their households.* Manuscript 151, 1897.

God's Part and Yours. Christian parents, I entreat you to awake. . . . If you neglect your duty and shirk your responsibility, expecting the Lord to do your work, you will be disappointed. When you have faithfully done all that you can do, bring your children to Jesus; and with earnest, persevering faith, make intercession for them. The Lord will be your helper; He will work with your efforts; in His strength you will gain the victory. . . .

When parents shall manifest such an interest for their children as God would have them, He will hear their prayers and work with their efforts; but God does not propose to do the work which He has left for parents to do. *Review and Herald,* Sept. 13, 1881.

The Creator Will Help You. Mothers, remember that in your work the Creator of the universe will give you help. In His strength, and through His name, you can lead your children to be overcomers. Teach them to look to God for strength. Tell them that He hears their prayers. Teach them to overcome evil with good. Teach them to exert an influence that is elevating and ennobling. Lead them to unite with God, and then they will have strength to resist the strongest temptation. They will then receive the reward of the overcomer. *Review and Herald,* July 9, 1901.

Your compassionate Redeemer is watching you in love and sympathy, ready to hear your prayers and render you the assistance which you need in your lifework. Love, joy, peace, long-suffering, gentleness, faith, and charity are the elements of the Christian character. These precious graces are the fruits of the Spirit. They are the Christian's crown and shield. *Pacific Health Journal,* September 1890.

A Word of Encouragement to Those Who Have Erred. Those who have been training their children in an improper way need not despair; let them become converted to God and seek for the true spirit of obedience, and they will be enabled to make decided reforms. In conforming your own customs to the saving principles of God's holy law, you will have an influence upon your children. *Signs of the Times,* Sept. 17, 1894.

Some Children Will Refuse to Heed Parental Counsel. Parents may do everything in their power to give their children every privilege and instruction, in order that they may give their hearts to God; yet the children may refuse to walk in the light and, by their evil course, cast unfavorable reflections upon their parents who love them, and whose hearts yearn after their salvation.

It is Satan who tempts children to follow in a course of sin and disobedience. . . . If they refuse to walk in the light, if they refuse to submit their will and way to God, and persist in following a course of sin in their impenitence, the light and privileges they have had will rise up in judgment against them, because they did not walk in the light, and knew not whither they went. Satan is leading them, and they become a subject of remark in the world. People will say, "Why, look at those children! Their parents are very religious, but you see they are worse than my children, and I do not profess to be a Christian." In this way children who receive good instruction and yet do not heed it cast a reproach upon their parents, dishonoring them, and putting them to shame before an ungodly world. They also bring a reproach upon the religion of Jesus Christ through their wicked course of action. *Youth's Instructor,* Aug. 10, 1893.

Parents, This Is Your Work. Parents, it is your work to develop in your children patience, constancy, and genuine love. In dealing aright with the children God has given you, you are helping them lay the foundation for pure, well-balanced characters. You are instilling into their minds principles which they will one day follow in their own families. The effect of your well-directed efforts will be seen as they conduct their households in the way of the Lord. *Review and Herald,* June 6, 1899.

CHAPTER 34

Ways in Which Character Is Ruined

Parents May Sow the Seed of Ruin. Mistaken parents are teaching their children lessons which will prove ruinous to them, and are also planting thorns for their own feet. . . . To a great extent, parents hold in their own hands the future happiness of their children. Upon them rests the important work of forming the character of these children. The instructions given in childhood will follow them all through life. Parents sow the seed which will spring up and bear fruit either for good or evil. They can fit their sons and daughters for happiness or for misery. *Testimonies for the Church,* vol. 1, p. 393.

By Indulgence or Iron Rule. Children are often indulged from their babyhood, and wrong habits become fixed. The parents have been bending the sapling. By their course of training the character develops, either into deformity or into symmetry and beauty. But while many err upon the side of indulgence, others go to the opposite extreme and rule their children with a rod of iron. Neither of these follow out the Bible directions, but both are doing a fearful work. They are molding the minds of their children and must render an account in the day of God for the manner in which they have done this. Eternity will reveal the results of the work done in this life. *Ibid.,* vol. 4, pp. 368, 369.

By Failing to Train for God. In failing to train their children to keep the way of the Lord, to do those things which He has commanded, parents neglect a solemn duty. Manuscript 12, 1898.

Some [children] have been left to do as they pleased; others have been found fault with and discouraged. But little pleasantness, and cheerfulness, and words of approval have been given them. Manuscript 34, 1893.

Oh, if mothers would only work with wisdom, with calmness and determination, to train and subdue the carnal tempers of their children, what an amount of sin would be nipped in the bud, and what a host of church trials would be saved! . . . Many souls will be eternally lost because of the neglect of parents to properly discipline their children, and to teach them submission to authority in their youth. Petting faults and soothing outbreaks is not laying the ax at the root of the evil, but proves the ruin of thousands of souls. Oh, how will parents answer to God for this fearful neglect of their duty! *Testimonies for the Church,* vol. 4, p. 92.

By Negligence That Dallies With Sin. Children need watchful care and guidance as never before, for Satan is striving to gain the control of their minds and hearts and to drive out the Spirit of God. The fearful state of the youth of this age constitutes one of the strongest signs that we are living in the last days, but the ruin of many may be traced directly to the wrong management of the parents. The spirit of murmuring against reproof has been taking root and is bearing its fruit of insubordination. While the parents are not pleased with the characters their children are developing, they fail to see the errors that make them what they are. . . .

God condemns the negligence that dallies with sin and crime, and the insensibility that is slow to detect its baleful presence in the families of professed Christians. *Ibid.,* pp. 199, 200.

By Lack of Restraint. Because they do not properly restrain and direct their children, thousands are coming up with deformed characters, with lax morals, and with little education in the practical duties of life. They are left to do as they please with their impulses, their time, and their mental powers. The loss to the cause of God in these neglected talents lies at the door of fathers and mothers; and what excuse will they render to Him whose stewards they are, entrusted with the sacred duty of fitting the souls under their charge to improve all their powers to the glory of their Creator? *Ibid.,* vol. 5, p. 326.

The parents have thought they loved their children, but have proved themselves their worst enemies. They have let evil go unrestrained. They have allowed their children to cherish sin, which is like cherishing and petting a viper, that will not only sting the victim who cherishes it, but all with whom he is connected. *Fundamentals of Christian Education,* pp. 52, 53.

By Overlooking Glaring Wrongs. Instead of uniting with those who bear the burdens, to lift up the standard of morals, and working with heart and soul in the fear of God to correct the wrongs in their children, many parents soothe their own consciences by saying, "My children are no worse than others." They seek to conceal the glaring wrongs which God hates, lest their children shall become offended and take some desperate course. If the spirit of rebellion is in their hearts, far better subdue it now than permit it to increase and strengthen by indulgence. If parents would do their duty, we should see a different state of things. Many of these parents have backslidden from God. They do not have wisdom from Him to perceive the devices of Satan and to resist his snares. *Testimonies for the Church,* vol. 4, pp. 650, 651.

By Petting and Indulging Children. Parents frequently pet and indulge their young children because it appears easier to manage them in that way. It is smoother work to let them have their own way than to check the unruly inclinations that rise so strongly in their breasts. Yet this course is cowardly. It is a wicked thing thus to shirk responsibility; for the time will come when these children, whose unchecked inclinations have strengthened into absolute vices, will bring reproach and disgrace upon themselves and their families. They go out into busy life unprepared for its temptations, not strong enough to endure perplexities and troubles; passionate, overbearing, undisciplined, they seek to bend others to their will, and, failing in this, consider themselves ill-used by the world, and turn against it. *Ibid.,* p. 201.

By Sowing Seeds of Vanity. Wherever we go, we see children indulged, petted, and praised without discretion. This tends to make them vain, bold, and conceited. The seeds of vanity are easily sown in the human heart by injudicious parents and guardians, who praise and indulge the young under their charge, with no thought of the future. Self-will and pride are evils that turned angels into demons and barred the gates of heaven against them. And yet parents, unconsciously, are systematically training their children to be the agents of Satan. *Pacific Health Journal,* January 1890.

By Becoming Slaves to Teenage Children. How many toil-worn, burdened parents have become slaves to their children, while, in harmony with their education and training, the children live to please, amuse, and glorify themselves. Parents sow the seed in the hearts of their children which yields a harvest that they do not care to reap. Under this training, at the age of ten, twelve, or sixteen, children think themselves very wise, imagine that they are prodigies, and regard themselves as altogether too knowing to be in subjection to their parents, and too elevated to stoop to the duties of everyday life. The love of pleasure controls their minds; and selfishness, pride, and rebellion work out their bitter results in their lives. They accept the insinuations of Satan and cultivate an unhallowed ambition to make a great show in the world. *Youth's Instructor,* July 20, 1893.

By Misguided Love and Sympathy. Parents may indulge their affection for their children at the expense of obedience to God's holy law. Guided by this affection, they disobey God by allowing their children to carry out wrong impulses, and withhold the instruction and discipline which God has commanded them to give. When parents thus disregard the commands of God, they imperil their own souls and the souls of their children. *Review and Herald,* Apr. 6, 1897.

Weakness in requiring obedience, and false love and sympathy—the false notion that to indulge and not to restrain is wisdom—constitute a system of training that grieves angels; but it delights Satan, for it brings hundreds and thousands of children into his ranks. This is why he blinds the eyes of parents, benumbs their sensibilities, and confuses their minds. They see that their sons and daughters are not pleasant, lovely, obedient, and care-taking; yet children accumulate in their homes, to poison their lives, fill their hearts with grief, and add to the number whom Satan is using to allure souls to destruction. *Testimonies for the Church,* vol. 1, p. 393.

By Failure to Require Obedience. If ungrateful children are fed and clothed and allowed to go uncorrected, they are emboldened to continue in their course of evil. And inasmuch as their parents or guardians thus favor them and do not require obedience, they are partakers with them in their wicked deeds. Such children might just as well be with the wicked, whose iniquitous course they choose to follow, as to remain in Christian homes, to poison others. In this age of wickedness every Christian must stand firm in condemnation of the evil, Satanic actions of wayward children. Evil youth should not be treated as kind and obedient, but as disturbers of the peace and corrupters of their companions. Manuscript 119, 1901.

By Allowing the Children to Follow Their Own Minds. The prevailing influence in society is in favor of allowing the youth to follow the natural turn of their own minds. *Messages to Young People,* pp. 373, 374.

They [parents] think that by gratifying the wishes of their children and letting them follow their own inclinations, they can gain their love. What an error! Children thus indulged grow up unrestrained in their desires, unyielding in their dispositions, selfish, exacting, and overbearing, a curse to themselves and to all around them. *Testimonies for the Church,* vol. 1, p. 393.

By Allowing Wrong Attitudes. The lessons of childhood, good or bad, are not learned in vain. Character is developed in youth for good or evil. At home there may be praise and false flattery; in the world each stands on his own merits. The pampered ones, to whom all home authority has yielded, are there daily subjected to mortification by being obliged to yield to others. Many are even then taught their true place by these practical lessons of life. Through rebuffs, disappointments, and plain language from their superiors, they often find their true level and are humbled to understand and accept their proper place. But this is a severe and unnecessary ordeal for them to pass through and could have been prevented by proper training in their youth.

The majority of these ill-disciplined ones go through life at cross-purposes with the world, making a failure where they should have succeeded. They grow to feel that the world owes them a grudge because it does not flatter and caress them, and they take revenge by holding a grudge against the world and bidding it defiance. Circumstances sometimes oblige them to affect a humility they do not feel; but it does not fit them with a natural grace, and their true characters are sure to be exposed sooner or later. . . .

Why will parents educate their children in such a manner that they will be at war with those who are brought in contact with them? *Ibid.,* vol. 4, pp. 201, 202.

By Training as Devotees of Society. Children are not to be trained to be the devotees of society. They are not to be sacrificed to Molech, but they are to become members of the Lord's family. Parents are to be filled with the compassion of Christ, that they may work for the salvation of the souls that are placed under their influence. They are not to have their minds all engrossed in the fashions and practices of the world. They are not to educate their children to attend parties and concerts and dances, to have and attend feasts, because after this manner the Gentiles walk. *Review and Herald,* Mar. 13, 1894.

By Permitting Selfish Seeking of Happiness. There are many youth who might have been a blessing to society and an honor to the cause of God if they had been started in life with right ideas as to what constituted success. But instead of being controlled by reason and principle, they had been trained to yield to wayward inclination, and sought only to gratify themselves by indulging in selfish pleasure, thinking thus to obtain happiness. But they failed to attain their object, for seeking happiness in the path of selfishness will bring but misery. They are useless in society, useless in the cause of God. Their prospects both for this world and the next are of a most discouraging order, for by selfish love of pleasure they lose both this world and the next. *Youth's Instructor,* July 20, 1893.

By a Lack of Piety at Home. In professedly Christian homes, where fathers and mothers would be supposed to be diligent students of the Scriptures, in order that they might know every specification and restriction in the Word of God, there is manifest neglect of following the instruction of the Word and of bringing up the children in the nurture and admonition of the Lord. Professedly Christian parents fail to practice piety at home. How can fathers and mothers represent Christ's character in the home life when they are content to reach a cheap, low standard? The seal of the living God will be placed upon those only who bear a likeness to Christ in character. *Review and Herald,* May 21, 1895.

If Parents Were Obedient to God. The Lord will not vindicate the misrule of parents. Today hundreds of children swell the ranks of the enemy, living and working apart from the purpose of God. They are disobedient, unthankful, unholy; but the sin lies at the door of their parents. Christian parents, thousands of children are perishing in their sins because of the failure of their parents to rule the home wisely. If parents were obedient to the unseen Leader of the armies of Israel, whose glory was enshrouded in the pillar of cloud, the unhappy state of affairs now existing in so many families would not be seen. *Review and Herald,* June 6, 1899.

CHAPTER 35

How Parents May Build Strong Characters

Devote Best Time and Thought to It. The parents receive the child a helpless burden in their arms; he knows nothing, and he is to be taught to love God, is to be brought up in the nurture and admonition of the Lord. He is to be fashioned after the divine model.

When parents see the importance of their work in training their children, when they see that it involves eternal interest, they will feel that they must devote their best time and thought to this work. *Signs of the Times,* Mar. 16, 1891.

Gain an Understanding of Principles Involved. The lessons learned, the habits formed, during the years of infancy and childhood have more to do with the formation of the character and the direction of the life than have all the instruction and training of after years.

Parents need to consider this. They should understand the principles that underlie the care and training of children. They should be capable of rearing them in physical, mental, and moral health. *The Ministry of Healing,* p. 380.

Shun Superficiality. We are living in an age when almost everything is superficial. There is but little stability and firmness of character, because the training and education of children from their cradle is superficial. Their character is built upon sliding sand. Self-denial and self-control have not been molded into their characters. They have been petted and indulged until they are spoiled for practical life. The love of pleasure controls minds, and children are flattered and indulged to their ruin. *Health Reformer,* December 1872.

Fortify Children Through Prayer and Faith. You have brought children into the world who have had no voice in regard to their existence. You have made yourselves responsible in a great measure for their future happiness, their eternal well-being. The burden is upon you, whether you are sensible of it or not, to train these children for God—to watch with jealous care the first approach of the wily foe, and be prepared to raise a standard against him. Build a fortification of prayer and faith about your children, and exercise diligent watching thereunto. You are not secure a moment against the attacks of Satan. You have no time to rest from watchful, earnest labor. You should not sleep a moment at your post. This is a most important warfare. Eternal consequences are involved. It is life or death with you and your family. *Testimonies for the Church,* vol. 2, pp. 397, 398.

Take a Firm, Decided Stand. Parents generally put too much confidence in their children; for often when the parents are confiding in them, they are in concealed iniquity. Parents, watch your children with a jealous care. Exhort, reprove, counsel them when you rise up, and when you sit down; when you go out, and when you come in; "line upon line, precept upon precept, here a little, and there a little." Subdue your children when they are young. With many parents this is sadly neglected. They do not take as firm and decided a stand as they should in regard to their children. *Ibid.,* vol. 1, p. 156.

Patiently Sow Precious Seed. "Whatsoever a man soweth, that shall he also reap." Parents, your work is to win the confidence of your children, and in love patiently sow the precious seed. Do your work with contentment, never complaining of the hardship, care, and toil. If by patient, kindly, Christlike efforts you may present one soul perfect in Christ Jesus, your life will not have been in vain. Keep your own soul hopeful and patient. Let no discouragement be traced in your features or attitude. You have in your hands the making of a character, through the help of God, that may work in the Master's vineyard and win many souls to Jesus. Ever encourage your children to reach a high standard in all their habits and tendencies. Be patient with their imperfections, as God is patient with you in your imperfections, bearing with you, watching over you, that you may bring forth fruit unto His glory. Encourage your children to strive to add to their attainments the virtues they lack. Manuscript 136, 1898.

Teach Submission to Law. Fathers and mothers, be sensible. Teach your children that they must be subordinate to law. Manuscript, 136, 1898.

It is not mercy or kindness to permit a child to have its own way, to submit to its rule, and to neglect to correct it on the ground that you love it too well to punish it. What kind of love is it that permits your child to develop traits of character that will make him and everyone else miserable? Away with such love! True love will look out for the present and eternal good of the soul. *Review and Herald,* July 16, 1895.

What right have parents to bring children into the world to neglect and to let them grow up without culture and Christian training? Parents should be responsible. Teach them control; teach them that they are to be managed, and not to manage. Manuscript 9, 1893.

Coordinate the Physical, Mental, and Spiritual. The physical, mental, and spiritual capabilities should be developed in order to form a properly balanced character. Children should be watched, guarded, and disciplined in order to successfully accomplish this. *Testimonies for the Church,* vol. 4, pp. 197, 198.

The physical constitution of Jesus, as well as His spiritual development, is brought before us in these words, "the child grew," and "increased in stature." In childhood and youth attention should be given to physical development. Parents should so train their children in good habits of eating and drinking, dressing, and exercise, that a good foundation will be laid for sound health in afterlife. The physical organism should have special care, that the powers of the body may not be dwarfed, but developed to their full extent. This places the children and youth in a favorable position, so that, with proper religious training, they may, like Christ, wax strong in spirit. *Youth's Instructor,* July 27, 1893.

Health Is Related to Intellect and Morals. In order to arouse the moral sensibilities of your children to the claims that God has upon them, you should imprint upon their minds and hearts how to obey the laws of God in their physical frames; for health has a great deal to do with their intellect and morals. If they have health and purity of heart, they are then better prepared to live and be a blessing to the world. To balance their minds in the right direction and at the right time is a most important work, for very much depends on the decision made at the critical moment.

How important, then, that the minds of parents should be as free as possible from perplexing, wearing care in needless things, that they may think and act with calm consideration, wisdom, and love, making the physical and moral health of their children the first and highest consideration. *Health Reformer,* December 1872.

Parents wonder that children are so much more difficult to control than they used to be, when in most cases their own criminal management has made them so. The quality of food they bring upon their tables and encourage their children to eat is constantly exciting their animal passions and weakening the moral and intellectual faculties. *Pacific Health Journal,* October 1897.

Pure Food for the Mind Is Essential. Educate the faculties and tastes of your dear ones; seek to preoccupy their minds, so that there shall be no place for low, debasing thoughts or indulgences. The grace of Christ is the only antidote or preventive of evil. You may choose, if you will, whether the minds of your children shall be occupied with pure, uncorrupted thoughts or with the evils that are existing everywhere—pride and forgetfulness of their Redeemer. The mind, like the body, must have pure food in order to have health and strength. Give your children something to think of that is out of and above themselves. The mind that lives in a pure, holy atmosphere will not become trifling, frivolous, vain, and selfish. Letter 27, 1890.

We are living in a time when everything that is false and superficial is exalted above the real, the natural, and the enduring. The mind must be kept free from everything that would lead it in a wrong direction. It should not be encumbered with trashy stories, which do not add strength to the mental powers. The thoughts will be of the same character as the food we provide for the mind. *Testimonies for the Church,* vol. 5, p. 544.

A Brilliant Intellect Is Not Sufficient. You may be pleased with the brilliant intellect of your child; but unless it is under the control of a sanctified heart, it will work at cross-purposes with God. Nothing but a high sense of the claims of God upon us can give us the proper stability of character, penetration of mind, and depth of understanding essential to success, both in this world and in the world to come. *Review and Herald,* Apr. 23, 1889.

Aim at High Points in Character Development. If we teach our children to be industrious, half the danger is over, for idleness leads into all manner of temptation to sin. Let us educate our children to be simple in manner without being bold, to be benevolent and self-sacrificing without being extravagant, to be economical without becoming avaricious. And above all, let us teach them the claims which God has upon them, that it is their duty to carry religion into every department of life, that they should love God supremely, and love their neighbor, not neglecting the little courtesies of life which are essential to happiness. *Pacific Health Journal,* May 1890.

Pray for Heavenly Wisdom. Parents should reflect and pray earnestly to God for wisdom and divine aid to properly train their children, that they may develop characters that God will approve. Their anxiety should not be how they can educate their children that they may be praised and honored of the world, but how they can educate them to form beautiful characters that God can approve. Much prayer and study are needed for heavenly wisdom to know how to deal with young minds, for very much is depending upon the direction parents give to the minds and wills of their children. *Health Reformer,* December 1872.

Moral and Spiritual Guidance Must Be Given. Parents need to be impressed with their obligation to give to the world children having well-developed character—children who will have moral power to resist temptation, and whose life will be an honor to God and a blessing to their fellowmen. Those who enter upon active life with firm principles will be prepared to stand unsullied amid the moral pollutions of this corrupt age. *Christian Temperance and Bible Hygiene,* p. 75.

Teach Children to Choose for Themselves. Let the youth and the little children be taught to choose for themselves that royal robe woven in heaven's loom—the "fine linen, clean and white" (Revelation 19:8), which all the holy ones of earth will wear. This robe, Christ's own spotless character, is freely offered to every human being. But all who receive it will receive and wear it here.

Let the children be taught that as they open their minds to pure, loving thoughts and do loving and helpful deeds, they are clothing themselves with His beautiful garment of character. This apparel will make them beautiful and beloved here, and will hereafter be their title of admission to the palace of the King. *Education,* p. 249.

SECTION 9

FUNDAMENTAL ELEMENTS OF
CHARACTER BUILDING

CHAPTER 36

Advantage of the Early Years

Early Childhood Is the Most Important Period. Too much importance cannot be placed on the early training of children. The lessons that the child learns during the first seven years of life have more to do with forming his character than all that it learns in future years. Manuscript 2, 1903.

From babyhood the character of the child is to be molded and fashioned in accordance with the divine plan. Virtues are to be instilled into his opening mind. *Signs of the Times,* Sept. 25, 1901.

The parents' work must begin with the child in its infancy, that it may receive the right impress of character ere the world shall place its stamp on mind and heart. *Review and Herald,* Aug. 30, 1881.

The Most Susceptible Age. It is during the first years of a child's life that his mind is most susceptible to impressions either good or evil. During these years decided progress is made in either a right direction or a wrong one. On one hand, much worthless information may be gained; on the other, much solid, valuable knowledge. The strength of intellect, the substantial knowledge, are possessions which the gold of Ophir could not buy. Their price is above gold or silver. *Counsels to Parents, Teachers, and Students,* p. 132.

First Impressions Are Seldom Forgotten. Neither infants, children, or youth should hear an impatient word from father, mother, or any member of the household; for they receive impressions very early in life, and what parents make them today, they will be tomorrow, and the next day, and the next. The first lessons impressed upon the child are seldom forgotten. . . .

The impressions made on the heart early in life are seen in after years. They may be buried, but they will seldom be obliterated. Manuscript 57, 1897.

The Foundation Is Laid in the First Three Years. Mothers, be sure that you properly discipline your children during the first three years of their lives. Do not allow them to form their wishes and desires. The mother must be mind for her child. The first three years is the time in which to bend the tiny twig. Mothers should understand the importance attaching to this period. It is then that the foundation is laid.

If these first lessons have been defective, as they very often are, for Christ's sake, for the sake of your children's future and eternal good, seek to repair the wrong you have done. If you have waited until your children were three years old to begin to teach them self-control and obedience, seek to do it now, even though it will be much harder. Manuscript 64, 1899.

Not So Difficult as Generally Supposed. Much parental anxiety and grief might be saved if children were taught from their cradles that their wills were not to be made law, and their whims continually indulged. It is not so difficult as is generally supposed to teach the little child to stifle its outburst of temper and subdue its fits of passion. *Pacific Health Journal,* April 1890.

Do Not Postpone This Work. Many neglect their duty during the first years of their children's lives, thinking that when they get older, they will then be very careful to repress wrong and educate them in the right. But the very time for them to do this work is when the children are babes in their arms. It is not right for parents to pet and humor their children; neither is it right for them to abuse them. A firm, decided, straightforward course of action will be productive of the best results. *Testimonies for the Church,* vol. 4, p. 313.

When I have called attention of parents to the wrong habits which they were encouraging in their very young children, some parents have appeared entirely indifferent; others have said with a smile, "Little darlings! I cannot bear to cross them in any way. They will do better when they get older. They will then be ashamed of these passionate outbursts. It is not best to be too particular and strict with the little ones. They will outgrow these habits of telling lies and deceiving and being indolent and selfish." A very easy way indeed for mothers to dispose of the matter, but this does not meet the will of God. Manuscript 43, 1900.

Thwart Satan's Effort to Claim Infant Children. Parents, you fail generally to begin your work early enough. You let Satan preoccupy the soil of the heart by putting in the first crop of seed. *Review and Herald,* Apr. 14, 1885.

You have a work to do that Satan shall not gain the control of your children and take them away from you before they are out of your arms. Mothers, you should see to it that the powers of darkness do not control your little ones. You should set your will that the enemy shall not raise his banner of darkness in your home. *Signs of the Times,* July 22, 1889.

In Preparing Also for Practical Life. There are but very few who take time to carefully consider what an amount of knowledge both of temporal and eternal things may be gained by the child during its first twelve or fifteen years. Not only should children in these first years of life be obtaining book knowledge, but they should be learning the arts essential for practical life; the latter should not be neglected for the former. Manuscript 43, 1900.

Napoleon's Heritage. The character of Napoleon Bonaparte was greatly influenced by his training in childhood. Unwise instructors inspired him with a love for conquest, forming mimic armies and placing him at their head as commander. Here was laid the foundation for his career of strife and bloodshed. Had the same care and effort been directed to making him a good man, imbuing his young heart with the spirit of the Gospel, how widely different might have been his history. *Signs of the Times,* Oct. 11, 1910.

Hume and Voltaire. It is said that Hume, the skeptic, was in early life a conscientious believer in the Word of God. Being connected with a debating society, he was appointed to present the arguments in favor of infidelity. He studied with earnestness and perseverance, and his keen and active mind became imbued with the sophistry of skepticism. Erelong he came to believe its delusive teachings, and his whole afterlife bore the dark impress of infidelity.

When Voltaire was five years old, he committed to memory an infidel poem, and the pernicious influence was never effaced from his mind. He became one of Satan's most successful agents to lead men away from God. Thousands will rise up in the judgment and charge the ruin of their souls upon the infidel Voltaire.

By the thoughts and feelings cherished in early years every youth is determining his own life history. Correct, virtuous, manly habits formed in youth will become a part of the character and will usually mark the course of the individual through life. The youth may become vicious or virtuous, as they choose. They may as well be distinguished for true and noble deeds as for great crime and wickedness. *Ibid.*

Hannah's Reward. Opportunities of inestimable worth, interests infinitely precious, are committed to every mother. During the first three years of the life of Samuel the prophet, his mother carefully taught him to distinguish between good and evil. By every familiar object surrounding him she sought to lead his thoughts up to the Creator. In fulfillment of her vow to give her son to the Lord, with great self-denial she placed him under the care of Eli the high priest, to be trained for service in the house of God. . . . His early training led him to choose to maintain his Christian integrity. What a reward was Hannah's! And what an encouragement to faithfulness is her example! *Review and Herald,* Sept. 8, 1904.

How Joseph's Mind Was Garrisoned. The lessons given Joseph in his youth by Jacob in expressing his firm trust in God and relating to him again and again the precious evidences of His loving-kindness and unceasing care were the very lessons he needed in his exile among an idolatrous people. In the testing time he put these lessons to a practical use. When under the severest trial, he looked to his heavenly Father, whom he had learned to trust. Had the precepts and example of the father of Joseph been of an opposite character, the pen of inspiration would never have traced upon the pages of sacred history the story of integrity and virtue that shines forth in the character of Joseph. The early impressions made upon his mind garrisoned his heart in the hour of fierce temptation and led him to exclaim, "How can I do this great wickedness, and sin against God?" *Good Health,* January 1880.

The Fruitage of Wise Training. It is a sad fact that any weakness and indecision on the part of the mother is quickly seen by the children, and the tempter then works upon their minds, leading them to persist in following their inclination. If parents would cultivate the qualities necessary for them to use in the proper training of their children, if they would plainly lay before the children the rules they must follow, and not suffer these rules to be broken, the Lord would cooperate with and bless both parents and children. Manuscript 133, 1898.

At a very early age children become susceptible to demoralizing influences, but parents who profess to be Christians do not seem to discern the evil of their own course of management. Oh, that they might realize that the bias which is given to a child in its earliest years gives a tendency to character and shapes the destiny either for eternal life or eternal death! Children are susceptible to moral and spiritual impressions, and those who are wisely trained in childhood may be erring at times, but they will not go far astray. *Signs of the Times,* Apr. 16, 1896.

CHAPTER 37

The Power of Habit

How Habits Are Established. Any one act, either good or evil, does not form the character; but thoughts and feelings indulged prepare the way for acts and deeds of the same kind. *Youth's Instructor,* Dec. 15, 1886.

It is . . . by a repetition of acts that habits are established and character confirmed. *Signs of the Times,* Aug. 6, 1912.

The Time to Establish Good Habits. The character is formed, to a great extent, in early years. The habits then established have more influence than any natural endowment, in making men either giants or dwarfs in intellect; for the very best talents may, through wrong habits, become warped and enfeebled. The earlier in life one contracts hurtful habits, the more firmly will they hold their victim in slavery, and the more certainly will they lower his standard of spirituality. On the other hand, if correct and virtuous habits are formed in youth, they will generally mark the course of the possessor through life. In most cases, it will be found that those who in later life reverence God and honor the right learned that lesson before there was time for the world to stamp its images of sin upon the soul. Those of mature age are generally as insensible to new impressions as is the hardened rock, but youth is impressible. *Christian Temperance and Bible Hygiene,* p. 45.

Habits May Be Modified, but Seldom Changed. What the child sees and hears is drawing deep lines upon the tender mind, which no after circumstances in life can entirely efface. The intellect is now taking shape, and the affections receiving direction and strength. Repeated acts in a given course become habits. These may be modified by severe training, in afterlife, but are seldom changed. *Good Health,* January 1880.

Once formed, habits become more and more firmly impressed upon the character. The intellect is continually receiving its mold from opportunities and advantages, ill or well improved. Day by day we form characters which place the students as well-disciplined soldiers under the banner of Prince Emmanuel, or rebels under the banner of the prince of darkness. Which shall it be? Manuscript 69, 1897.

Persevering Effort Is Necessary. What we venture to do once, we are more apt to do again. Habits of sobriety, of self-control, of economy, of close application, of sound, sensible conversation, of patience and true courtesy, are not gained without diligent, close watching over self. It is much easier to become demoralized and depraved than to conquer defects, keeping self in control and cherishing true virtues. Persevering efforts will be required if the Christian graces are ever perfected in our lives. *Testimonies for the Church,* vol. 4, p. 452.

Corrupt Children Endanger Others. God-fearing parents will deliberate and plan as to how to train their children to right habits. They will choose companions for their children, rather than leave them in their inexperience to choose for themselves. *Review and Herald,* June 24, 1890.

If, in their early childhood, children are not perseveringly and patiently trained in the right way, they will form wrong habits. These habits will develop in their future life and will corrupt others. Those whose minds have received a low cast, who have been cheapened by wrong home influences, by deceptive practices, carry their wrong habits with them through life. If they make a profession of religion, these habits will be revealed in their religious life. *Review and Herald,* Mar. 30, 1897.

King Saul, a Sad Example. The history of Israel's first king presents a sad example of the power of early wrong habits. In his youth Saul did not love and fear God; and that impetuous spirit, not early trained to submission, was ever ready to rebel against divine authority. Those who in their youth cherish a sacred regard for the will of God, and who faithfully perform the duties of their position, will be prepared for higher service in afterlife. But men cannot for years pervert the powers that God has given them, and then, when they choose to change, find these powers fresh and free for an entirely opposite course. *Patriarchs and Prophets,* p. 622.

A child may receive sound religious instruction; but if parents, teachers, or guardians permit his character to be biased by a wrong habit, that habit, if not overcome, will become a predominant power, and the child is lost. *Testimonies for the Church,* vol. 5, p. 53.

Small Actions Are Important. Every course of action has a twofold character and importance. It is virtuous or vicious, right or wrong, according to the motive which prompts it. A wrong action, by frequent repetition, leaves a permanent impression upon the mind of the actor, and also on the minds of those who are connected with him in any relation, either spiritual or temporal. The parents or teachers who give no attention to the small actions that are not right establish those habits in the youth. *Review and Herald,* May 17, 1898.

Parents should deal faithfully with the souls committed to their trust. They should not encourage in their children pride, extravagance, or love of show. They should not teach them, or suffer them to learn, little pranks which appear cunning in small children, but which they will have to unlearn, and for which they must be corrected when they are older. *Testimonies for the Church,* vol. 1, p. 396.

Little pranks and errors may seem to be amusing when the child is a baby, and they may be permitted and encouraged; but as the child grows older, they become disgusting and offensive. Letter 1, 1877.

Bad Habits Are More Easily Formed Than Good. All the learning they may acquire will never undo the evil resulting from lax discipline in childhood. One neglect, often repeated, forms habit. One wrong act prepares the way for another. Bad habits are more easily formed than good ones and are given up with more difficulty. *Review and Herald,* Dec. 5, 1899.

Young children, if left to themselves, learn the bad more readily than the good. Bad habits agree best with the natural heart, and things which they see and hear in infancy and childhood are deeply imprinted upon their minds. *Pacific Health Journal,* September 1897.

Early Habits Decide Future Victory or Defeat. We shall be individually, for time and eternity, what our habits make us. The lives of those who form right habits, and are faithful in the performance of every duty, will be as shining lights, shedding bright beams upon the pathway of others; but if habits of unfaithfulness are indulged, if lax, indolent, neglectful habits are allowed to strengthen, a cloud darker than midnight will settle on the prospects in this life, and forever debar the individual from the future life. *Testimonies for the Church,* vol. 4, p. 452.

In childhood and youth the character is most impressible. The power of self-control should then be acquired. By the fireside and at the family board, influences are exerted whose results are as enduring as eternity.

More than any natural endowment, the habits established in early years decide whether a man will be victorious or vanquished in the battle of life. *The Desire of Ages,* p. 101.

CHAPTER 38

Study Age, Disposition, and Temperament

Do Not Hurry Children Out of Childhood. Parents should never hurry their children out of their childhood. Let the lessons given them be of that character which will inspire their hearts with noble purposes; but let them be children and grow up with that simple trust, candor, and truthfulness which will prepare them to enter the kingdom of heaven. *Good Health,* March 1880.

There Is a Beauty Appropriate to Each Period. Parents and teachers should aim so to cultivate the tendencies of the youth that at each stage of life they may represent the beauty appropriate to that period, unfolding naturally, as do the plants in the garden. *Education,* p. 107.

One of Christ's most beautiful and impressive parables is that of the sower and the seed. . . . The truths which this parable teaches were made a living reality in Christ's own life. In both His physical and His spiritual nature He followed the divine order of growth, illustrated by the plant, as He wishes all youth to do. Although He was the Majesty of heaven, the King of glory, He became a babe in Bethlehem, and for a time represented the helpless infant in its mother's care.

In childhood Jesus did the works of an obedient child. He spoke and acted with the wisdom of a child, and not of a man, honoring His parents and carrying out their wishes in helpful ways, according to the ability of a child. But at each stage of His development He was perfect, with the simple, natural grace of a sinless life. The Sacred Record says of His childhood, "The child grew, and waxed strong in spirit, filled with wisdom: and the grace of God was upon him." And of His youth it is recorded, "Jesus increased in wisdom and stature, and in favour with God and man." Luke 2:40, 52. *Counsels to Parents, Teachers, and Students,* pp. 140, 141.

Diversity of Disposition in Family Members. Marked diversities of disposition and character frequently exist in the same family, for it is in the order of God that persons of varied temperament should associate together. When this is the case, each member of the household should sacredly regard the feelings and respect the right of the others. By this means mutual consideration and forbearance will be cultivated, prejudices will be softened, and rough points of character smoothed. Harmony may be secured, and the blending of the varied temperaments may be a benefit to each. *Signs of the Times,* Sept. 9, 1886.

Study Individual Minds and Characters. Every child brought into the world increases the responsibility of the parents. . . . Their dispositions, their tendencies, their traits of character are to be studied. Very carefully should the discriminating powers of the parents be educated, that they may be enabled to repress the wrong tendencies and encourage right impressions and correct principles.

Violence or harshness is not required in this work. Self-control must be cultivated and leave its impression on the mind and heart of the child. Manuscript 12, 1898.

It is a very nice work to deal with human minds. All children cannot be treated in the same way, for that restraint which must be kept upon one would crush out the life of another. Manuscript 32, 1899.

Stimulate Weak Traits; Repress Wrong Ones. There are few well-balanced minds, because parents are wickedly negligent of their duty to stimulate weak traits and repress wrong ones. They do not remember that they are under the most solemn obligation to watch the tendencies of each child, that it is their duty to train their children to right habits and right ways of thinking. *Signs of the Times,* Jan. 31, 1884.

Learn the Disposition of Each Child. Children must have constant care, but you need not let them see that you are ever guarding them. Learn the disposition of each as revealed in their association with one another, and then seek to correct their faults by encouraging opposite traits. Children should be taught that the development of both the mental and the physical powers rests with themselves; it is the result of effort. They should early learn that happiness is not found in selfish gratification; it follows only in the wake of duty. At the same time the mother should seek to make her children happy. *Signs of the Times,* Feb. 9, 1882.

Mental Needs Are as Important as Physical. Some parents attend carefully to the temporal wants of their children; they kindly and faithfully nurse them in sickness, and then think their duty done. Here they mistake. Their work has but just begun. The wants of the mind should be cared for. It requires skill to apply the proper remedies to cure a wounded mind.

Children have trials just as hard to bear, just as grievous in character, as those of older persons. Parents themselves do not feel the same at all times. Their minds are often perplexed. They labor under mistaken views, and feelings. Satan buffets them, and they yield to his temptations. They speak irritably and in a manner to excite wrath in their children, and are sometimes exacting and fretful. The poor children partake of the same spirit, and the parents are not prepared to help them, for they were the cause of the trouble. Sometimes everything seems to go wrong. There is fretfulness all around, and all have a miserable, unhappy time. The parents lay the blame upon their poor children and think them very disobedient and unruly, the worst children in the world, when the cause of the disturbance is in themselves. *Testimonies for the Church,* vol. 1, p. 384.

Encourage Amiability. The ill-balanced mind, the hasty temper, the fretfulness, envy, or jealousy, bear witness to parental neglect. These evil traits of character bring great unhappiness to their possessors. How many fail to receive from companions and friends the love which they might have, if they were more amiable. How many create trouble wherever they go, and in whatever they are engaged! *Fundamentals of Christian Education,* p. 67.

Varied Temperaments Need Varied Discipline. Children have varied temperaments, and parents cannot always give the same manner of discipline to each. There are different qualities of mind, and they should be made a prayerful study that they may be molded so as to accomplish the purpose God designed. *Good Health,* July 1880.

Mothers, . . . take time to get acquainted with your children. Study their dispositions and temperaments, that you may know how to deal with them. Some children need more attention than others. *Review and Herald,* July 9, 1901.

Dealing With Unpromising Children. There are some children who need more patient discipline and kindly training than others. They have received as a legacy unpromising traits of character, and because of this they need the more of sympathy and love. By persevering labor these wayward ones may be prepared for a place in the work of the Master. They may possess undeveloped powers which, when aroused, will enable them to fill places far in advance of those from whom more has been expected.

If you have children with peculiar temperaments, do not, because of this, let the blight of discouragement rest upon their lives. . . . Help them by the manifestation of forbearance and sympathy. Strengthen them by loving words and kindly deeds to overcome their defects of character. *Counsels to Parents, Teachers, and Students,* pp. 115, 116.

You Can Train More Than You Think. Just as soon as the mother loves Jesus, she wants to train her children for Him. You can train the disposition of children much more than you think you can from their earliest years. That precious name of Jesus should be a household word. Manuscript 17, 1893.

CHAPTER 39

The Will a Factor in Success

Every Child Should Understand the Power of the Will.
The will is the governing power in the nature of man, bringing all the other faculties under its sway. The will is not the taste or the inclination, but it is the deciding power, which works in the children of men unto obedience to God, or unto disobedience. *Testimonies for the Church,* vol. 5, p. 513.

Every child should understand the true force of the will. He should be led to see how great is the responsibility involved in this gift. The will is . . . the power of decision, or choice. *Education,* p. 289.

Success Comes When the Will Is Yielded to God. Every human being possessed of reason has power to choose the right. In every experience of life God's word to us is, "Choose you this day whom ye will serve." Joshua 24:15. Everyone may place his will on the side of the will of God, may choose to obey Him, and by thus linking himself with divine agencies, he may stand where nothing can force him to do evil. In every youth, every child, lies the power, by the help of God, to form a character of integrity and to live a life of usefulness.

The parent or teacher who by such instruction trains the child to self-control will be the most useful and permanently successful. To the superficial observer his work may not appear to the best advantage; it may not be valued so highly as that of the one who holds the mind and will of the child under absolute authority; but after years will show the result of the better method of training. *Ibid.*

Do Not Weaken, but Direct the Child's Will. Save all the strength of the will, for the human being needs it all; but give it proper direction. Treat it wisely and tenderly, as a sacred treasure. Do not hammer it in pieces, but by precept and true example wisely fashion and mold it until the child comes to years of responsibility. *Counsels to Parents, Teachers, and Students,* p. 116.

Children should early be trained to submit their will and inclination to the will and authority of their parents. When parents teach their children this lesson, they are educating them to submit to God's will and obey His requirements, and fitting them to be members of Christ's family. Manuscript 119, 1899.

To Be Guided, Not Crushed. To direct the child's development without hindering it by undue control should be the study of both parent and teacher. Too much management is as bad as too little. The effort to "break the will" of a child is a terrible mistake. Minds are constituted differently; while force may secure outward submission, the result with many children is a more determined rebellion of the heart. Even should the parent or teacher succeed in gaining the control he seeks, the outcome may be no less harmful to the child. . . .

Since the surrender of the will is so much more difficult for some pupils than for others, the teacher should make obedience to his requirements as easy as possible. The will should be guided and molded, but not ignored or crushed. *Education,* pp. 288, 289.

Lead; Never Drive. Allow the children under your care to have an individuality, as well as yourselves. Ever try to lead them, but never drive them. *Testimonies for the Church,* vol. 5, p. 653.

Exercise of Will Expands and Strengthens Mind. A child may be so trained as to have . . . no will of his own. Even his individuality may be merged in the one who superintends his training; his will, to all intents and purposes, is subject to the will of the teacher. Children who are thus educated will ever be deficient in moral energy and individual responsibility. They have not been taught to move from reason and principle; their wills have been controlled by another, and the mind has not been called out, that it might expand and strengthen by exercise. They have not been directed and disciplined with respect to their peculiar constitutions and capabilities of mind, to put forth their strongest powers when required. *Counsels to Parents, Teachers, and Students,* p. 74.

When There Is a Clash of Wills. If the child has a stubborn will, the mother, if she understands her responsibility, will realize that this stubborn will is part of the inheritance she has given him. She will not look upon his will as something that must be broken. There are times when the determination of the mother meets the determination of the child, when the firm, matured will of the mother meets the unreasoning will of the child, and when either the mother rules because of her advantage of age and experience, or there is a ruling of the older will by the younger, undisciplined will of the child. At such times there is need of great wisdom; for by unwise management, by stern compulsion, the child may be spoiled for this life and the next. By a lack of wisdom everything may be lost.

This is a crisis that should seldom be permitted to come, for both mother and child will have a hard struggle. Great care should be shown to avoid such an issue. But once such an issue is entered into, the child must be led to yield to the superior wisdom of the parent. The mother is to keep her words under perfect control. There

are to be no loud-voiced commands. Nothing is to be done
that will develop a defiant spirit in the child. The mother
must study how to deal with him in such a way that he will
be drawn to Jesus. She must pray in faith that Satan shall not
be victor over the child's will. The heavenly angels are
watching the scene.

The mother must realize that God is her helper, that love
is her success, her power. If she is a wise Christian, she will
not attempt to force the child into submission. She will pray;
and as she prays, she will be conscious of a renewal of spiritual life within herself. And she will see that at the same time
the power that is working in her is working also in the child.
And the child, in the place of being compelled, is led and
grows gentler; and the battle is gained. Each kindly thought,
each patient action, each word of wise restraint, is like apples
of gold in pictures of silver. The mother has gained a victory
more precious than language can express. She has renewed
light and increased experience. The "true Light, which
lighteth every man that cometh into the world," has subdued
her will. There is peace after the storm, like the shining of
the sun after rain. Letter 55, 1902.

Parents Should Retain Youthful Feelings. Too few
realize the importance of retaining, as far as possible, their
own youthful feelings, and not becoming harsh and
unsympathizing in their nature. God would be pleased
to have parents mingle the graceful simplicity of a child
with the strength, wisdom, and maturity of manhood and
womanhood. Some never had a genuine childhood. They
never enjoyed the freedom, simplicity, and freshness of
budding life. They were scolded and snubbed, reproved
and beaten, until the innocency and trustful frankness of

the child was exchanged for fear, envy, jealousy, and deceitfulness. Such seldom have the characteristics that will make the childhood of their own dear ones happy. *Good Health,* March 1880.

A Great Mistake. A great mistake is made when the lines of control are placed in the child's hands, and he is allowed to bear sway and control in the home. This is giving undue direction to that wonderful thing, the will power. But this has been done and will continue to be done because fathers and mothers are blind in their discernment and calculation. Manuscript 126, 1897.

A Mother Who Yielded to Her Crying Child. Your child . . . needs the hand of wisdom to guide him aright. He has been allowed to cry for what he wanted, until he has formed the habit of doing this. He has been allowed to cry for his father. Again and again, in his hearing, others have been told how he cries for his father, until he makes it a point of doing this. Had I your child, in three weeks he would be transformed. I would let him understand that my word was law, and kindly but firmly I would carry out my purposes. I would not submit my will to the child's will. You have a work to do here, and you have lost much by not taking hold of it before. Letter 5, 1884.

Unhappy Life of the Spoiled Child. Every child that is not carefully and prayerfully disciplined will be unhappy in this probationary time and will form such unlovely traits of character that the Lord cannot unite them with His family in heaven. There is a very great burden to be carried all through the life of a spoiled child. In trial, in disappointment, in temptation, he will follow his undisciplined, misdirected will. Manuscript 126, 1897.

Children who are allowed to have their own way are

not happy. The unsubdued heart has not within itself the elements of rest and contentment. The mind and heart must be disciplined and brought under proper restraint, in order for the character to harmonize with the wise laws that govern our being. Restlessness and discontent are the fruits of indulgence and selfishness. *Testimonies for the Church,* vol. 4, p. 202.

The Background of Many Trials. The sad trials, which prove so dangerous to the prosperity of a church, and which cause the unbelieving to stumble and turn away with doubt and dissatisfaction, usually arise from an unsubdued and rebellious spirit, the offspring of parental indulgence in early youth. How many lives are wrecked, how many crimes are committed, under the influence of a quick-rising passion that might have been checked in childhood, when the mind was impressible, when the heart was easily influenced for right and was subject to a fond mother's will. Inefficient training of children lies at the foundation of a vast amount of moral wretchedness. *Ibid.*

CHAPTER 40

Exemplify Christian Principles

Children Will Imitate Parents. Fathers and mothers, you are teachers; your children are the pupils. Your tones of voice, your deportment, your spirit, are copied by your little ones. *Signs of the Times,* Mar. 11, 1886.

Children imitate their parents; hence great care should be taken to give them correct models. Parents who are kind and polite at home, while at the same time they are firm and decided, will see the same traits manifested in their children. If they are upright, honest, and honorable, their children will be quite likely to resemble them in these particulars. If they reverence and worship God, their children, trained in the same way, will not forget to serve Him also. *Testimonies for the Church,* vol. 5, pp. 319, 320.

In the family, fathers and mothers should ever present before their children the example they wish to be imitated. They should manifest one to the other a tender respect in word, and look, and action. They should make it manifest that the Holy Spirit is controlling them, by representing to their children the character of Jesus Christ. The powers of imitation are strong; and in childhood and youth, when this faculty is most active, a perfect pattern should be set before the young. Children should have confidence in their parents, and thus take in the lessons they would inculcate. *Review and Herald,* Mar. 13, 1894.

Teach by Precept and Example. The mother, in the education of her children, is in a continual school. While teaching her children, she is herself learning daily. The lessons which she gives her children in self-control must be practiced by herself. In dealing with the varied minds and moods of her children, she needs keen perceptive powers or she will be in danger of misjudging and of dealing partially with her children. The law of kindness she should practice in her home life if she would have her children courteous and kind. Thus they have lessons repeated, by precept and example daily. *Pacific Health Journal,* June 1890.

The teachers in the school will do something toward educating your children, but your example will do more than can be accomplished by any other means. Your conversation, the way in which you manage your business matters, the likes and dislikes to which you give expression, all help in molding the character. The kindly disposition, the self-control, the self-possession, the courtesy your child sees in you, will be daily lessons to him. Like time, this education is ever going on, and the tendency of this everyday school should be to make your child what he ought to be. *Review and Herald,* June 27, 1899.

Be careful that you are not rude to your children. . . . Require obedience, and do not allow yourself to speak carelessly to your children, because your manners and your words are their lesson book. Help them gently, tenderly over this period of their life. Let the sunshine of your presence make sunshine in their hearts. These growing boys and girls feel very sensitive, and by roughness you may mar their whole life. Be careful, mothers; never scold, for that never helps. Manuscript 127, 1898.

Parents to Be Patterns of Self-control. Children should be kept as free from excitement as possible; therefore the mother must be calm and unhurried, free from all excitement and nervous haste. This is a school of discipline to herself as well as to the child. While teaching the little ones the lesson of self-denial, she is educating herself to be a pattern to her children. While with tender interest she is working the soil of their hearts, that she may subdue the natural sinful inclinations, she is cultivating in her own words and in her own deportment the graces of the Spirit. Manuscript 43, 1900.

One victory gained over yourself will be of great value and encouragement to your children. You may stand on vantage ground, saying, I am God's husbandry; I am God's building. I place myself under His hand to be fashioned after the divine similitude, that I may be a coworker with God in fashioning the minds and characters of my children so that it will be easier for them to walk in the way of the Lord. . . . Fathers and mothers, when you can control yourselves, you will gain great victories in controlling your children. Letter 75, 1898.

The Fruits of Self-control. Parents, every time you lose self-control and speak and act impatiently, you sin against God. The recording angel writes every impatient, unguarded word spoken before them, carelessly or in jest; every word that is not chaste and elevated, he marks as a spot against your Christian character. Speak kindly to your children. Remember how sensitive you are, how little you can bear to be blamed, and do not lay upon them that which you cannot bear; for they are weaker than you and cannot endure as much. The fruits of self-control, thoughtfulness, and painstaking on your part will be a hundredfold.

Let your pleasant, cheerful words ever be like sunbeams in your family. *Signs of the Times,* Apr. 10, 1884.

If parents desire their children to be right and do right, they must be right themselves in theory and in practice. *Good Health,* January 1880.

Children Are Influenced by Deportment of Professing Christians. There are children of Sabbathkeepers who have been taught from their youth to observe the Sabbath. Some of these are very good children, faithful to duty as far as temporal matters are concerned; but they feel no deep conviction of sin and no need of repentance from sin. Such are in a dangerous condition. They are watching the deportment and efforts of professed Christians. They see some who make high professions, but who are not conscientious Christians, and they compare their own views and actions with these stumbling blocks; and as there are no outbreaking sins in their own lives, they flatter themselves that they are about right. *Testimonies for the Church,* vol. 4, p. 40.

It is because so many parents and teachers profess to believe the Word of God while their lives deny its power, that the teaching of Scripture has no greater effect upon the youth. At times the youth are brought to feel the power of the Word. They see the preciousness of the love of Christ. They see the beauty of His character, the possibilities of a life given to His service. But in contrast they see the life of those who profess to revere God's precepts. *Education,* p. 259.

Parents Must Say "No" to Temptation. Mothers, by not following the practices of the world, you may set before your children an example of faithfulness to God, and so teach them to say no. Teach your children the meaning of the precept, "If sinners entice thee, consent thou not." But if you would have your children able to say no to temptation, you yourself must be able to say no. It is as needful for the man to say no, as for the child. *Review and Herald,* Mar. 31, 1891.

Exemplify Gentleness. Parents, be kind and gentle with your children, and they will learn gentleness. Let us demonstrate in our homes that we are Christians. I value as worthless that profession that is not carried out in the home life in kindness and forbearance and love. Manuscript 97, 1909.

Watch Tone of Voice as Well as the Words. Let not one word of fretfulness, harshness, or passion escape your lips. The grace of Christ awaits your demand. His Spirit will take control of your heart and conscience, presiding over your words and deeds. Never forfeit your self-respect by hasty, thoughtless words. See that your words are pure, your conversation holy. Give your children an example of that which you wish them to be. . . . Let there be peace, pleasant words, and cheerful countenances. Letter 28, 1890.

Parents cannot with safety be in any way overbearing. They must not show a masterly, criticizing, faultfinding spirit. The words they speak, the tone in which they speak, are lessons, either for good or ill, to their children. Fathers and mothers, if cross words fall from your lips, you are teaching your children to speak in the same way, and the refining influence of the Holy Spirit is made of none effect. Patient continuance in well-doing is essential if you would do your duty to your children. Letter 8a, 1896.

Parents Are God's Agents in Molding Character. The intellects of your children are taking shape, the affections and characters are being molded, but after what pattern? Let the parents remember that they are agents in these transactions. And when they may be sleeping in the grave, their work left behind is enduring, and will bear testimony of them whether it is good or bad. *Pacific Health Journal,* June 1890.

Stamping the Image of the Divine. You must instruct, warn, and counsel, ever remembering that your looks, words, and actions have a direct bearing upon the future course of your dear ones. Your work is not done to paint a form of beauty upon canvas or to chisel it from marble, but to impress upon a human soul the image of the Divine. *Signs of the Times,* May 25, 1882.

SECTION 10

DISCIPLINE AND ITS ADMINISTRATION

CHAPTER 41

Objectives of Discipline

Self-government the Paramount Objective. The object of discipline is the training of the child for self-government. He should be taught self-reliance and self-control. Therefore as soon as he is capable of understanding, his reason should be enlisted on the side of obedience. Let all dealing with him be such as to show obedience to be just and reasonable. Help him to see that all things are under law, and that disobedience leads, in the end, to disaster and suffering. When God says, "Thou shalt not," He in love warns us of the consequence of disobedience, in order to save us from harm and loss. *Education,* p. 287.

Enlisting the Power of the Will. The true object of reproof is gained only when the wrongdoer himself is led to see his fault and his will is enlisted for its correction. When this is accomplished, point him to the source of pardon and power. *Ibid.,* p. 291.

Those who train their pupils to feel that the power lies in themselves to become men and women of honor and usefulness will be the most permanently successful. *Fundamentals of Christian Education,* p. 58.

Correct Habits, Inclinations, Evil Tendencies. It is the work of the parents to restrain and guide and control. They cannot commit a worse evil than to permit their children to gratify all their childish wishes and fancies, and leave them to follow their own inclinations; they cannot do them a greater wrong than to leave upon their minds the impression that they are to live to please and amuse themselves, to choose their own ways and find their own pleasure and society. . . . The youth need

223

parents who will educate and discipline them, correct their wrong habits and inclinations, and prune away their evil tendencies. Manuscript 12, 1898.

Break Down Satan's Stronghold. Mothers, the destiny of your children rests to a great extent in your hands. If you fail in duty, you may place them in Satan's ranks and make them his agents to ruin other souls. Or your faithful discipline and godly example may lead them to Christ, and they in turn will influence others, and thus many souls may be saved through your instrumentality. *Signs of the Times,* Feb. 9, 1882.

Let us look carefully and begin to catch up our dropped stitches. Let us break down the strongholds of the enemy. Let us mercifully correct our loved ones and keep them from the power of the enemy. Do not be discouraged. *Review and Herald,* July 16, 1895.

Teach Respect to Parental and Divine Authority. Children . . . should be trained, educated, and disciplined until they become obedient to their parents, giving respect to their authority. In this way respect for divine authority will be implanted in their hearts, and the family training will be like a preparatory training for the family in heaven. The training of childhood and youth should be of such a character that children will be prepared to take up their religious duties, and thus become fitted to enter into the courts above. *Review and Herald,* Mar. 13, 1894.

He who is the fountain of all knowledge has stated the condition of our fitness to enter the heaven of bliss, in the words, "Blessed are they that do his commandments, that they may have right to the tree of life, and may enter in through the gates into the city." Obedience to God's commandments is the price of heaven, and obedience to their parents in the Lord is the all-important lesson for children to learn. Manuscript 12a, 1896.

Obedience From Principle, Not Compulsion. Tell your children exactly what you require of them. Then let them understand that your word is law and must be obeyed. Thus you are training them to respect the commandments of God, which plainly declare, "Thou shalt," and "Thou shalt not." It is far better for your boy to obey from principle than from compulsion. *Review and Herald,* Sept. 15, 1904.

A Lesson in Implicit Confidence. Isaac is bound by the trembling, loving hands of his pitying father, because God has said it. The son submits to the sacrifice, because he believes in the integrity of his father. . . .

This act of faith in Abraham is recorded for our benefit. It teaches us the great lesson of confidence in the requirements of God, however close and cutting they may be; and it teaches children perfect submission to their parents and to God. By Abraham's obedience we are taught that nothing is too precious for us to give to God. *Testimonies for the Church,* vol. 3, p. 368.

Youth Will Respond to Trust. The youth must be impressed with the idea that they are trusted. They have a sense of honor, and they want to be respected, and it is their right. If pupils receive the impression that they cannot go out or come in, sit at the table, or be anywhere, even in their rooms, except they are watched, a critical eye is upon them to criticize and report, it will have the influence to demoralize, and pastime will have no pleasure in it. This knowledge of a continual oversight is more than a parental guardianship, and far worse; for wise parents can, through tact, often discern beneath the surface and see the working of the restless mind under the longings of youth, or under the forces of temptations, and set their plans to work to counteract evils. But this constant watchfulness is not natural, and produces evils that it is seeking to avoid. The healthfulness of youth requires exercise, cheerfulness, and a happy, pleasant atmosphere surrounding them, for the development of physical health and symmetrical character. *Fundamentals of Christian Education,* p. 114.

Self-government Versus Absolute Authority. There are many families of children who appear to be well trained, while under the training discipline; but when the system which has held them to set rules is broken up, they seem to be incapable of thinking, acting, or deciding for themselves. These children have been so long under iron rule, not allowed to think and act for themselves in those things in which it was highly proper that they should, that they have no confidence in themselves to move out upon their own judgment, having an opinion of their own. And when they go out from their parents to act for themselves, they are easily led by others' judgment in the wrong direction. They have not stability of character. They have not been thrown upon their own judgment as fast and as far as practicable, and therefore their minds have not been properly developed and strengthened. They have so long been absolutely controlled by their parents that they rely wholly upon them; their parents are mind and judgment for them.

On the other hand, the young should not be left to think and act independently of the judgment of their parents and teachers. Children should be taught to respect experienced judgment and to be guided by their parents and teachers. . . . They should be so educated that their minds will be united with the minds of their parents and teachers, and so instructed that they can see the propriety of heeding their counsel. Then when they go forth from the guiding hand of their parents and teachers, their characters will not be like the reed trembling in the wind.

The severe training of youth—without properly directing them to think and act for themselves as their own capacity and turn of mind will allow, that by this means they may have growth of thought, feelings of self-respect, and confidence in their own ability to perform—will ever produce a class who are weak in mental and moral power. And when they stand in the world to act for themselves, they will reveal the fact that they were trained, like the animals, and not educated. Their wills, instead of being guided, were forced into subjection by the harsh discipline of parents and teachers. *Testimonies for the Church,* vol. 3, pp. 132, 133.

Evil Results When One Mind Dominates Another. Those parents and teachers who boast of having complete control of the minds and wills of the children under their care would cease their boastings could they trace out the future lives of the children who are thus brought into subjection by force or through fear. These are almost wholly unprepared to share in the stern responsibilities of life. When these youth are no longer under their parents and teachers, and are compelled to think and act for themselves, they are almost sure to take a wrong course and yield to the power of temptation. They do not make this life a success, and the same deficiencies are seen in their religious life. Could the instructors of children and youth have the future result of their mistaken discipline mapped out before them, they would change their plan of education. That class of teachers who are gratified that they have almost complete control of the wills of their scholars are not the most successful teachers, although the appearance for the time being may be flattering.

God never designed that one human mind should be under the complete control of another. And those who make efforts to have the individuality of their pupils merged in themselves, and to be mind, will, and conscience for them, assume fearful responsibilities. These scholars may, upon certain occasions, appear like well-drilled soldiers. But when the restraint is removed, there will be seen a want of independent action from firm principle existing in them. *Ibid.,* pp. 133, 134.

Through Skill and Patient Effort. It requires skill and patient effort to mold the young in the right manner. Especially do children who have come into the world burdened with a heritage of evil, the direct results of the sins of their parents, need the most careful culture to develop and strengthen their moral and intellectual faculties. And the responsibility of the parents is heavy indeed. Evil tendencies are to be carefully restrained and tenderly rebuked; the mind is to be stimulated in favor of the right. The child should be encouraged in attempting to govern himself. And all this is to be done judiciously, or the purpose desired will be frustrated. *Christian Temperance and Bible Hygiene,* p. 138.

CHAPTER 42

The Time to Begin Discipline

Disobedient Children a Sign of the Last Days. One of the signs of the "last days" is the disobedience of children to their parents. And do parents realize their responsibility? Many seem to lose sight of the watch care they should ever have over their children, and suffer them to indulge in evil passions and to disobey them. *Review and Herald,* Sept. 19, 1854.

Children are the heritage of the Lord, and unless parents give them such a training as will enable them to keep the way of the Lord, they neglect solemn duty. It is not the will or purpose of God that children shall become coarse, rough, uncourteous, disobedient, unthankful, unholy, heady, highminded, lovers of pleasures more than lovers of God. The Scriptures state that this condition of society shall be a sign of the last days. *Signs of the Times,* Sept. 17, 1894.

Indulgent Parents Disqualify for Heaven's Order. There is perfect order in heaven, perfect concord and agreement. If parents so neglect to bring their children under proper authority here, how can they hope that they will be considered fit companions for the holy angels in a world of peace and harmony? *Testimonies for the Church,* vol. 4, p. 199.

Those who have had no respect for order or discipline in this life would have no respect for the order which is observed in heaven. They can never be admitted into heaven, for all worthy of an entrance there will love order and respect discipline. The characters formed in this life will determine the future destiny. When Christ shall come, He will not change the character of any individual. . . . Parents should neglect no duty on their part to benefit their children. They should so train them that they may be a blessing to society here and may reap the reward of eternal life hereafter. *Ibid.,* p. 429.

When Discipline Should Begin. The moment that the child begins to choose his own will and way, that moment his education in discipline is to begin. This may be called an unconscious education. It is then that a work, conscious and powerful, is to begin. The greatest burden of this work necessarily rests on the mother. She has the first care of the child, and she is to lay the foundation of an education that will help the child to develop a strong, symmetrical character. . . .

Frequently mere babies show a most determined will. If this will is not brought into subjection to a wiser authority than the child's untrained desires, Satan takes control of the mind and fashions the disposition in harmony with his will. Letter 9, 1904.

Neglecting the work of disciplining and training until a perverse disposition has become strengthened is doing the children a most serious wrong; for they grow up selfish, exacting, and unlovable. They cannot enjoy their own company any better than can others; therefore they will ever be filled with discontent. The work of the mother must commence at an early age, giving Satan no chance to control the minds and dispositions of their little ones. Manuscript 43, 1900.

Repress First Appearance of Evil. Parents, you should commence your first lesson of discipline when your children are babes in your arms. Teach them to yield their will to yours. This can be done by bearing an even hand and manifesting firmness. Parents should have perfect control over their own spirits and, with mildness and yet firmness, bend the will of the child until it shall expect nothing else but to yield to their wishes.

Parents do not commence in season. The first manifestation of temper is not subdued, and the children grow stubborn, which increases with their growth and strengthens with their strength. *Testimonies for the Church,* vol. 1, p. 218.

"Too Young to Punish?" Eli did not manage his household according to God's rules for family government. He followed his own judgment. The fond father overlooked the faults and sins of his sons in their childhood, flattering himself that after a time they would outgrow their evil tendencies. Many are now making a similar mistake. They think they know a better way of training their children than that which God has given in His Word. They foster wrong tendencies in them, urging as an excuse, "They are too young to be punished. Wait till they become older and can be reasoned with." Thus wrong habits are left to strengthen until they become second nature. The children grow up without restraint, with traits of character that are a lifelong curse to them and are liable to be reproduced in others.

There is no greater curse upon households than to allow the youth to have their own way. When parents regard every wish of their children and indulge them in what they know is not for their good, the children soon lose all respect for their parents, all regard for the authority of God or man, and are led captive at the will of Satan. *Patriarchs and Prophets,* pp. 578, 579.

Put Home Training Ahead of Other Pursuits. Many point to the children of ministers, teachers, and other men of high repute for learning and piety, and urge that if these men, with their superior advantages, fail in family government, those who are less favorably situated need not hope to succeed. The question to be settled is,

Have these men given to their children that which is their right—a good example, faithful instruction, and proper restraint? It is by a neglect of these essentials that such parents give to society children who are unbalanced in mind, impatient of restraint, and ignorant of the duties of practical life. In this they are doing the world an injury which outweighs all the good that their labors accomplish. Those children transmit their own perversity of character as an inheritance to their offspring, and at the same time their evil example and influence corrupt society and make havoc in the church. We cannot think that any man, however great his ability and usefulness, is best serving God or the world while his time is given to other pursuits, to the neglect of his own children. *Signs of the Times,* Feb. 9, 1882.

Heavenly Cooperation Is Promised. God will bless a just and correct discipline. But "without me," says Christ, "ye can do nothing." The heavenly intelligences cannot cooperate with fathers and mothers who are neglecting to train their children, who are allowing Satan to handle that little piece of infant machinery, that youthful mind, as an instrument through whom he can work to counteract the working of the Holy Spirit. Manuscript 126, 1897.

CHAPTER 43

Discipline in the Home

Well-ordered, Well-disciplined Families. It is the duty of those who claim to be Christians to present to the world well-ordered, well-disciplined families—families that will show the power of true Christianity. *Review and Herald,* Apr. 13, 1897.

It is no easy matter to train and educate children wisely. As parents try to keep judgment and the fear of the Lord before them, difficulties will arise. The children will reveal the perversity bound up in their hearts. They show love of folly, of independence, a hatred of restraint and discipline. They practice deception and utter falsehoods. Too many parents, instead of punishing the children for these faults, make themselves blind in order that they shall not see beneath the surface or discern the true meaning of these things. Therefore the children continue in their deceptive practices, forming characters that God cannot approve.

The standard raised in God's Word is set aside by parents who dislike, as some have termed it, to use the strait jacket in the education of their children. Many parents have a settled dislike for the holy principles of the Word of God, because these principles place too much responsibility on them. But the after sight, which all parents are obliged to have, shows that God's ways are the best, and that the only path of safety and happiness is found in obedience to His will. *Review and Herald,* Mar. 30, 1897.

Restraint of Children Is No Easy Task. In the present state of things in society, it is no easy task for parents to restrain their children and instruct them according to the Bible rule of right. When they would train their children in harmony with the precepts of the Word of God and, like Abraham of old, command their households after them, the children think their parents overcareful and unnecessarily exacting. *Signs of the Times,* Apr. 17, 1884.

False Ideas Regarding Restraint. If you want the blessing of God, parents, do as did Abraham. Repress the evil, and encourage the good. Some commanding may be necessary in the place of consulting the inclination and pleasure of the children. Letter 53, 1887.

To allow a child to follow his natural impulses is to allow him to deteriorate and to become proficient in evil. Wise parents will not say to their children, "Follow your own choice; go where you will, and do what you will"; but, "Listen to the instruction of the Lord." Wise rules and regulations must be made and enforced, that the beauty of the home life may not be spoiled. *Counsels to Parents, Teachers, and Students,* p. 112.

Why Achan's Family Perished. Have you considered why it was that all who were connected with Achan were also subjects of the punishment of God? It was because they had not been trained and educated according to the directions given them in the great standard of the law of God. Achan's parents had educated their son in such a way that he felt free to disobey the word of the Lord. The principles inculcated in his life led him to deal with his children in such a way that they also were corrupted. Mind acts and reacts upon mind, and the punishment, which included the relations of Achan with himself, reveals the fact that all were involved in the transgression. Manuscript 67, 1894.

Blind Parental Affection the Greatest Obstacle in Training. The sin of parental neglect is almost universal. Blind affection for those who are connected with us by the ties of nature too often exists. This affection is carried to great lengths; it is not balanced by the wisdom or the fear of God. Blind parental affection is the greatest obstacle in the way of the proper training of children. It prevents the discipline and training which are required by the Lord. At times, because of this affection, parents seemed to be bereft of their reason. It is like the tender mercies of the wicked—cruelty disguised in the garb of so-called love. It is the dangerous undercurrent which carries children to ruin. *Review and Herald,* Apr. 6, 1897.

Parents are in constant danger of indulging natural affections at the expense of obedience to God's law. Many parents, to please their children, allow what God forbids. *Review and Herald,* Jan. 29, 1901.

Parents Responsible for What Children Might Have Been. If as teachers in the home the father and mother allow children to take the lines of control into their own hands and to become wayward, they are held responsible for what their children might otherwise have been. *Review and Herald,* Sept. 15, 1904.

Those who follow their own inclination, in blind affection for their children, indulging them in the gratification of their selfish desires, and do not bring to bear the authority of God to rebuke sin and correct evil, make it manifest that they are honoring their wicked children more than they honor God. They are more anxious to shield their reputation than to glorify God, more desirous to please their children than to please the Lord. . . .

Those who have too little courage to reprove wrong, or who through indolence or lack of interest make no earnest effort to purify the family or the church of God, are held accountable for the evil that may result from their neglect of duty. We are just as responsible for evils that we might have checked in others by exercise of parental or pastoral authority, as if the acts had been our own. *Patriarchs and Prophets,* p. 578.

No Place for Partiality. It is very natural for parents to be partial to their own children. Especially if these parents feel that they themselves possess superior ability, they will regard their children as superior to other children. Hence much that would be severely censured in others is passed over in their own children as smart and witty. While this partiality is natural, it is unjust and unchristian. A great wrong is done our children when we permit their faults to go uncorrected. *Signs of the Times,* Nov. 24, 1881.

Make No Compromise With Evil. It should be made plain that the government of God knows no compromise with evil. Neither in the home nor in the school should disobedience be tolerated. No parent or teacher who has at heart the well-being of those under his care will compromise with the stubborn self-will that defies authority or resorts to subterfuge or evasion in order to escape obedience. It is not love but sentimentalism that palters with wrongdoing, seeks by coaxing or bribes to secure compliance, and finally accepts some substitute in place of the thing required. *Education,* p. 290.

In too many families today there is too much self-indulgence and disobedience passed by without being corrected, or else there is manifested an overbearing, masterful spirit that creates the worst evils in the dispositions of children. Parents correct them at times in such an inconsiderate way that their lives are made miserable, and they lose all respect for father, mother, brothers, and sisters. Letter 75, 1898.

Parents Fail to Understand Correct Principles. It is heart-saddening to see the imbecility of parents in the exercise of their God-given authority. Men who in everything else are consistent and intelligent fail to understand the principles that should be brought into the training of their little ones. They fail to give them right instruction at the very time when right instruction, a godly example, and firm decision are most needed to lead in right lines the inexperienced minds that are ignorant of the deceptive and dangerous influences that they must meet with everywhere. Manuscript 119, 1899.

The greatest suffering has come upon the human family because parents have departed from the divine plan to follow their own imaginings and imperfectly developed ideas. Many parents follow impulse. They forget that the present and future good of their children requires intelligent discipline. Manuscript 49, 1901.

God Accepts No Excuse for Mismanagement. Rebellion is too frequently established in the hearts of children through the wrong discipline of the parents, when if a proper course had been taken, the children would have formed good and harmonious characters. *Testimonies for the Church,* vol. 3, pp. 532, 533.

While parents have the power to discipline, educate, and train their children, let them exert that power for God. He requires from them pure, faultless, undeviating obedience. He will tolerate nothing else. He will make no excuse for the mismanagement of children. *Review and Herald,* Apr. 13, 1897.

Overcome Natural Spirit of Obstinacy. Some children are naturally more obstinate than others and will not yield to discipline, and in consequence they make themselves very unattractive and disagreeable. If the mother has not wisdom to deal with this phase of character, a most unhappy state of affairs will follow; for such children will have their own way to their destruction. But how terrible for a child to cherish a spirit of obstinacy not only in childhood, but in more mature years, and because of a lack of agreement in childhood, nourish bitterness and unkindness in manhood and womanhood toward the mother who failed to bring her children under restraint. Manuscript 18, 1891.

Never Tell Child, "I Cannot Do Anything With You." Never let your child hear you say, "I cannot do anything with you." As long as we may have access to the throne of God, we as parents should be ashamed to utter any such word. Cry unto Jesus, and He will help you to bring your little ones to Him. *Review and Herald,* July 16, 1895.

Family Government to Be Diligently Studied. I have heard mothers say that they had not the ability to govern which others have, that it is a peculiar talent which they do not possess. Those who realize their deficiency in this respect should make the subject of family government their most diligent study. And yet the most valuable suggestions of others should not be adopted without thought and discrimination. They may not be equally adapted to the circumstances of every mother, or to the peculiar disposition and temperament of each child in the family. Let the mother study with care the experience of others, note the difference between their methods and her own, and carefully test those that may appear to be of real value. If one mode of discipline does not produce the desired results, let another plan be tried, and the effects carefully noted.

Mothers, above all others, should accustom themselves to thought and investigation. If they will persevere in this course, they will find that they are acquiring the faculty in which they thought themselves deficient, that they are learning to form aright the characters of their children. The result of the labor and thought given to this work will be seen in their obedience, their simplicity, their modesty and purity; and it will richly repay all the effort made. *Signs of the Times,* Mar. 11, 1886.

Parents to Be United in Discipline. The mother should ever have the cooperation of the father in her efforts to lay the foundation of a good Christian character in her children. A doting father should not close his eyes to the faults of his children because it is not pleasant to administer correction. *Testimonies for the Church,* vol. 1, p. 547.

Right principles must be established in the mind of the child. If the parents are united in this work of discipline, the child will understand what is required of him. But if the father, by word or look, shows that he does not approve of the discipline the mother gives, if he feels that she is too strict, and thinks that he must make up for the harshness by petting and indulgence, the child will be ruined. Deception will be practiced by the sympathizing parents, and the child will soon learn that he can do as he pleases. Parents who are committing this sin against their children are accountable for the ruin of their souls. Manuscript 58, 1899.

Combined Influence of Affection and Authority. Let the light of heavenly grace irradiate your character, that there may be sunlight in the home. Let there be peace, pleasant words, and cheerful countenances. This is not blind affection, not that tenderness which encourages sin by unwise indulgence, and which is the veriest cruelty, not that false love which allows the children to rule and makes the parents slaves to their caprices. There should be no parental partiality, no oppression; the combined influence of affection and authority will place the right mold upon the family. *Review and Herald,* Sept. 15, 1891.

Represent God's Character in Discipline. Be firm, be decided in carrying out Bible instruction, but be free from all passion. Bear in mind that when you become harsh and unreasonable before your little ones, you teach them to be the same. God requires you to educate your children, bringing into your discipline all the generalship of a wise teacher who is under the control of God. If the converting power of God is exercised in your home, you yourselves will be constant learners. You will represent the character of Christ, and your efforts in this direction will please God. Never neglect the work that should be done for the younger members of the Lord's family. You are, parents, the light of your home. Then let your light shine forth in pleasant words, in soothing tones of the voice. Take all the sting out of them by prayer to God for self-control. And angels will be in your home, for they will observe your light. The discipline you give your children will go forth in strong, clear currents from your correctly managed home to the world. Manuscript 142, 1898.

No Deviation From Right Principles. Anciently, parental authority was regarded; children were then in subjection to their parents and feared and reverenced them; but in these last days the order is reversed. Some parents are in subjection to their children. They fear to cross the will of their children, and therefore yield to them. But just as long as children are under the roof of the parents, dependent upon them, they should be subject to their control. Parents should move with decision, requiring that their views of right be followed out. *Testimonies for the Church,* vol. 1, pp. 216, 217.

Take Extreme Steps if Willful Disobedience Is Unchecked. Some indulgent, ease-loving parents fear to exercise wholesome authority over their unruly sons, lest they run away from home. It would be better for some to do this than to remain at home to live upon the bounties provided by the parents, and at the same time trample upon all authority, both human and divine. It might be a most profitable experience for such children to have to the full that independence which they think so desirable, to learn that it costs exertion to live. Let the parents say to the boy who threatens to run away from home, "My son, if you are determined to leave home rather than comply with just and proper rules, we will not hinder you. If you think to find the world more friendly than the parents who have cared for you from infancy, you must learn your mistake for yourself. When you wish to come to your father's house, to be subject to his authority, you will be welcome. Obligations are mutual. While you have food and clothing and parental care, you are in return under obligation to submit to home rules and wholesome discipline. My house cannot be polluted with the stench of tobacco, with profanity or drunkenness. I desire that angels of God shall come into my home. If you are fully determined to serve Satan, you will be as well off with those whose society you love as you will be at home."

Such a course would check the downward career of thousands. But too often children know that they may do their worst, and yet an unwise mother will plead for them and conceal their transgressions. Many a rebellious son exults because his parents have not the courage to restrain him. . . . They do not enforce obedience. Such parents are encouraging their children in dissipation and are dishonoring God by their unwise indulgence. It is these rebellious, corrupt youth that form the most difficult element to control in schools and colleges. *Review and Herald,* June 13, 1882.

Be Not Weary in Well-doing. The work of parents is continuous. It should not be laid hold of vigorously for one day and neglected the next. Many are ready to begin the work, but are not willing to persevere in it. They are eager to do some great thing, to make some great sacrifice; but they shrink from the unceasing care and effort in the little things of everyday life, the hourly pruning and training of the wayward tendencies, the work of giving instruction, reproof, or encouragement, little by little, as it is needed. They wish to see children correct their faults and form right characters at once, reaching the mountaintop at a bound, and not by successive steps; and because their hopes are not immediately realized, they become disheartened. Let all such persons take courage as they remember the words of the apostle, "Let us not be weary in well doing: for in due season we shall reap, if we faint not." *Signs of the Times,* Nov. 24, 1881.

Sabbathkeeping children may become impatient of restraint and think their parents too strict; hard feelings may even arise in their hearts and discontented, unhappy thoughts may be cherished by them against those who are working for their present and their future and eternal good. But if life shall be spared a few years, they will bless their parents for that strict care and faithful watchfulness over them in their years of inexperience. *Testimonies for the Church,* vol. 1, p. 400.

Read Admonitions From God's Word. When children err, parents should take time to read to them tenderly from the Word of God such admonitions as are particularly applicable to their case. When they are tried, tempted, or discouraged, cite them to its precious words of comfort, and gently lead them to put their trust in Jesus. Thus the young mind may be directed to that which is pure and ennobling. And as the great problems of life, and the dealings of God with the human race, are unfolded to the understanding, the reasoning powers are exercised, the judgment enlisted, while lessons of divine truth are impressed upon the heart. Thus parents may be daily molding the characters of their children, that they may have a fitness for the future life. *Review and Herald,* June 13, 1882.

CHAPTER 44

Administration of Corrective Discipline

Ask the Lord to Come In and Rule. Exact obedience in your family; but while you do this, seek the Lord with your children, and ask Him to come in and rule. Your children may have done something that demands punishment; but if you deal with them in the spirit of Christ, their arms will be thrown about your neck; they will humble themselves before the Lord and will acknowledge their wrong. That is enough. They do not then need punishment. Let us thank the Lord that He has opened the way by which we may reach every soul. Manuscript 21, 1909.

If your children are disobedient, they should be corrected. . . . Before correcting them, go by yourself, and ask the Lord to soften and subdue the hearts of your children and to give you wisdom in dealing with them. Never in a single instance have I known this method to fail. You cannot make a child understand spiritual things when the heart is stirred with passion. Manuscript 27, 1911.

Instruct Children Patiently. The Lord wants the hearts of these children from their very babyhood to be given to His service. While they are too young to reason with, divert their minds as best you can; and as they become older, teach them by precept and example that you cannot indulge their wrong desires.

Instruct them patiently. Sometimes they will have to be punished, but never do it in such a way that they will feel that they have been punished in anger. By such a course you only work a greater evil. Many unhappy differences in the family circle might be avoided if parents would obey the counsel of the Lord in the training of their children. Manuscript 93, 1909.

Parents to Be Under Discipline to God. Mothers, however provoking your children may be in their ignorance, do not give way to impatience. Teach them patiently and lovingly. Be firm with them. Do not let Satan control them. Discipline them only when you are under the discipline of God. Christ will be victor in the lives of your children if you will learn of Him who is meek and lowly, pure and undefiled. Letter 272, 1903.

But if you attempt to govern without exercising self-control, without system, thought, and prayer, you will most assuredly reap the bitter consequences. *Signs of the Times,* Feb. 9, 1882.

Never Correct in Anger. You should correct your children in love. Do not let them have their own way until you get angry, and then punish them. Such correction only helps on the evil, instead of remedying it. *Review and Herald,* Sept. 19, 1854.

To manifest passion toward an erring child is to increase the evil. It arouses the worst passions of the child and leads him to feel that you do not care for him. He reasons with himself that you could not treat him so if you cared.

And think you that God takes no cognizance of the way in which these children are corrected? He knows, and He knows also what might be the blessed results if the work of correction were done in a way to win rather than to repel. . . .

Do not, I beg of you, correct your children in anger. That is the time of all times when you should act with humility and patience and prayer. Then is the time to kneel down with the children and ask the Lord for pardon. Seek to win them to Christ by the manifestation of kindness and love, and you will see that a higher power than that of earth is cooperating with your efforts. Manuscript 53, 1912.

When you are obliged to correct a child, do not raise the voice to a high key. . . . Do not lose your self-control. The parent who, when correcting a child, gives way to anger is more at fault than the child. *Signs of the Times,* Feb. 17, 1904.

Scolding and Fretting Never Help. Harsh, angry words are not of heavenly origin. Scolding and fretting never help. Instead, they stir up the worst feelings of the human heart. When your children do wrong and are filled with rebellion, and you are tempted to speak and act harshly, wait before you correct them. Give them an opportunity to think, and allow your temper to cool.

As you deal kindly and tenderly with your children, they and you will receive the blessing of the Lord. And think you that in the day of God's judgment anyone will regret that he has been patient and kind with his children? Manuscript 114, 1903.

Nervousness Is No Excuse for Impatience. Parents sometimes excuse their own wrong course because they do not feel well. They are nervous and think they cannot be patient and calm and speak pleasantly. In this they deceive themselves and please Satan, who exults that the grace of God is not regarded by them as sufficient to overcome natural infirmities. They can and should at all times control themselves. God requires it of them. *Testimonies for the Church,* vol. 1, p. 385.

Sometimes when fatigued by labor or oppressed with care, parents do not maintain a calm spirit, but manifest a lack of forbearance that displeases God and brings a cloud over the family. Parents, when you feel fretful, you should not commit so great a sin as to poison the whole family with this dangerous irritability. At such times set a double watch over yourselves and resolve that none but pleasant, cheerful words shall escape your lips. By thus exercising self-control, you will grow stronger. Your nervous system will not be so sensitive. . . . Jesus knows our infirmities and has Himself shared our experience in all things but in sin; therefore He has prepared for us a path suited to our strength and capacity.

Sometimes everything seems to go wrong in the family circle. There is fretfulness all around, and all seem very miserable and unhappy. The parents lay the blame upon their poor children and think them very disobedient and unruly, the worst children in the world, when the cause of the disturbance is in themselves. God requires them to exercise self-control. They should realize that when they yield to impatience and fretfulness, they cause others to suffer. Those around them are affected by the spirit they manifest, and if they in their turn act out the same spirit, the evil is increased. *Signs of the Times,* Apr. 17, 1884.

There Is Sometimes Power in Silence. Those who desire to control others must first control themselves. . . . When a parent or teacher becomes impatient and is in danger of speaking unwisely, let him remain silent. There is wonderful power in silence. *Education,* p. 292.

Give Few Commands; Then Require Obedience. Let mothers be careful not to make unnecessary requirements to exhibit their own authority before others. Give few commands, but see that these are obeyed. *Signs of the Times,* Feb. 9, 1882.

Do not . . . in your discipline of children release them from that which you have required them to do. Do not let your mind become so absorbed in other things as to cause you to grow careless. And do not become wearied in your guardianship because your children forget and do that which you have forbidden them to do. Manuscript 32, 1899.

In all your commands aim to secure the highest good of your children, and then see that these commands are obeyed. Your energy and decision must be unwavering, yet ever in subjection to the Spirit of Christ. *Signs of the Times,* Sept. 13, 1910.

Dealing With a Negligent Child. When you ask your child to do a certain thing, and he answers, "Yes, I will do it," and then neglects to fulfill his word, you must not leave the matter thus. You must call your child to account for this neglect. If you pass it by without notice, you educate your child to habits of neglect and unfaithfulness. God has given to every child a stewardship. Children are to obey their parents. They are to help bear the burdens and responsibilities of the home; and when they neglect to do their appointed work, they should be called to account and required to perform it. Manuscript 127, 1899.

Results of Hasty, Spasmodic Discipline. When children have done wrong, they themselves are convicted of their sin and feel humiliated and distressed. To scold them for their faults will often result in making them stubborn and secretive. Like unruly colts, they seem determined to make trouble, and scolding will do them no good. Parents should seek to divert their minds into some other channel.

But the trouble is, parents are not uniform in their management, but move more from impulse than from principle. They fly into a passion and do not set an example before their children that Christian parents should. One day they pass over the wrongdoings of their children, and the next day they manifest no patience or self-control. They do not keep the way of the Lord to do justice and judgment. They are often more guilty than are their children.

Some children will soon forget a wrong that is done to them by father and mother; but other children who are differently constituted cannot forget severe, unreasonable punishment which they did not deserve. Thus their souls are injured, and their minds bewildered. The mother loses her opportunities to instill right principles into the mind of the child, because she did not maintain self-control and manifest a well-balanced mind in her deportment and words. Manuscript 38, 1895.

Be so calm, so free from anger, that they will be convinced that you love them, even though you punish them. Manuscript 2, 1903.

Inducements Are Sometimes Better Than Punishment. I have felt such a deep interest in this line of work that I have adopted children in order that they might be trained in right lines. Instead of punishing them when they did wrong, I would hold out inducements to them to do right. One was in the habit of throwing herself on the floor if she could not have her own way. I said to her, "If you will not lose your temper once today, your uncle White and I will take you in the carriage, and we will have a happy day in the country. But if you throw yourself on the floor once, you will forfeit your right to the pleasure." I worked in this way for these children, and now I feel thankful that I had the privilege of doing this work. Manuscript 95, 1909.

Deal With Wrong Promptly, Wisely, Firmly. Disobedience must be punished. Wrongdoing must be corrected. The iniquity that is bound up in the heart of a child must be met and overcome by parents and teachers. Wrong must be dealt with promptly and wisely, with firmness and decision. Hatred of restraint, love of self-indulgence, indifference to things of eternity, must be carefully dealt with. Unless evil is eradicated, the soul will be lost. And more than this: he who gives himself up to follow in Satan's lead seeks constantly to entice others. From our children's earliest years we should seek to subdue in them the spirit of the world. Letter 166, 1901.

The Rod Is Sometimes Necessary. The mother may ask, "Shall I never punish my child?"

Whipping may be necessary when other resorts fail, yet she should not use the rod if it is possible to avoid doing so. But if milder measures prove insufficient, punishment that will bring the child to its senses should in love be administered. Frequently one such correction will be enough for a lifetime, to show the child that he does not hold the lines of control.

And when this step becomes necessary, the child should be seriously impressed with the thought that this is not done for the gratification of the parent, or to indulge arbitrary authority, but for the child's own good. He should be taught that every fault uncorrected will bring unhappiness to himself and will displease God. Under such discipline children will find their greatest happiness in submitting their wills to the will of the heavenly Father. *Counsels to Parents, Teachers, and Students,* pp. 116, 117.

As the Last Resort. Many times you will find that if you will reason with them kindly, they will not need to be whipped. And such method of dealing will lead them to have confidence in you. They will make you their confidant. They will come to you and say, I did wrong today at such a time, and I want you to forgive me and to ask God to forgive me. I have gone through scenes like this, and therefore I know. . . . I am thankful that I had courage, when they did wrong, to deal with them firmly, to pray with them, and to keep the standards of God's Word before them. I am glad that I presented to them the promises made to the over-comer, and the rewards offered to those who are faithful. Manuscript 27, 1911.

Never Strike a Passionate Blow. Never give your child a passionate blow, unless you want him to learn to fight and quarrel. As parents you stand in the place of God to your children, and you are to be on guard. Manuscript 32, 1899.

You may have to punish with the rod; this is sometimes essential, but defer any settlement of the difficulty until you have settled the case with yourselves. Ask yourself, Have I submitted my way and will to God? Have I placed myself where God can manage me, so that I may have wisdom, patience, kindness, and love in dealing with the refractory elements in the home? Manuscript 79, 1901.

Caution to a Quick-tempered Father. Bro. L., have you considered what a child is, and whither it is going? Your children are the younger members of the Lord's family—brothers and sisters entrusted to your care by your heavenly Father for you to train and educate for heaven. When you are handling them so roughly as you have frequently done, do you consider that God will call you to account for this dealing? You should not use your children thus roughly. A child is not a horse or a dog to be ordered about according to your imperious will, or to be controlled under all circumstances by a stick or whip, or by blows with the hand. Some children are so vicious in their tempers that the infliction of pain is necessary, but very many cases are made much worse by this manner of discipline. . . .

Never raise your hand to give them a blow unless you can with a clear conscience bow before God and ask His blessing upon the correction you are about to give. Encourage love in the hearts of your children. Present before them high and correct motives for self-restraint. Do not give them the impression that they must submit to control because it is your arbitrary will, because they are weak, and you are strong, because you are the father, they the children. If you wish to ruin your family, continue to govern by brute force, and you will surely succeed. *Testimonies for the Church,* vol. 2, pp. 259, 260.

Never Shake an Offending Child. Parents have not given their children the right education. Frequently they manifest the same imperfections which are seen in the children. They eat improperly, and this calls their nervous energies to the stomach, and they have no vitality to expand in other directions. They cannot properly control their children because of their own impatience; neither can they teach them the right way. Perhaps they take hold of them roughly and give them an impatient blow. I have said that to shake a child would shake two evil spirits in, while it would shake one out. If a child is wrong, to shake it only makes it worse. It will not subdue it. *Ibid.,* p. 365.

First Use Reason and Prayer. First reason with your children, clearly point out their wrongs, and impress upon them that they have not only sinned against you, but against God. With your heart full of pity and sorrow for your erring children, pray with them before correcting them. Then they will see that you do not punish them because they have put you to inconvenience, or because you wish to vent your displeasure upon them, but from a sense of duty, for their good; and they will love and respect you. *Signs of the Times,* Apr. 10, 1884.

That prayer may make such an impression on their minds that they will see that you are not unreasonable. And if the children see that you are not unreasonable, you have gained a great victory. This is the work that is to be carried on in our family circles in these last days. Manuscript 73, 1909.

The Effectiveness of Prayer in a Disciplinary Crisis. Do not threaten them with the wrath of God if they do wrong, but bring them in your prayers to Christ. Manuscript 27, 1893.

Before you cause your child physical pain, you will, if you are a Christian father or mother, reveal the love you have for your erring one. As you bow before God with your child, you will present before the sympathizing Redeemer His own words, "Suffer the little children to come unto me, and forbid them not; for of such is the kingdom of God." Mark 10:14. That prayer will bring angels to your side. Your child will not forget these experiences, and the blessing of God will rest upon such instruction, leading him to Christ. When children realize that their parents are trying to help them, they will bend their energies in the right direction. *Counsels to Parents, Teachers, and Students,* pp. 117, 118.

Personal Experiences in Discipline. I never allowed my children to think that they could plague me in their childhood. I also brought up in my family others from other families, but I never allowed those children to think that they could plague their mother. Never did I allow myself to say a harsh word or to become impatient or fretful over the children. They never got the better of

me once—not once, to provoke me to anger. When my spirit
was stirred, or when I felt anything like being provoked, I
would say, "Children, we shall let this rest now; we shall not
say anything more about it now. Before we retire, we shall
talk it over." Having all this time to reflect, by evening they
had cooled off, and I could handle them very nicely. . . .

There is a right way, and there is a wrong way. I never
lifted a hand to my children, before I talked with them; and
if they broke down, and if they saw their mistake (and they
always did when I brought it before them and prayed with
them), and if they were subdued (and they always were when
I did this), then I had them under my control. I never found
them otherwise. When I prayed with them, they would
break all to pieces, and they would throw their arms around
my neck and cry. . . .

I never allowed, in correcting my children, even my
voice to be changed in any way. When I saw something
wrong, I waited until the "heat" was over, and then I would
take them after they had had a chance for reflection and were
ashamed. They would get ashamed, if I gave them an hour
or two to think of these things. I always went away and
prayed. I would not speak to them then.

After they had been left to themselves for a while, they
would come to me about it. "Well," I would say, "we will
wait until evening." At that time we would have a season of
prayer, and then I would tell them that they hurt their own
souls and grieved the Spirit of God by their wrong course of
action. Manuscript 82, 1901.

Take Time for Prayer. When I have felt roiled and
was tempted to speak words that I would be ashamed of,

I would keep silent and pass right out of the room and ask God to give me patience to teach these children. Then I could go back and talk with them, and tell them they must not do this wrong again. We can take such a position in this matter that we shall not provoke the children to wrath. We should speak kindly and patiently, remembering all the time how wayward we are and how we want to be treated by our heavenly Father.

Now these are the lessons that parents must learn, and when you have learned these, you will be the very best students in the school of Christ, and your children will be the very best children. In this way you can teach them to have respect for God and to keep His law, because you will have excellent government over them, and in doing this you are bringing up into society children who will be a blessing to all around them. You are fitting them to be laborers together with God. Manuscript 19, 1887.

Joy May Follow the Pain of Discipline. The true way of dealing with trial is not by seeking to escape it, but by transforming it. This applies to all discipline, the earlier as well as the later. The neglect of the child's earliest training, and the consequent strengthening of wrong tendencies, makes his after education more difficult and causes discipline to be too often a painful process. Painful it must be to the lower nature, crossing, as it does, the natural desires and inclinations; but the pain may be lost sight of in a higher joy.

Let the child and the youth be taught that every mistake, every fault, every difficulty, conquered, becomes a stepping-stone to better and higher things. It is through such experiences that all who have ever made life worth the living have achieved success. *Education,* pp. 295, 296.

Follow the Divine Guidebook. Parents who would properly rear their children need wisdom from heaven in order to act judiciously in all matters pertaining to home discipline. *Pacific Health Journal,* January 1890.

The Bible is a guide in the management of children. Here, if parents desire, they may find a course marked out for the education and training of their children, that they may make no blunders. . . . When this Guidebook is followed, parents, instead of giving unlimited indulgence to their children, will use more often the chastening rod; instead of being blind to their faults, their perverse tempers, and alive only to their virtues, they will have clear discernment and will look upon these things in the light of the Bible. They will know that they must command their children in the right way. Manuscript 57, 1897.

God cannot take rebels into His kingdom; therefore He makes obedience to His commands a special requirement. Parents should diligently teach their children what saith the Lord. Then God will show to angels and to men that He will build a safeguard round about His people. Manuscript 64, 1899.

Your Part and God's Part. Parents, when you have faithfully done your duty, to the extent of your ability, you may then in faith ask the Lord to do that for your children which you cannot do. *Signs of the Times,* Feb. 9, 1882.

After you have done your duty faithfully to your children, then carry them to God and ask Him to help you. Tell Him that you have done your part, and then in faith ask God to do His part, that which you cannot do. Ask Him to temper their dispositions, to make them mild and gentle by His Holy Spirit. He will hear you pray. He will love to answer your prayers. Through His Word He has enjoined it upon you to correct your children, to "spare not for their crying," and His Word is to be heeded in these things. *Review and Herald,* Sept. 19, 1854.

CHAPTER 45

With Love and Firmness

Two Ways and Their End. There are two ways to deal with children—ways that differ widely in principle and results. Faithfulness and love, united with wisdom and firmness, in accordance with the teachings of God's Word, will bring happiness in this life and in the next. Neglect of duty, injudicious indulgence, failure to restrain or correct the follies of youth, will result in unhappiness and final ruin to the children and disappointment and anguish to the parents. *Review and Herald,* Aug. 30, 1881.

Love has a twin sister, which is duty. Love and duty stand side by side. Love exercised while duty is neglected will make children headstrong, willful, perverse, selfish, and disobedient. If stern duty is left to stand alone without love to soften and win, it will have a similar result. Duty and love must be blended in order that children may be properly disciplined. *Testimonies for the Church,* vol. 3, p. 195.

Uncorrected Faults Bring Unhappiness. Wherever it seems necessary to deny the wishes or oppose the will of a child, he should be seriously impressed with the thought that this is not done for the gratification of the parents, or to indulge arbitrary authority, but for his own good. He should be taught that every fault uncorrected will bring unhappiness to himself and will displease God. Under such discipline children will find their greatest happiness in submitting their own will to the will of their heavenly Father. *Fundamentals of Christian Education,* p. 68.

Youth who follow their own impulse and inclination

can have no real happiness in this life, and in the end will lose eternal life. *Review and Herald,* June 27, 1899.

Kindness to Be the Law of the Home. God's method of government is an example of how children are to be trained. There is no oppression in the Lord's service, and there is to be no oppression in the home or in the school. Yet neither parents nor teachers should allow disregard of their word to pass unnoticed. Should they neglect to correct the children for doing wrong, God would hold them accountable for their neglect. But let them be sparing of censure. Let kindness be the law of the home and of the school. Let the children be taught to keep the law of the Lord, and let a firm, loving influence restrain them from evil. *Counsels to Parents, Teachers, and Students,* p. 155.

Have Consideration for Childish Ignorance. Fathers and mothers, in the home you are to represent God's disposition. You are to require obedience, not with a storm of words, but in a kind, loving manner. You are to be so full of compassion that your children will be drawn to you. Manuscript 79, 1901.

Be pleasant in the home. Restrain every word that would arouse unholy temper. "Fathers, provoke not your children to wrath," is a divine injunction. Remember that your children are young in years and experience. In controlling and disciplining them, be firm, but kind. *Review and Herald,* Apr. 21, 1904.

Children do not always discern right from wrong, and when they do wrong, they are often treated harshly, instead of being kindly instructed. Manuscript 12, 1898.

No license is given in God's Word for parental severity or oppression or for filial disobedience. The law of God, in the home life and in the government of nations, flows from a heart of infinite love. Letter 8a, 1896.

Sympathy for the Unpromising Child. I see the necessity of parents dealing in the wisdom of Christ with their erring children. . . . It is the unpromising ones who need the greatest patience and kindness, the most tender sympathy. But many parents reveal a cold, unpitying spirit, which will never lead the erring to repentance. Let the hearts of parents be softened by the grace of Christ, and His love will find a way to the heart. Manuscript 22, 1890.

The Saviour's rule—"As ye would that men should do to you, do ye also to them likewise" (Luke 6:31)—should be the rule of all who undertake the training of children and youth. They are the younger members of the Lord's family, heirs with us of the grace of life. Christ's rule should be sacredly observed toward the dullest, the youngest, the most blundering, and even toward the erring and rebellious. *Education*, pp. 292, 293.

Help Children to Overcome. God has a tender regard for the children. He wants them to gain victories every day. Let us all endeavor to help the children to be overcomers. Do not let offenses come to them from the very members of their own family. Do not permit your actions and your words to be of a nature that your children will be provoked to wrath. Yet they must be faithfully disciplined and corrected when they do wrong. Manuscript 47, 1908.

Give Praise Whenever Possible. Praise the children when they do well, for judicious commendation is as great a help to them as it is to those older in years and understanding. Never be cross-grained in the sanctuary of the home. Be kind and tenderhearted, showing Christian politeness, thanking and commending your children for the help they give you. Manuscript 14, 1905.

Be pleasant. Never speak loud, passionate words. In

restraining and disciplining your children, be firm, but kind. Encourage them to do their duty as members of the family firm. Express your appreciation of the efforts they put forth to restrain their inclinations to do wrong. Manuscript 22, 1904.

Be just what you wish your children to be when they shall have charge of families of their own. Speak as you would have them speak. Manuscript 42, 1903.

Guard Tones of the Voice. Speak always in a calm, earnest voice, in which no trace of passion is expressed. Passion is not necessary to secure prompt obedience. Letter 69, 1896.

Fathers and mothers, you are responsible for your children. Be careful under what influences you place them. Do not, by scolding or fretting, lose your own influence over them for good. You are to guide them, not to stir up the passions of their mind. Whatever provocation you may have, be sure that the tone of your voice betrays no irritation. Do not let them see in you a manifestation of the spirit of Satan. This will not help you to fit and train your children for the future, immortal life. Manuscript 47, 1908.

Justice to Be Blended With Mercy. God is our lawgiver and king, and parents are to place themselves under His rule. This rule forbids all oppression from parents and all disobedience from children. The Lord is full of loving-kindness, mercy, and truth. His law is holy, just, and good, and must be obeyed by parents and children. The rules which should regulate the lives of parents and children flow from a heart of infinite love, and God's rich blessings will rest upon those parents who administer His law in their homes, and upon the children who obey this law. The combined influence of mercy and justice is to be felt. "Mercy and truth are met together; righteousness and peace have kissed each other." Households under this discipline will walk in the way of the Lord, to do justice and judgment. *Signs of the Times,* Aug. 23, 1899.

The parent who permits his rule to become a despotism is making a terrible mistake. He wrongs not only his children but himself, quenching in their young hearts the love that would flow out in acts and words of affection. Kindness, forbearance, and love, manifested to children, will be reflected back upon the parents. That which they sow, they will also reap. . . .

While you seek to administer justice, remember that she has a twin sister, which is mercy. The two stand side by side and should not be separated. *Review and Herald,* Aug. 30, 1881.

Severity Arouses Combative Spirit. Counsel to Stern Parents. Severity and justice, unmingled with love, will not lead your children to do right. Notice how quickly the combative spirit is aroused in them. Now there is a better way to manage them than by mere compulsion. Justice has a twin sister, which is love. Let love and justice clasp hands in all your management, and you will surely have the help of God to cooperate with your efforts. The Lord, your gracious Redeemer, wants to bless you, and give you His mind, and His grace, and His salvation, that you may have a character which God can approve. Letter 19a, 1891.

The authority of the parents should be absolute, yet this power is not to be abused. In the control of his children the father should not be governed by caprice, but by the Bible standard. When he permits his own harsh traits of character to bear sway, he becomes a despot. *Review and Herald,* Aug. 30, 1881.

Reprove, but With Affectionate Tenderness. No doubt you will see faults and waywardness on the part of your children. Some parents will tell you that they talk to and punish their children, but they cannot see that it does them any real good. Let such parents try new methods. Let them mingle kindness and affection and love with their family government, and yet let them be as firm as a rock to right principles. Manuscript 38, 1895.

None who deal with the young should be ironhearted, but affectionate, tender, pitiful, courteous, winning, and companionable; yet they should know that reproofs must be given, and that even rebuke may have to be spoken to cut off some evil-doing. Manuscript 68, 1897.

I am instructed to say to parents, Raise the standard of behavior in your own homes. Teach your children to obey. Rule them by the combined influence of affection and Christlike authority. Let your lives be such that of you may be spoken the words of commendation spoken of Cornelius, of whom it is said that he "feared God with all his house." *Review and Herald,* Apr. 21, 1904.

Exercise Neither Severity nor Excessive Indulgence. We have no sympathy with that discipline which would discourage children by hard censure, or irritate them by passionate correction, and then, as the impulse changes, smother them with kisses, or harm them by injurious gratification. Excessive indulgence and undue severity are alike to be avoided. While vigilance and firmness are indispensable, so also are sympathy and tenderness. Parents, remember that you deal with children who are struggling with temptation, and that to them these evil promptings are as hard to resist as are those that assail persons of mature years. Children who really desire to do right may fail again and again, and as often need encouragement to energy and perseverance. Watch the working of these young minds with prayerful solicitude. Strengthen every good impulse; encourage every noble action. *Signs of the Times,* Nov. 24, 1881.

Maintain Uniform Firmness, Unimpassioned Control. Children have sensitive, loving natures. They are easily pleased and easily made unhappy. By gentle discipline in loving words and acts, mothers may bind their children to their hearts. Uniform firmness and unimpassioned control are necessary to the discipline of every family. Say what you mean calmly, move with consideration, and carry out what you say without deviation.

It will pay to manifest affection in your association with your children. Do not repel them by lack of sympathy in their childish sports, joys, and griefs. Never let a frown gather upon your brow, or a harsh word escape your lips. *Testimonies for the Church,* vol. 3, p. 532.

Even kindness must have its limits. Authority must be sustained by a firm severity, or it will be received by many with mockery and contempt. The so-called tenderness, the coaxing and the indulgence used toward youth, by parents and guardians, is the worst evil which can come upon them. Firmness, decision, positive requirements, are essential in every family. *Ibid.,* vol. 5, p. 45.

Remember Your Own Mistakes. Let father and mother remember that they themselves are but grown-up children. Though great light has shone upon their pathway and they have had long experience, yet how easily are they stirred to envy, jealousy, and evil surmisings. Because of their own mistakes and errors they should learn to deal gently with their erring children. Manuscript 53, Undated.

You may feel annoyed sometimes because your children go contrary to what you have told them. But have you ever thought that many times you go contrary to what the Lord has commanded you to do? Manuscript 45, 1911.

How to Win Love and Confidence. There is danger that both parents and teachers will command and dictate too much, while they fail to come sufficiently into social relation with their children or scholars. They often hold themselves too much reserved and exercise their authority in a cold, unsympathizing manner, which cannot win the hearts of their children and pupils. If they would gather the children close to them, and show that they love them, and would manifest an interest in all their efforts, and even in their sports, sometimes even being a child among them, they would make the children very happy and would gain their love and win their confidence. And the children would more quickly learn to respect and love the authority of their parents and teachers. *Counsels to Parents, Teachers, and Students,* pp. 76, 77.

Seek to Imitate Christ. He [Christ] identified Himself with the lowly, the needy, and the afflicted. He took little children in His arms and descended to the level of the young. His large heart of love could comprehend their trials and necessities, and He enjoyed their happiness. His spirit, wearied with the bustle and confusion of the crowded city, tired of association with crafty and hypocritical men, found rest and peace in the society of innocent children. His presence never repulsed them. The Majesty of heaven condescended to answer their questions, and simplified His important lessons to meet their childish understanding. He planted in their young, expanding minds the seeds of truth that would spring up and produce a plentiful harvest in their riper years. *Testimonies for the Church,* vol. 4, p. 141.

An Errant Youth Who Needed Sympathy. Your letters I have read with interest and sympathy. I would say your son now needs a father as he has never needed one before. He has erred; you know it, and he knows that you know it; and words that you would have spoken to him in his innocency with safety, and which would not have produced any bad results, would now seem like unkindness and be sharp as a knife. . . . I know that parents feel the shame of the wrongdoing of a child that has dishonored them very keenly, but does the erring one wound and bruise the heart of the earthly parent any more than we as the children of God bruise our heavenly Parent, who has given us and is still giving us His love, inviting us to return and repent of our sins and iniquities and He will pardon our transgression?

Do not withdraw your love now. That love and sympathy is needed now as never before. When others look with coldness and put the worst construction upon the misdeeds of your boy, should not the father and mother in pitying tenderness seek to guide his footsteps into safe paths? I do not know the character of your son's sins, but I am safe in saying, whatever they may be, Let no comments from human lips, no pressure from human actions, of those who think they are doing justice, lead you to pursue a course which can be interpreted by your son that you feel too much mortified and dishonored to ever take him back into confidence and to forget his transgressions. Let nothing cause you to lose hope, nothing to cut off your love and tenderness for the erring one. Just because he is erring, he needs you, and he wants a father and a mother to help him to recover himself from the snare of Satan. Hold him fast by faith and love, and cling to the all-pitying Redeemer, remembering that he has One who has an interest in him, even above your own. . . .

Do not talk discouragement and hopelessness. Talk courage. Tell him he can redeem himself, that you, his father and mother, will help him to take hold from above to plant his feet on the solid Rock, Christ Jesus, to find a sure support and unfailing strength in Jesus. If his fault be ever so grievous, it will not cure your son to press this constantly upon him. A right course of action is needed to save a soul from death and keep a soul from committing a multitude of sins. Letter 18e, 1890.

Seek Divine Help to Overcome Hasty Temper. I wish to say to every father and mother, If you have a hasty temper, seek God for help to overcome it. When you are provoked to impatience, go to your chamber, and kneel down and ask God to help you that you may have a right influence over your children. Manuscript 33, 1909.

Mothers, when you yield to impatience and deal harshly with your children, you are not learning of Christ, but of another master. Jesus says, "Take my yoke upon you and learn of me; for I am meek and lowly in heart; and ye shall find rest unto your souls. For my yoke is easy, and my burden is light." When you find your work hard, when you complain of difficulties and trials, when you say that you have no strength to withstand temptation, that you cannot overcome impatience, and that the Christian life is uphill work, be sure that you are not bearing the yoke of Christ; you are bearing the yoke of another master. *Signs of the Times,* July 22, 1889.

Reflecting the Divine Image. The church needs men of a meek and quiet spirit, who are long-suffering and patient. Let them learn these attributes in dealing with their families. Let parents think a great deal more of their children's eternal interests than they do of their present comfort. Let them look upon their children as younger members of the Lord's family, and train and discipline them in such a way as will lead them to reflect the divine image. *Review and Herald,* July 16, 1895.

SECTION 11

FAULTY DISCIPLINE

CHAPTER 46

Evils of Indulgence

True Love Is Not Indulgent. Love is the key to a child's heart, but the love that leads parents to indulge their children in unlawful desires is not a love that will work for their good. The earnest affection which springs from love to Jesus will enable parents to exercise judicious authority and to require prompt obedience. The hearts of parents and children need to be welded together, so that as a family they may be a channel through which wisdom, virtue, forbearance, kindness, and love may flow. *Review and Herald,* June 24, 1890.

Too Much Freedom Makes Prodigal Sons. The reason that children do not become godly is because they are allowed too much freedom. Their will and inclination is indulged. . . . Many prodigal sons become such because of indulgence in the home, because their parents have not been doers of the Word. The mind and purpose are to be sustained by firm, undeviating, sanctified principles. Consistency and affection are to be enforced by a lovely and consistent example. Letter 117, 1898.

The More Indulgence, the Harder the Management. Parents, make home happy for your children. By this I do not mean that you are to indulge them. The more they are indulged, the harder they will be to manage, and the more difficult it will be for them to live true, noble lives when they go out into the world. If you allow them to do as they please, their purity and loveliness of character will quickly fade. Teach them to obey. Let them see that your authority must be respected.

This may seem to bring them a little unhappiness now, but it will save them from much unhappiness in the future. Manuscript 2, 1903.

To indulge a child when young and erring is a sin. A child should be kept under control. Letter 144, 1906.

If children are allowed to have their own way, they receive the idea that they must be waited upon, cared for, indulged, and amused. They think that their wishes and their will must be gratified. Manuscript 27, 1896.

Should she [the mother] not let her child have his own way now and then, let him do just as he wishes, permit him to be disobedient? Certainly not, for just so sure as she does, she lets Satan plant his hellish banner in her house. She must fight the battle of that child which he cannot fight himself. That is her work, to rebuke the devil, to seek God earnestly, and never to let Satan take her child right out of her arms and place him in his arms. Manuscript 70, Undated.

Indulgence Causes Restlessness and Discontent. In some families the wishes of the child are law. Everything he desires is given him. Everything he dislikes he is encouraged to dislike. These indulgences are supposed to make the child happy, but it is these very things that make him restless, discontented, and satisfied with nothing. Indulgence has spoiled his appetite for plain, healthful food, for the plain, healthful use of his time; gratification has done the work of unsettling that character for time and for eternity. Manuscript 126, 1897.

Elisha's Effective Rebuke for Disrespect. The idea that we must submit to ways of perverse children is a mistake. Elisha, at the very commencement of his work, was mocked and derided by the youth of Bethel. He was a man of great mildness, but the Spirit of God impelled him to pronounce a curse upon those railers. They had heard of Elijah's ascension, and they made this solemn event the subject of jeers. Elisha evinced that he was not to be trifled with, by old or young, in his sacred calling. When they told him he had better go up, as Elijah had done before him, he cursed them in the name of the Lord. The awful judgment that came upon them was of God.

After this, Elisha had no further trouble in his mission. For fifty years he passed in and out of the gate of Bethel, and went to and fro from city to city, passing through crowds of the worst and rudest of idle, dissolute youth; but no one ever mocked him or made light of his qualifications as the prophet of the Most High. *Testimonies for the Church,* vol. 5, p. 44.

Do Not Yield to Coaxing. Parents will have much to answer for in the day of accounts because of their wicked indulgence of their children. Many gratify every unreasonable wish, because it is easier to be rid of their importunity in this way than in any other. A child should be so trained that a refusal would be received in the right spirit and accepted as final. *Pacific Health Journal,* May 1890.

Do Not Take Child's Word Before That of Others. Parents should not pass lightly over the sins of their children. When these sins are pointed out by some faithful friend, the parent should not feel that his rights are invaded, that he has received a personal offense. The habits of every youth and every child affect the welfare of society. The wrong course of one youth may lead many others in an evil way. *Review and Herald,* June 13, 1882.

Do not allow your children to see that you take their word before the statements of older Christians. You cannot do them a greater injury. By saying, I believe my children before I believe those whom I have evidence are children of God, you encourage in them the habit of falsifying. *Review and Herald,* Apr. 13, 1897.

The Heritage of a Spoiled Child. It is impossible to depict the evil that results from leaving a child to its own will. Some who go astray because of neglect in childhood will later, through the inculcation of practical lessons, come to their senses; but many are lost forever because in childhood and youth they received only a partial, one-sided culture. The child who is spoiled has a heavy burden to carry throughout his life. In trial, in disappointment, in temptation, he will follow his undisciplined, misdirected will. Children who have never learned to obey will have weak, impulsive characters. They seek to rule, but have not learned to submit. They are without moral strength to restrain their wayward tempers, to correct their wrong habits, or to subdue their uncontrolled wills. The blunders of untrained, undisciplined childhood become the inheritance of manhood and womanhood. The perverted intellect can scarcely discern between the true and the false. *Counsels to Parents, Teachers, and Students,* pp. 112, 113.

CHAPTER 47

Lax Discipline and Its Fruitage

Faulty Training Affects Entire Religious Life. A woe rests upon parents who have not trained their children to be God-fearing, but have allowed them to grow to manhood and womanhood undisciplined and uncontrolled. During their own childhood they were allowed to manifest passion and willfulness and to act from impulse, and they bring this same spirit into their own homes. They are defective in temper, and passionate in government. Even in their acceptance of Christ they have not overcome the passions that were allowed to rule in their childish hearts. They carry the results of their early training through their entire religious life. It is a most difficult thing to remove the impress thus made upon the plant of the Lord; for as the twig is bent, the tree is inclined. If such parents accept the truth, they have a hard battle to fight. They may be transformed in character, but the whole of their religious experience is affected by the lax discipline exercised over them in their early lives. And their children have to suffer because of their defective training; for they stamp their faults upon them to the third and fourth generation. *Review and Herald,* Oct. 9, 1900.

The Eli's of Today. When parents sanction and thus perpetuate the wrongs in their children as did Eli, God will surely bring them to the place where they will see that they have not only ruined their own influence, but also the influence of the youth whom they should have restrained. . . . They will have bitter lessons to learn. Manuscript 33, 1903.

Oh, that the Eli's of today, who are everywhere to be found pleading excuses for the waywardness of their children, would promptly assert their own God-given authority to restrain and correct them. Let parents and guardians, who overlook and excuse sin in those under their care, remember that they thus become accessory to these wrongs. If, instead of unlimited indulgence, the chastening rod were oftener used, not in passion, but with love and prayer, we would see happier families and a better state of society. *Signs of the Times,* Nov. 24, 1881.

The neglect of Eli is brought plainly before every father and mother in the land. As the result of his unsanctified affection or his unwillingness to do a disagreeable duty, he reaped a harvest of iniquity in his perverse sons. Both the parent who permitted the wickedness and the children who practiced it were guilty before God, and He would accept no sacrifice or offering for their transgression. *Review and Herald,* May 4, 1886.

Society Cursed by Defective Characters. Oh! when will parents be wise? When will they see and realize the character of their work in neglecting to require obedience and respect according to the instructions of God's Word? The results of this lax training are seen in the children as they go out into the world and take their place at the head of families of their own. They perpetuate the mistakes of their parents. Their defective traits have full scope; and they transmit to others the wrong tastes, habits, and tempers that were permitted to develop in their own characters. Thus they became a curse instead of a blessing to society. *Testimonies for the Church,* vol. 5, pp. 324, 325.

The wickedness which exists in the world today may be traced to the neglect of parents to discipline themselves and their children. Thousands upon thousands of Satan's victims are what they are because of the injudicious way in which they were managed during their childhood. The stern rebuke of God is upon this mismanagement. Manuscript 49, 1901.

Slackening the Reins of Discipline. Children who are misruled, who are not educated to obey and respect, link themselves with the world and take their parents in hand, putting a bridle on them, and leading them where they choose. Too often, at the very time when the children should show unquestioning respect and obedience to the counsel of their parents, the parents slacken the reins of discipline. Parents who have hitherto been bright examples of consistent piety are now led by their children. Their firmness is gone. Fathers who have borne the cross of Christ, and kept the marks of the Lord Jesus on them in singleness of purpose, are led by their children in questionable and uncertain paths. *Review and Herald,* Apr. 13, 1897.

Indulging the Older Children. Fathers and mothers who should understand the responsibility which rests upon them relax their discipline to meet the inclinations of their growing sons and daughters. The will of the child is the law recognized. Mothers who have been firm, consistent, and unbending in their adherence to principle, maintaining simplicity and fidelity, become indulgent as their children merge into manhood and womanhood. In their love of display they give their children to Satan with their own hands, like the apostate Jews making them pass through the fire to Molech. Manuscript 119, 1899.

Dishonoring God to Gain Child's Favor. Fathers and mothers are giving way to the inclination of godless children, and assisting them with money and facilities to make an appearance in the world.

Oh, what an account such parents will have to render to God! They dishonor God and show all honor to their wayward children, opening their doors to amusements which they have in the past condemned from principle. They have allowed card playing, dancing parties, and balls to win their children to the world. At the time when their influence over their children should be strongest, bearing a testimony of what true Christianity means, like Eli they bring themselves under the curse of God by dishonoring Him and disregarding His requirements, in order to gain the favor of their children. But a fashionable piety will not be of much value in the hour of death. Although some ministers of the gospel may approve this kind of religion, parents will find that they are leaving the crown of glory to obtain laurels that are of no value. God help fathers and mothers to arouse to their duty! *Review and Herald,* Apr. 13, 1897.

Be What You Wish Your Children to Be. Be what you wish your children to be. Parents have perpetuated by precept and example their own stamp of character to their posterity. The fitful, coarse, uncourteous tempers and words are impressed upon children, and children's children, and thus the defects in the management of parents testify against them from generation to generation. *Signs of the Times,* Sept. 17, 1894.

CHAPTER 48

The Child's Reaction

To Provocation. Children are exhorted to obey their parents in the Lord, but parents are also enjoined, "Provoke not your children to wrath, lest they be discouraged." Manuscript 38, 1895.

Often we do more to provoke than to win. I have seen a mother snatch from the hand of her child something that was giving it special pleasure. The child did not know the reason for this, and naturally felt abused. Then followed a quarrel between parent and child, and a sharp chastisement ended the scene as far as outward appearance was concerned; but that battle left an impression on the tender mind that would not be easily effaced. This mother acted unwisely. She did not reason from cause to effect. Her harsh, injudicious action stirred the worst passions in the heart of her child, and on every similar occasion these passions would be aroused and strengthened. *Counsels to Parents, Teachers, and Students,* p. 117.

To Faultfinding. You have no right to bring a gloomy cloud over the happiness of your children by faultfinding or severe censure for trifling mistakes. Actual wrong should be made to appear just as sinful as it is, and a firm, decided course should be pursued to prevent its recurrence; yet children should not be left in a hopeless state of mind, but with a degree of courage that they can improve and gain your confidence and approval. Children may wish to do right, they may purpose in their hearts to be obedient; but they need help and encouragement. *Signs of the Times,* Apr. 10, 1884.

To Too Harsh Discipline. Oh, how God is dishonored in a family where there is no true understanding as to what constitutes family discipline, and children are confused as to what is discipline and government. It is true that too harsh discipline, too much criticism, unrequired laws and regulations, lead to disrespect of authority and to the disregarding finally of those regulations that Christ would have fulfilled. *Review and Herald,* Mar. 13, 1894.

When parents show a rough, severe, masterly spirit, a spirit of obstinacy and stubbornness is aroused in the children. Thus the parents fail to exert over their children the softening influence that they might.

Parents, can you not see that harsh words provoke resistance? What would you do if treated as inconsiderately as you treat your little ones? It is your duty to study from cause to effect. When you scolded your children, when with angry blows you struck those who were too small to defend themselves, did you ask yourself what effect such treatment would have upon you? Have you thought how sensitive you are in regard to words of censure or blame? how quickly you feel hurt if you think that someone fails to recognize your capabilities? You are but grown-up children. Then think how your children must feel when you speak harsh, cutting words to them, severely punishing them for faults that are not half so grievous in the sight of God as is your treatment of them. Manuscript 42, 1903.

Many parents professing to be Christians are not converted. Christ does not abide in their hearts by faith! Their harshness, their imprudence, their unsubdued tempers, disgust their children and make them averse to all their religious instruction. Letter 18b, 1891.

To Continual Censure. In our efforts to correct evil, we should guard against a tendency to faultfinding or censure. Continual censure bewilders, but does not reform. With many minds, and often those of the finest susceptibility, an atmosphere of unsympathetic criticism is fatal to effort. Flowers do not unfold under the breath of a blighting wind.

A child frequently censured for some special fault comes to regard that fault as his peculiarity, something against which it is vain to strive. Thus are created discouragement and hopelessness, often concealed under an appearance of indifference or bravado. *Education,* p. 291.

To Ordering and Scolding. Some parents raise many a storm by their lack of self-control. Instead of kindly asking the children to do this or that, they order them in a scolding tone, and at the same time a censure or reproof is on their lips which the children have not merited. Parents, this course pursued toward your children destroys their cheerfulness and ambition. They do your bidding, not from love, but because they dare not do otherwise. Their heart is not in the matter. It is a drudgery instead of a pleasure, and this often leads them to forget to follow out all your directions, which increases your irritation and makes it still worse for the children. The faultfinding is repeated, their bad conduct arrayed before them in glowing colors, until discouragement comes over them, and they are not particular whether they please or not. A spirit of "I don't care" seizes them, and they seek that pleasure and enjoyment away from home, away from their parents, which they do not find at home. They mingle with street company and are soon as corrupt as the worst. *Testimonies for the Church,* vol. 1, pp. 384, 385.

To an Arbitrary Course of Action. The will of the parents must be under the discipline of Christ. Molded and controlled by God's pure Holy Spirit, they may establish unquestioned dominion over the children. But if the parents are severe and exacting in their discipline, they do a work which they themselves can never undo. By their arbitrary course of action, they stir up a sense of injustice. Manuscript 7, 1899.

To Injustice. Children are sensitive to the least injustice, and some become discouraged under it and will neither heed the loud, angry voice of command, nor care for threatenings of punishment. Rebellion is too frequently established in the hearts of children through the wrong discipline of the parents, when if a proper course had been taken, the children would have formed good and harmonious characters. A mother who does not have perfect control of herself is unfit to have the management of children. *Testimonies for the Church,* vol. 3, pp. 532, 533.

To a Jerk or Blow. When the mother gives her child a jerk or blow, do you think it enables him to see the beauty of the Christian character? No indeed; it only tends to raise evil feelings in the heart, and the child is not corrected at all. Manuscript 45, 1911.

To Harsh, Unsympathetic Words. Christ is ready to teach the father and the mother to be true educators. Those who learn in His school . . . will never speak in a harsh, unsympathetic tone; for words spoken in this manner grate upon the ear, wear upon the nerves, cause mental suffering, and create a state of mind that makes it impossible to curb the temper of the child to whom such words are spoken. This is often the reason why children speak disrespectfully to parents. Letter 47a, 1902.

To Ridicule and Taunting. They [parents] are not authorized to fret and scold and ridicule. They should never taunt their children with perverse traits of character, which they themselves have transmitted to them. This mode of discipline will never cure the evil. Parents, bring the precepts of God's Word to admonish and reprove your wayward children. Show them a "Thus saith the Lord" for your requirements. A reproof which comes as the word of God is far more effective than one falling in harsh, angry tones from the lips of parents. *Fundamentals of Christian Education,* pp. 67, 68.

To Impatience. Impatience in the parents excites impatience in the children. Passion manifested by the parents creates passion in the children and stirs up the evils of their nature. . . . Every time they lose self-control and speak and act impatiently, they sin against God. *Testimonies for the Church,* vol. 1, p. 398.

To Alternate Scolding and Coaxing. I have frequently seen children who were denied something that they wanted throw themselves upon the floor in a pet, kicking and screaming, while the injudicious mother alternately coaxed and scolded in the hope of restoring her child to good nature. This treatment only fosters the child's passion. The next time it goes over the same ground with increased willfulness, confident of gaining the day as before. Thus the rod is spared and the child is spoiled.

The mother should not allow her child to gain an advantage over her in a single instance. And, in order to maintain this authority, it is not necessary to resort to harsh measures; a firm, steady hand and a kindness which convinces the child of your love will accomplish the purpose. *Pacific Health Journal,* April 1890.

To Lack of Firmness and Decision. Great harm is done by a lack of firmness and decision. I have known parents to say, You cannot have this or that, and then relent, thinking they may be too strict, and give the child the very thing they at first refused. A lifelong injury is thus inflicted. It is an important law of the mind—one which should not be overlooked—that when a desired object is so firmly denied as to remove all hope, the mind will soon cease to long for it, and will be occupied in other pursuits. But as long as there is any hope of gaining the desired object, an effort will be made to obtain it. . . .

When it is necessary for parents to give a direct command, the penalty of disobedience should be as unvarying as are the laws of nature. Children who are under this firm, decisive rule know that when a thing is forbidden or denied, no teasing or artifice will secure their object. Hence they soon learn to submit and are much happier in so doing. The children of undecided and overindulgent parents have a constant hope that coaxing, crying, or sullenness may gain their object, or that they may venture to disobey without suffering the penalty. Thus they are kept in a state of desire, hope, and uncertainty, which makes them restless, irritable, and insubordinate. God holds such parents guilty of wrecking the happiness of their children. This wicked mismanagement is the key to the impenitence and irreligion of thousands. It has proved the ruin of many who have professed the Christian name. *Signs of the Times,* Feb. 9, 1882.

To Unnecessary Restrictions. When parents become old and have young children to bring up, the father is likely to feel that the children must follow in the sturdy, rugged path in which he himself is traveling. It is difficult for him to realize that his children are in need of having life made pleasant and happy for them by their parents.

Many parents deny the children an indulgence in that which is safe and innocent, and are so afraid of encouraging them in cultivating desires for unlawful things that they will not even allow their children to have the enjoyment that children should have. Through fear of evil results, they refuse permission to indulge in some simple pleasure that would have saved the very evil they seek to avoid; and thus the children think there is no use in expecting any favors, and therefore will not ask for them. They steal away to the pleasures they think will be forbidden. Confidence between parents and children is thus destroyed. *Signs of the Times,* Aug. 27, 1912.

To the Denial of Reasonable Privileges. If fathers and mothers have not themselves had a happy childhood, why should they shadow the lives of their children because of their own great loss in this respect? The father may think that this is the only course that will be safe to pursue; but let him remember that all minds are not constituted alike, and the greater the efforts made to restrict, the more uncontrollable will be the desire to obtain that which is denied, and the result will be disobedience to parental authority. The father will be grieved by what he considers the wayward course of his son, and his heart will feel sore over his rebellion. But would it not be well for him to consider the fact that the first cause of his son's disobedience was his own unwillingness to indulge him in that in which there was no sin? The parent thinks that sufficient reason is given for his son's abstaining from his indulgence since he has denied it to him. But parents should remember that their children are intelligent beings, and they should deal with them as they themselves would like to be dealt with. *Ibid.*

To Severity. Parents who exercise a spirit of dominion [domination] and authority, transmitted to them from their own parents, which leads them to be exacting in their discipline and instruction, will not train their children aright. By their severity in dealing with their errors, they stir up the worst passions of the human heart and leave their children with a sense of injustice and wrong. They meet in their children the very disposition that they themselves have imparted to them.

Such parents drive their children away from God, by talking to them on religious subjects; for the Christian religion is made unattractive and even repulsive by this misrepresentation of truth. Children will say, "Well, if that is religion, I do not want anything of it." It is thus that enmity is often created in the heart against religion; and because of an arbitrary enforcement of authority, children are led to despise the law and the government of heaven. Parents have fixed the eternal destiny of their children by their own misrule. *Review and Herald,* Mar. 13, 1894.

To Quiet, Kind Manner. If parents desire their children to be pleasant, they should never speak to them in a scolding manner. The mother often allows herself to become irritable and nervous. Often she snatches at the child and speaks in a harsh manner. If a child is treated in a quiet, kind manner, it will do much to preserve in him a pleasant temper. *Review and Herald,* May 17, 1898.

To Loving Entreaty. The father, as priest of the household, should deal gently and patiently with his children. He should be careful not to arouse in them a combative disposition. He must not allow transgression to go uncorrected, and yet there is a way to correct without stirring up the worst passions in the human heart. Let him in love talk with his children, telling them how grieved the Saviour is over their course; and then let him kneel with them before the mercy seat and present them to Christ, praying that He will have compassion on them and lead them to repent and ask forgiveness. Such disciplining will nearly always break the most stubborn heart.

God desires us to deal with our children in simplicity. We are liable to forget that children have not had the advantage of the long years of training that older people have had. If the little ones do not act in accordance with our ideas in every respect, we sometimes think that they deserve a scolding. But this will not mend matters. Take them to the Saviour, and tell Him all about it; then believe that His blessing will rest upon them. Manuscript 70, 1903.

CHAPTER 49

Attitude of Relatives

Indulgent Relatives Are a Problem. Be careful how you relinquish the government of your children to others. No one can properly relieve you of your God-given responsibility. Many children have been utterly ruined by the interference of relatives or friends in their home government. Mothers should never allow their sisters or mothers to interfere with the wise management of their children. Though the mother may have received the very best training at the hands of her mother, yet, in nine cases out of ten, as a grandmother she would spoil her daughter's children, by indulgence and injudicious praise. All the patient effort of the mother may be undone by this course of treatment. It is proverbial that grandparents, as a rule, are unfit to bring up their grandchildren. Men and women should pay all the respect and deference due to their parents; but in the matter of the management of their own children, they should allow no interference, but hold the reins of government in their own hands. *Pacific Health Journal,* January 1890.

When They Laugh at Disrespect and Passion. Wherever I go, I am pained by the neglect of proper home discipline and restraint. Little children are allowed to answer back, to manifest disrespect and impertinence, using language that no child should ever be permitted to address to its superiors. Parents who permit the use of unbecoming language are more worthy of blame than their children. Impertinence should not be tolerated in a child even once. But fathers and mothers, uncles and aunts and grandparents laugh at the exhibition of passion in the little creature of a year old. Its imperfect utterance of disrespect, its childish stubbornness, are thought cunning. Thus wrong habits are confirmed, and the child grows up to be an object of dislike to all around him. *Signs of the Times,* Feb. 9, 1882.

When They Discourage Proper Correction. I tremble especially for mothers, as I see them so blind, and feeling so little the responsibilities that devolve upon a mother. They see Satan working in the self-willed child of even but a few months of age. Filled with spiteful passion, Satan seems to be taking full possession. But there may be in the house perhaps a grandmother, an aunt, or some other relative or friend, who will seek to make that parent believe that it would be cruelty to correct that child; whereas just the opposite is true; and it is the greatest cruelty to let Satan have the possession of that tender, helpless child. Satan must be rebuked. His hold on the child must be broken. If correction is needed, be faithful, be true. The love of God, true pity for the child, will lead to the faithful discharge of duty. *Review and Herald,* Apr. 14, 1885.

Perplexities of a Family Community. It is not the best policy for children of one, two, or three families that are connected by marriage to settle within a few miles of one another. The influence is not good on the parties. The business of one is the business of all. The perplexities and troubles which every family must experience more or less, and which, as far as possible, should be confined within the limits of the family circle, are extended to family connections and have a bearing upon the religious meetings. There are matters which should not be known to a third person, however friendly and closely connected he may be. Individuals and families should bear them. But the close relationship of several families, brought into constant intercourse, has a tendency to break down the dignity which should be maintained in every family. In performing the delicate duty of reproving and admonishing, there will be danger of injuring feelings, unless it be done with the greatest tenderness and care. The best models of character are liable to errors and mistakes, and great care should be exercised that too much is not made of little things.

Such family and church relationship . . . is very pleasant to the natural feelings; but it is not the best, all things considered, for the development of symmetrical Christian characters. . . . All parties would be much happier to be separated and to visit occasionally, and their influence upon one another would be tenfold greater.

United as these families are by marriage, and mingling as they do in one another's society, each is awake to the faults and errors of the others, and feels in duty bound to correct them; and because these relatives are really dear to one another, they are grieved over little things that they would not notice in those not so closely connected. Keen sufferings of mind are endured, because feelings will arise with some that they have not been treated impartially, and with all that consideration which they deserved. Petty jealousies sometimes arise, and molehills become mountains. These little misunderstandings and petty variances cause more severe suffering of mind than do trials that come from other sources. *Testimonies for the Church,* vol. 3, pp. 55, 56.

SECTION 12

DEVELOPMENT OF
THE MENTAL POWER

CHAPTER 50

What Comprises True Education?

The Breadth of True Education. True education means more than taking a certain course of study. It is broad. It includes the harmonious development of all the physical powers and the mental faculties. It teaches the love and fear of God and is a preparation for the faithful discharge of life's duties. *Counsels to Parents, Teachers, and Students,* p. 64.

Proper education includes not only mental discipline, but that training which will secure sound morals and correct deportment. *Ibid.,* p. 331.

The first great lesson in all education is to know and understand the will of God. We should bring into every day of life the effort to gain this knowledge. To learn science through human interpretation alone is to obtain a false education, but to learn of God and Christ is to learn the science of heaven. The confusion in education has come because the wisdom and knowledge of God have not been exalted. *Ibid.,* p. 447.

Influence Counter to Selfish Rivalry and Greed. At such a time as this, what is the trend of the education given? To what motive is appeal most often made? To self-seeking. Much of the education given is a perversion of the name. In true education the selfish ambition, the greed for power, the disregard for the rights and needs of humanity, that are the curse of our world, find a counterinfluence. God's plan of life has a place for every human being. Each is to improve his talents to the utmost; and faithfulness in doing this, be the gifts few or many, entitles one to honor.

In God's plan there is no place for selfish rivalry. Those who measure themselves by themselves, and compare themselves among themselves, are not wise. (2 Corinthians 10:12.) Whatever we do is to be done "as of the ability which God giveth." 1 Peter 4:11. It is to be done "heartily, as to the Lord, and not unto men; knowing that of the Lord ye shall receive the reward of the inheritance: for ye serve the Lord Christ." Colossians 3:23, 24. Precious the service done and the education gained in carrying out these principles. But how widely different is much of the education now given! From the child's earliest years it is an appeal to emulation and rivalry; it fosters selfishness, the root of all evil. *Education,* pp. 225, 226.

The Model Was Given in Eden. The system of education instituted at the beginning of the world was to be a model for man throughout all aftertime. As an illustration of its principles a model school was established in Eden, the home of our first parents. The Garden of Eden was the schoolroom, nature was the lesson book, the Creator Himself was the instructor. *Ibid.,* p. 20.

Exemplified in the Master Teacher. In the training of His disciples the Saviour followed the system of education established at the beginning. The Twelve first chosen, with a few others who through ministry to their needs were from time to time connected with them, formed the family of Jesus. They were with Him in the house, at the table, in the closet, in the field. They accompanied Him on His journeys, shared His trials and hardships, and, as much as in them was, entered into His work.

Sometimes He taught them as they sat together on the mountainside, sometimes beside the sea, or from the fisherman's boat, sometimes as they walked by the way. Whenever He spoke to the multitude, the disciples formed the inner circle. They pressed close beside Him, that they might lose nothing of His instruction. They were attentive listeners, eager to understand the truths they were to teach in all lands and to all ages. *Ibid.,* pp. 84, 85.

True Education Is Both Practical and Literary. In childhood and youth practical and literary training should be combined, and the mind stored with knowledge. . . .

Children should be taught to have a part in domestic duties. They should be instructed how to help father and mother in the little things that they can do. Their minds should be trained to think, their memories taxed to remember their appointed work; and in the training to habits of usefulness in the home, they are being educated in doing practical duties appropriate to their age. *Fundamentals of Christian Education,* pp. 368, 369.

It Is Not the Natural Choice of Youth. The kind of education that fits the youth for practical life, they naturally do not choose. They urge their desires, their likes and dislikes, their preferences and inclinations; but if parents have correct views of God, of the truth, and of the influences and associations that should surround their children, they will feel that upon them rests the God-given responsibility of carefully guiding the inexperienced youth. *Counsels to Parents, Teachers, and Students,* p. 132.

It Is Not a Method of Escape From Life's Burdens. Let the youth be impressed with the thought that education is not to teach them how to escape life's disagreeable tasks and heavy burdens; that its purpose is to lighten the work by teaching better methods and higher aims. Teach them that life's true aim is not to secure the greatest possible gain for themselves, but to honor their Maker in doing their part of the world's work, and lending a helpful hand to those weaker or more ignorant. *Education,* pp. 221, 222.

Education Should Awaken the Spirit of Service. Above any other agency, service for Christ's sake in the little things of everyday experience has power to mold the character and to direct the life into lines of unselfish ministry. To awaken this spirit, to encourage and rightly to direct it, is the parents' and the teacher's work. No more important work could be committed to them. The spirit of ministry is the spirit of heaven, and with every effort to develop and encourage it angels will cooperate.

Such an education must be based upon the Word of God. Here only are its principles given in their fullness. The Bible should be made the foundation of study and of teaching. The essential knowledge is a knowledge of God and of Him whom He has sent. *The Ministry of Healing,* p. 401.

It Places Moral Training Above Intellectual Culture. Children are in great need of proper education in order that they may be of use in the world. But any effort that exalts intellectual culture above moral training is misdirected. Instructing, cultivating, polishing, and refining the youth and children should be the main burden of both parents and teachers. *Counsels to Parents, Teachers, and Students,* pp. 84, 85.

Its Goal Is Character Building. The highest class of education is that which will give such knowledge and discipline as will lead to the best development of character, and will fit the soul for that life which measures with the life of God. Eternity is not to be lost out of our reckoning. The highest education is that which will teach our children and youth the science of Christianity, which will give them an experimental knowledge of God's ways, and will impart to them the lessons that Christ gave to His disciples of the paternal character of God. *Ibid., pp. 45, 46.*

It Is a Training That Directs and Develops. There is a time for training children and a time for educating youth, and it is essential that in school both of these be combined in a great degree. Children may be trained for the service of sin or for the service of righteousness. The early education of youth shapes their characters both in their secular and in their religious life. Solomon says, "Train up a child in the way he should go; and when he is old, he will not depart from it." This language is positive. The training which Solomon enjoins is to direct, educate, and develop.

In order for parents and teachers to do this work, they must themselves understand "the way" the child should go. This embraces more than merely having a knowledge of books. It takes in everything that is good, virtuous, righteous, and holy. It comprehends the practice of temperance, godliness, brotherly kindness, and love to God and to one another. In order to attain this object, the physical, mental, moral, and religious education of children must have attention. *Testimonies for the Church, vol. 3, pp. 131, 132.*

It Prepares Workers for God. Upon fathers and mothers devolves the responsibility of giving a Christian education to the children entrusted to them. In no case are they to let any line of business so absorb mind and time and talents that their children are allowed to drift until they are separated far from God. They are not to allow their children to slip out of their grasp into the hands of unbelievers.

They are to do all in their power to keep them from imbibing the spirit of the world. They are to train them to become workers together with God. They are to be God's human hand, fitting themselves and their children for an endless life. *Fundamentals of Christian Education,* p. 545.

It Teaches the Love and Fear of God. Christian parents, will you not for Christ's sake examine your desires, your aims for your children, and see if they will bear the test of God's law? The most essential education is that which will teach them the love and the fear of God. *Review and Herald,* June 24, 1890.

It Is Regarded by Many as Old-fashioned. The education that is lasting as eternity is almost wholly neglected as old-fashioned and undesirable. The educating of the children to take hold of the work of character building in reference to their present good, their present peace and happiness, and to guide their feet in the path cast up for the ransomed of the Lord to walk in, is considered not fashionable and, therefore, not essential. In order to have your children enter the gates of the City of God as conquerors, they must be educated to fear God and keep His commandments in the present life. *Fundamentals of Christian Education,* p. 111.

It Is Ever Progressing, Never Completed. Our lifework here is a preparation for the life eternal. The education begun here will not be completed in this life; it will be going forward through all eternity—ever progressing, never completed. More and more fully will be revealed the wisdom and love of God in the plan of redemption. The Saviour, as He leads His children to the fountains of living waters, will impart rich stores of knowledge. And day by day the wonderful works of God, the evidences of His power in creating and sustaining the universe, will open before the mind in new beauty. In the light that shines from the throne, mysteries will disappear, and the soul will be filled with astonishment at the simplicity of the things that were never before comprehended. *The Ministry of Healing,* p. 466.

CHAPTER 51

Preparing for School

The First Eight or Ten Years. Children should not be long confined within doors, nor should they be required to apply themselves closely to study until a good foundation has been laid for physical development. For the first eight or ten years of a child's life the field or garden is the best schoolroom, the mother the best teacher, nature the best lesson book. Even when the child is old enough to attend school, his health should be regarded as of greater importance than a knowledge of books. He should be surrounded with the conditions most favorable to both physical and mental growth. *Education,* p. 208.

It is customary to send very young children to school. They are required to study from books things that tax their young minds. . . . This course is not wise. A nervous child should not be overtaxed in any direction. *Fundamentals of Christian Education,* p. 416.

The Child's Program During Infancy. During the first six or seven years of a child's life, special attention should be given to its physical training, rather than the intellect. After this period, if the physical constitution is good, the education of both should receive attention. Infancy extends to the age of six or seven years. Up to this period children should be left, like little lambs, to roam around the house and in the yards, in the buoyancy of their spirits, skipping and jumping, free from care and trouble.

Parents, especially mothers, should be the only teachers of such infant minds. They should not educate from books. The children generally will be inquisitive to learn the things of nature. They will ask questions in regard to things they see and hear, and parents should improve the opportunity to instruct and patiently answer those little inquiries. They can in this manner get the advantage of the enemy and fortify the minds of their children by sowing good seed in their hearts, leaving no room for the bad to take root. The mother's loving instruction at a tender age is what is needed by children in the formation of character. *Pacific Health Journal,* September 1897.

Lessons During the Transition Period. The mother should be the teacher, and home the school where every child receives his first lessons; and these lessons should include habits of industry. Mothers, let the little ones play in the open air; let them listen to the songs of the birds and learn the love of God as expressed in His beautiful works. Teach them simple lessons from the book of nature and the things about them; and as their minds expand, lessons from books may be added and firmly fixed in the memory. But let them also learn, even in their earliest years, to be useful. Train them to think that, as members of the household, they are to act an interested, helpful part in sharing the domestic burdens, and to seek healthful exercise in the performance of necessary home duties. *Fundamentals of Christian Education,* pp. 416, 417.

It Need Not Be a Painful Process. Such a training is of untold value to a child, and this training need not be a painful process. It can be so given that the child will find pleasure in learning to be helpful. Mothers can amuse their children while teaching them to perform little offices of love, little home duties. This is the mother's work—patiently to instruct her children, line upon line, precept upon precept, here a little, and there a little.

And in doing this work, the mother herself will gain an invaluable training and discipline. Letter 55, 1902.

Morals Imperiled by School Associates. Do not send your little ones to school too early. The mother should be careful how she trusts the molding of the infant mind to other hands. *Christian Temperance and Bible Hygiene,* p. 67.

Many mothers feel that they have not time to instruct their children, and in order to get them out of the way, and get rid of their noise and trouble, they send them to school. . . .

Not only has the physical and mental health of children been endangered by being sent to school at too early a period, but they have been the losers in a moral point of view. They have had opportunities to become acquainted with children who were uncultivated in their manners. They were thrown into the society of the coarse and rough, who lie, swear, steal and deceive, and who delight to impart their knowledge of vice to those younger than themselves. Young children, if left to themselves, learn the bad more readily than the good. Bad habits agree best with the natural heart, and the things which they see and hear in infancy and childhood are deeply imprinted upon their minds; and the bad seed sown in their young hearts will take root and will become sharp thorns to wound the hearts of their parents. *Solemn Appeal,* pp. 130, 132.

CHAPTER 52

Choosing the School

We Sustain Terrible Losses. At times I find myself wishing that God would speak to parents with an audible voice as He spoke to the wife of Manoah, telling them what they must do in training their children. We are sustaining terrible losses in every branch of the work through the neglect of home training. It was this that impressed upon our minds the need of schools where a religious influence should predominate. If anything can be done to counteract the great evil, in the strength of Jesus we will do it. Manuscript 119, 1899.

Facing a Momentous Issue. Parents, guardians, place your children in training schools where the influences are similar to those of a rightly conducted home school; schools in which the teachers will carry them forward from point to point, and in which the spiritual atmosphere is a savor of life unto life. . . . Whether or not our youth who have received wise instruction and training from godly parents will continue to be sanctified through the truth depends largely upon the influence that, after leaving their homes, they meet among those to whom they look for Christian instruction. *Testimonies for the Church,* vol. 8, pp. 225, 226.

Which Class of Educators? There are two classes of educators in the world. One class is those whom God makes channels of light, and the other class is those whom Satan uses as his agents, who are wise to do evil. One class contemplates the character of God and increases in the knowledge of Jesus, whom God hath sent into the world. This class becomes wholly given up to those things which bring heavenly enlightenment, heavenly wisdom, to the uplifting of the soul. Every capability of their nature is submitted to God, and their thoughts are brought into captivity to Christ. The other class is in league with the prince of darkness, who is ever on the alert that he may find an opportunity to teach others the knowledge of evil. *Fundamentals of Christian Education,* p. 174.

Choose the School Where God Is the Foundation. In planning for the education of their children outside the home, parents should realize that it is no longer safe to send them to the public school, and should endeavor to send them to schools where they will obtain an education based on a Scriptural foundation. Upon every Christian parent there rests the solemn obligation of giving to his children an education that will lead them to gain a knowledge of the Lord and to become partakers of the divine nature through obedience to God's will and way. *Counsels to Parents, Teachers, and Students,* p. 205.

Consider God's Counsel to Israel. While the judgments of God were falling upon the land of Egypt, the Lord directed the Israelites not only to keep their children within their houses, but to bring in even their cattle from the fields. . . .

As the Israelites kept their children within their houses during the time when the judgments of God were in the land of Egypt, so in this time of peril we are to keep our children separate and distinct from the world. We are to teach them that the commandments of God mean much more than we realize. Those who keep them will not imitate the practices of the transgressors of God's law.

Parents must regard God's Word with respect, obeying its teachings. To the parents in this day, as well as to the

Israelites, God declares: "These words . . . shall be in thine heart; and thou shalt teach them diligently unto thy children, and shalt talk of them when thou sittest in thine house, and when thou walkest by the way, and when thou liest down, and when thou risest up. And thou shalt bind them for a sign upon thine hand, and they shall be as frontlets between thine eyes. And thou shalt write them upon the posts of thy house, and on thy gates."

Notwithstanding this plain instruction, some of God's people permit their children to attend the public schools, where they mingle with those who are corrupt in morals. In these schools their children can neither study the Bible nor learn its principles. Christian parents, you must make provision for your children to be educated in Bible principles. Manuscript 100, 1902.

Bible Truth Neutralized; the Child Confused. Do our children receive from the teachers in the public schools ideas that are in harmony with the Word of God? Is sin presented as an offense against God? Is obedience to all the commandments of God taught as the beginning of all wisdom? We send our children to the Sabbath school that they may be instructed in regard to the truth, and then as they go to the day school, lessons containing falsehood are given them to learn. These things confuse the mind, and should not be; for if the young receive ideas that pervert the truth, how will the influence of this education be counteracted?

Can we wonder that under such circumstances some of the youth among us do not appreciate religious advantages? Can we wonder that they drift into temptation? Can we wonder that, neglected as they have been, their energies are devoted to amusements which do them no good, that their religious aspirations are weakened, and their spiritual life darkened? The mind will be of the same character as that upon which it feeds, the harvest of the same nature as the seed sown. Do not these facts sufficiently show the necessity of guarding from the earliest years the education of the youth? Would it not be better for the youth to grow up in a degree of ignorance as to what is commonly accepted as education than for them to become careless in regard to the truth of God? *Testimonies for the Church,* vol. 6, pp. 193, 194.

Schools in All Our Churches. In all our churches there should be schools, and teachers in these schools who are missionaries. It is essential that teachers be trained to act well their part in the important work of educating the children of Sabbathkeepers, not only in the sciences, but in the Scriptures. These schools, established in different localities and conducted by God-fearing men or women, as the case demands, should be built on the same principles as were the schools of the prophets. *Counsels to Parents, Teachers, and Students,* p. 168.

Church Schools in the Cities. It is of the greatest importance that church schools shall be established, to which the children may be sent and still be under the watch care of their mothers and have opportunity to practice the lessons of helpfulness that it is God's design they shall learn in the home. . . .

Much more can be done to save and educate the children of those who at present cannot get away from the cities. This is a matter worthy of our best efforts. Church schools are to be established for the children in the cities, and in connection with these schools provision is to be made for the teaching of higher studies, where these are called for. *Review and Herald,* Dec. 17, 1903.

Provide Schools for Small Churches. Many families, who, for the purpose of educating their children, move to places where our large schools are established, would do better service for the Master by remaining where they are. They should encourage the church of which they are members to establish a church school where the children within their borders could receive an all-round, practical Christian education. It would be vastly better for their children, for themselves, and for the cause of God, if they would remain in the smaller churches, where their help is needed, instead of going to the larger churches, where, because they are not needed, there is a constant temptation to fall into spiritual inactivity.

Wherever there are a few Sabbathkeepers, the parents should unite in providing a place for a day school where their children and youth can be instructed. They should employ a Christian teacher, who, as a consecrated missionary, shall educate the children in such a way as to lead them to become missionaries. Let teachers be employed who will give a thorough education in the common branches, the Bible being made the foundation and the life of all study. *Testimonies for the Church,* vol. 6, p. 198.

In localities where believers are few, let two or three churches unite in erecting a humble building for a church school. *Ibid.,* p. 109.

If parents will realize the importance of these small educating centers, cooperating to do the work that the Lord desires to be done at this time, the plans of the enemy for our children will be frustrated. Manuscript 33, 1908.

Home Church Schools. As far as possible, all our children should have the privilege of a Christian education. To provide this we must sometimes establish home church schools. It would be well if several families in a neighborhood would unite to employ a humble, God-fearing teacher to give to the parents that help that is needed in educating their children. This will be a great blessing to many isolated groups of Sabbathkeepers, and a plan more pleasing to the Lord than that which has been sometimes followed, of sending young children away from their homes to attend one of our larger schools.

Our small companies of Sabbathkeepers are needed to hold up the light before their neighbors; and the children are needed in their homes, where they may be a help to their parents when the hours of study are ended. The well-ordered Christian home, where young children can have parental discipline that is after the Lord's order, is the best place for them. *Counsels to Parents, Teachers, and Students,* p. 158.

A Problem for Isolated Members. Some families of Sabbathkeepers live alone or far separated from others of like faith. These have sometimes sent their children to our boarding schools, where they have received help and have returned to be a blessing in their own home. But some cannot send their children away from home to be educated. In such cases parents should endeavor to employ an exemplary religious teacher, who will feel it a pleasure to work for the Master in any capacity and be willing to cultivate any part of the Lord's vineyard. Fathers and mothers should cooperate with the teacher, laboring earnestly for the conversion of their children. *Testimonies for the Church,* vol. 6, pp. 198, 199.

Work as for Life to Save Children. In some countries parents are compelled by law to send their children to school. In these countries, in localities where there is a church, schools should be established, if there are no more than six children to attend. Work as if you were working for your life to save the children from being drowned in the polluting, corrupting influences of the world.

We are far behind our duty in this important matter. In many places schools should have been in operation years ago. Many localities would thus have had representatives of the truth who would have given character to the work of the Lord. Instead of centering so many large buildings in a few places, schools should have been established in many localities.

Let these schools now be started under wise direction, that the children and youth may be educated in their own churches. It is a grievous offense to God that there has been so great neglect in this line, when Providence has so abundantly supplied us with facilities with which to work. *Ibid.*, pp. 199, 200.

An Established School Not to Be Abandoned. The schoolwork in a place where a church school has been established should never be given up unless God plainly directs that this should be done. Adverse influences may seem to conspire against the school, but with God's help the teacher can do a grand, saving work in changing the order of things. *Counsels to Parents, Teachers, and Students*, p. 157.

To Uplift Disobedient, Unruly Children. Sometimes there is in the school a disorderly element that makes the work very hard. Children who have not received a right education make much trouble, and by their perversity make the heart of the teacher sad. But let him not become discouraged. Test and trial bring experience. If the children are disobedient and unruly, there is all the more need of strenuous effort. The fact that there are children with such characters is one of the reasons why church schools should be established. The children whom parents have neglected to educate and discipline must be saved if possible. *Ibid.,* p. 153.

To Convert Worldly Youth. Years ago school buildings should have been erected in other places besides ————, not large buildings, but buildings suitable for church schools, in which the children and youth could receive a true education. The lesson books used should be of a character to bring the law of God to the attention. The Bible should be made the foundation of education. In this work the light and strength and power of the truth will be magnified. Youth from the world, whose minds have not been depraved by habits of sensuality, will connect with these schools and will there be converted. . . . This kind of missionary work, I am instructed, will have a most telling influence in extending the light and knowledge of truth. Manuscript 150, 1899.

To Maintain the Highest Standards. The character of the work done in our church schools should be of the very highest order. Jesus Christ, the Restorer, is the only remedy for a wrong education; and the lessons taught in His Word should ever be kept before the youth in the most attractive form. The school discipline should supplement the home training, and both at home and at school simplicity and godliness should be maintained. *Counsels to Parents, Teachers, and Students,* p. 174.

To Prepare for the Higher Grade Above. To parents He sends the warning cry, Gather your children into your own houses; gather them away from those who are disregarding the commandments of God, who are teaching and practicing evil. Get out of the large cities as fast as possible. Establish church schools. Give your children the Word of God as the foundation of all their education. This is full of beautiful lessons, and if pupils make it their study in the primary grade below, they will be prepared for the higher grade above. *Testimonies for the Church,* vol. 6, p. 195.

God Has Made Provision. Our schools are the Lord's special instrumentality to fit the children and youth for missionary work. Parents should understand their responsibility and help their children to appreciate the great privileges and blessings that God has provided for them in educational advantages. *Counsels to Parents, Teachers, and Students,* p. 149.

CHAPTER 53

The Church's Responsibility

The Church as a Watchman. The Lord would use the church school as an aid to the parents in educating and preparing their children for this time before us. Then let the church take hold of the schoolwork in earnest and make it what the Lord desires it to be. *Counsels to Parents, Teachers, and Students,* p. 167.

God has appointed the church as a watchman, to have a jealous care over the youth and children, and as a sentinel to see the approach of the enemy and give warning of danger. But the church does not realize the situation. She is sleeping on guard. In this time of peril fathers and mothers must arouse and work as for life, or many of the youth will be forever lost. *Ibid.,* p. 165.

God's Law Must Be Upheld. The church has a special work to do in educating and training its children that they may not, in attending school, or in any other association, be influenced by those of corrupt habits. The world is full of iniquity and disregard of the requirements of God. . . .

The Protestant churches have accepted the spurious Sabbath, the child of the Papacy, and have exalted it above God's holy, sanctified day. It is our work to make plain to our children that the first day of the week is not the true Sabbath, and that its observance, after light has come to us as to what is the true Sabbath, is a plain contradiction of the law of God. *Testimonies for the Church,* vol. 6, p. 193.

Skilled Workers Must Be Trained for Christ. As a church, as individuals, if we would stand clear in the judgment, we must make more liberal efforts for the training of our young people, that they may be better fitted for the various branches of the great work committed to our hands. We should lay wise plans, in order that the ingenious minds of those who have talent may be strengthened and disciplined and polished after the highest order, that the work of Christ may not be hindered for lack of skillful laborers, who will do their work with earnestness and fidelity. *Counsels to Parents, Teachers, and Students,* p. 43.

All to Share the Expense. Let all share the expense. Let the church see that those who ought to receive its benefits are attending the school. Poor families should be assisted. We cannot call ourselves true missionaries if we neglect those at our very doors, who are at the most critical age, and who need our aid to secure knowledge and experience that will fit them for the service of God. The Lord would have painstaking efforts made in the education of our children. *Testimonies for the Church,* vol. 6, p. 217.

Lift Financial Load of Training Worthy Youth. The churches in different localities should feel that a solemn responsibility rests upon them to train youth and educate talent to engage in missionary work. When they see those in the church who give promise of making useful workers, but who are not able to support themselves in the school, they should assume the responsibility of sending them to one of our training schools. There is excellent ability in the churches that needs to be brought into service. There are persons who would do good service in the Lord's vineyard, but many are too poor to obtain without assistance the education that they require. The churches should feel it a privilege to take a part in defraying the expenses of such.

Those who have the truth in their hearts are always openhearted, helping where it is necessary. They lead out, and others imitate their example. If there are some who should have the benefit of the school, but who cannot pay full price for their tuition, let the churches show their liberality by helping them. *Counsels to Parents, Teachers, and Students,* p. 69.

A School Fund for Advanced Education. Let a fund be created by generous contributions for the establishment of schools for the advancement of educational work. We need men well trained, well educated, to work in the interests of the churches. They should present the fact that we cannot trust our youth to go to seminaries and colleges established by other denominations, that we must gather them into schools where their religious training shall not be neglected. *Ibid.,* pp. 44, 45.

Give to Missions, but Do Not Neglect Youth at Home. Shall the members of the church give means to advance the cause of Christ among others and leave their own children to carry on the work and service of Satan? *Testimonies for the Church,* vol. 6, p. 217.

While we should put forth earnest efforts for the masses of the people around us, and push the work into foreign fields, no amount of labor in this line can excuse us for neglecting the education of our children and youth. They are to be trained to become workers for God. Both parents and teachers, by precept and example, are so to instill the principles of truth and honesty into the minds and hearts of the young, that they will become men and women who are as true as steel to God and His cause. *Counsels to Parents, Teachers, and Students,* p. 165.

Pray in Faith; God Will Open Ways. Some may ask, "How are such schools to be established?" We are not a rich people, but if we pray in faith and let the Lord work in our behalf, He will open ways before us to establish small schools in retired places for the education of our youth, not only in the Scriptures and in book learning, but in many lines of manual labor. *Ibid.,* p. 204.

"Let Us Arise and Build."⋆ We should establish the work in right lines here at Crystal Springs [Sanitarium, California]. Here are our children. Shall we allow them to be contaminated by the world—by its iniquity, its disregard of God's commandments? I ask those who are planning to send their children to the public schools, where they are liable to be contaminated, How can you take such a risk?

We desire to erect a church school building for our children. Because of the many calls for means, it seems a difficult matter to secure sufficient money or to arouse an interest great enough to build a small, convenient schoolhouse. I have told the school committee that I would lease to them some land for as long a time as they care to use it for school purposes. I hope that interest enough will be aroused to enable us to erect a building where our children can be taught the Word of God, which is the lifeblood and the flesh of the Son of God. . . . Will you not take an interest in the erection of this school building in which the Word of God is to be taught? One man, when asked how much he was willing to give to the school in labor, said that if we would give him three dollars a day and his board and lodging, he would help us. But we do not want offers of this kind. Help will come to us. We expect to have a school building, in which the Bible can be taught, in which prayers can be offered to God, and in which the children can be instructed in

Bible principles. We expect that everyone who can take hold with us will want to have a share in erecting this building. We expect to train a little army of workers on this hillside. Manuscript 100, 1902.

Help With Labor as Well as Finances. We know that all are interested in the success of this enterprise. Let those who have spare time give a few days in helping to build this schoolhouse. Not enough money has been subscribed yet to pay merely for the necessary material. We are glad for what has been given, but we now ask everyone to take hold of this matter interestedly, so that we shall soon have a place where our children can study the Bible, which is the foundation of all true education. The fear of the Lord—the very first lesson to be taught—is the beginning of wisdom.

There is no reason why this matter should drag. Let everyone take hold to help, persevering with unflagging interest until the building is completed. Let everyone do something. Some may have to get up as early as four o'clock in the morning in order to help. Usually I begin my work before that time. As soon as it is daylight, some could begin work on the building, putting in an hour or two before breakfast. Others could not do this, perhaps, but all can do something to show their interest in making it possible for the children to be educated in a school where they can be disciplined and trained for God's service. His blessing will surely rest upon every such effort. . . .

Brethren and sisters, what will you do to help build a church school? We believe that everyone will regard it as a privilege and a blessing to have this school building. Let us catch the spirit of the work, saying, We will arise and build. If all will take hold of the work unitedly, we shall soon have a schoolhouse in which from day to day our children will be taught the way of the Lord. As we do our best, the blessing of God will rest upon us. Shall we not arise and build? *Ibid.*

---

* NOTE: This is a portion of an address given July 14, 1902, urging the building of a church school near her own home.

CHAPTER 54

Teachers and Parents in Partnership

Need for a Sympathetic Understanding. The teachers in the home and the teachers in the school should have a sympathetic understanding of one another's work. They should labor together harmoniously, imbued with the same missionary spirit, striving together to benefit the children physically, mentally, and spiritually, and to develop characters that will stand the test of temptation. *Counsels to Parents, Teachers, and Students,* p. 157.

Parents should remember that much more will be accomplished by the work of the church school if they themselves realize the advantage that their children will obtain in such a school, and unite wholeheartedly with the teacher. By prayer, by patience, by forbearance, parents can undo much of the wrong caused by impatience and unwise indulgence. Let parents and teacher take hold of the work together, the parents remembering that they themselves will be helped by the presence in the community of an earnest, God-fearing teacher. *Ibid.,* pp. 155, 156.

Disunion May Nullify Good Influence. A spirit of disunion cherished in the hearts of a few will communicate itself to others and undo the influence for good that would be exerted by the school. Unless parents are ready and anxious to cooperate with the teacher for the salvation of their children, they are not prepared to have a school established among them. *Testimonies for the Church,* vol. 6, p. 202.

Teamwork Begins in the Home. The work of cooperation should begin with the father and mother themselves, in the home life. In the training of their children they have a joint responsibility, and it should be their constant endeavor to act together. Let them yield themselves to God, seeking help from Him to sustain each other. Let them teach their children to be true to God, true to principle, and thus true to themselves and to all with whom they are connected. With such training, children when sent to school will not be a cause of disturbance or anxiety. They will be a support to their teachers and an example and encouragement to their fellow pupils. *Education,* p. 283.

The children will carry with them into the schoolroom the influence of your training. As godly parents and godly teachers work in harmony, the hearts of the children are prepared to take a deep interest in the work of God in the church. The graces cultivated in the home are carried into the church, and God is glorified. Letter 29, 1902.

If parents are so engrossed in the business and pleasures of this life that they neglect the proper discipline of their children, the work of the teacher is not only made very hard and trying, but often rendered wholly fruitless. *Review and Herald,* June 13, 1882.

The Teacher's Work Is Supplemental. In the formation of character no other influences count so much as the influence of the home. The teacher's work should supplement that of the parents, but is not to take its place. In all that concerns the well-being of the child, it should be the effort of parents and teachers to cooperate. *Education,* p. 283.

The instruction given the child in the home is to be such as will help the teacher. In the home the child is to be taught the importance of neatness, order, and thoroughness; and these lessons are to be repeated in the school. Manuscript 45, 1912.

When the child is old enough to be sent to school, the teacher should cooperate with the parents, and manual training should be continued as part of the school studies. There are many students who object to this kind of work in the schools. They think useful employment, like learning a trade, degrading; but such have an incorrect idea of what constitutes true dignity. *Counsels to Parents, Teachers, and Students,* p. 146.

The Home May Be Blessed Through the School. If he [the teacher] labors patiently, earnestly, perseveringly, in Christ's lines, the reformatory work done in the school may extend to the homes of the children, bringing into them a purer, more heavenly atmosphere. This is indeed missionary work of the highest order. *Ibid.,* p. 157.

The watchful teacher will find many opportunities for directing pupils to acts of helpfulness. By little children especially the teacher is regarded with almost unbounded confidence and respect. Whatever he may suggest as to ways of helping in the home, faithfulness in the daily tasks, ministry to the sick or the poor, can hardly fail of bringing forth fruit. And thus again a double gain will be secured. The kindly suggestion will react upon its author. Gratitude and cooperation on the part of the parents will lighten the teacher's burden and brighten his path. *Education,* p. 213.

Parents May Lighten the Teacher's Work. If parents faithfully act their part, the work of the teacher will be greatly lightened. His hope and courage will be increased. Parents whose hearts are filled with the love of Christ will refrain from finding fault and will do all in their power to encourage and help the one whom they have chosen as teacher for their children. They will be willing to believe that he is just as conscientious in his work as they are in theirs. *Counsels to Parents, Teachers, and Students,* p. 157.

When parents realize their responsibilities, there will be far less left for the teachers to do. *Ibid.,* p. 148.

Parents May Be Counselors to the Teacher. We are to talk the love of God in our homes; we are to teach it in our schools. The principles of the Word of God are to be brought into the home and school life. If parents fully understood their duty of submission to the Lord's revealed will, they would be wise counselors in our school and in educational matters; for their experience in home training would teach them how to guard against the temptations that come to children and youth. Teachers and parents would thus become laborers together with God in the work of educating the youth for heaven. Letter 356, 1907.

The parents' intimate knowledge both of the character of the children and of their physical peculiarities or infirmities, if imparted to the teacher, would be an assistance to him. It is to be regretted that so many fail of realizing this. By most parents little interest is shown either to inform themselves as to the teacher's qualification, or to cooperate with him in his work. *Education,* p. 284.

They [parents] must feel it their duty to cooperate with the teacher, to encourage wise discipline, and to pray much for the one who is teaching their children. *Fundamentals of Christian Education,* p. 270.

Teachers May Be Advisers to Parents. Since parents so rarely acquaint themselves with the teacher, it is the more important that the teacher seek the acquaintance of parents. He should visit the homes of his pupils and gain a knowledge of the influences and surroundings among which they live. By coming personally in touch with their homes and lives, he may strengthen the ties that bind him to his pupils, and may learn how to deal more successfully with their different dispositions and temperaments.

As he interests himself in the home education, the teacher imparts a double benefit. Many parents, absorbed in work and care, lose sight of their opportunities to influence for good the lives of their children. The teacher can do much to arouse these parents to their possibilities and privileges. He will find others to whom the sense of their responsibility is a heavy burden, so anxious are they that their children shall become good and useful men and women. Often the teacher can assist these parents in bearing their burden; and, by counseling together, both teacher and parents will be encouraged and strengthened. *Education,* pp. 284, 285.

CHAPTER 55

Unity in Discipline

The Teacher Needs Tact in Management. Among the youth will be found great diversity of character and education. Some have lived in an element of arbitrary restraint and harshness, which has developed in them a spirit of obstinacy and defiance. Others have been household pets, allowed by overfond parents to follow their own inclinations. Every defect has been excused, until their character is deformed. To deal successfully with these different minds, the teacher needs to exercise great tact and delicacy in management, as well as firmness in government.

Dislike and even contempt for proper regulations will often be manifested. Some will exercise all their ingenuity in evading penalties, while others will display a reckless indifference to the consequences of transgression. All this will call for more patience and greater exertion on the part of those who are entrusted with their education. *Testimonies for the Church,* vol. 5, pp. 88, 89.

Let Rules Be Few and Well Considered. In the school as well as in the home there should be wise discipline. The teacher must make rules to guide the conduct of his pupils. These rules should be few and well considered, and once made they should be enforced. Every principle involved in them should be so placed before the student that he will be convinced of its justice. *Counsels to Parents, Teachers, and Students,* p. 153.

The Teacher Must Enforce Obedience. In the school, as well as in the home, the question of discipline should be understood. We should hope that in the schoolroom there would never be occasion to use the rod. But if in a school there are those who stubbornly resist all counsel and entreaty, all prayers and burden of soul in their behalf, then it is necessary to make them understand that they must obey.

Some teachers do not think it best to enforce obedience. They think that their duty is merely to educate. True, they should educate. But what does the education of children amount to if, when they disregard the principles placed before them, the teacher does not feel that he has a right to exercise authority. *Review and Herald,* Sept. 15, 1904.

He Needs the Cooperation of Parents. The teacher should not be left to carry the burden of his work alone. He needs the sympathy, the kindness, the cooperation, and the love of every church member. The parents should encourage the teacher by showing that they appreciate his efforts. Never should they say or do anything that will encourage insubordination in their children.

But I know that many parents do not cooperate with the teacher. They do not foster in the home the good influence exerted in the school. Instead of carrying out in the home the good influence exerted in the school, they allow their children to do as they please, to go hither and thither without restraint. And if the teacher exercises authority in requiring obedience, the children carry to their parents an exaggerated, distorted account of the way in which they have been dealt with. The teacher may have done only that which it was his painful duty to do; but the parents sympathize with their children, even though they are in the wrong. And often those parents who themselves rule in anger are the most unreasonable when their children are restrained and disciplined in school. *Counsels to Parents, Teachers, and Students,* pp. 153, 154.

When parents justify the complaints of their children against the authority and discipline of the school, they do not see that they are increasing the demoralizing power which now prevails to such a fearful extent. Every influence surrounding the youth needs to be on the right side, for youthful depravity is increasing. *Testimonies for the Church,* vol. 5, p. 112.

Let Them Sustain the Faithful Teachers. Parents who have never felt the care which they should feel for the souls of their children, and who have never given them proper restraint and instruction, are the very ones who manifest the most bitter opposition when their children are restrained, reproved, or corrected at school. Some of these children are a disgrace to the church and a disgrace to the name of Adventists. *Ibid., p.* 51.

Let them [parents] teach their children to be true to God, true to principle, and thus true to themselves and to all with whom they are connected. . . .

Parents who give this training are not the ones likely to be found criticizing the teacher. They feel that both the interest of their children and justice to the school demand that, so far as possible, they sustain and honor the one who shares their responsibility. *Education,* p. 283.

Never Criticize the Teacher Before Children. Parents, when the church school teacher tries to train and discipline your children that they may gain eternal life, do not in their presence criticize his actions, even though you may think him too severe. If you desire them to give their hearts to the Saviour, cooperate with the teacher's efforts for their salvation. How much better it is for children, instead of hearing criticism, to hear from the lips of their mother words of commendation regarding the work of the teacher. Such words make lasting impressions and influence the children to respect the teacher. *Counsels to Parents, Teachers, and Students,* pp. 154, 155.

If criticism or suggestion in regard to the teacher's work becomes necessary, it should be made to him in private. If this proves ineffective, let the matter be referred to those who are responsible for the management of the school. Nothing should be said or done to weaken the children's respect for the one upon whom their well-being in so great degree depends. *Ibid.,* pp. 161, 162.

If parents would place themselves in the position of the teachers, and see how difficult it must necessarily be to manage and discipline a school of hundreds of students of every grade and class of minds, they might, upon reflection, see things differently. *Testimonies for the Church,* vol. 4, p. 429.

Insubordination Often Begins in the Home. In allowing children to do as they please, parents may think themselves affectionate, but they are practicing the veriest cruelty. Children are able to reason, and their souls are hurt by inconsiderate kindness, however proper this kindness may be in the eyes of the parents. As the children grow older, their insubordination grows. Their teachers may try to correct them, but too often the parents side with the children, and the evil continues to grow, clothed, if possible, with a still darker covering of deception than before. Other children are led astray by the wrong course of these children, and yet the parents cannot see the wrong. The words of their children are listened to before the words of teachers, who mourn over the wrong. *Review and Herald,* Jan. 20, 1901.

Teacher's Work Doubled by Noncooperative Parents. The neglect of parents to train their children makes the work of the teacher doubly hard. The children bear the stamp of the unruly, unamiable traits revealed by their parents. Neglected at home, they regard the discipline of the school as oppressive and severe. Such children, if not carefully guarded, will leaven other children by their undisciplined, deformed characters. . . . The good that children might receive in school to counteract their defective home training is undermined by the sympathy which their parents show for them in their wrongdoing.

Shall parents who believe the Word of God continue their crooked management and confirm in their children their evil propensities? Fathers and mothers professing the truth for this time might better come to their senses and no longer be partakers in this evil, no longer carry out Satan's devices by accepting the false testimony of their unconverted children. It is enough for teachers to have the children's influence to contend with, without having the parents' influence also. *Review and Herald,* Oct. 9, 1900.

CHAPTER 56

Academy and College Training

Many Losing the Way in Worldly Institutions. It is a terrible fact, and one that should make the hearts of parents tremble, that in so many schools and colleges to which the youth are sent for mental culture and discipline, influences prevail which misshape the character, divert the mind from life's true aims, and debase the morals. Through contact with the irreligious, the pleasure loving, and the corrupt, many, many youth lose the simplicity and purity, the faith in God, and the spirit of self-sacrifice that Christian fathers and mothers have cherished and guarded by careful instruction and earnest prayer.

Many who enter school with the purpose of fitting themselves for some line of unselfish ministry become absorbed in secular studies. An ambition is aroused to win distinction in scholarship and to gain position and honor in the world. The purpose for which they entered school is lost sight of, and the life is given up to selfish and worldly pursuits. And often habits are formed that ruin the life both for this world and for the world to come. *The Ministry of Healing,* p. 403.

Religious Home Influences Are Effaced. You pray, "Lead us not into temptation." Then do not consent for your children to be placed where they will meet unnecessary temptation. Do not send them away to schools where they will be associated with influences that will be as tares sown in the field of their heart.

In the home school, during their early years, train and discipline your children in the fear of God. And then be

328

careful lest you place them where the religious impressions they have received will be effaced, and the love of God taken out of their hearts. Let no inducement of high wages or of apparently great educational advantages lead you to send your children away from your influence, to places where they will be exposed to great temptations. "What shall it profit a man, if he shall gain the whole world, and lose his own soul? Or what shall a man give in exchange for his soul?" Mark 8:36, 37. Manuscript 30, 1904.

Our Colleges Are Ordained of God. When I was shown by the angel of God that an institution should be established for the education of our youth, I saw that it would be one of the greatest means ordained of God for the salvation of souls. . . . If the influence in our college is what it should be, the youth who are educated there will be enabled to discern God and glorify Him in all His works; and while engaged in cultivating the faculties which God has given them, they will be preparing to render Him more efficient service. *Testimonies for the Church,* vol. 4, pp. 419–422.

The youth are to be encouraged to attend our schools, which should become more and more like the schools of the prophets. Our schools have been established by the Lord. *Fundamentals of Christian Education,* p. 489.

Advantages of Experience in School Home. To a great extent children who are to receive an education in our schools will make far more permanent advancement if separated from the family circle where they have received an erroneous education. It may be necessary for some families to locate where they can board their children and save expense, but in many cases it would prove a hindrance rather than a blessing to their children. *Ibid.,* p. 313.

School Home for Wayward Daughter. The enemy has had his way with your daughter until his toils have bound her about like bands of steel, and it will require a strong, persevering effort to save her soul. If you have success in this case, there must be no halfway work. The habits of years cannot easily be broken. She should be placed where a steady, firm, abiding influence is constantly exercised. I would advise you to put her in the college at ———; let her have the discipline of the boardinghouse. It is where she ought to have been years ago.

The boardinghouse is conducted upon a plan that makes it a good home. This home may not suit the inclinations of some, but it is because they have been educated to false theories, to self-indulgence and self-gratification; and all their habits and customs have been in a wrong channel. But, my dear sister, we are nearing the end of time; and we want now, not to meet the world's tastes and practices, but to meet the mind of God, to see what saith the Scriptures, and then to walk according to the light which God has given us. Our inclinations, our customs and practices, are not to have the preference. God's Word is our standard. *Testimonies for the Church,* vol. 5, p. 506.

Resident Students. It seems that some teachers think that none of the children and young people whose parents live in the vicinity of a school should have school privileges unless they live with their teachers in the school home. This is to me a new and strange idea.

There are young people whose home influences have been such that it would be greatly to their advantage to live for a time in a well-regulated school home. And for those who live where they must of necessity leave their own homes in order to enjoy school privileges, the school homes are a great blessing. But the parental home where God is feared and obeyed is, and ever should be, the best place for young children, where under the proper training of their parents they may enjoy the care and discipline of a religious family, administered by their own parents. . . .

Regarding the youth that are of suitable age to attend a boarding school, let us avoid making unnecessary and arbitrary rules that would separate from their parents those who live in the vicinity of our schools. . . .

Unless the parents are convinced that it would be for the best interests of their children to place them under the school home discipline, they should be permitted to keep them under their own control as far as possible. In some places parents living near the school may see that their children would be benefited by living at the school home, where they can receive certain lines of instruction that they could not receive so well in their own homes. But let it not be urged that children must in all cases be separated from their parents in order to get the advantages of any one of our schools. . . .

Parents are the natural guardians of their children, and they have a solemn responsibility to oversee their education and training.

Can we not understand that the parents, who have watched for years the development of their children, should know best the kind of training and management they should have in order to bring out and cultivate the best traits of character in them? I should advise that children from homes within two or three miles of a school should be allowed to attend the school while living at home and having the benefits of parental influence. Wherever possible, let the family be held together. Letter 60, 1910.

All Children to Have Educational Privileges. The church is asleep and does not realize the magnitude of this matter of educating the children and youth. "Why," says one, "what is the need of being so particular to educate our youth thoroughly? It seems to me that if you take a few who have decided to follow a literary calling or some other calling that requires a certain discipline, and give due attention to them, that is all that is necessary. It is not required that the whole mass of our youth be so well trained. Will not this answer every essential requirement?" I answer, No, most decidedly not. . . . All our youth should be permitted to have the blessings and privileges of an education at our schools, that they may be inspired to become laborers together with God. They all need an education, that they may be fitted for usefulness, qualified for places of responsibility in both private and public life. *Review and Herald,* Feb. 13, 1913.

A Balanced School Program. The faculties of the mind need cultivation, that they may be exercised to the glory of God. Careful attention should be given to the culture of the intellect, that the various organs of the mind may have equal strength, by being brought into exercise, each in its distinctive office. If parents allow their children to follow the bent of their own minds, their own inclination and pleasure, to the neglect of duty, their characters will be formed after this pattern, and they will not be competent for any responsible position in life. The desires and inclinations of the young should be restrained, their weak points of character strengthened, and their overstrong tendencies repressed.

If one faculty is suffered to remain dormant, or is turned out of its proper course, the purpose of God is not carried out. All the faculties should be well developed. Care should be given to each, for each has a bearing upon the others, and all must be exercised in order that the mind may be properly balanced. If one or two organs are cultivated and kept in continual use because it is the choice of your children to put the strength of the mind in one direction to the neglect of other mental powers, they will come to maturity with unbalanced minds and inharmonious characters. They will be apt and strong in one direction, but greatly deficient in other directions just as important. They will not be competent men and women. Their deficiencies will be marked and will mar the entire character. *Testimonies for the Church,* vol. 3, p. 26.

Evils of Constant, Year-round Study. Many parents keep their children at school nearly the year round. These children go through the routine of study mechanically, but do not retain that which they learn. Many of these constant students seem almost destitute of intellectual life. The monotony of continual study wearies the mind, and they take but little interest in their lessons; and to many the application to books becomes painful. They have not an inward love of thought and an ambition to acquire knowledge. They do not encourage in themselves habits of reflection and investigation. . . .

Close reasoners and logical thinkers are few, for the reason that false influences have checked the development of the intellect. The supposition of parents and teachers that continued study would strengthen the intellect has proved erroneous, for in many cases it has had the opposite effect. *Counsels to Parents, Teachers, and Students,* pp. 84, 85.

Censure Often Justly Belongs to Parents. The teacher should not be expected to do the parents' work.

There has been, with many parents, a fearful neglect of duty. Like Eli, they fail to exercise proper restraint; and then they send their undisciplined children to college, to receive the training which the parents should have given them at home.

The teachers have a task which few appreciate. If they succeed in reforming these wayward youth, they receive but little credit. If the youth choose the society of the evil-disposed and go on from bad to worse, then the teachers are censured and the school is denounced. In many cases the censure justly belongs to the parents. They had the first and most favorable opportunity to control and train their children, when the spirit was teachable, and the mind and heart were easily impressed. But through the slothfulness of the parents, the children are permitted to follow their own will, until they become hardened in an evil course. *Ibid.,* p. 91.

Parents to Sustain Teacher's Authority. One of the greatest difficulties with which teachers have had to contend is the failure on the part of parents to cooperate in administering the discipline of the college. If the parents would stand pledged to sustain the authority of the teacher, much insubordination, vice, and profligacy would be prevented. Parents should require their children to respect and obey rightful authority. They should labor with unremitting care and diligence to instruct, guide, and restrain their children, until right habits are firmly established. With such training the youth would be in subjection to the institutions of society and the general restraints of moral obligation. *Testimonies for the Church,* vol. 5, p. 89.

It is not to be left to children to judge whether the discipline of the college is reasonable or unreasonable.

If the parents have confidence enough in the teachers and in the system of education adopted by the school to send their children to it, let them show good sense and moral stamina and support the teacher in enforcing discipline. . . .

Parents who are wise will feel very grateful that there are schools where lawlessness of any kind will not be tolerated, and where children will be trained to obedience rather than indulgence, and where good influences will be brought to bear upon them.

There are some parents who purpose sending their demoralized children to school because they are incorrigible at home. Will these parents support the teachers in their work of discipline, or will they stand ready to believe every false report? Manuscript 119, 1899.

They Should Support School Discipline. Some parents who have sent their children to ———— have told them that if anything unreasonable were required of them not to submit, whoever might require it. What a lesson is this to give to children! In their inexperience how can they judge between what is reasonable and unreasonable?

They may wish to be away at night, no one knows where, and if required by teachers or guardians to give an account of themselves, will call this unreasonable and an infringement on their rights. Their independence must not be interfered with. What power can rules or authority have upon these youth, while they consider any discipline an unreasonable restriction of their liberty?

In many cases these youth have remained in school but a short period, returning home with an unfinished education, that they may have liberty to follow the bent of their untrained, undisciplined wills which they could not have at school. The lessons of indulgence taught them by an unwise father or mother have done their work for time and for eternity, and the loss of these souls will be set to their account. *Ibid.*

An Education Outside the College Curriculum.

Children and youth should cultivate habits of thoroughness in the matter of education. The college course does not embrace all the education which they are to receive. They may be constantly learning lessons from the things they see and hear. They may study from cause to effect, from the surroundings and the circumstances of life. They may learn every day something they must avoid, and something they may practice that will elevate and ennoble them, giving solidity to the character and strengthening in them those principles which are the foundation of noble manhood and womanhood.

If they enter upon their education with careless purposes, well content to pass along without any particular effort on their part, then they will not reach the standard God would have them attain. *Youth's Instructor,* Apr. 21, 1886.

PRIMARY IMPORTANCE
OF PHYSICAL DEVELOPMENT

CHAPTER 57

Exercise and Health*

Well-regulated Employment and Amusement. In order for children and youth to have health, cheerfulness, vivacity, and well-developed muscles and brains, they should be much in the open air and have well-regulated employment and amusement. *Counsels to Parents, Teachers, and Students,* p. 83.

Children should have occupation for their time. Proper mental labor and physical outdoor exercise will not break the constitution of your boys. Useful labor and an acquaintance with the mysteries of housework will be beneficial to your girls, and some outdoor employment is positively necessary to their constitution and health. *Testimonies for the Church,* vol. 4, p. 97.

Exercise and Fresh Air. Those who do not use their limbs every day will realize a weakness when they do attempt to exercise. The veins and muscles are not in a condition to perform their work and keep all the living machinery in healthful action, each organ in the system doing its part. The limbs will strengthen with use. Moderate exercise every day will impart strength to the muscles, which without exercise become flabby and enfeebled. By active exercise in the open air every day, the liver, kidneys, and lungs also will be strengthened to perform their work.

Bring to your aid the power of the will, which will resist cold and will give energy to the nervous system. In a short time you will so realize the benefit of exercise and pure air that you would not live without these blessings. Your lungs, deprived of air, will be like a hungry person deprived of food. Indeed, we can live longer without food than without air, which is the food that God has provided for the lungs. *Ibid.,* vol. 2, p. 533.

Students Especially Need Physical Activity. Inactivity weakens the system. God made men and women to be active and useful. Nothing can increase the strength of the young like proper exercise of all the muscles in useful labor. *Signs of the Times,* Aug. 19, 1875.

All Faculties Are Strengthened by Exercise. Children and youth who are kept at school and confined to books cannot have sound physical constitutions. The exercise of the brain in study, without corresponding physical exercise, has a tendency to attract the blood to the brain, and the circulation of the blood through the system becomes unbalanced. The brain has too much blood, and the extremities too little. There should be rules regulating the studies of children and youth to certain hours, and then a portion of their time should be spent in physical labor. And if their habits of eating, dressing, and sleeping are in accordance with physical law, they can obtain an education without sacrificing physical and mental health. *Counsels to Parents, Teachers, and Students,* p. 83.

Let children be taught, when quite young, to bear the smaller responsibilities of life, and the faculties thus employed will strengthen by exercise. Thus the youth may become efficient helpers in the greater work which the Lord shall afterward call them to do. . . .

Few have been trained to habits of industry, thoughtfulness, and caretaking. Indolence, inaction, is the greatest curse to children of this age. Wholesome, useful labor will be a great blessing, by promoting the formation of good habits and a noble character. *Review and Herald,* Aug. 30, 1881.

Plan for Variety and Change in Work. The active mind and hands of youth must have employment, and if they are not directed to tasks that are useful, that will develop them and bless others, they will find employment in that which will work injury to them in both body and mind.

The youth should cheerfully share the burdens of life with their parents, and by so doing preserve a clear conscience, which is positively necessary to physical and moral health. In doing this, they should be guarded from being taxed in the same direction for any great length of time. If the youth are kept steadily at one kind of employment, until the task becomes irksome, less will be accomplished than might have been through a change of work or a season of relaxation. If the mind is too severely taxed, it will cease to become strong and will degenerate. By a change in the work, health and vigor may be retained. There will be no need to cast aside the useful for the useless, for selfish amusements are dangerous to the morals. *Youth's Instructor,* July 27, 1893.

Weariness, Normal Result of Labor. Mothers, there is nothing that leads to such evils as to lift the burdens from your daughters and give them nothing special to do, and let them choose their own employment, perhaps a little crochet or some other fancywork to busy themselves. Let them have exercise of the limbs and muscles. If it wearies them, what then? Are you not wearied in your work? Will weariness hurt your children, unless overworked, more than it hurts you? No, indeed. *Testimonies for the Church,* vol. 2, p. 371.

They may be weary, but how sweet is rest after a

proper amount of labor. Sleep, nature's sweet restorer, invigorates the tired body and prepares it for the next day's duties. *Signs of the Times,* Apr. 10, 1884.

Why Poverty Is Often a Blessing. Riches and idleness are thought by some to be blessings indeed; but those who are always busy, and who cheerfully go about their daily tasks, are the most happy and enjoy the best health. . . . The sentence that man must toil for his daily bread, and the promise of future happiness and glory, both came from the same throne, and both are blessings. *Christian Temperance and Bible Hygiene,* p. 97.

Poverty, in many cases, is a blessing; for it prevents youth and children from being ruined by inaction. The physical as well as the mental powers should be cultivated and properly developed. The first and constant care of parents should be to see that their children have firm constitutions, that they may be sound men and women. It is impossible to attain this object without physical exercise.

For their own physical health and moral good, children should be taught to work, even if there is no necessity so far as want is concerned. If they would have pure and virtuous characters, they must have the discipline of well-regulated labor, which will bring into exercise all the muscles. The satisfaction that children will have in being useful, and in denying themselves to help others, will be the most healthful pleasure they ever enjoyed. *Testimonies for the Church,* vol. 3, p. 151.

Mental and Physical Activities Equalized. Students should not be permitted to take so many studies that they will have no time for physical training. The health cannot be preserved unless some portion of each day is given to muscular exertion in the open air. Stated hours should be devoted to manual labor of some kind, anything that will call into action all parts of the body. Equalize the taxation of the mental and the physical powers, and the mind of the student will be refreshed. If he is diseased, physical exercise will often help the system to recover its normal condition. When students leave college, they should have better health and a better understanding of the laws of life than when they enter it. The health should be as sacredly guarded as the character. *Christian Temperance and Bible Hygiene,* pp. 82, 83.

Youthful Energy—How Rashly Squandered. The youth in the freshness and vigor of life little realize the value of their abounding energy. A treasure more precious than gold, more essential to advancement than learning or rank or riches—how lightly is it held! how rashly squandered! . . .

In the study of physiology, pupils should be led to see the value of physical energy and how it can be so preserved and developed as to contribute in the highest degree to success in life's great struggle. *Education,* pp. 195, 196.

Activity Not to Be Repressed but Guided. Our children stand, as it were, at the parting of the ways. On every hand the world's enticements to self-seeking and self-indulgence call them away from the path cast up for the ransomed of the Lord. Whether their lives shall be a blessing or a curse depends upon the choice they make. Overflowing with energy, eager to test their untried capabilities, they must find some outlet for their superabounding life. Active they will be for good or for evil.

God's Word does not repress activity, but guides it aright. God does not bid the youth to be less aspiring

The elements of character that make a man truly successful and honored among men—the irrepressible desire for some greater good, the indomitable will, the strenuous application, the untiring perseverance—are not to be discouraged. By the grace of God they are to be directed to the attainment of objects as much higher than mere selfish and worldly interests as the heavens are higher than the earth. *The Ministry of Healing*, p. 396.

★ NOTE: See *The Adventist Home,* pp. 493-530, Section 17, "Relaxation and Recreation."

CHAPTER 58

Training for Practical Life

Why God Appointed Labor for Adam and Eve. The Lord made Adam and Eve and placed them in the Garden of Eden to dress the garden and keep it for the Lord. It was for their happiness to have some employment, or else the Lord would not have appointed them their work. Manuscript 24b, 1894.

When in counsel with the Father before the world was, it was designed that the Lord God should plant a garden for Adam and Eve in Eden and give them the task of caring for the fruit trees and cultivating and training the vegetation. Useful labor was to be their safeguard, and it was to be perpetuated through all generations to the close of earth's history. *Signs of the Times,* Aug. 13, 1896.

Example of Jesus as the Perfect Workman. In His earth-life, Christ was . . . obedient and helpful in the home. He learned the carpenter's trade and worked with His own hands in the little shop at Nazareth. . . . The Bible says of Jesus, "And the child grew, and waxed strong in spirit, filled with wisdom: and the grace of God was upon him." As He worked in childhood and youth, mind and body were developed. He did not use His physical powers recklessly, but gave them such exercise as would keep them in health, that He might do the best work in every line. He was not willing to be defective, even in the handling of tools. He was perfect as a workman, as He was perfect in character. *Fundamentals of Christian Education,* pp. 417, 418.

Every article He made was well made, the different parts fitting exactly, the whole able to bear test. *Evangelism,* p. 378.

He Toiled Daily With Patient Hands. Jesus made the lowly paths of human life sacred by His example. . . . His life was one of diligent industry. He, the Majesty of heaven, walked the streets, clad in the simple garb of the common laborer. He toiled up and down the mountain steeps, going to and from His humble work. Angels were not sent to bear Him on their pinions up the tiresome ascent, or to lend their strength in performing His lowly task. Yet when He went forth to contribute to the support of the family by His daily toil, He possessed the same power as when He wrought the miracle of feeding the five thousand hungry souls on the shore of Galilee.

But He did not employ His divine power to lessen His burdens or lighten His toil. He had taken upon Himself the form of humanity with all its attendant ills, and He flinched not from its severest trials. He lived in a peasant's home, He was clothed in coarse garments, He mingled with the lowly, He toiled daily with patient hands. His example shows us that it is man's duty to be industrious, that labor is honorable. *The Health Reformer,* October 1876.

For a long time Jesus dwelt at Nazareth, unhonored or unknown, that He might teach men how to live near God while discharging the humble duties of life. It was a mystery to angels that Christ, the Majesty of heaven, should condescend, not only to take upon Himself humanity, but to assume its heaviest burdens and most humiliating offices. This He did in order to become like one of us, that He might be acquainted with the toil, the sorrows, and fatigue of the children of men. *Ibid.*

Awaken Ambition for Useful Accomplishments. In the children and youth an ambition should be awakened to take their exercise in doing something that will be beneficial to themselves and helpful to others. The exercise that develops mind and character, that teaches the hands to be useful, that trains the youth to bear their share of life's burdens, is that which gives physical strength and quickens every faculty. And there is a reward in virtuous industry, in the cultivation of the habit of living to do good. *Counsels to Parents, Teachers, and Students,* p. 147.

The youth need to be taught that life means earnest work, responsibility, caretaking. They need a training that will make them practical—men and women who can cope with emergencies. They should be taught that the discipline of systematic, well-regulated labor is essential, not only as a safeguard against the vicissitudes of life, but as an aid to all-round development. *Education,* p. 215.

Physical Labor Is Not Degrading. It is a popular error with a large class to regard work as degrading; therefore young men are very anxious to educate themselves to become teachers, clerks, merchants, lawyers, and to occupy almost any position that does not require physical labor. Young women regard housework as belittling. And although the physical exercise required to perform household labor, if not too severe, is calculated to promote health, yet they seek for an education that will fit them to become teachers or clerks, or they learn some trade that will confine them indoors, to sedentary employment. *Counsels to Parents, Teachers, and Students,* p. 291.

The world is full of young men and women who pride themselves upon their ignorance of any useful labor; and they are, almost invariably, frivolous, vain, fond of display, unhappy, unsatisfied, and too often dissipated and unprincipled. Such characters are a blot upon society and a disgrace to their parents. *The Health Reformer,* December 1877.

None of us should be ashamed of work, however small and servile it may appear. Labor is ennobling. All who toil with head or hands are working men or working women. And all are doing their duty and honoring their religion as much while working at the washtub or washing dishes as they are in going to meeting. While the hands are engaged in the most common labor, the mind may be elevated and ennobled by pure and holy thoughts. *Testimonies for the Church,* vol. 4, p. 590.

Youth to Be Masters, Not Slaves of Labor. The youth should be led to see the true dignity of labor. *Education,* p. 214.

One great reason why physical toil is looked down on is the slipshod, unthinking way in which it is so often performed. It is done from necessity, not from choice. The worker puts no heart into it, and he neither preserves self-respect nor wins the respect of others. Manual training should correct this error. It should develop habits of accuracy and thoroughness. Pupils should learn tact and system; they should learn to economize time and to make every move count. They should not only be taught the best methods, but be inspired with ambition constantly to improve. Let it be their aim to make their work as nearly perfect as human brains and hands can make it.

Such training will make the youth masters and not slaves of labor. It will lighten the lot of the hard toiler and will ennoble even the humblest occupation. He who regards work as mere drudgery and settles down to it with self-complacent ignorance, making no effort to improve, will find it indeed a burden. But those who recognize science in the humblest work will see in it nobility and beauty and will take pleasure in performing it with faithfulness and efficiency. *Ibid.,* p. 222.

Wealth Not to Excuse From Practical Training. In many cases parents who are wealthy do not feel the importance of giving their children an education in the practical duties of life as well as in the sciences. They do not see the necessity, for the good of their children's minds and morals, and for their future usefulness, of giving them a thorough understanding of useful labor. This is due their children, that, should misfortune come, they could stand forth in noble independence, knowing how to use their hands. If they have a capital of strength, they cannot be poor, even if they have not a dollar.

Many who in youth were in affluent circumstances may be robbed of all their riches, and be left with parents and brothers and sisters dependent upon them for sustenance. Then how important that every youth be educated to labor, that they may be prepared for any emergency! Riches are indeed a curse when their possessors let them stand in the way of their sons and daughters obtaining a knowledge of useful labor, that they may be qualified for practical life. *Testimonies for the Church,* vol. 3, p. 150.

Children to Share Domestic Duties. The faithful mother will not, cannot, be a devotee to fashion, neither will she be a domestic slave, to humor the whims of her children and excuse them from labor. She will teach them to share with her domestic duties, that they may have a knowledge of practical life. If the children share the labor with their mother, they will learn to regard useful employment as essential to happiness, ennobling rather than degrading. But if the mother educates her daughters to be indolent, while she bears the heavy burdens of domestic life, she is teaching them to look down upon her as their servant, to wait on them and do the things they should do. The mother should ever retain her dignity. *Pacific Health Journal,* June 1890.

Some mothers are at fault in releasing their daughters from toil and care. By so doing they encourage them in indolence. The excuse these mothers sometimes plead is, "My daughters are not strong." But they take the sure course to make them weak and inefficient. Well-directed labor is just what they require to make them strong, vigorous, cheerful, happy, and courageous to meet the various trials with which this life is beset. *Signs of the Times,* Aug. 19, 1875.

Assign Useful Tasks to Children. The carelessness of parents in neglecting to furnish employment to their children has resulted in untold evil, imperiling the lives of many youth and sadly crippling their usefulness.

God desires both parents and teachers to train children in the practical duties of everyday life. Encourage industry. Girls—and even boys who do not have outdoor work—should learn how to help the mother. From childhood, boys and girls should be taught to bear heavier and still heavier burdens, intelligently helping in the work of the family firm. Mothers, patiently show your children how to use their hands. Let them understand that their hands are to be used as skillfully as are yours in the household work. *Review and Herald,* Sept. 8, 1904.

Each child in the family should have a part of the home burden to bear and should be taught to perform his task faithfully and cheerfully. If the work is portioned out in this way, and the children grow up accustomed to bearing suitable responsibilities, no member of the household will be overburdened, and everything will move off pleasantly and smoothly in the home. A proper economy will be maintained, for each one will be acquainted with, and interested in, the details of the home. *Signs of the Times,* Aug. 23, 1877.

Cooking and Sewing, Basic Lessons. Mothers should take their daughters with them into the kitchen and give them a thorough education in the cooking department. They should also instruct them in the art of substantial sewing. They should teach them how to cut garments economically and put them together neatly. Some mothers, rather than to take this trouble to patiently instruct their inexperienced daughters, prefer to do it all themselves. But in so doing, they leave the essential branches of education neglected and commit a great wrong against their children; for in afterlife they feel embarrassment because of their lack of knowledge in these things. *Appeal to Mothers,* p. 15.

Give Training to Both Boys and Girls. Since both men and women have a part in homemaking, boys as well as girls should gain a knowledge of household duties. To make a bed and put a room in order, to wash dishes, to prepare a meal, to wash and repair his own clothing, is a training that need not make any boy less manly; it will make him happier and more useful. And if girls, in turn, could learn to harness and drive a horse,* and to use the saw and the hammer, as well as the rake and the hoe, they would be better fitted to meet the emergencies of life. *Education,* pp. 216, 217.

It is as essential for our daughters to learn the proper use of time as it is for our sons, and they are equally accountable to God for the manner in which they occupy it. Life is given us for wise improvement of the talents we possess. *The Health Reformer,* December 1877.

See Privileges in Conserving Mother's Strength. Every day there is housework to be done—cooking, washing dishes, sweeping, and dusting. Mothers, have you taught your daughters to do these daily duties? . . . Their muscles need exercise. In the place of getting exercise by jumping and playing ball or croquet, let their exercise be to some purpose. Manuscript 129, 1898.

Teach the children to bear their share of the burdens of the household. Keep them occupied at some useful employment. Show them how to do their work easily and well. Help them to realize that by lightening the burdens of their mother, they are preserving her strength and prolonging her life. Many a weary mother has been laid away in an untimely grave for no other reason than that her children were not taught to share her burdens. By encouraging a spirit of unselfish service in the home, parents are drawing their children closer to Christ, who is the embodiment of unselfishness. Manuscript 70, 1903.

An Experiment in Happiness. Children, seat your mother in the easy chair, and tell her to show you what she would have done first. What a surprise this would be to many weary, overtaxed mothers! Never will children and youth feel the peace of contentment until by the faithful performance of home duties they relieve the tired hands and weary heart and brain of the mother. These are steps on the ladder of progress that will carry them forward to receive the higher education.

It is the faithful performance of everyday duties that brings the satisfaction and peace that come to the true home worker. Those who neglect to bear part of the responsibilities of the home are the ones who are troubled with loneliness and discontent; for they have not learned the truth that those who are happy are happy because they share the daily routine of work which rests upon the mother or other members of the family. Many are leaving unlearned the most useful lessons, which it is essential for their future good to understand. Manuscript 129, 1898.

The Rewards of Faithfulness in Home Duties. A faithful fulfillment of home duties, filling the position you can occupy to the best advantage, be it ever so simple and humble, is truly elevating. This divine influence is needed. In this there is peace and sacred joy. It possesses healing power. It will secretly and insensibly soothe the wounds of the soul and even the sufferings of the body. Peace of mind, which comes from pure and holy motives and actions, will give free and vigorous spring to all the organs of the body. Inward peace and a conscience void of offense toward God will quicken and invigorate the intellect, like dew distilled upon the tender plants. The will is then rightly directed and controlled and is more decided and yet free from perverseness. The meditations are pleasing because they are sanctified. The serenity of mind which you may possess will bless all with whom you associate. This peace and calmness will, in time, become natural and will reflect its precious rays upon all around you, to be again reflected upon you. The more you taste this heavenly peace and quietude of mind, the more it will increase. It is an animated, living pleasure which does not throw all the moral energies into a stupor, but awakens them to increased activity. Perfect peace is an attribute of Heaven which angels possess. *Testimonies for the Church,* vol. 2, pp. 326, 327.

There Will Be Activity in Heaven. The angels are workers; they are ministers of God to the children of men. Those slothful servants who look forward to a heaven of inaction have false ideas of what constitutes heaven. The Creator has prepared no place for the gratification of sinful indolence. Heaven is a place of interested activity; yet to the weary and heavy laden, to those who have fought the good fight of faith, it will be a glorious rest; for the youth and vigor of immortality will be theirs, and against sin and Satan they will no longer have to contend. To these energetic workers a state of eternal indolence would be irksome. It would be no heaven to them. The path of toil appointed to the Christian on earth may be hard and wearisome, but it is honored by the footprints of the Redeemer, and he is safe who follows in that sacred way. *Christian Temperance and Bible Hygiene,* p. 99.

---

* NOTE: This was written in 1903. The principles are fully applicable today.

CHAPTER 59

Teaching Useful Trades

Every Child Should Learn Some Trade. The careless-ness of parents in failing to furnish employment to the children that they have taken the responsibility of bringing into the world has resulted in untold evil, imperiling the lives of many youth and greatly crippling their usefulness. It is a great mistake to permit young men to grow up without learning some trade. Manuscript 121, 1901.

From the pillar of cloud Jesus gave directions through Moses to the Hebrews that they should educate their children to work, that they should teach them trades, and that none should be idle. Manuscript 24b, 1894.

You should help your children to acquire a knowledge, that, if necessary, they could live by their own labor. You should teach them to be decided in following the calls of duty. *Signs of the Times,* Aug. 19, 1875.

Teach Use of Tools. When children reach a suitable age, they should be provided with tools. If their work is made interesting, they will be found apt pupils in the use of tools. If the father is a carpenter, he should give his boys lessons in house building, ever bringing into his instruction lessons from the Bible, the words of Scripture in which the Lord compares human beings to His building. Manuscript 45, 1912.

Train Sons in Agriculture. Fathers should train their sons to engage with them in their trades and employments. Farmers should not think that agriculture is a business that is not elevated enough for their sons. Agriculture should be advanced by scientific knowledge.

Farming has been pronounced unprofitable. People say that the soil does not pay for the labor expended upon it, and they bemoan the hard fate of those who till the soil. . . . But should persons of proper ability take hold of this line of employment, and make a study of the soil, and learn how to plant, to cultivate, and to gather in the harvest, more encouraging results might be seen. Many say, "We have tried agriculture and know what its results are," and yet these very ones need to know how to cultivate the soil and to bring science into their work. Their plowshares should cut deeper, broader furrows, and they need to learn that in tilling the soil they need not become common and coarse in their natures. . . . Let them learn to put in the seed in its season, to give attention to vegetation, and to follow the plan that God has devised. *Signs of the Times,* Aug. 13, 1896.

Training of Outstanding Value. No line of manual training is of more value than agriculture. A greater effort should be made to create and to encourage an interest in agricultural pursuits. Let the teacher call attention to what the Bible says about agriculture; that it was God's plan for man to till the earth; that the first man, the ruler of the whole world, was given a garden to cultivate; and that many of the world's greatest men, its real nobility, have been tillers of the soil. Show the opportunities in such a life. . . .

He who earns his livelihood by agriculture escapes many temptations and enjoys unnumbered privileges and blessings denied to those whose work lies in the great cities. And in these days of mammoth trusts and business competition, there are few who enjoy so real an independence and so great certainty of fair return for their labor as does the tiller of the soil. *Education,* p. 219.

Fresh Produce Is of Special Value. Families and institutions should learn to do more in the cultivation and improvement of land. If people only knew the value of the products of the ground, which the earth brings forth in their season, more diligent efforts would be made to cultivate the soil. All should be acquainted with the special value of fruits and vegetables fresh from the orchard and garden. *Counsels on Diet and Foods,* p. 312.

Schools to Give Instruction in Useful Trades. Manual training is deserving of far more attention than it has received. Schools should be established that, in addition to the highest mental and moral culture, shall provide the best possible facilities for physical development and industrial training. Instruction should be given in agriculture, manufactures—covering as many as possible of the most useful trades—also in household economy, healthful cookery, sewing, hygienic dressmaking, the treatment of the sick, and kindred lines. Gardens, workshops, and treatment rooms should be provided, and the work in every line should be under the direction of skilled instructors.

The work should have a definite aim and should be thorough. While every person needs some knowledge of different handicrafts, it is indispensable that he become proficient in at least one. Every youth, on leaving school, should have acquired a knowledge of some trade or occupation by which, if need be, he may earn a livelihood. *Education,* p. 218.

A Training of Double Value. There should have been connected with the schools establishments for carrying on various branches of labor, that the students might have employment and the necessary exercise out of school hours. . . . Then a practical knowledge of business could have been obtained while their literary education was being gained. *Counsels to Parents, Teachers, and Students,* pp. 83, 84.

Industrial Knowledge Is of More Value Than Scientific. There should have been experienced teachers to give lessons to young ladies in the cooking department. Young girls should have been instructed to cut, make, and mend garments, and thus become educated for the practical duties of life.

For young men, there should be establishments where they could learn different trades, which would bring into exercise their muscles as well as their mental powers. If the youth can have but a one-sided education, which is of the greater consequence—a knowledge of the sciences, with all the disadvantages to health and life, or a knowledge of labor for practical life? We unhesitatingly answer, The latter. If one must be neglected, let it be the study of books. *Testimonies for the Church,* vol. 3, p. 156.

There may be those who have had wrong training and those who have wrong ideas in regard to the training of children. These children and youth want the very best training, and you must bring the physical labor right in with the mental—the two should go together. Manuscript 19, 1887.

Jesus Was an Example of Contented Industry. It requires much more grace and stern discipline of character to work for God in the capacity of mechanic, merchant, lawyer, or farmer, carrying the precepts of Christianity into the ordinary business of life, than to labor as an acknowledged missionary in the open field, where one's position is understood and half its difficulties obviated by that very fact. It requires strong spiritual nerve and muscle to carry religion into the workshop and business office, sanctifying the details of everyday life, and ordering every worldly transaction to the standard of a Bible Christian.

Jesus, in His thirty years of seclusion at Nazareth, toiled and rested, ate and slept, from week to week and from year to year, the same as His humble contemporaries. He called no attention to Himself as a marked personage; yet He was the world's Redeemer, the adored of angels, doing, all the time, His Father's work, living out a lesson that should remain for humanity to copy to the end of time.

This essential lesson of contented industry in the necessary duties of life, however humble, is yet to be learned by the greater portion of Christ's followers. If there is no human eye to criticize our work, nor voice to praise or blame, it should be done just as well as if the Infinite One Himself were personally to inspect it. We should be as faithful in the minor details of our business as we would in the larger affairs of life. *Health Reformer,* October 1876.

CHAPTER 60

Knowledge of and Obedience to the Laws of Life

Wonders of the Human Body. We are God's workmanship, and His Word declares that we are "fearfully and wonderfully made." He has prepared this living habitation for the mind; it is "curiously wrought," a temple which the Lord Himself has fitted up for the indwelling of His Holy Spirit. The mind controls the whole man. All our actions, good or bad, have their source in the mind. It is the mind that worships God and allies us to heavenly beings. Yet many spend all their lives without becoming intelligent in regard to the casket [the human body] that contains this treasure.

All the physical organs are the servants of the mind, and the nerves are the messengers that transmit its orders to every part of the body, guiding the motions of the living machinery. *Fundamentals of Christian Education,* pp. 425, 426.

As the mechanism of the body is studied, attention should be directed to its wonderful adaptation of means to ends, the harmonious action and dependence of the various organs. As the interest of the student is thus awakened, and he is led to see the importance of physical culture, much can be done by the teacher to secure proper development and right habits. *Education,* p. 198.

The Health to Be Guarded. Since the mind and the soul find expression through the body, both mental and spiritual vigor are in great degree dependent upon physical strength and activity; whatever promotes physical health, promotes the development of a strong mind and a well-balanced character. Without health, no one can as distinctly understand or as completely fulfill his obligations to himself, to his fellow beings, or to his Creator. Therefore the health should be as faithfully guarded as the character. A knowledge of physiology and hygiene should be the basis of all educational effort. *Ibid.,* p. 195.

Many Unwilling to Study the Laws of Health. Many are unwilling to put forth the needed effort to obtain a knowledge of the laws of life and the simple means to be employed for the restoration of health. They do not place themselves in right relation to life. When sickness is the result of their transgression of natural law, they do not seek to correct their errors, and then ask the blessing of God. *Christian Temperance and Bible Hygiene,* pp. 112, 113.

We should educate ourselves, not only to live in harmony with the laws of health, but to teach others the better way. Many, even of those who profess to believe the special truths for this time, are lamentably ignorant with regard to health and temperance. They need to be educated, line upon line, precept upon precept. The subject must be kept fresh before them. This matter must not be passed over as nonessential, for nearly every family needs to be stirred up on the question. The conscience must be aroused to the duty of practicing the principles of true reform. *Ibid.,* p. 117.

The principles of hygiene as applied to diet, exercise, the care of children, the treatment of the sick, and many like matters should be given much more attention than they ordinarily receive. *Education,* p. 197.

To Study Preventive Measures. Far too little thought is given to the causes underlying the mortality, the disease and degeneracy, that exist today even in the most civilized and favored lands. The human race is deteriorating. . . . Most of the evils that are bringing misery and ruin to the race might be prevented, and the power to deal with them rests to a great degree with parents. *The Ministry of Healing,* p. 380.

Teach Children to Reason From Cause to Effect. Teach your children to reason from cause to effect. Show them that if they violate the laws of their being, they must pay the penalty in suffering. If you cannot see as rapid improvement as you desire, do not be discouraged, but instruct them patiently, and press on until victory is gained. *Counsels to Parents, Teacher, and Students,* p. 126.

Those who study and practice the principles of right living will be greatly blessed, both physically and spiritually. An understanding of the philosophy of health is a safeguard against many of the evils that are continually increasing. *Ibid.,* p. 138.

Let the Instruction Be Progressive. Children should be early taught, in simple, easy lessons, the rudiments of physiology and hygiene. The work should be begun by the mother in the home and should be faithfully carried forward in the school. As the pupils advance in years, instruction in this line should be continued until they are qualified to care for the house they live in. They should understand the importance of guarding against disease by preserving the vigor of every organ and should also be taught how to deal with common diseases and accidents. *Education,* p. 196.

Factual Knowledge Is Not Sufficient. The student of physiology should be taught that the object of his study is not merely to gain a knowledge of facts and principles. This alone will prove of little benefit. He may understand the importance of ventilation, his room may be supplied with pure air; but unless he fills his lungs properly he will suffer the results of imperfect respiration. So the necessity of cleanliness may be understood, and needful facilities may be supplied; but all will be without avail unless put to use. The great requisite in teaching these principles is to impress the pupil with their importance, so that he will conscientiously put them in practice. *Ibid.,* p. 200.

Knowledge of Nature's Laws Is Necessary. There are matters not usually included in the study of physiology that should be considered—matters of far greater value to the student than are many of the technicalities commonly taught under this head. As the foundation principle of all education in these lines, the youth should be taught that the laws of nature are the laws of God—as truly divine as are the precepts of the Decalogue. The laws that govern our physical organism, God has written upon every nerve, muscle, and fiber of the body. Every careless and willful violation of these laws is a sin against our Creator. How necessary, then, that a thorough knowledge of these laws should be imparted! *Ibid.,* p. 196, 197.

Regularity in Eating and Sleeping. The importance of regularity in the time for eating and sleeping should not be overlooked. Since the work of building up the body takes place during the hours of rest, it is essential, especially in youth, that sleep should be regular and abundant. *Ibid.,* p. 205.

In regulating the hours for sleep, there should be no haphazard work. Students should not form the habit of burning the midnight oil and taking the hours of the day for sleep. If they have been accustomed to doing this at home, they should correct the habit, going to bed at a seasonable hour. They will then rise in the morning refreshed for the duties of the day. *Counsels to Parents, Teachers, and Students,* p. 297.

Insist on Right Health Habits. Right habits of eating and drinking and dressing must be insisted upon. Wrong habits render the youth less susceptible to Bible instruction. The children are to be guarded against the indulgence of appetite, and especially against the use of stimulants and narcotics. The tables of Christian parents should not be loaded down with food containing condiments and spices. *Ibid.,* p. 126.

We are not to indulge in any habit that will weaken physical or mental strength, or abuse our powers in any way. We are to do all in our power to keep ourselves in health, in order that we may have sweetness of disposition, a clear mind, and be able to distinguish between the sacred and the common, and honor God in our bodies and in our spirits, which are His. *Youth's Instructor,* Aug. 24, 1893.

Importance of Correct Posture. Among the first things to be aimed at should be a correct position, both in sitting and in standing. God made man upright, and He desires him to possess not only the physical but the mental and moral benefit, the grace and dignity and self-possession, the courage and self-reliance, which an erect bearing so greatly tends to promote. Let the teacher give instruction on this point by example and by precept. Show what a correct position is, and insist that it shall be maintained. *Education,* p. 198.

Respiration and Vocal Culture. Next in importance to right position are respiration and vocal culture. The one who sits and stands erect is more likely than others to breathe properly. But the teacher should impress upon his pupils the importance of deep breathing. Show how the healthy action of the respiratory organs, assisting the circulation of the blood, invigorates the whole system, excites the appetite, promotes digestion, and induces sound, sweet sleep, thus not only refreshing the body, but soothing and tranquilizing the mind. And while the importance of deep breathing is shown, the practice should be insisted upon. Let exercises be given which will promote this, and see that the habit becomes established. . . .

The training of the voice has an important place in physical culture, since it tends to expand and strengthen the lungs, and thus to ward off disease. To ensure correct delivery in reading and speaking, see that the abdominal muscles have full play in breathing, and that the respiratory organs are unrestricted. Let the strain come on the muscles of the abdomen rather than on those of the throat. Great weariness and serious disease of the throat and lungs may thus be prevented. Careful attention should be given to securing distinct articulation, smooth, well-modulated tones, and a not-too-rapid delivery. This will not only promote health, but will add greatly to the agreeableness and efficiency of the student's work. *Ibid.,* pp. 198, 199.

Three Essentials for Family Happiness. In the study of hygiene the earnest teacher will improve every opportunity to show the necessity of perfect cleanliness both in personal habits and in all one's surroundings. The value of the daily bath in promoting health and in stimulating mental action should be emphasized. Attention should be given also to sunlight and ventilation, the hygiene of the sleeping room and the kitchen. Teach the pupils that a healthful sleeping room, a thoroughly clean kitchen, and a tastefully arranged, wholesomely supplied table will go farther toward securing the happiness of the family and the regard of every sensible visitor than any amount of expensive furnishing in the drawing room. That "the life is more than meat, and the body is more than raiment" (Luke 12:23) is a lesson no less needed now than when given by the divine Teacher eighteen hundred years ago. *Ibid.,* p. 200.

Seek to Understand Nature's Remedies. Pure air, sunlight, abstemiousness, rest, exercise, proper diet, the use of water, trust in divine power—these are the true remedies. Every person should have a knowledge of nature's remedial agencies and how to apply them. It is essential both to understand the principles involved in the treatment of the sick and to have a practical training that will enable one rightly to use this knowledge.

The use of natural remedies requires an amount of care and effort that many are not willing to give. Nature's process of healing and upbuilding is gradual, and to the impatient it seems slow. The surrender of hurtful indulgences requires sacrifice. But in the end it will be found that nature, untrammeled, does her work wisely and well. Those who persevere in obedience to her laws will reap the reward in health of body and health of mind. *The Ministry of Healing,* p. 127.

A Comprehensive Code. In regard to that which we can do for ourselves, there is a point that requires careful, thoughtful consideration. I must become acquainted with myself. I must be a learner always as to how to take care of this building, the body God has given me, that I may preserve it in the very best condition of health. I must eat those things which will be for my very best good physically, and I must take special care to have my clothing such as will conduce to a healthful circulation of the blood. I must not deprive myself of exercise and air. I must get all the sunlight that it is possible for me to obtain. I must have wisdom to be a faithful guardian of my body.

I should do a very unwise thing to enter a cool room when in a perspiration; I should show myself an unwise steward to allow myself to sit in a draft, and thus expose myself so as to take cold. I should be unwise to sit with cold feet and limbs and thus drive back the blood from the extremities to the brain or internal organs. I should always protect my feet in damp weather. I should eat regularly of the most healthful food which will make the best quality of blood, and I should not work intemperately if it is in my power to avoid doing so. And when I violate the laws God has established in my being, I am to repent and reform, and place myself in the most favorable condition under the doctors God has provided—pure air, pure water, and the healing, precious sunlight. *Medical Ministry,* p. 230.

We Are Individually Responsible to God. Our bodies are Christ's purchased possession, and we are not at liberty to do with them as we please. All who understand the laws of health should realize their obligation to obey these laws, which God has established in their being. Obedience to the laws of health is to be made a matter of personal duty. We ourselves must suffer the results of violated law. We must individually answer to God for our habits and practices. Therefore the question with us is not, "What is the world's practice?" but, "How shall I as an individual treat the habitation that God has given me?" *The Ministry of Healing,* p. 310.

MAINTAINING PHYSICAL FITNESS

CHAPTER 61

The Homemaker
in the Kitchen *

The High Calling of the Homemaker. There can be no employment more important than that of housework. To cook well, to present healthful food upon the table in an inviting manner, requires intelligence and experience. The one who prepares the food that is to be placed in our stomachs, to be converted into blood to nourish the system, occupies a most important and elevated position. *Testimonies for the Church,* vol. 3, p. 158.

It is essential for every youth to have a thorough acquaintance with everyday duties. If need be, a young woman can dispense with a knowledge of French and algebra, or even of the piano; but it is indispensable that she learn to make good bread, to fashion neatly fitting garments, and to perform efficiently the many duties that pertain to homemaking.

To the health and happiness of the whole family nothing is more vital than skill and intelligence on the part of the cook. By ill-prepared, unwholesome food she may hinder and even ruin both the adult's usefulness and the child's development. Or by providing food adapted to the needs of the body, and at the same time inviting and palatable, she can accomplish as much in the right as otherwise she accomplished in the wrong direction. So, in many ways, life's happiness is bound up with faithfulness in common duties. *Education,* p. 216.

The Science of Cooking Is an Essential Art. The science of cooking is not a small matter. . . . This art should be regarded as the most valuable of all the arts, because it is so closely connected with life. It should receive more attention; for in order to make good blood, the system requires good food. The foundation of that which keeps people in health is the medical missionary work of good cooking.

Often health reform is made health deform by the unpalatable preparation of food. The lack of knowledge regarding healthful cookery must be remedied before health reform is a success.

Good cooks are few. Many, many mothers need to take lessons in cooking, that they may set before the family well-prepared, neatly served food. *Counsels on Diet and Foods,* p. 263.

Seek to Become Mistress of the Art. Our sisters often do not know how to cook. To such I would say, I would go to the very best cook that could be found in the country, and remain there if necessary for weeks, until I had become mistress of the art—an intelligent, skillful cook. I would pursue this course if I were forty years old. It is your duty to know how to cook, and it is your duty to teach your daughters to cook. *Testimonies for the Church,* vol. 2, p. 370.

Study and Practice. Food can be prepared simply and healthfully, but it requires skill to make it both palatable and nourishing. In order to learn how to cook, women should study and then patiently reduce what they learn to practice. People are suffering because they will not take the trouble to do this. I say to such, It is time for you to rouse your dormant energies and inform yourselves. Do not think the time wasted which is devoted to obtaining a thorough knowledge and experience in the preparation of healthful, palatable food. No matter how long an experience you have had in cooking, if you still have the responsibilities of a family, it is your duty to learn how to care for them properly. *Christian Temperance and Bible Hygiene,* p. 49.

Both Variety and Simplicity Are Essential. The meals should be varied. The same dishes, prepared in the same way, should not appear on the table meal after meal and day after day. The meals are eaten with greater relish, and the system is better nourished, when the food is varied. *The Ministry of Healing,* p. 300.

Our bodies are constructed from what we eat; and in order to make tissues of good quality, we must have the right kind of food, and it must be prepared with such skill as will best adapt it to the wants of the system. It is a religious duty for those who cook to learn how to prepare healthful food in a variety of ways, so that it may be both palatable and healthful. *Christian Temperance and Bible Hygiene,* pp. 48, 49.

Even in the table arrangements, fashion and show exert their baleful influence. The healthful preparation of food becomes a secondary matter. The serving of a great variety of dishes absorbs time, money, and taxing labor, without accomplishing any good. It may be fashionable to have half a dozen courses at a meal, but the custom is ruinous to health. It is a fashion that sensible men and women should condemn, by both precept and example. . . . How much better it would be for the health of the household if the table preparations were more simple. *Ibid.,* p. 73.

Results of Poor Cooking. Poor cookery is wearing away the life energies of thousands. More souls are lost from this cause than many realize. In deranges the system and produces disease. In the condition thus induced, heavenly things cannot be readily discerned. *Ibid.,* p. 49.

Scanty, ill-cooked food depraves the blood by weakening the bloodmaking organs. It deranges the system and brings on disease, with its accompaniment of irritable nerves and bad tempers. The victims of poor cookery are numbered by thousands and tens of thousands. Over many graves might be written: "Died because of poor cooking," "Died of an abused stomach." *The Ministry of Healing,* p. 302.

Teach Your Children How to Cook. Do not neglect to teach your children how to cook. In so doing, you impart to them principles which they must have in their religious education. In giving your children lessons in physiology, and teaching them how to cook with simplicity and yet with skill, you are laying the foundation for the most useful branches of education. Skill is required to make good light bread. There is religion in good cooking, and I question the religion of that class who are too ignorant and too careless to learn to cook. *Testimonies for the Church,* vol. 2, p. 537.

Instruct Them Patiently and Cheerfully. Mothers should take their daughters into the kitchen with them when very young, and teach them the art of cooking. The mother cannot expect her daughters to understand the mysteries of housekeeping without education. She should instruct them patiently, lovingly, and make the work as agreeable as she can by her cheerful countenance and encouraging words of approval. *Ibid.,* vol. 1, p. 684.

If they fail once, twice, or thrice, censure not. Already discouragement is doing its work and tempting them to say, "It is of no use; I can't do it." This is not the time for censure. The will is becoming weakened. It needs the spur of encouraging, cheerful, hopeful words, as, "Never mind the mistakes you have made. You are but a learner, and must expect to make blunders. Try again. Put your mind on what you are doing. Be very careful, and you will certainly succeed." *Ibid.,* pp. 684, 685.

How Interest and Ardor May Be Cooled.

Many mothers do not realize the importance of this branch of knowledge, and rather than have the trouble and care of instructing their children and bearing with their failings and errors while learning, they prefer to do all themselves. And when their daughters make a failure in their efforts, they send them away with, "It is no use; you can't do this or that. You perplex and trouble me more than you help me."

Thus the first efforts of the learners are repulsed, and the first failure so cools their interest and ardor to learn, that they dread another trial, and will propose to sew, knit, clean house, anything but cook. Here the mother was greatly at fault. She should have patiently instructed them, that they might, by practice, obtain an experience which would remove the awkwardness and remedy the unskillful movements of the inexperienced worker. *Ibid.,* p. 685.

The Most Necessary Preparation Young Women Can Make for Practical Life.

Young ladies should be thoroughly instructed in cooking. Whatever may be their circumstances in life, here is knowledge which may be put to a practical use. It is a branch of education which has the most direct influence upon human life, especially the lives of those held most dear. *Ibid.,* pp. 683, 684.

I prize my seamstress; I value my copyist; but my cook, who knows well how to prepare the food to sustain life and nourish brain, bone, and muscle, fills the most important place among the helpers in my family. *Ibid.,* vol. 2, p. 370.

Young women think that it is menial to cook and do other kinds of housework; and, for this reason, many girls who marry and have the care of families have little idea of the duties devolving upon a wife and mother. *The Ministry of Healing,* p. 302.

Thus Build a Barrier Against Folly and Vice. When you are teaching them [your daughters] the art of cookery, you are building around them a barrier that will preserve them from the folly and vice which they may otherwise be tempted to engage in. *Testimonies for the Church,* vol. 2, p. 370.

Men as Well as Women Should Learn to Cook. Men, as well as women, need to understand the simple, healthful preparation of food. Their business often calls them where they cannot obtain wholesome food; then, if they have a knowledge of cookery, they can use it to good purpose. *The Ministry of Healing,* p. 323.

Both young men and young women should be taught how to cook economically and to dispense with everything in the line of flesh food. *Counsels to Parents, Teachers, and Students,* p. 313.

Study Economy; Avoid Waste. In every line of cooking the question that should be considered is, "How shall the food be prepared in the most natural and inexpensive manner?" And there should be careful study that the fragments of food left over from the table be not wasted. Study how, that in some way these fragments of food shall not be lost. This skill, economy, and tact is a fortune. In the warmer parts of the season, prepare less food. Use more dry substance. There are many poor families, who, although they have scarcely enough to eat, can often be enlightened as to why they are poor; there are so many jots and tittles wasted. *Counsels on Diet and Foods,* p. 258.

Serious Questions for Reflection. "Whether therefore ye eat, or drink, or whatsoever ye do, do all to the glory of God." Do you do this when you prepare food for your tables and call your family to partake of it? Are you placing before your children only the food that you know will make the very best blood? Is it that food that will preserve their systems in the least feverish condition? Is it that which will place them in the very best relation to life and health? Is this the food that you are studying to place before your children? Or do you, regardless of their future good, provide for them unhealthful, stimulating, irritating food? *Testimonies for the Church,* vol. 2, p. 359, 360.

★ NOTE: *Counsels on Diet and Foods* presents detailed counsels on the whole food question.

CHAPTER 62

Eating to Live

God Appointed the Inclinations and Appetites. Our natural inclinations and appetites . . . were divinely appointed, and when given to man, were pure and holy. It was God's design that reason should rule the appetites, and that they should minister to our happiness. And when they are regulated and controlled by a sanctified reason, they are holiness unto the Lord. *Temperance,* p. 12.

A Subject of Divine Solicitude. The education of the Israelites included all their habits of life. Everything that concerned their well-being was the subject of divine solicitude and came within the province of divine law. Even in providing their food, God sought their highest good. The manna with which He fed them in the wilderness was of a nature to promote physical, mental, and moral strength. . . . Notwithstanding the hardships of their wilderness life, there was not a feeble one in all their tribes. *Education,* p. 38.

Built From the Food We Eat. Our bodies are built up from the food we eat. There is a constant breaking down of the tissues of the body; every movement of every organ involves waste, and this waste is repaired from our food. Each organ of the body requires its share of nutrition. The brain must be supplied with its portion; the bones, muscles, and nerves demand theirs. It is a wonderful process that transforms the food into blood and uses this blood to build up the varied parts of the body; but this process is going on continually, supplying with life and strength each nerve, muscle, and tissue. *The Ministry of Healing,* p. 295.

Begin With Correct Infant Feeding. The importance of training children to right dietetic habits can hardly be over-estimated. The little ones need to learn that they eat to live, not live to eat. The training should begin with the infant in its mother's arms. The child should be given food only at regular intervals, and less frequently as it grows older. It should not be given sweets, or the food of older persons, which it is unable to digest. Care and regularity in the feeding of infants will not only promote health, and thus tend to make them quiet and sweet-tempered, but will lay the foundation of habits that will be a blessing to them in after years. *Ibid.,* p. 383.

Educate Tastes and Appetite. As children emerge from babyhood, great care should still be taken in educating their tastes and appetite. Often they are permitted to eat what they choose and when they choose, without reference to health. The pains and money so often lavished upon unwholesome dainties lead the young to think that the highest object in life, and that which yields the greatest amount of happiness, is to be able to indulge the appetite. The result of this training is gluttony, then comes sickness. . . .

Parents should train the appetites of their children and should not permit the use of unwholesome foods. *Ibid.,* p. 384.

Spiritual, Mental, and Physical Powers Influenced by Diet. Mothers who gratify the desires of their children at the expense of health and happy tempers are sowing seeds of evil that will spring up and bear fruit. Self-indulgence grows with the growth of the little ones, and both mental and physical vigor are sacrificed. Mothers who do this work reap with bitterness the seed they have sown. They see their children grow up unfitted in mind and character to act a noble and useful part in society or in the home. The spiritual as well as the mental and physical powers suffer under the influence of unhealthful food. The conscience becomes stupefied, and the susceptibility to good impressions is impaired. *Counsels on Diet and Foods,* p. 230.

Choose the Best Foods. In order to know what are the best foods, we must study God's original plan for man's diet. He who created man and who understands his needs appointed Adam his food. . . . Grains, fruits, nuts, and vegetables constitute the diet chosen for us by our Creator. *The Ministry of Healing,* pp. 295, 296.

Prepare Them in a Simple, Appetizing Way. God has furnished man with abundant means for the gratification of an unperverted appetite. He has spread before him the products of the earth—a bountiful variety of food that is palatable to the taste and nutritious to the system. Of these our benevolent heavenly Father says we may freely eat. Fruits, grains, and vegetables, prepared in a simple way, free from spice and grease of all kinds, make, with milk or cream, the most healthful diet. They impart nourishment to the body and give a power of endurance and a vigor of intellect that are not produced by a stimulating diet. *Counsels on Diet and Foods,* p. 92.

Appetite Not a Safe Guide. Those foods should be chosen that best supply the elements needed for building up the body. In this choice appetite is not a safe guide. Through wrong habits of eating, the appetite has become perverted. Often it demands food that impairs health and causes weakness instead of strength. . . . The disease and suffering that everywhere prevail are largely due to popular errors in regard to diet. *The Ministry of Healing,* p. 295.

Children Who Followed an Untrained Appetite. While upon the cars, I heard parents remark that the appetites of their children were delicate, and unless they had meat and cake, they could not eat. When the noon meal was taken, I observed the quality of food given to these children. It was fine wheaten bread, sliced ham coated with black pepper, spiced pickles, cake, and preserves. The pale, sallow complexion of these children plainly indicated the abuses the stomach was suffering. Two of these children observed another family of children eating cheese with their food, and they lost their appetite for what was before them until their indulgent mother begged a piece of the cheese to give to her children, fearing the dear children would fail to make out their meal. The mother remarked, "My children love this or that so much, and I let them have what they want; for the appetite craves the kinds of food the system requires."

This might be correct if the appetite had never been perverted. There is a natural and a depraved appetite. Parents who have taught their children to eat unhealthful, stimulating food all their lives—until the taste is perverted, and they crave clay, slate pencils, burned coffee, tea grounds, cinnamon, cloves, and spices—cannot claim that the appetite demands what the system requires. The appetite has been falsely educated, until it is depraved. The fine organs of the stomach have been stimulated and burned, until they have lost their delicate sensitiveness. Simple, healthful food seems to them insipid. The abused stomach will not perform the work given it, unless urged to it by the most stimulating substances. If these children had been trained from their infancy to take only healthful food, prepared in the most simple manner, preserving its natural properties as much as possible, and avoiding flesh meats, grease, and all spices, the taste and appetite would be unimpaired. In its natural state, it might indicate, in a great degree, the food best adapted to the wants of the system." *Counsels on Diet and Foods,* p. 239.

What About Flesh Foods? We do not mark out any precise line to be followed in diet; but we do say that in countries where there are fruits, grains, and nuts in abundance, flesh food is not the right food for God's people. I have been instructed that flesh food has a tendency to animalize the nature, to rob men and women of that love and sympathy which they should feel for everyone, and to give the lower passions control over the higher powers of the being. If meat eating was ever healthful, it is not safe now. *Testimonies for the Church,* vol. 9, p. 159.

Reasons for Discarding Flesh Foods. Those who eat flesh are but eating grains and vegetables at second hand, for the animal receives from these things the nutrition that produces growth. The life that was in the grains and vegetables passes into the eater. We receive it by eating the flesh of the animal. How much better to get it direct, by eating the food that God provided for our use!

Flesh was never the best food; but its use is now doubly objectionable, since disease in animals is so rapidly increasing. Those who use flesh foods little know what they are eating. Often if they could see the animals when living and know the quality of the meat they eat, they would turn from it with loathing. People are continually eating flesh that is filled with tuberculous and cancerous germs. Tuberculosis, cancer, and other fatal diseases are thus communicated. *The Ministry of Healing,* p. 313.

Effects Not Immediately Realized. The effects of a flesh diet may not be immediately realized, but this is no evidence that it is not harmful. Few can be made to believe that it is the meat they have eaten which has poisoned their blood and caused their suffering. Many die of diseases wholly due to meat eating, while the real cause is not suspected by themselves or by others. *Ibid.,* p. 315.

Return to the Original Wholesome Diet. Is it not time that all should aim to dispense with flesh foods? How can those who are seeking to become pure, refined, and holy, that they may have the companionship of heavenly angels, continue to use as food anything that has so harmful an effect on soul and body? How can they take the life of God's creatures that they may consume the flesh as a luxury? Let them, rather, return to the wholesome and delicious food given to man in the beginning. *Ibid.,* p. 317.

The Course of Those Awaiting Christ's Coming. Among those who are waiting for the coming of the Lord, meat eating will eventually be done away; flesh will cease to form a part of their diet. We should ever keep this end in view and endeavor to work steadily toward it. I cannot think that in the practice of flesh eating we are in harmony with the light which God has been pleased to give us. *Counsels on Diet and Foods,* pp. 380, 381.

Back to God's Design. Again and again I have been shown that God is bringing His people back to His original design, that is, not to subsist on the flesh of dead animals. He would have us teach people a better way. . . . If meat is discarded, if the taste is not educated in that direction, if a liking for fruits and grains is encouraged, it will soon be as God in the beginning designed it should be. No meat will be used by His people. *Ibid., p. 82.*

Instruction Concerning a Change in Diet. It is a mistake to suppose that muscular strength depends on the use of animal food. The needs of the system can be better supplied, and more vigorous health can be enjoyed without its use. The grains, with fruits, nuts, and vegetables, contain all the nutritive properties necessary to make good blood. These elements are not so well or so fully supplied by a flesh diet. Had the use of flesh been essential to health and strength, animal food would have been included in the diet appointed man in the beginning.

When the use of flesh food is discontinued, there is often a sense of weakness, a lack of vigor. Many urge this as evidence that flesh food is essential; but it is because foods of this class are stimulating, because they fever the blood and excite the nerves, that they are so missed. Some will find it as difficult to leave off flesh eating as it is for the drunkard to give up his dram, but they will be the better for the change.

When flesh food is discarded, its place should be supplied with a variety of grains, nuts, vegetables, and fruits, that will be both nourishing and appetizing. This is especially necessary in the case of those who are weak, or who are taxed with continuous labor. *The Ministry of Healing,* p. 316.

Well-prepared Substitutes Are Helpful. Especially where meat is not made a principal article of food is good cooking an essential requirement. Something must be prepared to take the place of meat, and these substitutes for meat must be well prepared, so that meat will not be desired. Letter 60a, 1896.

I am acquainted with families who have changed from a meat diet to one that is impoverished. Their food is so poorly prepared that the stomach loathes it, and such have told me that the health reform did not agree with them; that they were decreasing in physical strength. Here is one reason why some have not been successful in their efforts to simplify their food. They have a poverty-stricken diet. Food is prepared without painstaking, and there is a continual sameness.

There should not be many kinds at any one meal, but all meals should not be composed of the same kinds of foods without variation. Food should be prepared with simplicity, yet with a nicety which will invite the appetite. *Testimonies for the Church,* vol. 2, p. 63.

Overcoming the Unnatural Appetite. Persons who have accustomed themselves to a rich, highly stimulating diet have an unnatural taste, and they cannot at once relish food that is plain and simple. It will take time for the taste to become natural and for the stomach to recover from the abuse it has suffered. But those who persevere in the use of wholesome food will, after a time, find it palatable. Its delicate and delicious flavors will be appreciated, and it will be eaten with greater enjoyment than can be derived from unwholesome dainties. And the stomach, in a healthy condition, neither fevered nor overtaxed, can readily perform its task. *The Ministry of Healing,* pp. 298, 299.

Healthful Eating Is Not a Sacrifice. While the children should be taught to control the appetite, and to eat with reference to health, let it be made plain that they are denying themselves only that which would do them harm. They give up hurtful things for something better. Let the table be made inviting and attractive as it is supplied with the good things which God has so bountifully bestowed. *Ibid.,* p. 385.

Consider the Season, Climate, Occupation. Not all foods wholesome in themselves are equally suited to our needs under all circumstances. Care should be taken in the selection of food. Our diet should be suited to the season, to the climate in which we live, and to the occupation we follow. Some foods that are adapted for use at one season or in one climate are not suited to another. So there are different foods best suited for persons in different occupations. Often food that can be used with benefit by those engaged in hard physical labor is unsuitable for persons of sedentary pursuits or intense mental application. God has given us an ample variety of healthful foods, and each person should choose from it the things that experience and sound judgment prove to be best suited to his own necessities. *Ibid.,* pp. 296, 297.

Prepare Food With Intelligence and Skill. It is wrong to eat merely to gratify the appetite, but no indifference should be manifested regarding the quality of the food or the manner of its preparation. If the food eaten is not relished, the body will not be so well nourished. The food should be carefully chosen and prepared with intelligence and skill. *Ibid.,* p. 300.

"We Can Pick Up Anything." In many families great preparations are made for visitors. A variety of food is prepared for the table. This food is tempting to those unaccustomed to such a variety of rich food. . . .

I have a knowledge of the course pursued by some who make these extra preparations for visitors. In their own families they observe no regularity. The meals are prepared to suit the convenience of the wife and mother. The happiness of the husband and children is not studied. Though such a parade is made for visitors, anything is thought to be good enough for "only us." A table against the wall, a cold meal placed on it, with no effort to make it inviting, is too often seen. "Only for us," they say. "We can pick up anything." Manuscript 1, 1876.

Make the Mealtime a Pleasant Social Occasion. Mealtime should be a season for social intercourse and refreshment. Everything that can burden or irritate should be banished. Let trust and kindliness and gratitude to the Giver of all good be cherished, and the conversation will be cheerful, a pleasant flow of thought that will uplift without wearying. *Education,* p. 206.

The table is not a place where rebellion should be cultivated in the children by some unreasonable course pursued by the parents. The whole family should eat with gladness, with gratitude, remembering that those who love and obey God will partake of the marriage supper of the Lamb in the kingdom of God, and Jesus Himself will serve them. Letter 19, 1892.

Regularity in Eating. Irregularities in eating destroy the healthful tone of the digestive organs, to the detriment of health and cheerfulness. *The Ministry of Healing,* p. 384.

In no case should the meals be irregular. If dinner is eaten an hour or two before the usual time, the stomach is unprepared for the new burden; for it has not yet disposed of the food eaten at the previous meal and has not vital force for the new work. Thus the system is overtaxed.

Neither should the meals be delayed one or two hours, to suit circumstances, or in order that a certain amount of work may be accomplished. The stomach calls for food at the time it is accustomed to receive it. If that time is delayed, the vitality of the system decreases and finally reaches so low an ebb that the appetite is entirely gone. If food is then taken, the stomach is unable to properly care for it. The food cannot be converted into good blood. If all would eat at regular periods, not tasting anything between meals, they would be ready for their meals and would find a pleasure in eating that would repay them for their effort. *Counsels on Diet and Foods,* p. 179.

Teach Children When, How, and What to Eat. Children are generally untaught in regard to the importance of when, how, and what they should eat. They are permitted to indulge their tastes freely, to eat at all hours, to help themselves to fruit when it tempts their eyes; and this, with the pie, cake, bread and butter, and sweetmeats eaten almost constantly, makes them gourmands and dyspeptics. The digestive organs, like a mill which is continually kept running, become enfeebled, vital force is called from the brain to aid the stomach in its overwork, and thus the mental powers are weakened. The unnatural stimulation and wear of the vital forces make them nervous, impatient of restraint, self-willed, and irritable. They can scarcely be trusted out of their parents' sight. In many cases the moral powers seem deadened, and it is difficult to arouse them to a sense of the shame and grievous nature of sin; they slip easily into habits of prevarication, deceit, and often open lying.

Parents deplore these things in their children, but do not realize that it is their own bad management which has brought about the evil. They have not seen the necessity of restraining the appetites and passions of their children, and they have grown and strengthened with their years. Mothers prepare with their own hands and place before their children food which has a tendency to injure them physically and mentally. *Pacific Health Journal,* May 1890.

Never Eat Between Meals. The stomach must have careful attention. It must not be kept in continual operation. Give this misused and much-abused organ some peace and quiet and rest. . . .

After the regular meal is eaten, the stomach should be allowed to rest for five hours. Not a particle of food should be introduced into the stomach till the next meal. In this interval the stomach will perform its work and will then be in a condition to receive more food. *Counsels on Diet and Foods,* pp. 173, 179.

Mothers make a great mistake in permitting them [their children] to eat between meals. The stomach becomes deranged by this practice, and the foundation is laid for future suffering. Their fretfulness may have been caused by unwholesome food, still undigested; but the mother feels that she cannot spend time to reason upon the matter and correct her injurious management. Neither can she stop to soothe their impatient worrying. She gives the little sufferers a piece of cake or some other dainty to quiet them, but this only increases the evil. . . .

Mothers often complain of the delicate health of their children, and consult the physician; when, if they would but exercise a little common sense, they would see that the trouble is caused by errors in diet. *Christian Temperance and Bible Hygiene,* p. 61.

Late "Snacks" a Pernicious Habit. Another pernicious habit is that of eating just before bedtime. The regular meals may have been taken; but because there is a sense of faintness, more food is taken. By indulgence this wrong practice becomes a habit and often so firmly fixed that it is thought impossible to sleep without food. As a result of eating late suppers, the digestive process is continued through the sleeping hours. But though the stomach works constantly, its work is not properly accomplished. The sleep is often disturbed with unpleasant dreams, and in the morning the person awakes unrefreshed and with little relish for breakfast. When we lie down to rest, the stomach should have its work all done, that it, as well as the other organs of the body, may enjoy rest. For persons of sedentary habits late suppers are particularly harmful. With them the disturbance created is often the beginning of disease that ends in death. *The Ministry of Healing,* pp. 303, 304.

A Mother Counseled That Breakfast Is Important. Your child has a nervous temperament, and her diet should be carefully guarded. She should not be allowed to choose that food which will gratify the taste without affording proper nourishment. . . . Never let her go from home to school without her breakfast. Do not venture to give full scope to your inclinations in this matter. Place yourself entirely under the control of God, and He will help you to bring all your desires into harmony with His requirements. Letter 69, 1896.

It is the custom and order of society to take a slight breakfast. But this is not the best way to treat the stomach. At breakfast time the stomach is in a better condition to take care of more food than at the second or third meal of the day. The habit of eating a sparing breakfast and a large dinner is wrong. Make your breakfast correspond more nearly to the heartiest meal of the day. *Counsels on Diet and Foods,* p. 173.

Provide an Abundance of the Best Foods. Children and youth should not be underfed in the least degree; they should have an abundance of healthful food, but this does not mean that it is proper to place before them rich cakes and pastries. They should have the best of exercise and the best of food, for these have an important bearing upon the condition of the mental and moral powers. A proper, wholesome diet will be one of the means whereby healthful digestion may be preserved. Letter 19, 1892.

Partake of This in Moderation. Parents often make a mistake by giving their children too much food. Children treated in this way will grow up dyspeptics. Moderation in the use of even good food is essential. Parents, place before your children the amount they should eat. Leave it not with them to eat just as much as they may feel inclined. . . . Parents, unless this point is guarded, your children will have dull perceptions. They may attend school, but they will be unable to learn as they ought; for the strength which should go to the brain is used in taking care of the extra food that burdens the stomach. Parents need to be educated to see that too much food given to children makes them feeble instead of robust. Manuscript 155, 1899.

Parents, Not Children, to Dictate Here. Teach them to deny appetite, to be grateful for the plain, simple diet God gives them. It is not for you to allow them to dictate to you what they should eat, but you should dictate what is best for them. It is a sin for you to allow your children to murmur and complain about good wholesome food, just because it does not suit their depraved appetites. Letter 23, 1888.

Do not let the child receive the impression that, because he is your child, he must therefore be deferred to and permitted to choose and direct his own way. He should not be permitted to choose articles of food that are not good for him, simply because he likes them. The experience of parents should have a controlling power in the life of the child. *Signs of the Times,* Aug. 13, 1896.

Respect Child's Preference, if Reasonable. It rests with us individually to decide whether our lives shall be controlled by the mind or by the body. The youth must, each for himself, make the choice that shapes his life; and no pains should be spared that he may understand the forces with which he has to deal, and the influences which mold character and destiny. *Education,* p. 202.

In the education of children and youth they should be taught that the habits of eating, drinking, and dressing which have been formed after the world's standard are not in accordance with the laws of health and life, and must be held in control by reason and intellect. The power of appetite and strength of habit should not be permitted to overpower the dictates of reason. In order to secure this object, the youth must have higher aims and motives than mere animal gratification in eating and drinking. *Good Health,* July 1889.

Far-reaching Effects of Perverted Appetite. Some are not impressed with the necessity of eating and drinking to the glory of God. The indulgence of appetite affects them in all the relations of life. It is seen in the family, in the church, in the prayer meeting, and in the conduct of their children. It is the curse of their lives. It prevents them from understanding the truths for these last days. *Christian Temperance and Bible Hygiene,* p. 151.

Healthful Living, a Personal Obligation. What we eat and drink has an important bearing upon our lives and characters, and Christians should bring their habits of eating and drinking into conformity to the laws of nature. We must sense our obligations to God in these matters. Obedience to the laws of health should be made a matter of earnest study, for willing ignorance on this subject is sin. Each one should feel a personal obligation to carry out the laws of healthful living. Manuscript 47, 1896.

CHAPTER 63

Temperance in All Things

Intemperance Causes Most of Life's Ills. Intemperance is at the foundation of the larger share of the ills of life. It annually destroys tens of thousands. We do not speak of intemperance as limited only to the use of intoxicating liquors, but give it a broader meaning, including the hurtful indulgence of any appetite or passion. *Pacific Health Journal,* April 1890.

Through intemperance some sacrifice one half, and others two thirds of their physical, mental, and moral powers and become playthings for the enemy. *Messages to Young People,* p. 236.

Excessive Indulgence Is Sin. Excessive indulgence in eating, drinking, sleeping, or seeing is sin. The harmonious healthy action of all the powers of body and mind results in happiness; and the more elevated and refined the powers, the more pure and unalloyed the happiness. *Counsels on Diet and Foods,* p. 44.

Temperance Is a Principle of the Religious Life. Temperance in all things of this life is to be taught and practiced. Temperance in eating, drinking, sleeping, and dressing is one of the grand principles of the religious life. Truth brought into the sanctuary of the soul will guide in the treatment of the body. Nothing that concerns the health of the human agent is to be regarded with indifference. Our eternal welfare depends upon the use we make during this life of our time, strength, and influence. *Testimonies for the Church,* vol. 6, p. 375.

Only one lease of life is granted us here; and the inquiry with everyone should be, How can I invest my life that it may yield the greatest profit? *Pacific Health Journal,* April 1890.

Our first duty toward God and our fellow beings is that of self-development. Every faculty with which the Creator has endowed us should be cultivated to the highest degree of perfection, that we may be able to do the greatest amount of good of which we are capable. Hence that time is spent to good account which is directed to the establishment and preservation of sound physical and mental health. We cannot afford to dwarf or cripple a single function of mind or body by overwork or by abuse of any part of the living machinery. As surely as we do this, we must suffer the consequences. *Signs of the Times,* Nov. 17, 1890.

It Has a Wonderful Power. The observance of temperance and regularity in all things has a wonderful power. It will do more than circumstances or natural endowments in promoting that sweetness and serenity of disposition which count so much in smoothing life's pathway. At the same time the power of self-control thus acquired will be found one of the most valuable of equipments for grappling successfully with the stern duties and realities that await every human being. *Education,* p. 206.

An Aid to Clear Thinking. Every day men in positions of trust have decisions to make upon which depend results of great importance. Often they have to think rapidly, and this can be done successfully by those only who practice strict temperance. The mind strengthens under the correct treatment of the physical and mental powers. If the strain is not too great, new vigor comes with every taxation. *The Ministry of Healing,* p. 309.

Temperate Habits Yield Rich Rewards. The rising generation are surrounded with allurements calculated to tempt the appetite. Especially in our large cities, every form of indulgence is made easy and inviting. Those who,

like Daniel, refuse to defile themselves will reap the reward
of their temperate habits. With their greater physical stamina
and increased power of endurance, they have a bank of de-
posit upon which to draw in case of emergency.

Right physical habits promote mental superiority.
Intellectual power, physical strength, and longevity depend
upon immutable laws. There is no happen-so, no chance,
about this matter. Nature's God will not interfere to preserve
men from the consequences of violating nature's laws.
Christian Temperance and Bible Hygiene, p. 28.

For Perfect Health Be Temperate in All Things. In
order to preserve health, temperance in all things is necessary.
. . . Our heavenly Father sent the light of health reform to
guard against the evils resulting from a debased appetite, that
those who love purity and holiness may know how to use
with discretion the good things He has provided for them,
and that by exercising temperance in daily life, they may be
sanctified through the truth. *Ibid.,* p. 52.

Temperance Precedes Sanctification. God's people are
to learn the meaning of temperance in all things. . . . All self-
indulgence is to be cut away from their lives. Before they can
really understand the meaning of true sanctification and of
conformity to the will of Christ, they must, by cooperating
with God, obtain the mastery over wrong habits and practices. *Medical Ministry,* p. 275.

In Study. Intemperance in study is a species of in-
toxication; and those who indulge in it, like the drunkard, wander from safe paths and stumble and fall in
the darkness. The Lord would have every student bear
in mind that the eye must be kept single to the glory of
God. He is not to exhaust and waste his physical and

mental powers in seeking to acquire all possible knowledge of the sciences, but is to preserve the freshness and vigor of all his powers to engage in the work which the Lord has appointed him in helping souls to find the path of righteousness. *Counsels to Parents, Teachers, and Students,* pp. 405, 406.

In Work. We should practice temperance in our labor. It is not our duty to place ourselves where we shall be overworked. Some may at times be placed where this is necessary, but it should be the exception, not the rule. We are to practice temperance in all things. If we honor the Lord by acting our part, He will on His part preserve our health. We should have a sensible control of all our organs. By practicing temperance in eating, in drinking, in dressing, in labor, and in all things, we can do for ourselves what no physician can do for us. *Temperance,* p. 139.

As a rule, the labor of the day should not be prolonged into the evening. . . . I have been shown that those who do this often lose much more than they gain, for their energies are exhausted, and they labor on nervous excitement. They may not realize any immediate injury, but they are surely undermining their constitution. *Counsels on Health,* p. 99.

Those who make great exertions to accomplish just so much work in a given time, and continue to labor when their judgment tells them they should rest, are never gainers. They are living on borrowed capital. They are expending the vital force which they will need at a future time. And when the energy they have so recklessly used is demanded, they fail for want of it. The physical strength is gone, the mental powers fail. They realize that they have met with a loss, but do not know what it is. Their time of need has come, but their physical resources are exhausted. Everyone who violates the laws of health must sometime be a sufferer to a greater or less degree. God has provided us with constitutional force, which will be needed at different periods of our lives. If we recklessly exhaust this force by continual overtaxation, we shall sometime be the losers. *Fundamentals of Christian Education,* pp. 153, 154.

In Dressing. In all respects the dress should be healthful. "Above all things," God desires us to "be in health"—health of body and of soul. And we are to be workers together with Him for the health of both soul and body. Both are promoted by healthful dress.

It should have the grace, the beauty, the appropriateness of natural simplicity. Christ has warned us against the pride of life, but not against its grace and natural beauty. *The Ministry of Healing,* pp. 288, 289.

In Eating. True temperance teaches us to dispense entirely with everything hurtful, and to use judiciously that which is healthful. There are few who realize as they should how much their habits of diet have to do with their health, their character, their usefulness in this world, and their eternal destiny. The appetite should ever be in subjection to the moral and intellectual powers. The body should be servant to the mind, and not the mind to the body. *Temperance,* p. 138.

Those who eat and work intemperately and irrationally, talk and act irrationally. It is not necessary to drink alcoholic liquors in order to be intemperate. The sin of intemperate eating—eating too frequently, too much, and of rich, unwholesome food—destroys the healthy action of the digestive organs, affects the brain, and perverts the judgment, preventing rational, calm, healthy thinking and acting. *Christian Temperance and Bible Hygiene,* p. 155.

Special Care Not to Overeat. In nine cases out of ten there is more danger of eating too much than too little. . . . There are many sick who suffer from no disease. The cause of their sickness is indulgence of appetite. They think that if the food is healthful, they may eat as much as they please. This is a great mistake. Persons whose powers are debilitated should eat a moderate and even limited amount of food. The system will then be enabled to do its work easily and well, and a great deal of suffering will be saved. Manuscript 1, 1876.

Do Not Deny God by One Act of Intemperance. We have been bought with a price; therefore we are to glorify God in our body and in our spirit, which are His. We are not to deny Him by one act of intemperance, because the only-begotten Son of God has purchased us at an infinite cost, even the sacrifice of His life. He did not die for us in order that we might become slaves to evil habits, but that we might become the sons and daughters of God, serving Him with every power of the being. Letter 166, 1903.

Those who have a constant realization that they stand in this relation to God will not place in the stomach food which pleases the appetite, but which injures the digestive organs. They will not spoil the property of God by indulging improper habits of eating, drinking, or dressing. They will take great care of the human machinery, realizing that they must do this in order to work in copartnership with God. He wills that they shall be healthy, happy, and useful. But in order for them to be this, they must place their wills on the side of His will. *Temperance,* p. 214.

Carry Temperance Into All Details of Home Life. We urge that the principles of temperance be carried into all the details of home life; that the example of parents should be a lesson of temperance; that self-denial and self-control should be taught to the children and enforced upon them, so far as consistent, from babyhood. *Review and Herald,* Sept. 23, 1884.

In the family circle and in the church we should place Christian temperance on an elevated platform. It should be a living, working element, reforming habits, dispositions, and characters. *Temperance,* p. 165.

CHAPTER 64

The Home and the Temperance Crusade

Intemperance Is on the Rampage. Intemperance still continues its ravages. Iniquity in every form stands like a mighty barrier to prevent the progress of truth and righteousness. Social wrongs, born of ignorance and vice, are still causing untold misery and casting their baleful shadow upon both the church and the world. Depravity among the youth is increasing instead of decreasing. Nothing but earnest, continual effort will avail to remove this desolating curse. The conflict with interest and appetite, with evil habits and unholy passions, will be fierce and deadly; only those who shall move from principle can gain the victory in this warfare. *Temperance,* p. 234.

Intemperance is on the increase, in spite of the efforts made to control it. We cannot be too earnest in seeking to hinder its progress, to raise the fallen and shield the weak from temptation. With our feeble human hands we can do but little, but we have an unfailing Helper. We must not forget that the arm of Christ can reach to the very depths of human woe and degradation. He can give us help to conquer even this terrible demon of intemperance. *Christian Temperance and Bible Hygiene,* p. 21.

Total Abstinence Is the Answer. The only way in which any can be secure against the power of intemperance is to abstain wholly from wine, beer, and strong drinks. We must teach our children that in order to be manly they must let these things alone. God has shown us what constitutes true manliness. It is he that overcometh who will be honored, and whose name will not be blotted out of the book of life. *Ibid.,* p. 37.

Parents may, by earnest, persevering effort, unbiased by the customs of fashionable life, build a moral bulwark about their children that will defend them from the miseries and crimes caused by intemperance. Children should not be left to come up as they will, unduly developing traits that should be nipped in the bud; but they should be disciplined carefully, and educated to take their position upon the side of right, of reform and abstinence. In every crisis they will then have moral independence to breast the storm of opposition sure to assail those who take their stand in favor of true reform. *Temperance,* pp. 214, 215.

Intemperance Is Often a Result of Home Indulgence. Great efforts are made in our country to put down intemperance, but it is found a hard matter to overpower and chain the full-grown lion. If half these efforts were directed toward enlightening parents as to their responsibility in forming the habits and characters of their children, a thousandfold more good might result than from the present course. We bid all workers in the cause of temperance Godspeed; but we invite them to look deeper into the cause of the evil they war against, and go more thoroughly and consistently into reform. *Review and Herald,* Sept. 23, 1884.

In order to reach the root of intemperance we must go deeper than the use of alcohol or tobacco. Idleness, lack of aim, or evil associations may be the predisposing cause. Often it is found at the home table, in families that account themselves strictly temperate. Anything that disorders digestion, that creates undue mental excitement or in any way enfeebles the system, disturbing the balance of the mental and the physical powers, weakens the control of the mind over the body, and thus tends toward intemperance. The downfall of many a promising youth might be traced to unnatural appetites created by an unwholesome diet. *Education,* pp. 202, 203.

The tables of our American people are generally prepared in a manner to make drunkards. Appetite is the ruling principle with a large class. Whoever will indulge appetite in eating too often, and food not of a healthful quality, is weakening his power to resist the clamors of appetite and passion in other respects in proportion as he has strengthened the propensity to incorrect habits of eating. *Testimonies for the Church,* vol. 3, p. 563.

Tea and Coffee Are Contributing Factors. Through the intemperance begun at home, the digestive organs first become weakened, and soon ordinary food does not satisfy the appetite. Unhealthy conditions are established, and there is a craving for more stimulating food. Tea and coffee produce an immediate effect. Under the influence of these poisons the nervous system is excited; and in some cases, for the time being, the intellect seems to be invigorated, the imagination more vivid. Because these stimulants produce such agreeable results, many conclude that they really need them; but there is always a reaction. The nervous system has borrowed power from its future resources for present use, and all this temporary invigoration is followed by a corresponding depression. The suddenness of the relief obtained from tea and coffee is an evidence that what seems to be strength is only nervous excitement, and consequently must be an injury to the system. *Christian Temperance and Bible Hygiene,* p. 31.

Tobacco, a Subtle Poison. Tobacco using is a habit which frequently affects the nervous system in a more powerful manner than does the use of alcohol. It binds the victim in stronger bands of slavery than does the intoxicating cup; the habit is more difficult to overcome. Body and mind are, in many cases, more thoroughly intoxicated with the use of tobacco than with spirituous liquors; for it is a more subtle poison. *Testimonies for the Church,* vol. 3, p. 562.

Tobacco . . . affects the brain and benumbs the sensibilities, so that the mind cannot clearly discern spiritual things, especially those truths which would have a tendency to correct this filthy indulgence. Those who use tobacco in any form are not clear before God. In such a filthy practice it is impossible for them to glorify God in their bodies and spirits, which are His. *Counsels on Health,* p. 81.

Tobacco weakens the brain and paralyzes its fine sensibilities. Its use excites a thirst for strong drink, and in very many cases lays the foundation for the liquor habit. *Christian Temperance and Bible Hygiene,* p. 17.

Effects of Stimulants and Narcotics. The effect of stimulants and narcotics is to lessen physical strength, and whatever affects the body will affect the mind. A stimulant may for a time arouse the energies and produce mental and physical activity; but when the exhilarating influence is gone, both mind and body will be in a worse condition than before. Intoxicating liquors and tobacco have proved a terrible curse to our race, not only weakening the body and confusing the mind, but debasing the morals. As the control of reason is set aside, the animal passions will bear sway. The more freely these poisons are used, the more brutish will become the nature. *Signs of the Times,* Sept. 13, 1910.

Teach Children to Abhor Stimulants. Teach your children to abhor stimulants. How many are ignorantly fostering in them an appetite for these things! *Christian Temperance and Bible Hygiene,* p. 17.

God calls upon parents to guard their children against the indulgence of appetite, and especially against the use of stimulants and narcotics. The tables of Christian parents should never be loaded with food containing condiments and spices. They are to study to preserve the stomach from any abuse. *Review and Herald,* June 27, 1899.

In this fast age the less exciting the food the better. Temperance in all things and firm denial of appetite is the only path of safety. *Testimonies for the Church,* vol. 3, p. 561.

A Challenge to Parents. Parents may have transmitted to their children tendencies to appetite and passion, which will make more difficult the work of educating and training these children to be strictly temperate and to have pure and virtuous habits. If the appetite for unhealthy food and for stimulants and narcotics has been transmitted to them as a legacy from their parents, what a fearfully solemn responsibility rests upon the parents to counteract the evil tendencies which they have given to their children! How earnestly and diligently should the parents work to do their duty, in faith and hope, to their unfortunate offspring! *Ibid.,* pp. 567, 568.

Tastes and Appetites Must Be Educated. Parents should make it their first business to understand the laws of life and health, that nothing shall be done by them in the preparation of food, or through any other habits, which will develop wrong tendencies in their children. How carefully should mothers study to prepare their tables with the most simple, healthful food, that the digestive organs may not be weakened, the nervous forces unbalanced, and the instruction which they should give their children counteracted, by the food placed before them. This food either weakens or strengthens the organs

of the stomach and has much to do in controlling the physical and moral health of the children, who are God's blood-
bought property. *Ibid.,* p. 568.

What a sacred trust is committed to parents, to guard the
physical and moral constitutions of their children, so that the
nervous system may be well balanced, and the soul not be
endangered! *Ibid.*

Our sisters can do much in the great work for the salvation of others by spreading their tables with only healthful, nourishing food. They may employ their precious time
in educating the tastes and appetites of their children, in
forming habits of temperance in all things, and in encouraging self-denial and benevolence for the good of others.
Ibid., p. 489.

Negligent Parents Are Responsible. Many parents, to
avoid the task of patiently educating their children to habits
of self-denial, indulge them in eating and drinking whenever
they please. The desire to satisfy the taste and to gratify inclination does not lessen with the increase of years; and these
indulged youth, as they grow up, are governed by impulse,
slaves to appetite. When they take their place in society and
begin life for themselves, they are powerless to resist temptation. In the glutton, the tobacco devotee, . . . and the ine-
briate, we see the evil results of erroneous education. . . .

When we hear the sad lamentation of Christian men and
women over the terrible evils of intemperance, the questions
at once arise: Who have educated the youth? Who have fostered in them these unruly appetites? Who have neglected
the solemn responsibility of forming their character for usefulness in this life and for the society of heavenly angels in the
next? *Christian Temperance and Bible Hygiene,* p. 76.

The Real Work Begins at Home. It is in the home that the real work must begin. The greatest burden rests upon those who have the responsibility of educating the youth, of forming their character. Here is a work for mothers, in helping their children to form correct habits and pure tastes, to develop moral stamina, true moral worth. Teach them that they are not to be swayed by others, that they are not to yield to wrong influences, but to influence others for good, to ennoble and elevate those with whom they associate. Teach them that if they connect themselves with God, they will have strength from Him to resist the fiercest temptations. *Ibid.,* pp. 21, 22.

Temperance Is Not a Matter for Jesting. Many make the subject of temperance a matter of jest. They claim that the Lord does not concern Himself with such minor matters as our eating and drinking. But if the Lord had no care for these things, He would not have revealed Himself to the wife of Manoah, giving her definite instructions and twice enjoining upon her to beware lest she disregard them. Is not this sufficient evidence that He does care for these things? *Temperance,* pp. 233, 234.

Reform Begins With the Mother. The carefulness with which the mother should guard her habits of life is taught in the Scriptures. *The Ministry of Healing,* p. 372.

The reform should begin with the mother before the birth of her children; and if God's instructions were faithfully obeyed, intemperance would not exist. *Signs of the Times,* Sept. 13, 1910.

Not only the habits of the mother, but the training of the child were included in the angel's instruction to the Hebrew parents. It was not enough that Samson, the child who was to deliver Israel, should have a good legacy at his birth. This was to be followed by careful training.

From infancy he was to be trained to habits of strict temperance. . . .

The directions given concerning the Hebrew children teach us that nothing which affects the child's physical well-being is to be neglected. Nothing is unimportant. Every influence that affects the health of the body has its bearing upon mind and character. *The Ministry of Healing,* pp. 379, 380.

Temperance and self-control should be taught from the cradle. Upon the mother largely rests the burden of this work, and, aided by the father, she may carry it forward successfully. *Review and Herald,* July 9, 1901.

Continue the Lessons at Fireside and at School. It is a most difficult matter to unlearn the habits which have been indulged through life and have educated the appetite. The demon of intemperance is not easily conquered. It is of giant strength and hard to overcome. But let parents begin a crusade against intemperance at their own firesides, in their own families, in the principles they teach their children to follow from their very infancy, and they may hope for success. It will pay you, mothers, to use the precious hours which are given you of God in forming, developing, and training the characters of your children, and in teaching them to strictly adhere to the principles of temperance in eating and drinking. *Testimonies for the Church,* vol. 3, p. 567.

Instruction in this line should be given in every school and in every home. The youth and children should understand the effect of alcohol, tobacco, and other like poisons in breaking down the body, beclouding the mind, and sensualizing the soul. It should be made plain that no one who uses these things can long possess the full strength of his physical, mental, or moral faculties. *Education,* p. 202.

Make Plain the Effect of Small Deviations. It is the beginnings of evil that should be guarded against. In the instruction of the youth the effect of apparently small deviations from the right should be made very plain. . . . Let the youth be impressed with the thought that they are to be masters, and not slaves. Of the kingdom within them God has made them rulers, and they are to exercise their Heaven-appointed kingship. When such instruction is faithfully given, the results will extend far beyond the youth themselves. Influences will reach out that will save thousands of men and women who are on the very brink of ruin. *Ibid,* pp. 203, 204.

Build Moral Stamina to Resist Temptation. Individual effort on the right side is needed to subdue the growing evil of intemperance. Oh, that we could find words that would melt and burn their way into the heart of every parent in the land! *Pacific Health Journal,* May 1890.

Parents may lay for their children the foundation for a healthy, happy life. They may send them forth from their homes with moral stamina to resist temptation, and courage and strength to wrestle successfully with life's problems. They may inspire in them the purpose and develop the power to make their lives an honor to God and a blessing to the world. They may make straight paths for their feet, through sunshine and shadow, to the glorious heights above. *The Ministry of Healing,* p. 352.

God calls upon us to stand upon the broad platform of temperance in eating, drinking, and dressing. Parents, will you not awaken to your God-given responsibilities? Study the principles of health reform and teach your children that the path of self-denial is the only path of safety. Manuscript 86, 1897.

SECTION 15

FITTING ATTIRE

CHAPTER 65

The Blessings of Proper Dress

Appropriate and Becoming. In dress, as in all things else, it is our privilege to honor our Creator. He desires our clothing to be not only neat and healthful, but appropriate and becoming. *Education,* p. 248.

We should seek to make the best of our appearance. In the tabernacle service God specified every detail concerning the garments of those who ministered before Him. Thus we are taught that He has a preference in regard to the dress of those who serve Him. Very specific were the directions given in regard to Aaron's robes, for his dress was symbolic. So the dress of Christ's followers should be symbolic. In all things we are to be representatives of Him. Our appearance in every respect should be characterized by neatness, modesty, and purity. *Testimonies for the Church,* vol. 6, p. 96.

Illustrated by the Things of Nature. By the things of nature [the flowers, the lily] Christ illustrates the beauty that Heaven values, the modest grace, the simplicity, the purity, the appropriateness, that would make our attire pleasing to Him. *The Ministry of Healing,* p. 289.

Character May Be Judged by Style of Dress. The dress and its arrangement upon the person is generally found to be the index of the man or the woman. *Review and Herald,* Jan. 30, 1900.

We judge of a person's character by the style of dress worn. A modest, godly woman will dress modestly. A refined taste, a cultivated mind, will be revealed in the choice of a simple, appropriate attire. . . . The one who is simple and unpretending in her dress and in her manners shows that she understands that a true woman is characterized by moral worth. How charming, how interesting, is simplicity in dress, which in comeliness can be compared with the flowers of the field. *Review and Herald,* Nov. 17, 1904.

Guiding Principles Enunciated. I beg of our people to walk carefully and circumspectly before God. Follow the customs in dress so far as they conform to health principles. Let our sisters dress plainly, as many do, having the dress of good, durable material, appropriate for this age, and let not the dress question fill the mind. Our sisters should dress with simplicity. They should clothe themselves in modest apparel, with shamefacedness and sobriety. Give to the world a living illustration of the inward adorning of the grace of God. Manuscript 167, 1897.

Follow Prevailing Customs if Modest, Healthful, and Convenient. Christians should not take pains to make themselves a gazingstock by dressing differently from the world. But if, when following out their convictions of duty in respect to dressing modestly and healthfully, they find themselves out of fashion, they should not change their dress in order to be like the world; but they should manifest a noble independence and moral courage to be right, if all the world differ from them.

If the world introduce a modest, convenient, and healthful mode of dress, which is in accordance with the Bible, it will not change our relation to God or to the world to adopt such a style of dress. Christians should follow Christ and make their dress conform to God's Word. They should shun extremes. They should humbly pursue a straightforward course, irrespective of applause or of censure, and should cling to the right because of its own merits. *Testimonies for the Church,* vol. 1, pp. 458, 459.

Avoid Extremes. Do not occupy your time by endeavoring to follow all the foolish fashions in dress. Dress neatly and becomingly, but do not make yourself the subject of remarks either by being overdressed or by dressing in a lax, untidy manner. Act as though you knew that the eye of heaven is upon you, and that you are living under the approbation or disapprobation of God. Manuscript 53, 1912.

Care in Dress Not to Be Confused With Pride. There is a class who are continually harping upon pride and dress, who are careless of their own apparel, and who think it a virtue to be dirty, and dress without order and taste; and their clothing often looks as if it flew and lit upon their persons. Their garments are filthy, and yet such ones will ever be talking against pride. They class decency and neatness with pride. *Review and Herald,* Jan. 23, 1900.

Those who are careless and untidy in dress are seldom elevated in their conversation and possess but little refinement of feeling. They sometimes consider oddity and coarseness humility. *Review and Herald,* Jan. 30, 1900.

Christ Sounded a Caution. Christ noticed the devotion to dress, and He cautioned, yea, He commanded, His followers not to bestow too much thought upon it. "Why take ye thought for raiment? Consider the lilies of the field, how they grow; they toil not, neither do they spin; yet I say unto you, That even Solomon in all his glory was not arrayed like one of these." . . . Pride and extravagance in dress are sins to which woman is especially prone; hence these injunctions relate directly to her. Of how little value are gold or pearls or costly array, when compared with the meekness and loveliness of Christ! *Christian Temperance and Bible Hygiene,* pp. 93, 94.

Bible Instruction for God's People. I was directed to the following scriptures. Said the angel, "They are to instruct God's people." 1 Timothy 2:9, 10: "In like manner also that women adorn themselves in modest apparel, with shame-facedness and sobriety; not with broided hair, or gold, or pearls, or costly array; but (which becometh women profess-ing godliness) with good works." 1 Peter 3:3-5: "Whose adorning let it not be that outward adorning of plaiting of the hair and of wearing of gold, or of putting on of apparel; but let it be the hidden man of the heart, in that which is not corruptible, even the ornament of a meek and quiet spirit, which is in the sight of God of great price. For after this manner in the old time the holy women also, . . . adorned themselves." *Testimonies for the Church,* vol. 1, p. 189.

Many look upon these injunctions as too old-fashioned to be worthy of notice; but He who gave them to His disci-ples understood the dangers from the love of dress in our time, and sent to us the note of warning. Will we heed the warning and be wise? *Ibid.,* vol. 4, p. 630.

Those who are truly seeking to follow Christ will have conscientious scruples in regard to the dress they wear; they will strive to meet the requirements of this injunction [1 Peter 3:3-5] so plainly given by the Lord. *Messages to Young People,* pp. 345, 346.

Dangers in the Love of Dress. The love of dress endan-gers the morals and makes woman the opposite of the Christian lady, characterized by modesty and sobriety. Showy, extravagant dress too often encourages lust in the heart of the wearer and awakens base passions in the heart of the beholder. God sees that the ruin of the character is fre-quently preceded by the indulgence of pride and vanity in dress. He sees that the costly apparel stifles the desire to do good. *Testimonies for the Church,* vol. 4, p. 645.

The Witness of Simplicity in Dress. Simple, plain, unpretending dress will be a recommendation to my youthful sisters. In no better way can you let your light shine to others than in your simplicity of dress and deportment. You may show to all that, in comparison with eternal things, you place a proper estimate upon the things of this life. *Ibid.,* vol. 3, p. 376.

Modesty Will Shield From a Thousand Perils. My sisters, avoid even the appearance of evil. In this fast age, reeking with corruption, you are not safe unless you stand guarded. Virtue and modesty are rare. I appeal to you as followers of Christ, making an exalted profession, to cherish the precious, priceless gem of modesty. This will guard virtue. *Ibid.,* vol. 2, p. 458.

Chaste simplicity in dress, when united with modesty of demeanor, will go far toward surrounding a young woman with that atmosphere of sacred reserve which will be to her a shield from a thousand perils. *Education,* p. 248.

An Old-fashioned Idea. To train children to walk in the narrow path of purity and holiness is thought an altogether odd and old-fashioned idea. This is prevalent even among parents who profess to worship God, but their works testify that they are worshipers of mammon. They are ambitious to compete with their neighbors and to compare favorably, in the dress of themselves and their children, with the members of the church to which they belong. *Signs of the Times,* Sept. 10, 1894.

The Only Dress Admitted Into Heaven. There is a dress which every child and youth may innocently seek to obtain. It is the righteousness of the saints. If they will only be as willing and persevering in obtaining this as they are in fashioning their garments after the standard of worldly society, they will very soon be clothed with the righteousness of Christ, and their names will not be blotted out of the book of life. Mothers, as well as youth and children, need to pray, "Create in me a clean heart, O God, and renew a right spirit within me." [Psalm 51:10.] This purity of heart and loveliness of spirit are more precious than gold, both for time and for eternity. Only the pure in heart shall see God.

Then, mothers, teach your children, line upon line and precept upon precept, that the righteousness of Christ is the only dress in which they can be admitted into heaven, and that robed in this apparel they will be constantly doing duties in this life which will glorify God. *Christian Temperance and Bible Hygiene,* p. 95.

CHAPTER 66

Teaching the Fundamental Principles of Dress

A Necessary Part of Education. No education can be complete that does not teach right principles in regard to dress. Without such teaching, the work of education is too often retarded and perverted. Love of dress and devotion to fashion are among the teacher's most formidable rivals and most effective hindrances. *Education,* p. 246.

No Precise Style Given. No one precise style has been given me as the exact rule to guide all in their dress. Letter 19, 1897.

Neat, Attractive, Clean. The young should be encouraged to form correct habits in dress, that their appearance may be neat and attractive; they should be taught to keep their garments clean and neatly mended. All their habits should be such as to make them a help and comfort to others. *Testimonies for the Church,* vol. 6, p. 170.

Let the attire be appropriate and becoming. Though only a ten-cent calico, it should be kept neat and clean. *Ibid.,* vol. 4, p. 641.

Order and Correct Taste. In their dress they [Christians] avoid superfluity and display; but their clothing will be neat, not gaudy, modest, and arranged upon the person with order and taste. *Messages to Young People,* p. 349.

Correct taste is not to be despised or condemned. Our faith, if carried out, will lead us to be so plain in dress and zealous of good works that we shall be marked as peculiar. But when we lose taste for order and neatness in dress, we virtually leave the truth; for the truth never degrades but elevates. *Ibid.,* p. 353.

My sisters, your dress is telling either in favor of Christ and the sacred truth or in favor of the world. Which is it? *Review and Herald,* Nov. 17, 1904.

Good Taste in Colors and Figures. Taste should be manifested as to colors. Uniformity in this respect is desirable as far as convenient. Complexion, however, may be taken into account. Modest colors should be sought for. When figured material is used, figures that are large and fiery, showing vanity and shallow pride in those who choose them, should be avoided. And a fantastic taste in putting on different colors is bad. *Health Reformer.* Quoted in *Healthful Living,* p. 120.

Consider Durability and Service. Our clothing, while modest and simple, should be of good quality, of becoming colors, and suited for service. It should be chosen for durability rather than display. It should provide warmth and proper protection. The wise woman described in the Proverbs "is not afraid of the snow for her household: for all her household are clothed with double garments." [Proverbs 31:21, margin.] *The Ministry of Healing,* p. 288.

The Purchase of Good Material Is Economy. It is right to buy good material and have it carefully made. This is economy. But rich trimmings are not needed, and to indulge in them is to spend for self-gratification money that should be put into God's cause. *Counsels on Stewardship,* p. 301.

Remember the Needs of the Lord's Vineyard. We should dress neatly and tastefully; but, my sisters, when you are buying and making your own and your children's clothing, think of the work in the Lord's vineyard that is still waiting to be done. *Ibid.*

Worldlings spend much on dress. But the Lord has

charged His people to come out from the world and be separate. Gay or expensive apparel is not becoming to those who profess to believe that we are living in the last days. . . .

Practice economy in your outlay of means for dress. Remember that what you wear is constantly exerting an influence upon those with whom you come in contact. Do not lavish upon yourselves means that is greatly needed elsewhere. Do not spend the Lord's money to gratify a taste for expensive clothing. Manuscript 24, 1904.

Simplicity in Dress Recommends the Wearer's Religion. Simplicity of dress will make a sensible woman appear to the best advantage. *Review and Herald,* Nov. 17, 1904.

Dress as Christians should dress—simply, plainly adorn yourselves as becometh women professing godliness, with good works. *Review and Herald,* Dec. 6, 1881.

Many, in order to keep pace with absurd fashion, lose their taste for natural simplicity and are charmed with the artificial. They sacrifice time and money, the vigor of intellect, and true elevation of soul, and devote their entire being to the claims of fashionable life. *Health Reformer,* April 1872.

Dear youth, a disposition in you to dress according to the fashion, and to wear lace, and gold, and artificials for display, will not recommend to others your religion or the truth that you profess. People of discernment will look upon your attempts to beautify the external as proof of weak minds and proud hearts. *Testimonies for the Church,* vol. 1, pp. 135, 136.

There Should Be No Inappropriate Display. I would remind the youth who ornament their persons and wear feathers upon their hats that, because of their sins, our Saviour's head wore the shameful crown of thorns. When you devote precious time to trimming your apparel, remember that the King of glory wore a plain, seamless coat. You who weary yourselves in decorating your persons please bear in mind that Jesus was often weary from incessant toil and self-denial and self-sacrifice to bless the suffering and the needy. . . . It was on our account that He poured out His prayers to His Father with strong cries and tears. It was to save us from the very pride and love of vanity and pleasure which we now indulge, and which crowds out the love of Jesus, that those tears were shed, and that our Saviour's visage was marred with sorrow and anguish more than any of the sons of men. *Ibid.,* pp. 379, 380.

Unnecessary Trimmings. Do without the unnecessary trimmings, and lay aside for the advancement of the cause of God the means thus saved. Learn the lesson of self-denial, and teach it to your children. *Counsels on Stewardship,* pp. 301, 302.

A Point Clarified. The question has often been asked me if I believe it wrong to wear plain linen collars.* My answer has always been No. Some have taken the extreme meaning of what I have written about collars, and have maintained that it is wrong to wear one of any description. I was shown expensively wrought collars, and expensive and unnecessary ribbons and laces, which some Sabbathkeepers have worn, and still wear for the sake of show and fashion. In mentioning collars, I did not design to be understood that nothing like a collar should be worn, or in mentioning ribbons, that no ribbons at all should be worn. *Testimonies for the Church,* vol. 1, pp. 135, 136.

Extravagant or Extreme Trimmings. Our ministers and their wives should be an example in plainness of dress; they should dress neatly, comfortably, wearing good material, but avoiding anything like extravagance and trimmings, even if not expensive; for these things tell to our disadvantage. We should educate the youth to simplicity of dress, plainness with neatness. Let the extra trimmings be left out, even though the cost be but a trifle. *Testimonies to Ministers and Gospel Workers,* p. 180.

Not for Display. True refinement does not find satisfaction in the adorning of the body for display. *Christian Temperance and Bible Hygiene,* p. 93.

The Bible teaches modesty in dress. "In like manner also, that women adorn themselves in modest apparel." 1 Timothy 2:9. This forbids display in dress, gaudy colors, profuse ornamentation. Any device designed to attract attention to the wearer or to excite admiration is excluded from the modest apparel which God's Word enjoins. *Counsel to Parents, Teachers, and Students,* p. 302.

Self-denial in dress is a part of our Christian duty. To dress plainly and abstain from display of jewelry and ornaments of every kind is in keeping with our faith. Are we of the number who see the folly of worldlings in indulging in extravagance of dress as well as in love of amusements? *Testimonies for the Church,* vol. 3, p. 366.

Imperishable Ornaments Versus Gold or Pearls. There is an ornament that will never perish, that will promote the happiness of all around us in this life, and will shine with undimmed luster in the immortal future. It is the adorning of a meek and lowly spirit. God has bidden us wear the richest dress upon the soul. . . . Instead of seeking golden ornaments for the exterior, an earnest effort would be put forth to secure that wisdom which is of more value than fine gold. *Ibid.,* vol. 4, pp. 643, 644.

Of how little value are gold or pearls or costly array in comparison with the loveliness of Christ. Natural loveliness consists in symmetry, or the harmonious proportion of parts, each with the other; but spiritual loveliness consists in the harmony or likeness of our souls to Jesus. This will make its possessor more precious than fine gold, even the golden wedge of Ophir. The grace of Christ is indeed a priceless adornment. It elevates and ennobles its possessor and reflects beams of glory upon others, attracting them also to the Source of light and blessing. *Review and Herald,* Dec., 6, 1881.

The Attractiveness of Genuine Beauty. There is a natural tendency with all to be sentimental rather than practical. In view of this fact, it is important that parents, in the education of their children, should direct and train their minds to love truth, duty, and self-denial, and to possess noble independence, to choose to be right, if the majority choose to be wrong. . . .

If they preserve to themselves sound constitutions and amiable tempers, they will possess true beauty that they can wear with a divine grace. And they will have no need to be adorned with artificials, for these are always expressive of an absence of the inward adorning of true moral worth. A beautiful character is of value in the sight of God. Such beauty will attract, but not mislead. Such charms are fast colors; they never fade. *Signs of the Times,* Dec. 9, 1875.

The pure religion of Jesus requires of its followers the simplicity of natural beauty and the polish of natural refinement and elevated purity, rather than the artificial and false. *Testimonies for the Church,* vol. 3, p. 375.

Teach Children to Recognize Sensible Dress. Let us be faithful to the duties of the home life. Let your children understand that obedience must reign there. Teach them to distinguish between that which is sensible and that which is foolish in the matter of dress, and furnish them with clothes that are neat and simple. As a people who are preparing for the soon return of Christ, we should give to the world an example of modest dress in contrast with the prevailing fashion of the day. Talk these things over, and plan wisely what you will do; then carry out your plans in your families. Determine to be guided by higher principles than the notions and desires of your children. Manuscript 45, 1911.

If our hearts are united with Christ's heart, . . . nothing will be put upon the person to attract attention or to create controversy. *Testimonies to Ministers and Gospel Workers,* p. 131.

Provide Becoming Garments Appropriate for Age and Station in Life. My sister, bind your children to your heart by affection. Give them proper care and attention in all things. Furnish them with becoming garments, that they may not be mortified by their appearance, for this would be injurious to their self-respect. . . . It is always right to be neat and to be clad appropriately, in a manner becoming to your age and station in life. *Testimonies for the Church,* vol. 4, p. 142.

The Body Should Not Be Constricted. The dress should fit easily, obstructing neither the circulation of the blood nor a free, full, natural respiration. The feet should be suitably protected from cold and damp. Clad in this way, we can take exercise in the open air, even in the dew of morning or evening, or after a fall of rain or snow, without fear of taking cold. *Christian Temperance and Bible Hygiene,* pp. 89, 90.

The Dress of Young Children. If the dress of the child combines warmth, protection, and comfort, one of the chief causes of irritation and restlessness will be removed. The little one will have better health, and the mother will not find the care of the child so heavy a tax upon her strength and time.

Tight bands or waists hinder the action of the heart and lungs and should be avoided. No part of the body should at any time be made uncomfortable by clothing that compresses any organ or restricts its freedom of movement. The clothing of all children should be loose enough to admit of the freest and fullest respiration, and so arranged that the shoulders will support its weight. *The Ministry of Healing,* p. 382.

Let the Extremities Be Properly Clothed. Special attention should be given to the extremities, that they may be as thoroughly clothed as the chest and the region over the heart, where is the greatest amount of heat. Parents who dress their children with the extremities naked, or nearly so, are sacrificing the health and lives of their children to fashion. If these parts are not so warm as the body, the circulation is not equalized. When the extremities, which are remote from the vital organs, are not properly clad, the blood is driven to the head, causing headache or nosebleed; or there is a sense of fullness about the chest, producing cough or palpitation of the heart, on account of too much blood in that locality; or the stomach has too much blood, causing indigestion.

In order to follow the fashions, mothers dress their children with limbs nearly naked; and the blood is chilled back from its natural course and thrown upon the internal organs, breaking up the circulation and producing disease. The limbs were not formed by our Creator to endure exposure, as was the face. The Lord provided, . . . also, large veins and nerves for the limbs and feet, to contain a large amount of the current of human life, that the limbs might be uniformly as warm as the body. They should be so thoroughly clothed as to induce the blood to the extremities.

Satan invented the fashions which leave the limbs exposed, chilling back the life current from its original course. And parents bow at the shrine of fashion and so clothe their children that the nerves and veins become contracted, and do not answer the purpose that God designed they should. The result is habitually cold feet and hands. Those parents who follow fashion instead of reason will have an account to render to God for thus robbing their children of health. Even life itself is frequently sacrificed to the god of fashion. *Testimonies for the Church,* vol. 2, pp. 531, 532.

A Distinction in Dress of Men and Women. There is an increasing tendency to have women in their dress and appearance as near like the other sex as possible and to fashion their dress very much like that of men, but God pronounces it abomination. "In like manner also, that women adorn themselves in modest apparel, with shamefacedness and sobriety." 1 Timothy 2:9. . . .

God designed that there should be a plain distinction between the dress of men and women, and has considered the matter of sufficient importance to give explicit directions in regard to it; for the same dress worn by both sexes would cause confusion and great increase of crime. *Ibid.,* vol. 1, pp. 457–460.

Dressing for Church. Let none dishonor God's sanctuary by their showy apparel. *Ibid.,* vol. 5, p. 499.

All should be taught to be neat, clean, and orderly in their dress, but not to indulge in that external adorning which is wholly inappropriate for the sanctuary. There should be no display of the apparel, for this encourages irreverence. The attention of the people is often called to this or that fine article of dress, and thus thoughts are intruded that should have no place in the hearts of the worshipers. God is to be the subject of thought, the object of worship; and anything that attracts the mind from the solemn, sacred service is an offense to Him. The parading of bows and ribbons, ruffles and feathers, and gold and silver ornaments is a species of idolatry and is wholly inappropriate for the sacred service of God. *Ibid.*

Some receive the idea that in order to carry out that separation from the world that the Word of God requires, they must be neglectful of their apparel. There is a class of sisters who think they are carrying out the principle of nonconformity to the world by wearing an ordinary sun-bonnet, and the same dress worn by them through the week, upon the Sabbath when appearing in the assembly of the saints to engage in the worship of God. And some men who profess to be Christians view the matter of dress in the same light. These persons assemble with God's people upon the Sabbath, with their clothing dusty and soiled, and even with gaping rents in their garments, which are placed upon their persons in a slovenly manner.

This class, if they had an engagement to meet a friend honored by the world, by whom they wished to be especially favored, would exert themselves to appear in his presence with the best apparel that could be obtained; for this friend would feel insulted were they to come into his presence with their hair uncombed and garments uncleanly and in disorder. Yet these persons think that it is no matter in what dress they appear or what is the condition of their persons when they meet upon the Sabbath to worship the great God. *Review and Herald,* Jan. 30, 1900.

Dress Not to Be Made a Subject of Controversy. There is no need to make the dress question the main point of your religion. There is something richer to talk of. Talk of Christ; and when the heart is converted, every-thing that is out of harmony with the Word of God will drop off. *Evangelism,* p. 272.

It is not your dress that makes you of value in the Lord's sight. It is the inward adorning, the graces of the Spirit, the kind word, the thoughtful consideration for others that God values. *Counsels on Stewardship,* p. 301.

None to Be Conscience for Another, but Set a Worthy Example. Do not encourage a class who center their religion in dress. Let each one study the plain teachings of the Scriptures as to simplicity and plainness of dress and by faithful obedience to those teachings strive to set a worthy example to the world and to those new in the faith. God does not want any one person to be conscience for another.

Talk of the love and humility of Jesus, but do not encour-age the brethren and sisters to engage in picking flaws in the dress or appearance of one another. Some take delight in this work; and when their minds are turned in this direction, they begin to feel that they must become church tinkers. They climb upon the judgment seat, and as soon as they see one of their brethren and sisters, they look to find something to crit-icize. This is one of the most effectual means of becoming narrow-minded and of dwarfing spiritual growth. God would have them step down from the judgment seat, for He has never placed them there. *Historical Sketches of Seventh-day Adventist Foreign Missions,* pp. 122, 123.

The Heart Must Be Right. If we are Christians, we shall follow Christ, even though the path in which we are to walk cuts right across our natural inclinations. There is no use in telling you that you must not wear this or that, for if the love of these vain things is in your heart, your laying off your adornments will only be like cutting the foliage off a tree. The inclinations of the natural heart would again assert themselves. You must have a conscience of your own. *Review and Herald,* May 10, 1892.

Where Many Denominations Lost Their Power. Human reasoning has ever sought to evade or set aside the simple, direct instructions of the Word of God. In every age a majority of the professed followers of Christ have disregarded those precepts which enjoin self-denial and humility, which require modesty and simplicity of conversation, deportment, and apparel. The result has ever been the same—departure from the teachings of the gospel leads to the adoption of the fashions, customs, and principles of the world. Vital godliness gives place to a dead formalism. The presence and power of God, withdrawn from those world-loving circles, are found with a class of humble worshipers, who are willing to obey the teachings of the Sacred Word. Through successive generations this course has been pursued. One after another different denominations have risen and yielding their simplicity, have lost, in a great measure, their early power. *Messages to Young People,* p. 354.

God's Word the Standard. All matters of dress should be strictly guarded, following closely the Bible rule. Fashion has been the goddess who has ruled the outside world, and she often insinuates herself into the church. The church should make the Word of God her standard, and parents should think intelligently upon this subject. When they see their children inclined to follow worldly fashions, they should, like Abraham, resolutely command their households after them. Instead of uniting with the world, connect them with God. *Testimonies for the Church,* vol. 5, p. 499.

★ NOTE: See *Testimonies for the Church,* vol. 1, pp. 135, 136.

CHAPTER 67

The Fascinating
Power of Fashion

Fashion Is a Tyrannical Ruler. Fashion rules the world; and she is a tyrannical mistress, often compelling her devotees to submit to the greatest inconvenience and discomfort. Fashion taxes without reason and collects without mercy. She has a fascinating power and stands ready to criticize and ridicule all who do not follow in her wake. *Christian Temperance and Bible Hygiene,* p. 85.

The rich are ambitious to outdo one another in conforming to her ever-varying styles; the middle and poorer classes strive to approach the standard set by those supposed to be above them. Where means or strength is limited, and the ambition for gentility is great, the burden becomes almost insupportable. With many it matters not how becoming, or even beautiful, a garment may be, let the fashions change, and it must be remade or cast aside. *Education,* p. 246.

Satan, the instigator and prime mover in the ever-changing, never-satisfying decrees of fashion, is always busy devising something new that shall prove an injury to physical and moral health; and he triumphs that his devices succeed so well. Death laughs that the health-destroying folly and blind zeal of the worshipers at fashion's shrine bring them so easily under his dominion. Happiness and the favor of God are laid upon her altar. *Christian Temperance and Bible Hygiene,* p. 85.

The idolatry of dress is a moral disease. It must not be taken over into the new life. In most cases submission to the gospel requirements will demand a decided change in the dress. *Testimonies for the Church,* vol. 6, p. 96.

The Price Some Pay. How contrary to the principles given in the Scriptures are many of the modes of dress that fashion prescribes! Think of the styles that have prevailed for the last few hundreds of years or even for the last few decades. How many . . . would be pronounced inappropriate for a refined, God-fearing, self-respecting woman. . . . Many a poor girl, for the sake of a stylish gown, has deprived herself of warm underwear and paid the penalty with her life. Many another, coveting the display and elegance of the rich, has been enticed into paths of dishonesty and shame. Many a home is deprived of comforts, many a man is driven to embezzlement or bankruptcy, to satisfy the extravagant demands of the wife or children. *The Ministry of Healing,* p. 290.

Salvation Imperiled by Idolatry of Dress. Pride and vanity are manifested everywhere; but those who are inclined to look into the mirror to admire themselves will have little inclination to look into the law of God, the great moral mirror. This idolatry of dress destroys all that is humble, meek, and lovely in character. It consumes the precious hours that should be devoted to meditation, to searching the heart, to the prayerful study of God's Word. . . . No Christian can conform to the demoralizing fashions of the world without imperiling his soul's salvation. *Review and Herald,* Mar. 31, 1891.

Love of Display Demoralizes the Home. Aided by the grace of Christ, women are capable of doing a great and grand work. For this reason Satan works with his devices to invent fashionable dress, that love of display may so absorb the mind and heart and affection of even professed Christian mothers in this age, that they have no time to give to the education and training of their children or to the cultivation of their own minds and characters, that they may be examples to their children, patterns of good works. When Satan secures the time and affections of the mother, he is fully aware of how much he has gained. In nine cases out of ten he has secured the devotion of the whole family to dress and frivolous display. He reckons the children as among his spoils, for he has captivated the mother. Manuscript 43, 1900.

Little children hear more of dress than of their salvation, . . . for the mother is more familiar with fashion than with her Saviour. *Testimonies for the Church,* vol. 4, p. 643.

Parents and children are robbed of that which is best and sweetest and truest in life. For fashion's sake they are cheated out of a preparation for the life to come. *The Ministry of Healing,* p. 291.

Not Brave Enough to Stem the Tide. Many of the mother's burdens are the result of her effort to keep pace with the fashions of the day. Terrible is the effect of these fashions on the physical, mental, and moral health. Lacking the courage to stand firm for the right, women allow the current of popular feeling to draw them on in its wake. . . . Too often professedly Christian mothers sacrifice principle to their desire to follow the multitude who make fashion their god. Conscience protests, but they are not brave enough to take a decided stand against the wrong. *Review and Herald,* Nov. 17, 1904.

Parents—Take Care. Parents frequently dress their children in extravagant garments, with much display of ornaments, then openly admire the effect of their apparel and compliment them on their appearance. These foolish parents would be filled with consternation if they could see how Satan seconds their efforts and urges them on to greater follies. *Pacific Health Journal,* January 1890.

A Problem That Faces Many Mothers. Your daughters are inclined, if they see a dress different from that which they have, to desire a dress similar to that. Or perhaps they want something else that they see others have, which you do not feel would be in accordance with your faith to grant them. Will you allow them to tease this thing out of you, letting them mold you instead of molding them according to the principles of the gospel? Our children are very precious in the sight of God. Let us teach them the Word of God and train them in His ways. It is your privilege to teach your children to live so that they will have the commendation of Heaven. . . .

Let us not encourage our children to follow the fashions of the world; and if we will be faithful in giving them a right training, they will not do this. . . . The fashions of the world often take a ridiculous form, and you must take a firm position against them. Manuscript 45, 1911.

The Fruitage of the Love of Display. Love of dress and pleasure is wrecking the happiness of thousands. And some of those who profess to love and keep the commandments of God ape this class as near as they possibly can and retain the Christian name. Some of the young are so eager for display that they are even willing to give up the Christian name, if they can only follow out their inclination for vanity of dress and love of pleasure. *Testimonies for the Church,* vol. 3, p. 366.

Families who spend much time in dressing for display may be likened to the fig tree that Christ saw from afar. This fig tree flaunted its flourishing branches in the very face of justice; but when Christ came to look for fruit, He searched from the topmost twig to the lowest boughs and found nothing but leaves. It is fruit that He hungers for; fruit He must have. Manuscript 67, 1903.

Unsatisfying to Daughters of God. There is enough necessary and important labor in this world of need and suffering without wasting precious moments for ornamentation or
display. Daughters of the heavenly King, members of the
royal family, will feel a burden of responsibility to attain to a
higher life, that they may be brought into close connection
with Heaven and work in unison with the Redeemer of the
world. Those who are engaged in this work will not be satisfied with the fashions and follies which absorb the mind and
affections of women in these last days. If they are indeed the
daughters of God, they will be partakers of the divine nature.
They will be stirred with deepest pity, as was their divine
Redeemer, as they see the corrupting influences in society.
They will be in sympathy with Christ and in their sphere, as
they have ability and opportunity, will work to save perishing souls, as Christ worked in His exalted sphere for the benefit of man. *Testimonies for the Church,* vol. 3, pp. 483, 484.

PRESERVING MORAL INTEGRITY

CHAPTER 68

Prevalence of Corrupting Vices

An Age of Abounding Iniquity. We live amid the perils of the last days. Because iniquity abounds, the love of many waxes cold. The word "many" refers to the professed followers of Christ. They are affected by the prevailing iniquity and backslide from God, but it is not necessary that they should be thus affected. The cause of this declension is that they do not stand clear from this iniquity. The fact that their love of God is waxing cold because iniquity abounds shows that they are, in some sense, partakers in this iniquity, or it would not affect their love for God and their zeal and fervor in this cause. *Testimonies for the Church,* vol. 2, p. 346.

Influence of Debasing Books and Pictures. Many of the young are eager for books. They read everything they can obtain. Exciting love stories and impure pictures have a corrupting influence. Novels are eagerly perused by many; and, as the result, their imagination becomes defiled. In the cars photographs of females in a state of nudity are frequently circulated for sale. These disgusting pictures are also found in daguerrean saloons [photo shops] and are hung upon the walls of those who deal in engravings. This is an age when corruption is teeming everywhere. The lust of the eye and corrupt passions are aroused by beholding and by reading. The heart is corrupted through the imagination. The mind takes pleasure in contemplating scenes which awaken the lower and baser passions. These vile images, seen through defiled imagination, corrupt the morals and prepare the deluded, infatuated beings to give loose rein to lustful passions. Then follow sins and crimes which drag beings formed in the image of God down to a level with the beasts, sinking them at last in perdition. *Ibid.,* p. 410.

Licentiousness the Special Sin. A terrible picture of the condition of the world has been presented before me. Immorality abounds everywhere. Licentiousness is the special sin of this age. Never did vice lift its deformed head with such boldness as now. The people seem to be benumbed, and the lovers of virtue and true goodness are nearly discouraged by its boldness, strength, and prevalence. *Ibid.,* p. 346.

I was referred to Romans 1:18-32, as a true description of the world previous to the second appearing of Christ. *Appeal to Mothers,* p. 27.

It is sin, not trial and suffering, which separates God from His people and renders the soul incapable of enjoying and glorifying Him. It is sin that is destroying souls. Sin and vice exist in Sabbathkeeping families. *Testimonies for the Church,* vol. 2, pp. 390, 391.

Satan's Attack on Youth. It is the special work of Satan in these last days to take possession of the minds of youth, to corrupt the thoughts and inflame the passions; for he knows that by so doing he can lead to impure actions, and thus all the noble faculties of the mind will become debased, and he can control them to suit his own purposes. *Christian Temperance and Bible Hygiene,* p. 136.

An Index to the Future of Society. The youth of today are a sure index to the future of society; and as we view them, what can we hope for that future? The majority are fond of amusement and averse to work. . . . They have but little self-control and become excited and angry on the slightest occasion. Very many in every age and station of life are without principle or conscience; and with their idle, spendthrift habits they are rushing into vice and are corrupting society, until our world is becoming a second Sodom. If the appetites and passions were under the control of reason and religion, society would present a widely different aspect. God never designed that the present woeful condition of things should exist; it has been brought about through the gross violation of nature's laws. *Ibid., p. 45.*

The Problems of Self-abuse. Some who make a high profession do not understand the sin of self-abuse and its sure results. Long-established habit has blinded their understanding. They do not realize the exceeding sinfulness of this degrading sin. *Testimonies for the Church,* vol. 2, p. 347.

Youth and children of both sexes engage in moral pollution and practice this disgusting, soul-and-body-destroying vice. Many professed Christians are so benumbed by the same practice that their moral sensibilities cannot be aroused to understand that it is sin, and that if continued its sure results will be utter shipwreck of body and mind. Man, the noblest being upon the earth, formed in the image of God, transforms himself into a beast! He makes himself gross and corrupt. Every Christian will have to learn to restrain his passions and be controlled by principle. Unless he does this, he is unworthy of the Christian name. *Ibid.*

Moral pollution has done more than every other evil to cause the race to degenerate. It is practiced to an alarming extent and brings on disease of almost every description. Even very small children, infants, being born with natural irritability of the sexual organs, find momentary relief in handling them, which only increases the irritation and leads to a repetition of the act, until a habit is established which increases with their growth. *Ibid.,* p. 391.

Lustful Propensities Are Inherited. Parents do not generally suspect that their children understand anything about this vice. In very many cases the parents are the real sinners. They have abused their marriage privileges and by indulgence have strengthened their animal passions. And as these have strengthened, the moral and intellectual faculties have become weak. The spiritual has been overborne by the brutish. Children are born with the animal propensities largely developed, the parents' own stamp of character having been given to them. . . . Children born to these parents will almost invariably take naturally to the disgusting habits of secret vice. . . . The sins of the parents will be visited upon their children, because the parents have given them the stamp of their own lustful propensities. *Ibid.*

A Bewitching Slavery. I have felt deeply as I have seen the powerful influence of animal passions in controlling men and women of no ordinary intelligence and ability. They would be capable of engaging in a good work, of exerting a powerful influence, were they not enslaved by base passions. My confidence in humanity has been terribly shaken.

I have been shown that persons of apparently good deportment, not taking unwarrantable liberties with the other sex, were guilty of practicing secret vice nearly every day of their lives. They have not refrained from this terrible sin even while most solemn meetings have been in session. They have listened to the most solemn, impressive discourses upon the judgment, which seemed to bring them before the tribunal of God, causing them to fear and quake; yet hardly an hour would elapse before they would be engaged in their favorite, bewitching sin, polluting their own bodies. They were such slaves to this awful crime that they seemed devoid of power to control their passions. We have labored for some earnestly, we have entreated, we have wept and prayed over them; yet we have known that right amid all our earnest effort and distress, the force of sinful habit has obtained the mastery, and these sins have been committed. *Ibid.,* pp. 468, 469.

Knowledge of Vice Is Spread by Its Victims. Those who have become fully established in this soul-and-body-destroying vice can seldom rest until their burden of secret evil is imparted to those with whom they associate. Curiosity is at once aroused, and the knowledge of vice is passed from youth to youth, from child to child, until there is scarcely one to be found ignorant of the practice of this degrading sin. *Ibid.,* p. 392.

One corrupt mind can sow more evil seed in a short period of time than many can root out in a whole lifetime. *Ibid.,* p. 403.

CHAPTER 69

Effects of Harmful Practices

Vital Energy Is Depleted. The practice of secret habits surely destroys the vital forces of the system. All unnecessary vital action will be followed by corresponding depression. Among the young the vital capital, the brain, is so severely taxed at an early age that there is a deficiency and great exhaustion, which leaves the system exposed to disease of various kinds. *Appeal to Mothers,* p. 28.

Foundation Laid for Various Diseases Later in Life. If the practice is continued from the ages of fifteen and upward, nature will protest against the abuse she has suffered, and continues to suffer, and will make them pay the penalty for the transgression of her laws, especially from the ages of thirty to forty-five, by numerous pains in the system and various diseases, such as affection of the liver and lungs, neuralgia, rheumatism, affection of the spine, diseased kidneys, and cancerous humors. Some of nature's fine machinery gives way, leaving a heavier task for the remaining to perform, which disorders nature's fine arrangement; and there is often a sudden breaking down of the constitution, and death is the result. *Ibid.,* p. 18.

The Sixth Commandment Is Thoughtlessly Violated. To take one's life instantly is no greater sin in the sight of heaven than to destroy it gradually, but surely. Persons who bring upon themselves sure decay, by wrongdoing, will suffer the penalty here, and without a thorough repentance, will not be admitted into heaven hereafter any sooner than the one who destroys life

444

instantly. The will of God establishes the connection between cause and its effects. *Ibid.,* p. 26.

Pure-minded Also Subject to Disease. We do not include all the youth who are feeble as guilty of wrong habits. There are those who are pure-minded and conscientious who are sufferers from different causes over which they have no control. *Ibid.,* p. 23.

The Mental Powers Are Weakened. Fond and indulgent parents will sympathize with their children because they fancy their lessons are too great a task, and that their close application to study is ruining their health. True, it is not advisable to crowd the minds of the young with too many and too difficult studies. But, parents, have you looked no deeper into this matter than merely to adopt the idea suggested by your children? Have you not given too ready credence to the apparent reason for their indisposition? It becomes parents and guardians to look beneath the surface for the cause. *Testimonies for the Church,* vol. 4, pp. 96, 97.

The minds of some of these children are so weakened that they have but one half or one third of the brilliancy of intellect that they might have had, had they been virtuous and pure. They have thrown it away in self-abuse. *Ibid.,* vol. 2, p. 361.

High Resolve and Spiritual Life Destroyed. Secret vice is the destroyer of high resolve, earnest endeavor, and strength of will to form a good religious character. All who have any true sense of what is embraced in being a Christian know that the followers of Christ are under obligation as His disciples to bring all their passions, their physical powers and mental faculties into perfect subordination to His will. Those who are controlled by their passions cannot be followers of Christ. They are too much devoted to the service of their master, the originator of every evil, to leave their corrupt habits and choose the service of Christ. *Appeal to Mothers,* pp. 9, 10.

Religion May Be Formal, but It Is Destitute. Some who profess to be followers of Christ know that they are sinning against God and ruining their health, yet they are slaves to their own corrupt passions. They feel a guilty conscience and have less and less inclination to approach God in secret prayer. They may keep up the form of religion, yet be destitute of the grace of God in the heart. They have no devotedness to His service, no trust in Him, no living to His glory, no pleasure in His ordinances, and no delight in Him. *Ibid.,* p. 25.

Power of Self-government Seems Lost. Some will acknowledge the evil of sinful indulgences, yet will excuse themselves by saying that they cannot overcome their passions. This is a terrible admission for any person to make who names Christ. "Let everyone that nameth the name of Christ depart from iniquity." Why is this weakness? It is because the animal propensities have been strengthened by exercise, until they have gained the ascendancy over the higher powers. Men and women lack principle. They are dying spiritually, because they have so long pampered their natural appetites that their power of self-government seems gone. The lower passions of their nature have taken the reins, and that which should be the governing power has become the servant of corrupt passion. The soul is held in lowest bondage. Sensuality has quenched the desire for holiness and withered spiritual prosperity. *Testimonies for the Church,* vol. 2, p. 348.

Communication With Heaven Is Severed. Solemn messages from Heaven cannot forcibly impress the heart that is not fortified against the indulgence of this degrading vice. The sensitive nerves of the brain have lost their healthy tone by morbid excitation to gratify an unnatural desire for sensual indulgence. The brain nerves which communicate with the entire system are the only medium through which Heaven can communicate to man and affect his inmost life. Whatever disturbs the circulation of the electric currents in the nervous system lessens the strength of the vital powers, and the result is a deadening of the sensibilities of the mind. In consideration of these facts, how important that ministers and people who profess godliness should stand forth clear and untainted from this soul-debasing vice! *Ibid.,* p. 347.

Some Are Remorseful, but Self-respect Is Lost. The effect of such debasing habits is not the same upon all minds. There are some children who have the moral powers largely developed, who, by associating with children that practice self-abuse, become initiated into this vice. The effect upon such will be too frequently to make them melancholy, irritable, and jealous; yet such may not lose their respect for religious worship and may not show special infidelity in regard to spiritual things. They will at times suffer keenly from feelings of remorse, and will feel degraded in their own eyes, and lose their self-respect. *Ibid.,* p. 392.

The Mind May Be Fortified Against Temptation. Moral power is exceedingly weak when it comes in conflict with established habits. Impure thoughts have control of the imagination, and temptation is almost irresistible. If the mind were accustomed to contemplate elevating subjects, the imagination trained to behold pure and holy things, it would be fortified against temptation. It would linger upon the heavenly, the pure, the sacred, and could not be attracted to the base, corrupt, and vile. *Christian Temperance and Bible Hygiene,* p. 135.

Become Intelligent on These Things. Indulgence of the baser passions will lead very many to shut their eyes to the light, for they fear that they will see sins which they are unwilling to forsake. All may see if they will. If they choose darkness rather than light, their criminality will be none the less. Why do not men and women read and become intelligent upon these things, which so decidedly affect their physical, intellectual, and moral strength? God has given you a habitation to care for and preserve in the best condition for His service and glory. Your bodies are not your own. "What! know ye not that your body is the temple of the Holy Ghost, which is in you, which ye have of God, and ye are not your own? For ye are bought with a price; therefore glorify God in your body, and in your spirit, which are God's." "Know ye not that ye are the temple of God, and that the Spirit of God dwelleth in you? If any man defile the temple of God, him shall God destroy; for the temple of God is holy, which temple ye are." *Testimonies for the Church,* vol. 2, pp. 352, 353.

CHAPTER 70

Cautions and Counsels

Many Cases Have Been Revealed. Many cases have been presented before me, and as I have had a view of their inner lives, my soul has been sick and disgusted with the rotten-heartedness of human beings who profess godliness and talk of translation to heaven. I have frequently asked myself, Whom can I trust? Who is free from iniquity? *Testimonies for the Church,* vol. 2, p. 349.

I am filled with horror as the condition of families professing present truth is opened before me. The profligacy of youth and even children is almost incredible. Parents do not know that secret vice is destroying and defacing the image of God in their children. The sins which characterized the Sodomites exist among them. The parents are responsible, for they have not educated their children to love and obey God. They have not restrained them, nor diligently taught them the way of the Lord. They have allowed them to go out and to come in when they chose, and to associate with worldlings. These worldly influences which counteract parental teaching and authority are to be found largely in so-called good society. By their dress, looks, amusements, they surround themselves with an atmosphere which is opposed to Christ.

Our only safety is to stand as God's peculiar people. We must not yield one inch to the customs and fashions of this degenerate age, but stand in moral independence, making no compromise with its corrupt and idolatrous practices. *Ibid.,* vol. 5, p. 78.

The Ignorant to Be Enlightened. No matter how high a person's profession, those who are willing to be employed in gratifying the lust of the flesh cannot be Christians. As servants of Christ their employment and meditations and pleasure should consist in things more excellent. Many are ignorant of the sinfulness of these habits and their certain results. Such need to be enlightened. *Appeal to Mothers,* p. 25.

One Who Requested Prayer for Healing. My husband and I once attended a meeting where our sympathies were enlisted for a brother who was a great sufferer with the phthisic. He was pale and emaciated. He requested the prayers of the people of God. He said that his family were sick, and that he had lost a child. He spoke with feeling of his bereavement. He said that he had been waiting for some time to see Brother and Sister White. He had believed that if they would pray for him, he would be healed. After the meeting closed, the brethren called our attention to the case. They said that the church was assisting them, that his wife was sick, and his child had died. The brethren had met at his house and united in praying for the afflicted family. We were much worn and had the burden of labor upon us during the meeting and wished to be excused. I had resolved not to engage in prayer for anyone, unless the Spirit of the Lord should dictate in the matter. . . .

That night we bowed in prayer and presented his case before the Lord. We entreated that we might know the will of God concerning him. All we desired was that God might be glorified. Would the Lord have us pray for this afflicted man? We left the burden with the Lord and retired to rest. In a dream the case of that man was clearly presented. His course from his childhood up was shown, and that if we should pray, the Lord would not hear us; for he regarded iniquity in his heart. The next morning the man came for us to pray for him. We took him aside and told him we were sorry to be compelled to refuse his request. I related my dream, which he acknowledged was true. He had practiced self-abuse from his boyhood up, and he had continued the practice during his married life, but said he would try to break himself of it. This man had a long-established habit to overcome. He was in the middle age of life. His moral principles were so weak that when brought in conflict with long-established indulgence, they were overcome. . . .

Here was a man debasing himself daily and yet daring to venture into the presence of God and ask an increase of strength which he had vilely squandered, and which, if granted, he would consume upon his lust. What forbearance has God! If He should deal with man according to his corrupt ways, who could live in His sight? What if we had been less cautious and carried the case of this man before God while he was practicing iniquity, would the Lord have heard? Would He have answered? "For thou art not a God that hath pleasure in wickedness: neither shall evil dwell with thee. The foolish shall not stand in thy sight; thou hatest all workers of iniquity." . . .

This is not a solitary case. Even the marriage relation was not sufficient to preserve this man from the corrupt habits of his youth. I wish I could be convinced that such cases as the one I have presented are rare, but I know they are frequent. *Testimonies for the Church,* vol. 2, pp. 349-351.

A Self-murderer. A Mr. ——— professed to be a devoted follower of Christ. He was in very feeble health. Our feelings of sympathy were called out in his behalf. . . .

His case was shown me in vision. I saw that he was deceived in regard to himself, that he was not in favor with God. He had practiced self-abuse until he was a mere wreck of humanity. This vice was shown me as an abomination in the sight of God. . . .

[He] had practiced these habits so long he seemed to have lost the control of himself. He was naturally a smart man, possessing more than common abilities. But how were all his powers of body and mind brought into subjection by Satan and consumed upon his altar!

This man had gone so far he seemed to be left of God. He would go into the woods and spend days and nights in fasting and prayer that he might overcome this great sin, and then would return to his old habits. God did not hear his prayers. He asked God to do for him what had been in his power to do for himself. He had vowed to God, time and again, and had as often broken his vows and given himself up to his own corrupt lust, until God had left him to work his own ruin. He has since died. He was a self-murderer. The purity of heaven will never be marred with his society. *Appeal to Mothers,* pp. 24-28.

Appeal to an Indulged Daughter.* Your mind is impure. You were relieved from care and labor altogether too long. Household duties would have been one of the richest blessings that you could have had. Weariness would not have injured you one tenth as much as have your lascivious thoughts and conduct. You have received incorrect ideas in regard to girls and boys associating together, and it has been very congenial to your mind to be in the company of the boys. You are not pure in heart and mind. You have been injured by reading love stories and romances, and your mind has been fascinated by impure thoughts. Your imagination has become corrupt, until you seem to have no power to control your thoughts. Satan leads you captive as he pleases. . . .

Your conduct has not been chaste, modest, or becoming. You have not had the fear of God before your eyes. You have so often dissembled in order to accomplish your plans that you bear a violated conscience. My dear girl, unless you stop just where you are, ruin is surely before you. Cease your daydreaming, your castle-building. Stop your thoughts from running in the channel of folly and corruption.

You cannot safely associate with the boys. A tide of temptation is roused and surges in your breast, having a tendency to uproot principle, female virtue, and true modesty. If you go on in your willful, headstrong course, what will be your fate? . . . You are in danger, for you are just upon the point of sacrificing your eternal interests at the altar of passion. Passion is obtaining positive control of your entire being—passion of what quality? Of a base, destructive nature. By yielding to it, you will embitter the lives of your parents, bring sadness and shame to your sisters, sacrifice your own character, and forfeit heaven and a glorious immortal life. Are you ready to do this? . . .

You are forward. You love the boys and love to make them the theme of your conversation. "Out of the abundance of the heart the mouth speaketh." Habits have become powerful to control you, and you have learned to deceive in order to carry out your purposes and accomplish your desires. I do not consider your case hopeless; if I did, my pen would not be tracing these lines. In the strength of God, you can redeem the past. . . .

Keep clear of the boys. In their society your temptations become earnest and powerful. Put marriage out of your girl's head. You are in no sense fit for this. You need years of experience before you can be qualified to understand the duties and take up the burdens of married life. Positively guard your thoughts, your passions, and your affections. Do not degrade these to minister to lust. Elevate them to purity; devote them to God.

You may become a prudent, modest, virtuous girl, but not without earnest effort. You must watch, you must pray, you must meditate, you must investigate your motives and your actions. Closely analyze your feelings and your acts. Would you, in the presence of your father, perform an impure action? No, indeed. But you do this in the presence of your heavenly Father, who is so much more exalted, so holy, so pure. Yes; you corrupt your own body in the presence of the pure, sinless angels and in the presence of Christ; and you continue to do this irrespective of conscience, irrespective of the light and warnings given you. Remember, a record is made of all your acts. You must meet again the most secret things of your life. . . .

Again I warn you as one who must meet these lines in that day when the case of everyone shall be decided. Yield yourself to Christ without delay; He alone, by the power of His grace, can redeem you from ruin. He alone can bring your moral and mental powers into a state of health. Your heart may be warm with the love of God; your understanding, clear and mature; your conscience, illuminated, quick, and pure; your will, upright and sanctified, subject to the control of the Spirit of God. You can make yourself what you choose. If you will now face right about, cease to do evil and learn to do well, then you will be happy indeed; you will be successful in the battles of life and rise to glory and honor in the better life than this. "Choose you this day whom ye will serve." *Testimonies for the Church,* vol. 2, pp. 559-565.

Satan Works While Parents Sleep. This is a fast age. Little boys and girls commence paying attentions to one another when they should both be in the nursery, taking lessons in modesty of deportment. What is the effect of this common mixing up? Does it increase chastity in the youth who thus gather together? No, indeed! It increases the first lustful passions; after such meetings the youth are crazed by the devil and give themselves up to their vile practices.

Parents are asleep and know not that Satan has planted his hellish banner right in their households. What, I was led to inquire, will become of the youth in this corrupt age? I repeat, Parents are asleep. The children are infatuated with a lovesick sentimentalism, and the truth has no power to correct the wrong. What can be done to stay the tide of evil? Parents can do much if they will.

If a young girl just entering her teens is accosted with familiarity by a boy of her own age, or older, she should be taught to so resent this that no such advances will ever be repeated. When a girl's company is frequently sought by boys or young men, something is wrong. That young girl needs a mother to show her her place, to restrain her, and teach her what belongs to a girl of her age.

The corrupting doctrine which has prevailed, that, as viewed from a health standpoint, the sexes must mingle together, has done its mischievous work. When parents and guardians manifest one tithe of the shrewdness which Satan possesses, then can this association of sexes be nearer harmless. As it is, Satan is most successful in his efforts to bewitch the minds of the youth; and the mingling of boys and girls only increases the evil twenty-fold. *Ibid.,* pp. 482, 283.

The Picture Is Not Colored. Do not deceive yourselves into the belief that, after all, this matter is placed before you in an exaggerated light. I have not colored the picture. I have stated facts which will bear the test of the judgment. Awake! Awake! I beseech you, before it shall be too late for wrongs to be righted, and you and your children perish in the general ruin. Take hold of the solemn work, and bring to your aid every ray of light you can gather than has shone upon your pathway, and that you have not cherished; and, together with the aid of the light now shining, commence an investigation of your life and character as if you were before the tribunal of God. *Ibid.,* p. 401.

Until parents arouse, there is no hope for their children. *Ibid.,* p. 406.

---

* NOTE. These extracts from a letter to a self-willed girl who was practicing secret vice.

CHAPTER 71

Parental Vigilance and Help

Parents to Teach Self-control From Infancy. How important that we teach our children self-control from their very infancy, and teach them the lesson of submitting their wills to us. If they should be so unfortunate as to learn wrong habits, not knowing all the evil results, they can be reformed by appealing to their reason and convincing them that such habits ruin the constitution and affect the mind. We should show them that whatever persuasions corrupt persons may use to quiet their awakened fears and lead them to still indulge this pernicious habit, whatever may be their pretense, they are their enemies and the devil's agents. *Appeal to Mothers,* p. 10.

Keep Them Pure—Fortify Their Minds. It is a crime for mothers to allow themselves to remain in ignorance in regard to the habits of their children. If they are pure, keep them so. Fortify their young minds, and prepare them to detest this health-and-soul-destroying vice. *Ibid.,* p. 13.

Satan is controlling the minds of the young, and we must work resolutely and faithfully to save them. Very young children practice this vice, and it grows upon them and strengthens with their years, until every noble faculty of body and soul is being degraded. Many might have been saved if they had been carefully instructed in regard to the influence of this practice upon their health. They were ignorant of the fact that they were bringing much suffering upon themselves. . . .

Mothers, you cannot be too careful in preventing your

children from learning low habits. It is easier to learn evil than to eradicate it after it is learned. *Ibid.,* pp. 10, 11.

Exercise Determined Watchfulness and Close Inquiry. If your children practice this vice, they may be in danger of resorting to falsehood to deceive you. But, mothers, you must not be easily quieted and cease your investigations. You should not let the matter rest until you are fully satisfied. The health and souls of those you love are in peril, which makes this matter of the greatest importance. Determined watchfulness and close inquiry, notwithstanding the attempts to evade and conceal, will generally reveal the true state of the case. Then should the mother faithfully present this subject to them in its true light, showing its degrading downward tendency. Try to convince them that indulgence in this sin will destroy self-respect and nobleness of character, will ruin health and morals; and its foul stain will blot from the soul true love for God and the beauty of holiness. The mother should pursue this matter until she has sufficient evidence that the practice is at an end. *Ibid.,* p. 13, 14.

Avoid Haste and Censure as You Begin. You may inquire, How can we remedy the evils which already exist? How shall we begin the work? If you lack wisdom, go to God; He has promised to give liberally. Pray much, and fervently, for divine aid. One rule cannot be followed in every case. The exercise of sanctified judgment is now needful. Be not hasty and agitated and approach your children with censure. Such a course would only cause rebellion in them. You should feel deeply over any wrong course you have taken, which may have opened a door for Satan to lead your children by his temptations. If you have not instructed them in regard to the violation of the laws of health, blame rests upon you. You have neglected important duty, which result may be seen in the wrong practices of your children. *Ibid., pp.* 20, 21.

Instructing With Self-possession and Sympathy.

Before you engage in the work of teaching your children the lesson of self-control, you should learn it yourself. If you are easily agitated and become impatient, how can you appear reasonable to your children, while instructing them to control their passions? With self-possession and feelings of the deepest sympathy and pity, you should approach your erring children and faithfully present to them the sure work of ruin upon their constitutions if they continue the course they have begun—that as they debilitate the physical and mental, so also the moral must feel the decay, and they are sinning, not only against themselves, but against God.

You should make them feel, if possible, that it is God, the pure and holy God, that they have been sinning against; that the great Searcher of hearts is displeased with their course; that nothing is concealed from Him. If you can so impress your children that they will exercise that repentance which is acceptable to God, that godly sorrow which worketh repentance unto salvation, not to be repented of, the work will be thorough, the reform certain. They will not feel sorrow merely because their sins are known; but they will view their sinful practices in their aggravated character and will be led to confess them to God, without reserve, and will forsake them. They will feel to sorrow for their wrong course, because they have displeased God and sinned against Him and dishonored their bodies before Him who created them and has required them to present their bodies a living sacrifice, holy and acceptable unto Him, which is their reasonable service. *Ibid.,* pp. 21, 22.

Guard the Association of Children. Unless the minds of our children are firmly balanced by religious principle, their morals will become corrupted by the vicious examples with which they come in contact. *Christian Temperance and Bible Hygiene,* p. 134.

Shield them, as faithful mothers should, from becoming contaminated by associating with every young companion. Keep them, as precious jewels, from the corrupting influence of this age. If you are situated so that their intercourse with young associates cannot always be overruled, as you would wish to have it, then let them visit your children in your presence; and in no case allow these associates to lodge in the same bed or even in the same room. It will be far easier to prevent an evil than to cure it afterward. . . .

They [parents] let them visit other young friends, form their own acquaintances, and even go from their parental watch care, some distance from home, where they are allowed to do very much as they please. Satan improves all such opportunities and takes charge of the minds of these children whom mothers ignorantly expose to his artful snares. *Appeal to Mothers,* pp. 13, 14.

The Diet Is Important. You cannot arouse the moral sensibilities of your children while you are not careful in the selection of their food. The tables that parents usually prepare for their children are a snare to them. *Testimonies for the Church,* vol. 2, p. 400.

Indulgent parents do not teach their children self-denial. The very food they place before them is such as to irritate the stomach. The excitement thus produced is communicated to the brain, and as a result the passions are aroused. It cannot be too often repeated that whatever is taken into the stomach affects not only the body, but ultimately the mind as well. Gross and stimulating food fevers the blood, excites the nervous system, and too often dulls the moral perceptions, so that reason and conscience are overborne by the sensual impulses. It is difficult, and often wellnigh impossible, for one who is intemperate in diet to exercise patience and self-control. Hence the special importance of allowing children, whose characters are yet unformed, to have only such food as is healthful and unstimulating. It was in love that our heavenly Father sent the light of health reform to guard against the evils that result from unrestrained indulgence of appetite. *Christian Temperance and Bible Hygiene,* p. 134.

If ever there was a time when the diet should be of the most simple kind, it is now. Meat should not be placed before our children. Its influence is to excite and strengthen the lower passions and has a tendency to deaden the moral powers. *Testimonies for the Church,* vol. 2, p. 352.

Cleanliness Important. Frequent bathing is very beneficial, especially at night, just before retiring, or upon rising in the morning. It will take but a few moments to give the children a bath and to rub them until their bodies are in a glow. This brings the blood to the surface, relieving the brain; and there will be less inclination to indulge in impure practices. Teach the little ones that God is not pleased to see them with unclean bodies and untidy, torn garments. Tell them that He wants them to be pure without and within, that He may dwell with them. *Christian Temperance and Bible Hygiene,* pp. 141, 142.

Clean, Loose-fitting Clothing. Having the clothing neat and clean will be one means of keeping the thoughts pure and sweet. Every article of dress should be plain and simple, without unnecessary adornment, so that it will be but little work to wash and iron it. Especially should every article which comes in contact with the skin be kept clean and free from any offensive odor. Nothing of an irritating character should touch the bodies of children, nor should their clothing be allowed to bind them in any way. If more attention were given to this subject, far less impurity would be practiced. *Ibid.,* p. 142.

Do Not Release From Exercise. They [the youth] are excused from physical exercise to a great degree for fear they will overwork. The parents bear burdens themselves which their children should bear. Overwork is bad, but the result of indolence is more to be dreaded. Idleness leads to the indulgence of corrupt habits. Industry does not weary and exhaust one-fifth part as much as the pernicious habit of self-abuse. If simple, well-regulated labor exhausts your children, be assured, parents, there is something, aside from their labor, which is enervating their systems and producing a sense of constant weariness. Give your children physical labor, which will call into exercise the nerves and muscles. The weariness attending such labor will lessen their inclination to indulge in vicious habits. *Testimonies for the Church,* vol. 2, pp. 348, 349.

Indolence an Open Door to Temptation. Mothers, give your children enough to do. . . . Indolence will not be favorable to physical, mental, or moral health. It throws open the door and invites Satan in, which opportunity he improves, and draws the young into his snares. By indolence not only the moral strength is weakened, and the impulse of passion increased, but Satan's angels take possession of the whole citadel of the mind and compel conscience to surrender to vile passion. We should teach our children habits of patient industry. *Appeal to Mothers,* pp. 18, 19.

God Will Not Leave the Repentant to Perish. You should present encouragements before your children that a merciful God will accept true heart repentance and will bless their endeavors to cleanse themselves from all filthiness of the flesh and spirit. As Satan sees that he is losing control over the minds of your children, he will strongly tempt them and seek to bind them to continue to practice this bewitching vice. But with a firm purpose they must resist Satan's temptations to indulge the animal passions, because it is sin against God. They should not venture on forbidden ground, where Satan can claim control over them. If they in humility entreat God for purity of thought and a refined and sanctified imagination, He will hear them and grant their petitions. God has not left them to perish in their sins, but will help the weak and helpless, if they cast themselves in faith upon Him. *Ibid.,* pp. 22, 23.

CHAPTER 72

The Battle for Reform

Sincere Repentance and Determined Effort Necessary. Those who corrupt their own bodies cannot enjoy the favor of God until they sincerely repent, make an entire reform, and perfect holiness in the fear of the Lord. *Appeal to Mothers,* p. 29.

The only hope for those who practice vile habits is to forever leave them if they place any value upon health here and salvation hereafter. When these habits have been indulged in for quite a length of time, it requires a determined effort to resist temptation and refuse the corrupt indulgence. *Ibid.,* p. 27.

Thoughts Must Be Controlled.[1] You should control your thoughts. This will not be an easy task; you cannot accomplish it without close and even severe effort. . . . If you indulge in vain imaginations, permitting your mind to dwell upon impure subjects, you are, in a degree, as guilty before God as if your thoughts were carried into action. All that prevents the action is the lack of opportunity. Day and night dreaming and castle-building are bad and exceedingly dangerous habits. When once established, it is next to impossible to break up such habits and direct the thoughts to pure, holy, elevated themes. You will have to become a faithful sentinel over your eyes, ears, and all your senses if you would control your mind and prevent vain and corrupt thoughts from staining your soul. The power of grace alone can accomplish this most desirable work. *Testimonies for the Church,* vol. 2, p. 561.

Subject Passions and Affections to Reason.[2] Not only does God require you to control your thoughts, but also your passions and affections. Your salvation depends upon your governing yourself in these things. Passion and affection are powerful agents. If misapplied, if set in operation through wrong motives, if misplaced, they are powerful to accomplish your ruin and leave you a miserable wreck, without God and without hope.

The imagination must be positively and persistently controlled if the passions and affections are made subject to reason, conscience, and character. . . .

Unless you restrain your thoughts, your reading, and your words, your imagination will become hopelessly diseased. Read your Bible attentively, prayerfully, and be guided by its teachings. This is your safety. *Ibid.,* pp. 561-563.

Close Senses Against Evil. Those who would have that wisdom which is from God must become fools in the sinful knowledge of this age in order to be wise. They should shut their eyes that they may see and learn no evil. They should close their ears lest they hear that which is evil, and obtain that knowledge which would stain their purity of thoughts and acts, and guard their tongues lest they utter corrupt communications and guile be found in their mouths. *Appeal to Mothers,* p. 31.

Avoid reading and seeing things which will suggest impure thoughts. Cultivate the moral and intellectual powers. *Testimonies for the Church,* vol. 2, p. 410.

Avoid Inactivity Coupled With Excessive Study. Excessive study, by increasing the flow of blood to the brain, creates morbid excitability that tends to lessen the power of self-control and too often gives sway to impulse or caprice. Thus the door is opened to impurity. The misuse or nonuse of the physical powers is largely responsible for the tide of corruption that is overspreading the world. "Pride, fulness of bread, and abundance of idleness" are as deadly foes to human progress in this generation as when they led to the destruction of Sodom.

Teachers should understand these things and should instruct their pupils in these lines. Teach the students that right living depends on right thinking, and that physical activity is essential to purity of thought. *Education,* p. 209.

No Time for Vacillation. Purity of life and a character molded after the divine Pattern are not obtained without earnest effort and fixed principles. A vacillating person will not succeed in attaining Christian perfection. Such will be weighed in the balances and found wanting. Like a roaring lion, Satan is seeking for his prey. He tries his wiles upon every unsuspecting youth. . . . Satan tells the young that there is time enough yet, that they may indulge in sin and vice this once and never again; but that one indulgence will poison their whole life. Do not once venture on forbidden ground. In this perilous day of evil, when allurements to vice and corruption are on every hand, let the earnest, heartfelt cry of the young be raised to heaven: "Wherewithal shall a young man cleanse his way?" And may his ears be open and his heart inclined to obey the instruction given in the answer, "By taking heed thereto, according to thy word." *Testimonies for the Church,* vol. 2, pp. 408, 409.

All are accountable for their actions while in this world upon probation. All have power to control their actions if they will. If they are weak in virtue and purity of thoughts and acts, they can obtain help from the

Friend of the helpless. Jesus is acquainted with all the weaknesses of human nature, and, if entreated, will give strength to overcome the most powerful temptations. All can obtain this strength if they seek for it in humility. *Appeal to Mothers,* p. 31.

The only safety for the youth in this age of pollution is to make God their trust. Without divine help they will be unable to control human passions and appetites. In Christ is the very help needed, but how few will come to Him for that help. Said Jesus when upon the earth, "Ye will not come to me, that ye might have life." In Christ all can conquer. You can say with the apostle, "Nay, in all these things we are more than conquerors through him that loved us." Again, "But I keep under my body, and bring it into subjection." *Testimonies for the Church,* vol. 2, p. 409.

In Him True Pleasure May Be Found. The only sure safety for our children against every vicious practice is to seek to be admitted into the fold of Christ and to be taken under the watch care of the faithful and true Shepherd. He will save them from every evil, shield them from all dangers, if they will heed His voice. He says, "My sheep hear my voice, . . . and they follow me." In Christ they will find pasture, obtain strength and hope, and will not be troubled with restless longings for something to divert the mind and satisfy the heart. They have found the pearl of great price, and the mind is at peaceful rest. Their pleasures are of a pure, peaceful, elevated, heavenly character. They leave no painful reflections, no remorse. Such pleasures do not impair health or prostrate the mind, but are of a healthful nature.

Communion with and love for God, the practice of holiness, the destruction of sin, are all pleasant. The reading of God's Word will not fascinate the imagination and inflame the passions, like a fictitious storybook, but softens, soothes, elevates, and sanctifies the heart. When in trouble, when assailed by fierce temptations, they have the privilege of prayer. What an exalted privilege! Finite beings, of dust and ashes, admitted through the mediation of Christ, into the audience chamber of the Most High. In such exercises the soul is brought into a sacred nearness with God and is renewed in knowledge and true holiness and fortified against the assaults of the enemy. *Appeal to Mothers,* pp. 23, 24.

---

[1] NOTE. These are further extracts from a letter to the self-willed youth who was practicing secret vice.

[2] NOTE: See note on p. 452.

SECTION 17

AROUSING THE SPIRITUAL POWERS

CHAPTER 73

Responsibility for Eternal Interests

Ours Is a Day of Special Peril for Children. We are living in an unfortunate age for children. A heavy current is setting downward to perdition, and more than childhood's experience and strength is needed to press against this current, and not be borne down by it. The youth generally seem to be Satan's captives, and he and his angels are leading them to certain destruction. Satan and his hosts are warring against the government of God, and all who have a desire to yield their hearts to Him and obey His requirements Satan will try to perplex and overcome with his temptations, that they may become discouraged and give up the warfare. *Testimonies for the Church,* vol. 1, p. 397.

We never needed close connection with God more than we need it today. One of the greatest dangers that besets God's people has ever been from conformity to worldly maxims and customs. The youth especially are in constant peril. Fathers and mothers should be on their guard against the wiles of Satan. While he is seeking to accomplish the ruin of their children, let not parents flatter themselves that there is no particular danger. Let them not give thought and care to the things of this world, while the higher, eternal interests of their children are neglected. *Review and Herald,* June 13, 1882.

Parents in General Are Indifferent. It is a sad thing when parents grow cold in their spiritual life, and, because of waning piety and want of devotion to God, they do not realize the high responsibility that devolves upon them to patiently and thoroughly train their children to keep the way of the Lord. *Signs of the Times,* Sept. 17, 1894.

Parents in general are doing their best to unfit their children for the stern realities of life, for the difficulties that will surround them in the future, when they will be called upon to decide for right or wrong, and when strong temptations will be brought upon them. They will then be found weak where they should be strong. They will waver in principle and duty, and humanity will suffer from their weakness. *Pacific Health Journal,* January 1890.

The All-important Work Is Neglected. One great reason why there is so much evil in the world today is that parents occupy their minds with other things to the exclusion of the work that is all-important—the task of patiently and kindly teaching their children the way of the Lord. *Counsels to Parents, Teachers, and Students,* p. 129.

Mothers may have acquired knowledge of many things, but they have not acquired the essential knowledge unless they have a knowledge of Christ as a personal Saviour. If Christ is in the home, if mothers have made Him their counselor, they will educate their children from their very babyhood in the principles of true religion. *Signs of the Times,* July 22, 1889.

Satan Is Allowed to Control. Because men and women do not obey God, but choose their own way and follow their own perverted imagination, Satan is permitted to set up his hellish banner in their families and make his power felt through babes, children, and youth. His voice and will are expressed in the unsubdued wills and warped characters of the children, and through them he exerts a controlling power and carries out his plans. God is dishonored by the exhibition of perverse tempers, which exclude reverence for Him, and induce obedience to Satan's suggestions. The sin committed by parents in thus permitting Satan to bear sway is beyond conception. *Testimonies for the Church,* vol. 5, p. 325.

Many parents by their training, by their foolish indulgence and pampering of the tastes and appetite, are making themselves responsible for the crooked ways and dispositions of their children. Satan can control the whole being by that disposition to disobey the laws of God. Parents do not, like Abraham, command their households after them. And what is the result? Children and youth are standing under the rebel flag. They will not be ruled, but are determined to follow their own will. The only hope for children is to teach them to deny and not indulge self. Letter 117, 1898.

A Severe Battle Before Undisciplined Children. Children who are thus brought up undisciplined have everything to learn when they profess to be Christ's followers. Their whole religious experience is affected by their bringing up in childhood. The same self-will often appears; there is the same lack of self-denial, the same impatience under reproof, the same love of self and unwillingness to seek counsel of others, or to be influenced by other's judgment, the same indolence, shunning of burdens, lack of bearing responsibilities. All this is seen in their relation to the church. It is possible for such to overcome, but how hard the battle! How severe the conflict! How hard to pass through the course of thorough discipline which is necessary for them to reach the elevation of Christian character! Yet if they overcome at last, they will be permitted to see, before they are translated, how near the precipice of eternal destruction they came, because of the lack of right training in youth, the failure to learn submission in childhood. *Testimonies for the Church,* vol. 1, pp. 219, 220.

Fortify Against Corrupting Influences. Parents, you have taken the responsibility of bringing children into the world without any voice of theirs, and you are responsible for the lives and souls of your children. They have the attractions of the world to fascinate and allure. You can educate them so as to fortify them against its corrupting influence. You can train them to bear life's responsibilities and to realize their obligations to God, truth, and duty, and the bearing that their actions will have upon their future immortal life. *Signs of the Times,* Dec. 9, 1875.

The youth of our day are ignorant of Satan's devices. Parents should therefore be awake in these perilous times, working with perseverance and industry, to shut out the first approach of the foe. They should instruct their children when sitting in the house, or walking by the way, when rising up or lying down. *Signs of the Times,* Feb. 26, 1880.

Eternal vigilance must be exercised, that the children may be led in the paths of righteousness. Satan begins his work upon them from earliest childhood and creates desires for that which God has forbidden. The safety of children depends largely upon the vigilance, watchfulness, and care of the parents over them. *Review and Herald,* Mar. 13, 1894.

Parents should allow nothing to prevent them from giving to their children all the time that is necessary to make them understand what it means to obey and trust the Lord fully. *Counsels to Parents, Teachers, and Students,* p. 129.

Parents, Awake From Your Deathlike Slumber. From the indifference of their parents, many children are left to feel that their parents have no care for their souls. This ought not to be so, but those who have children should so manage their domestic and business affairs that nothing may come in between them and the children that would lessen the parents' influence in directing them to Christ. You should teach your children the lesson of the love of Jesus, that they may be pure in heart, in conduct, and conversation. . . .

The Lord would work upon the hearts of the children if the parents would but cooperate with the divine agencies, but He will not undertake to do that which has been appointed as your part of the work. Parents, you must awake from your deathlike slumber. *Review and Herald,* Oct. 25, 1892.

Our Great Hope Is Home Religion. Parents are asleep. Their children are going to destruction before their eyes, and the Lord would have His messengers present before the people, by precept and example, the necessity of home religion. Urge this matter home upon your congregations. Press the conviction of these solemn duties, so long neglected, home upon the conscience. This will break up the spirit of Pharisaism and resistance to the truth as nothing else can. Religion in the home is our great hope and makes the prospect bright for the conversion of the whole family to the truth of God. Manuscript 21, 1894.

Satan's Power May Be Broken. Parents have a more serious charge than they imagine. The inheritance of children is that of sin. Sin has separated them from God. Jesus gave His life that He might unite the broken links to God. As related to the first Adam, men receive from him nothing but guilt and the sentence of death. But Christ steps in and passes over the ground where Adam fell, enduring every test in man's behalf. . . . Christ's perfect example and the grace of God are given him to enable him to train his sons and daughters to be sons and daughters of God. It is by teaching them, line upon line, precept upon precept, how to give the heart and will up to Christ that Satan's power is broken. Letter 68, 1899.

Fathers and mothers, in full assurance of faith plead with your sons and daughters. Let them not hear one impatient word from your lips. If necessary, make to your children a heartfelt confession for having allowed them to follow in the path of vanity and to displease the Lord, who withheld not His Son from a lost world, that all might receive pardon and forgiveness of sin. . . .

Fathers and mothers who have in various ways indulged your children to their hurt, God desires you to redeem the time. Take heed while it is called today. Letter 66, 1910.

Parents Have the Noblest Missionary Field. Make it your lifework to form the characters of your children according to the divine Pattern. If they ever possess the inward adorning, the ornament of a meek and quiet spirit, it will be because you perseveringly trained them to love the teachings of God's Word and to seek the approval of Jesus above the approbation of the world. *Review and Herald,* Oct. 9, 1883.

As workers for God, our work is to begin with those nearest. It is to begin in our own home. There is no more important missionary field than this. Manuscript 19, 1900.

We need missionary fervor in our homes, that we may bring the Word of life before the members of our families and lead them to seek a home in the kingdom of God. Manuscript 101, 1908.

The management and instruction of children is the noblest missionary work that any man or woman can undertake. *Testimonies for the Church,* vol. 6, p. 205.

Parents as Artists to Shape Living Clay. How earnestly and perseveringly the artist labors to transfer to canvas a perfect likeness of his model; and how diligently the sculptor hews and chisels out the stone into a counterpart of the copy he is following. So the parents should labor to shape, polish, and refine their children after the pattern given them in Christ Jesus. As the patient artist studies, and works, and forms plans to make the results of his labors more perfect, so should the parent consider time well spent that is occupied in training the children for useful lives and fitting them for the immortal kingdom. The artist's work is small and unimportant compared with that of the parent. The one deals with lifeless material, from which he fashions forms of beauty; but the other deals with a human being whose life can be shaped for good or ill, to bless humanity or to curse it; to go out in darkness, or to live forever in a future sinless world. *Pacific Health Journal,* May 1890.

Make Perfection the Goal. Christ was once a little child. For His sake honor the children. Look upon them as a sacred charge, not to be petted and idolized, but to be taught to live pure, noble lives. They are God's property. He loves them, and He calls upon you to cooperate with Him in teaching them to form perfect characters. The Lord requires perfection from His redeemed family. He expects from us the perfection which Christ revealed in His humanity. Fathers and mothers especially need to understand the best methods of training children that they may cooperate with God. Manuscript 19, 1900.

Converted Parents Needed. Day and night I am burdened with the thought of our great need of converted parents. How many there are who need to humble their hearts before God and come into right relation to heaven if they would exert a saving influence over their families. They should know what they must do to inherit eternal life, if they would train their children for the inheritance of the redeemed. Every day they should be receiving the light of heaven into their souls, every day be receiving the impressions of the Holy Spirit upon heart and mind. Every day they should be receiving the Word of truth and letting it control the life. Manuscript 53, 1912.

Great responsibilities rest upon parents, and they should strive earnestly to fulfill their God-appointed mission. When they see the need of bending all the energies of the being to the work of training their children for God, a great deal of the frivolity and unnecessary pretense that is now seen will be put away. They will consider no sacrifice or toil too great that will enable them to prepare to meet the Lord with joy. This is a most precious part of their service as followers of God, and one that they cannot afford to neglect. Manuscript 27, 1911.

Look Constantly to Jesus. Parents, . . . use every spiritual sinew and muscle in the effort to save your little flock. The powers of hell will unite for its destruction, but God will lift up for you a standard against the enemy. Pray much more than you do. Lovingly, tenderly, teach your children to come to God as their heavenly Father. By your example teach them self-control and helpfulness. Tell them that Christ lived not to please Himself.

Gather up the rays of divine light that are shining upon your pathway. Walk in the light as Christ is in the light. As you take hold of the work of helping your children to serve God, the most provoking trials will come; but do not lose your hold; cling to Jesus. He says, "Let him take hold of my strength, that he may make peace with me; and he shall make peace with me." Isa. 27:5. Difficulties will arise; you will meet with obstacles; but look constantly to Jesus. When an emergency arises, ask, Lord, what shall I do now? If you refuse to fret or scold, the

Lord will show you the way. He will help you to use the talent of speech in so Christlike a way that peace and love will reign in the home. By following a consistent course of action, you may be evangelists in the home, ministers of grace to your children. *Counsels to Parents, Teachers, and Students,* pp. 156, 157.

This Work Pays. It costs something to bring children up in the way of God. It costs a mother's tears and a father's prayers. It calls for unflagging effort, for patient instruction, here a little and there a little. But this work pays. Parents can thus build around their children bulwarks which will preserve them from the evil that is flooding our world. *Review and Herald,* July 9, 1901.

CHAPTER 74

Every Home a Church

Parents to Be God's Representatives. Every family in the home life should be a church, a beautiful symbol of the church of God in heaven. If parents realized their responsibilities to their children, they would not under any circumstances scold and fret at them. This is not the kind of education any child should have. Many, many children have learned to be faultfinding, fretful, scolding, passionate children, because they were allowed to be passionate at home. Parents are to consider that they are in the place of God to their children, to encourage every right principle and repress every wrong thought. Letter 104, 1897.

If the moral qualities of children are neglected by parents and teachers, they are sure to be perverted. *Review and Herald,* Mar. 30, 1897.

Bible Religion the Only Safeguard. Generally speaking, the youth have but little moral strength. This is the result of neglected education in childhood. A knowledge of the character of God and our obligations to Him should not be regarded as a matter of minor consequence. The religion of the Bible is the only safeguard for the young. *Testimonies for the Church,* vol. 5, pp. 23, 24.

Happy are the parents whose lives are a true reflection of the divine, so that the promises and commands of God awaken in the child gratitude and reverence; the parents whose tenderness and justice and long-suffering interpret to the child the love and justice and long-suffering of God; and who, by teaching the child to love and trust and obey them, are teaching him to love and trust and obey his Father in heaven. Parents who impart to the child such a gift have endowed him with a treasure more precious than the wealth of all the ages—a treasure as enduring as eternity. *Prophets and Kings,* p. 245.

Profession Is Valueless Without Home Religion. The daily acts of life tell the measure and mold of our disposition and character. Where there is a lack of home religion, a profession of faith is valueless. Then let no unkind words fall from the lips of those who compose the home circle. Make the atmosphere fragrant with tender thoughtfulness of others. Only those will enter heaven who in probationary time have formed a character that breathes a heavenly influence. The saint in heaven must first be a saint upon earth. *Signs of the Times,* Nov. 14, 1892.

That which will make the character lovely in the home is that which will make it lovely in the heavenly mansions. The measure of your Christianity is gauged by the character of your home life. The grace of Christ enables its possessors to make the home a happy place, full of peace and rest. Unless you have the Spirit of Christ, you are none of His and will never see the redeemed saints in His kingdom, who are to be one with Him in the heaven of bliss. God desires you to consecrate yourself wholly to Him and represent His character in the home circle. *Ibid.*

The work of sanctification begins in the home. Those who are Christians in the home will be Christians in the church and in the world. There are many who do not grow in grace because they fail of cultivating home religion. *Signs of the Times,* Feb. 17, 1904.

Parents as Educators in the Home Church. I speak to fathers and mothers: You can be educators in your home churches; you can be spiritual missionary agencies. Let fathers and mothers feel the need of being home missionaries, the need of keeping the home atmosphere free from the influence of unkind and hasty speech, and the home school a place where angels of God can come in and bless and give success to the efforts put forth. Manuscript 33, 1908

Consider the family institution a training school, preparatory for the performance of religious duties. Your children are to act a part in church capacity, and every power of the mind, every physical capacity is to be kept strong and active for the service of Christ. They are to be taught to love truth because it is truth; they are to be sanctified through the truth, that they may stand in the grand review that shall take place erelong to determine the fitness of each to enter the higher school and become a member of the royal family, a child of the heavenly King. Manuscript 12, 1898.

They Must Lead Consistent Lives. Everything leaves its impress upon the youthful mind. The countenance is studied, the voice has its influence, and the deportment is closely imitated by them. Fretful and peevish fathers and mothers are giving their children lessons which at some period in their lives they would give all the world, were it theirs, could they unlearn. Children must see in the lives of their parents that consistency which is in accordance with their faith. By leading a consistent life and exercising self-control, parents may mold the characters of their children. *Testimonies for the Church,* vol. 4, p. 621.

Train Children as Workers for Christ. Those who are united by the ties of nature have the strongest claims upon each other. The members of the family should manifest kindness and the tenderest love. The words spoken and the deeds performed should be in accordance with Christian principles. In this way the home may be made a school, where workers for Christ may be trained.

The home is to be regarded as a sacred place. . . . Every day of our lives we should surrender ourselves to God. Thus we may gain special help and daily victories. The cross is to be borne daily. Every word should be guarded, for we are responsible to God to represent in our lives as far as possible the character of Christ. Manuscript 140, 1897.

A Fatal Mistake Many Make. Can we educate our sons and daughters for a life of respectable conventionality, a life professedly Christian, but lacking His self-sacrifice, a life on which the verdict of Him who is truth must be, "I know you not"? Thousands are doing this. They think to secure for their children the benefits of the gospel while they deny its spirit. But this cannot be. Those who reject the privilege of fellowship with Christ in service reject the only training that imparts a fitness for participation with Him in His glory. They reject the training that in this life gives strength and nobility of character. Many a father and mother, denying their children to the cross of Christ, have learned too late that they were thus giving them over to the enemy of God and man. They sealed their ruin, not alone for the future but for the present life. Temptation overcame them. They grew up a curse to the world, a grief and shame to those who gave them being. *Education,* pp. 264, 265.

We know not in what line our children may be called to serve. They may spend their lives within the circle of the home; they may engage in life's common vocations or go as teachers of the gospel to heathen lands; but all are alike called to be missionaries for God, ministers of mercy to the world. They are to obtain an education that will help them to stand by the side of Christ in unselfish service. *Prophets and Kings,* p. 245.

Teach Them to Rely on Divine Aid. If you wish your children to possess enlarged capacities to do good, teach them to have a right hold of the future world. If they are instructed to rely upon divine aid in their difficulties and dangers, they will not lack power to curb passion and to check the inward temptations to do wrong. Connection with the Source of wisdom will give light and the power of discernment between right and wrong. Those so endowed will become morally and intellectually strong and will have clearer views and better judgment even in temporal affairs. *Pacific Health Journal,* January 1890.

Salvation Assured Through Faith and Trust. We can have the salvation of God in our families; but we must believe for it, live for it, and have a continual, abiding faith and trust in God. . . . The restraint which God's Word imposes upon us is for our own interest. It increases the happiness of our families, and of all around us. It refines our taste, sanctifies our judgment, and brings peace of mind, and in the end, everlasting life. . . . Ministering angels will linger in our dwellings, and with joy carry heavenward the tidings of our advance in the divine life, and the recording angel will make a cheerful, happy record. *Signs of the Times,* Apr. 17, 1884.

The Spirit of Christ will be an abiding influence in the home life. If men and women will open their hearts to the heavenly influence of truth and love, these principles will flow forth again like streams in the desert, refreshing all and causing freshness to appear where now is barrenness and dearth. Manuscript 142, 1898.

Your children will carry forth from the home the precious influence of the home education. Then work in the home circle, in the first years of the children's lives, and they will carry your influence into the schoolroom; that influence will be felt by many others. Thus the Lord will be glorified. *Ibid.*

CHAPTER 75

Leading Little Children to Christ

How Early May Children Become Christians? In childhood the mind is readily impressed and molded, and it is then that boys and girls should be taught to love and honor God. Manuscript 115, 1903.

God wants every child of tender age to be His child, to be adopted into His family. Young though they may be, the youth may be members of the household of faith and have a most precious experience. They may have hearts that are tender and ready to receive impressions that will be lasting. They may have their hearts drawn out in confidence and love for Jesus, and live for the Saviour. Christ will make them little missionaries. The whole current of their thought may be changed, so that sin will not appear a thing to be enjoyed, but to be shunned and hated. *Counsels to Parents, Teachers, and Students,* p. 169.

Age of No Consequence. An eminent divine was once asked how old a child must be before there was reasonable hope of his being a Christian. "Age has nothing to do with it," was the answer. "Love to Jesus, trust, repose, confidence, are all qualities that agree with the child's nature. As soon as a child can love and trust his mother, then can he love and trust Jesus as the Friend of his mother. Jesus will be his Friend, loved and honored."

In view of the foregoing truthful statement, can parents be too careful in presenting precept and example before those watchful little eyes and sharp senses? Our religion should be made practical. It is needed in our homes as much as in the house of worship. There should be nothing cold, stern, and forbidding in our demeanor; but we should show, by kindness and sympathy, that we possess warm, loving hearts. Jesus should be the honored Guest in the family circle. We should talk with Him, bring all our burdens to Him, and converse of His love, His grace, and His perfection of character. What a lesson may be daily given by godly parents in taking all their troubles to Jesus, the Burden Bearer, instead of fretting and scolding over cares and perplexities they cannot help. The minds of the little ones may be taught to turn to Jesus as the flower turns its opening petals to the sun. *Good Health,* January 1880.

God's Love Should Be Taught in Every Lesson. The first lesson that children are to be taught is that God is their Father. This lesson should be given them in their earliest years. Parents are to realize that they are responsible before God for making their children acquainted with their heavenly Father. . . . That God is love is to be taught by every lesson. *Review and Herald,* June 6, 1899.

Fathers and mothers should teach the infant, the child, and the youth of the love of Jesus. Let the first baby lispings be of Christ. *Review and Herald,* Oct. 9, 1900.

Christ should be associated with all the lessons given to children. *Signs of the Times,* Feb. 9, 1882.

From the child's earliest years it is to be made acquainted with the things of God. In simple words let the mother tell it about Christ's life on earth. And more than this, let her bring into her daily life the teachings of the Saviour. Let her show her child, by her own example, that this life is a preparation for the life to come, a period granted to human beings in which they may form characters that will win for them entrance into the city of God. Manuscript 2, 1903.

They Need More Than Casual Notice. There has been altogether too little attention paid to our children and youth, and they have failed to develop as they should in the Christian life, because the church members have not looked upon them with tenderness and sympathy, desiring that they might be advanced in the divine life. *Review and Herald,* Feb. 13, 1913.

The Lord is not glorified when the children are neglected and passed by. . . . They require more than casual notice, more than a word of encouragement. They need painstaking, prayerful, careful labor. The heart that is filled with love and sympathy will reach the hearts of the youth who are apparently careless and hopeless. *Counsels on Sabbath School Work,* p. 77.

Jesus Says, "Train These Children for Me." Parents should seek to comprehend the fact that they are to train their children for the courts of God. When they are entrusted with children, it is the same as though Christ placed them in their arms and said, "Train these children for Me, that they may shine in the courts of God." One of the first sounds that should attract their attention is the name of Jesus, and in their earliest years they should be led to the footstool of prayer. Their minds should be filled with stories of the life of the Lord, and their imaginations encouraged in picturing the glories of the world to come. *Review and Herald,* Feb. 19, 1895.

They May Have a Christian Experience in Childhood. Help your children to prepare for the mansions that Christ has gone to prepare for those that love Him. Help them to fulfill God's purpose for them. Let your training be such that it will help them to be an honor to the One who died to secure for them eternal life in the kingdom of God. Teach them to respond to the invitation, "Take my yoke upon you, and learn of me; for I am meek and lowly in heart, and ye shall find rest unto your souls. For my yoke is easy, and my burden is light." Manuscript 138, 1903.

My brother and sister, you have a sacred work to do in the training of your children. While they are young, their hearts and minds are most susceptible to right impressions. . . . Teach them that they have an individual part to act and a Christian experience to gain even in their childhood. Letter 10, 1912.

Unless parents shall make it the first business of their lives to guide their children's feet into the path of righteousness from their earliest years, the wrong path will be chosen before the right. *Review and Herald,* Apr. 14, 1885.

Willing Obedience Is the Test of Conversion. Shall we not teach our children that willing obedience to the will of God proves whether those claiming to be Christians are Christians indeed? The Lord means every word He says. Manuscript 64, 1899.

God's Law the Foundation of Reformation. The law of God is to be the means of education in the family. Parents are under a most solemn obligation to walk in all the commandments of God, setting their children an example of the strictest integrity. . . .

The law of God is the foundation of all enduring reformation. We are to present to the world in clear, distinct lines the need of obedience to His law. The great reformative movement must begin in the home. Obedience to God's law is the great incentive to industry, economy, truthfulness, and just dealing between man and man. Letter 74, 1900.

Teach It to the Children. Have you taught your children from their babyhood to keep the command-

ments of God? . . . You are to teach them to form charac-
ters after the divine similitude, that Christ may reveal
Himself to them. He is willing to reveal Himself to children.
We know this from the history of Joseph, of Samuel, of
Daniel and his companions. Can we not see from the record
of their lives what God expects from children and youth?
Manuscript 62, 1901.

Parents . . . are under obligation to God to present their
children to Him fitted at a very early period to receive an intelligent knowledge of what is comprehended in being a follower of Jesus Christ. Manuscript 59, 1900.

Testimony of a Converted Child. Religion helps children to study better and to do more faithful work. A little girl
of twelve was telling, in a simple way, the evidence that she
was a Christian. "I did not like to study, but to play. I was
idle at school and often missed my lessons. Now I learn every
lesson well, to please God. I was mischievous at school, when
the teachers were not looking at me, making fun for the children to look at. Now I wish to please God by behaving well
and keeping the school laws. I was selfish at home, didn't like
to run errands, and was sulky when mother called me from
play to help her in work. Now it is a real joy for me to help
mother in any way and to show that I love her." *Counsels on
Sabbath School Work,* p. 79.

Beware of Procrastination. Parents, you should commence to discipline the minds of your children while they
are young, to the end that they may be Christians. . . .
Beware how you lull them to sleep over the pit of destruction, with the mistaken thought that they are not old enough
to be accountable, not old enough to repent of their sins and
profess Christ. *Testimonies for the Church,* vol. 1, p. 396.

Children of eight, ten, or twelve years are old enough

to be addressed on the subject of personal religion. Do not teach your children with reference to some future period when they shall be old enough to repent and believe the truth. If properly instructed, very young children may have correct views of their state as sinners and of the way of salvation through Christ. *Ibid.,* p. 400.

I was referred to the many precious promises on record for those who seek their Saviour early. Ecclesiastes 12:1: "Remember now thy Creator in the days of thy youth, while the evil days come not, nor the years draw nigh when thou shalt say, I have no pleasure in them." Proverbs 8:17: "I love them that love me, and those that seek me early shall find me." The great Shepherd of Israel is still saying, "Suffer little children to come unto me, and forbid them not: for of such is the kingdom of heaven." Teach your children that youth is the best time to seek the Lord. *Ibid.,* pp. 396, 397.

Direct From Infancy Through Youth. To allow a child to follow his natural impulses is to allow him to deteriorate and to become proficient in evil. The results of wrong training begin to be revealed in childhood. In early youth a selfish temper is developed, and as the youth grows to manhood, he grows in sin. A continual testimony against parental neglect is borne by children who have been permitted to follow a course of their own choosing. Such a downward course can be prevented only by surrounding them with influences that will counteract evil. From infancy to youth and from youth to manhood, a child should be under influences for good. *Review and Herald,* Sept. 15, 1904.

Fortify Children for Future Tests. Parents, ask yourselves the solemn question, "Have we educated our children to yield to paternal authority, and thus trained them to obey God, to love Him, to hold His law as the supreme guide of conduct and life? Have we educated them to be missionaries for Christ? To go about doing good?" Believing parents, your children will have to fight decisive battles for the Lord in the day of conflict; and while they win victories for the Prince of peace, they may be gaining triumphs for themselves. But if they have not been brought up in the fear of the Lord; if they have no knowledge of Christ, no connection with heaven, they will have no moral power, and they will yield to earthly potentates who have assumed to exalt themselves above the God of heaven in establishing a spurious sabbath to take the place of the Sabbath of Jehovah. *Review and Herald,* Apr. 23, 1889.

CHAPTER 76

Preparing for Church Membership

A Well-balanced Training. Instruction should be given as God has directed. Patiently, carefully, diligently, mercifully, children should be trained. Upon all parents rests the obligation of giving their children physical, mental, and spiritual instruction. It is essential ever to keep before children the claims of God.

Physical training, the development of the body, is far more easily given than spiritual training. . . .

Soul culture, which gives purity and elevation to the thoughts and fragrance to word and act, requires more painstaking effort. It takes patience to keep every evil motive weeded from the garden of the heart.

The spiritual training should in no case be neglected. Let us teach our children the beautiful lessons of God's Word, that through these they may gain a knowledge of Him. Let them understand that they should do nothing which is not right. Teach them to do justice and judgment. Tell them that you cannot permit them to take a wrong course. In the name of the Lord Jesus Christ present them to God at the throne of grace. Let them know that Jesus lives to make intercession for them. Encourage them to form characters fashioned after the divine similitude. *Review and Herald,* Sept. 15, 1904.

Knowledge of God and Christ Is Fundamental. The spiritual training should in no case be neglected, for "the fear of the Lord is the beginning of wisdom."

Psalm 111:10. By some, education is placed next to religion, but true education is religion. *Counsels to Parents, Teachers, and Students,* p. 108.

Define Practical Religious Experience. Practical instruction in religious experience is what Christian parents should be prepared to give their children. God requires this of you, and you neglect your duty if you fail to perform this work. Instruct your children in regard to God's chosen methods of discipline and the conditions of success in the Christian life. Teach them that they cannot serve God and have their minds absorbed in overcareful provision for this life; but do not let them cherish the thought that they have no need to toil and may spend their leisure moments in idleness. God's Word is plain on this point. *Testimonies for the Church,* vol. 5, p. 42.

Teach the Knowledge of God. To know God is eternal life. Are you teaching this to your children, or are you teaching them to meet the world's standard? Are you getting ready for the home that God is preparing for you? . . . Teach your children of the Saviour's life, death, and resurrection. Teach them to study the Bible. . . . Teach them to form characters that will live through the eternal ages. We must pray as we never have before that God will keep and bless our children. Manuscript 16, 1895.

Teach Daily Repentance and Forgiveness. It is not essential that all shall be able to specify to a certainty when their sins were forgiven. The lesson to be taught the children is that their errors and mistakes are to be brought to Jesus in their very childhood of life. Teach them to ask His forgiveness daily for any wrong that they have done, and that Jesus does hear the simple prayer of the penitent heart, and will pardon, and receive them, just as He received the children brought to Him when He was upon earth. Manuscript 5, 1896.

Teach Sound Doctrine. Those who have seen the truth and felt its importance, and have had an experience in the things of God, are to teach sound doctrine to their children. They should make them acquainted with the great pillars of our faith, the reasons why we are Seventh-day Adventists—why we are called, as were the children of Israel, to be a peculiar people, a holy nation, separate and distinct from all other people on the face of the earth. These things should be explained to the children in simple language, easy to be understood; and as they grow in years, the lessons imparted should be suited to their increasing capacity, until the foundations of truth have been laid broad and deep. *Testimonies for the Church,* vol. 5, p. 330.

Instruct Briefly and Frequently. Those who give instruction to children and youth should avoid tedious remarks. Short talks, right to the point, will have a happy influence. If there is much to be said, make up for brevity by frequency. A few interesting remarks, every now and then, will be more helpful than to give all the instruction at once. Long speeches tire the minds of the young. Too much talk will lead them even to loathe spiritual instruction, just as overeating burdens the stomach and lessens the appetite, leading to a loathing for food. *Gospel Workers,* pp. 208, 209.

The Evenings Are Precious Seasons. The home should be made a school of instruction rather than a place of monotonous drudgery. The evenings should be cherished as precious seasons, to be devoted to the instruction of the children in the way of righteousness. *Counsels on Sabbath School Work,* p. 48.

Recount God's Promises. We need to recognize the Holy Spirit as our enlightener. That Spirit loves to address the children and discover to them the treasures and beauties of the Word. The promises spoken by the great Teacher will captivate the senses and animate the soul of the child with a spiritual power that is divine. There will grow in the receptive mind a familiarity with divine things which will be as a barricade against the temptations of the enemy. *Counsels to Parents, Teachers, and Students,* p. 172.

Make Religious Instruction Pleasant. Religious instruction should be given to children from their earliest years. It should be given, not in a condemnatory spirit, but in a cheerful, happy spirit. Mothers need to be on the watch constantly, lest temptation shall come to the children in such a form as not to be recognized by them. The parents are to guard their children with wise, pleasant instruction. As the very best friends of these inexperienced ones, they should help them in the work of overcoming, for it means everything to them to be victorious. They should consider that their own dear children who are seeking to do right are younger members of the Lord's family, and they should feel an intense interest in helping them to make straight paths in the King's highway of obedience. With loving interest they should teach them day by day what it means to be children of God and to yield the will in obedience to Him. Teach them that obedience to God involves obedience to their parents. This must be a daily, hourly work. Parents, watch, watch and pray, and make your children your companions. *Testimonies for the Church,* vol. 6, pp. 93, 94.

Teach Spiritual Lessons From Homely Tasks. God has given to parents and teachers the work of educating the children and youth in these lines, and from every act of their lives they may be taught spiritual lessons. While training them in habits of physical cleanliness, we should teach them that God desires them to be clean in heart as well as in body. While sweeping a room, they may learn how the Lord purifies the heart. They would not close the doors and windows and leave in the room some purifying substance, but would open the doors and throw wide the windows, and with diligent effort expel all the dust. So the windows of impulse and feeling must be opened toward heaven, and the dust of selfishness and earthliness must be expelled. The grace of God must sweep through the chambers of the mind, and every element of the nature must be purified and vitalized by the Spirit of God. Disorder and untidiness in daily duties will lead to forgetfulness of God and to keeping the form of godliness in a profession of faith, having lost the reality. We are to watch and pray, else we shall grasp the shadow and lose the substance.

A living faith like threads of gold should run through the daily experience in the performance of little duties. *Ibid.,* pp. 170, 171.

Heart Education Versus Book Learning. It is right for the youth to feel that they must reach the highest development of their mental powers. We would not restrict the education to which God has set no limit. But our attainments will avail nothing if not put to use for the honor of God and the good of humanity. Unless our knowledge is a stepping-stone to the accomplishment of the highest purposes, it is worthless. . . .

Heart education is of more importance than the education gained from books. It is well, even essential, to obtain a knowledge of the world in which we live; but if we leave eternity out of our reckoning, we shall make a failure from which we can never recover. *Ibid.,* vol. 8, p. 311.

Mutual Benefits. Our children are the Lord's property; they have been bought with a price. This thought should be the mainspring of our labors for them. The most successful methods of assuring their salvation and keeping them out of the way of temptation is to instruct them constantly in the Word of God. And as parents become learners with their children, they will find their own growth in a knowledge of the truth more rapid. Unbelief will disappear; faith and activity will increase; assurance and confidence will deepen as they thus follow on to know the Lord. *Review and Herald,* May 6, 1909.

How Parents May Be Stumbling Blocks. What example do you give your children? What order do you have at home? Your children should be educated to be kind, thoughtful of others, gentle, easy to be entreated, and, above everything else, to respect religious things and feel the importance of the claims of God. *Testimonies for the Church,* vol. 5, p. 424.

Boys and girls may early reveal deep and symmetrical piety if the means which God has ordained for the guidance of every family is followed in His fear and love. They will demonstrate the value of correct training and discipline. But the impression made upon the mind of children by the words of the teacher of truth is often counteracted by the words and actions of the parents. The susceptible though wayward hearts of children are often impressed by the truth, but often temptations come to them through father or mother, and they fall a prey to Satan's devices. It is almost impossible to set the feet of children in safe paths when the parents do not cooperate. Evil sentiments, falling from the lips of injudicious parents, are the chief hindrance to genuine conversions among children. Manuscript 49, 1901.

Live in Harmony With Your Prayers. "If ye abide in me, and my words abide in you, ye shall ask what ye will, and it shall be done unto you." When you pray, present this promise. It is our privilege to come to Him with holy boldness. As in sincerity we ask Him to let His light shine upon us, He will hear and answer us. But we must live in harmony with our prayers. They are of no avail if we walk contrary to them. I have seen a father who, after reading a portion of scripture and offering prayer, would often, almost as soon as he had risen from his knees, begin to scold his children. How could God answer the prayer he had offered? And if, after scolding his children, a father offers prayer, does that prayer benefit the children? No; not unless it is a prayer of confession to God. Manuscript 114, 1903.

When Children Are Ready for Baptism. Never allow your children to suppose that they are not children of God until they are old enough to be baptized. Baptism does not make children Christians; neither does it convert them; it is but an outward sign, showing that they are sensible that they should be children of God by acknowledging that they believe in Jesus Christ as their Saviour and will henceforth live for Christ. Manuscript 5, 1896.

Parents whose children desire to be baptized have a work to do, both in self-examination and in giving faithful instruction to their children. Baptism is a most sacred and important ordinance, and there should be a thorough understanding as to its meaning. It means repentance for sin, and the entrance upon a new life in Christ Jesus. There should be no undue haste to receive the ordinance. Let both parents and children count the cost. In consenting to baptism of their children, parents sacredly pledge themselves to be faithful stewards over these children, to guide them in their character building. They pledge themselves to guard with special interest these lambs of the flock, that they may not dishonor the faith they profess. . . .

When the happiest period of their life has come, and they in their hearts love Jesus and wish to be baptized, then deal faithfully with them. Before they receive the ordinance, ask them if it is to be their first purpose in life to work for God. Then tell them how to begin. It is the first lessons that mean so much. In simplicity teach them how to do their first service for God. Make the work as easy to be understood as possible. Explain what it means to give up self to the Lord, to do just as His Word directs, under the counsel of Christian parents. *Testimonies for the Church,* vol. 6, pp. 93, 94.

Parents' Duty After Baptism. After faithful labor, if you are satisfied that your children understand the meaning of conversion and baptism and are truly converted, let them be baptized. But, I repeat, first of all prepare yourselves to act as faithful shepherds in guiding their inexperienced feet in the narrow way of obedience. God must work in the parents that they may give to their children a right example in love, courtesy, and Christian humility, and in an entire giving up of self to Christ. If you consent to the baptism of your children and then leave them to do as they choose, feeling no special duty to keep their feet in the straight path, you yourselves are responsible if they lose faith and courage and interest in the truth. *Ibid.,* pp. 94, 95.

God calls upon you to teach them to prepare to be members of the royal family, children of the heavenly King. Cooperate with God by working diligently for their salvation. If they err, do not scold them. Never taunt them with being baptized and yet doing wrong. Remember that they have much to learn in regard to the duties of a child of God. Manuscript 80, 1901.

Preparation for Special Convocations. Here is a work for families to engage in before coming up to our holy convocations. Let the preparation for eating and dressing be a secondary matter, but let deep heart-searching commence at home. Pray three times a day, and like Jacob, be importunate. At home is the place to find Jesus; then take Him with you to the meeting, and how precious will be the hours you spend there. But how can you expect to feel the presence of the Lord and see His power displayed, when the individual work of preparation for that time is neglected?

For your soul's sake, for Christ's sake, and for the sake of others, work at home. Pray as you are not accustomed to pray. Let the heart break before God. Set your house in order. Prepare your children for the occasion. Teach them that it is not of so much consequence that they appear with fine clothes as that they appear before God with clean hands and pure hearts. Remove every obstacle that may have been in their way—all differences that may have existed between themselves or between you and them. By so doing you will invite the Lord's presence into your homes, and holy angels will attend you as you go up to the meeting, and their light and presence will press back the darkness of evil angels. *Testimonies for the Church,* vol. 5, pp. 164, 165.

Sow the Seeds of Truth in Faith. The work of the sower is a work of faith. The mystery of the germination and growth of the seed he cannot understand, but he has confidence in the agencies by which God causes vegetation to flourish. He casts away the seed, expecting to gather it manyfold in an abundant harvest. So parents and teachers are to labor, expecting a harvest from the seed they sow. *Education,* p. 105.

We should ask the blessing of God on the seed sown, and the conviction of the Holy Spirit will take hold of even the little ones. If we exercise faith in God, we shall be enabled to lead them to the Lamb of God that taketh away the sin of the world. This is a work of the greatest consequence to the younger members of the Lord's family. *Testimonies for the Church,* vol. 6, p. 105.

MAINTAINING
THE RELIGIOUS EXPERIENCE

CHAPTER 77

The Bible in the Home

The Bible Is a Versatile Book. In its wide range of style and subjects, the Bible has something to interest every mind and appeal to every heart. In its pages are found history the most ancient; biography the truest to life; principles of government for the control of the state, for the regulation of the household—principles that human wisdom has never equaled. It contains philosophy the most profound; poetry the sweetest and the most sublime, the most impassioned and the most pathetic. Immeasurably superior in value to the productions of any human author are the Bible writings, even when thus considered; but of infinitely wider scope, of infinitely greater value, are they when viewed in their relation to the grand central thought. Viewed in the light of this thought, every topic has a new significance. In the most simply stated truths are involved principles that are as high as heaven and that compass eternity. *Education,* p. 125.

The Word of God abounds in precious jewels of truth, and parents should bring them forth from their casket and present them before their children in their true luster. . . . In the Word of God you have a treasure house from which you may draw precious stores, and as Christians you should furnish yourselves for every good work. *Signs of the Times,* Sept. 10, 1894.

In It God Provides a Rich Banquet. In giving us the privilege of studying His Word, the Lord has set before us a rich banquet. Many are the benefits derived from feasting on His Word, which is represented by Him as His flesh and blood, His spirit and life. By partaking of this Word, our spiritual strength is increased; we grow in grace and in a knowledge of the truth. Habits of self-control are formed and strengthened. The infirmities of childhood—fretfulness, willfulness, selfishness, hasty words, passionate acts—disappear, and in their place are developed the graces of Christian manhood and womanhood. *Counsels to Parents, Teachers, and Students,* p. 207.

The beautiful lessons of the Bible stories and parables, the pure, simple instruction of God's Holy Word, is the spiritual food for you and your children.

Oh, what a work is before you! Will you take hold of it in the love and fear of God? Will you put yourselves in communication with God through His Word? Letter 27, 1890.

It Is the Standard of Rectitude. The Word of God should be judiciously brought to bear upon the youthful minds and be their standard of rectitude, correcting their errors, enlightening and guiding their minds, which will be far more effectual in restraining and controlling the impulsive temperament than harsh words, which will provoke to wrath. This training of children to meet the Bible standard will require time, perseverance, and prayer. This should be attended to if some things about the house are neglected. *Signs of the Times,* Sept. 13, 1877.

The truths of the Bible, received, will uplift the mind from its earthliness and debasement. If the Word of God were appreciated as it should be, both young and old would possess an inward rectitude, a strength of principle, that would enable them to resist temptation. *Testimonies for the Church,* vol. 8, p. 319.

The Holy One of Israel has made known to us the statutes and laws which are to govern all human intelligences. These precepts, which have been pronounced "holy, and just, and good," are to form the standard of action in the home. There can be no departure from them without sin, for they are the foundation of the Christian religion. *Review and Herald,* Nov. 13, 1888.

It Strengthens the Intellect. If the Bible were studied as it should be, men would become strong in intellect. The subjects treated upon in the Word of God, the dignified simplicity of its utterance, the noble themes which it presents to the mind, develop faculties in man which cannot otherwise be developed. In the Bible a boundless field is opened for the imagination. The student will come from a contemplation of its grand themes, from association with its lofty imagery, more pure and elevated in thought and feeling than if he had spent the time reading any work of mere human origin, to say nothing of those of a trifling character. Youthful minds fail to reach their noblest development when they neglect the highest source of wisdom—the Word of God. The reason why we have so few men of good mind, of stability and solid worth, is that God is not feared, God is not loved, the principles of religion are not carried out in the life as they should be.

God would have us avail ourselves of every means of cultivating and strengthening our intellectual powers. . . . If the Bible were read more, if its truths were better understood, we should be a far more enlightened and intelligent people. Energy is imparted to the soul by searching its pages. *Christian Temperance and Bible Hygiene,* p. 126.

It Is the Foundation for Home, Social, and National Prosperity. The teaching of the Bible has a vital bearing upon man's prosperity in all the relations of this life. It unfolds the principles that are the cornerstone of a nation's prosperity—principles with which is bound up the well-being of society, and which are the safeguard of the family—principles without which no man can attain usefulness, happiness, and honor in this life, or can hope to secure the future, immortal life. There is no position in life, no phase of human experience, for which the teaching of the Bible is not an essential preparation. *Patriarchs and Prophets,* p. 599.

Knowledge of the Scriptures Is a Safeguard. From a child, Timothy knew the Scriptures; and this knowledge was a safeguard to him against the evil influences surrounding him and the temptation to choose pleasure and selfish gratification before duty. Such a safeguard all our children need, and it should be a part of the work of parents and of Christ's ambassadors to see that the children are properly instructed in the Word of God. *Testimonies for the Church,* vol. 4, p. 398.

Love for the Bible Is Not Natural. Youth are ignorant and inexperienced, and the love of the Bible and its sacred truths will not come naturally. Unless great pains are taken to build up around them barriers to shield them from Satan's devices, they are subject to his temptations and are led captive by him at his will. In their early years children are to be taught the claims of God's law and faith in Jesus our Redeemer to cleanse from the stains of sin. This faith must be taught day by day, by precept and example. *Ibid.,* vol. 5, p. 329.

Youth Especially Neglect Bible Study. Both old and young neglect the Bible. They do not make it their study, the rule of their life. Especially are the young guilty of this neglect. Most of them find time to read other books, but the book that points out the way to eternal life is not daily studied, Idle stories are attentively read, while the Bible is neglected. This book is our guide to a higher, holier life. The youth would pronounce it the most interesting book they ever read had not their imagination been perverted by the reading of fictitious stories.

Youthful minds fail to reach their noblest development when they neglect the highest source of wisdom—the Word of God. That we are in God's world, in the presence of the Creator; that we are made in His likeness; that He watches over us and loves us and cares for us—these are wonderful themes for thought and lead the mind into broad, exalted fields of meditation. He who opens mind and heart to the contemplation of such themes as these will never be satisfied with trivial, sensational subjects. *Counsels to Parents, Teachers, and Students,* pp. 138, 139.

Parental Disregard Is Reflected in Children. Even when quite young, children notice; and if the parents show that the Word of God is not their guide and counselor, if they disregard the messages brought to them, the same reckless spirit of, "I don't care; I will have my own way," will be shown by the children. Manuscript 49, 1898.

Give the Word Its Honored Place. As a people who have had great light, we are to be uplifting in our habits, in our words, in our domestic life and association. Give the Word its honored position as a guide in the home. Let it be regarded as the counselor in every difficulty, the standard of every practice. Will my brethren and sisters be convinced that there can never be true prosperity to any soul in the family circle unless the truth of God, the wisdom of righteousness, presides? Every effort should be made by fathers and mothers to bring their own minds up from the lazy habit of regarding the service of God as a burden. The power of the truth must be a sanctifying agency in the home. Letter 107, 1898.

Parents, give your children, line upon line, precept upon precept, the instruction contained in God's Holy Word. This is the work you pledged yourself to do when you were baptized. Let nothing of a worldly character keep you from doing this work. Do all in your power to save the souls of your children, whether they are bone of your bone and flesh of your flesh, or whether they have been received into your family by adoption. Manuscript 70, 1900.

Make It the Home Textbook. Parents, if you would educate your children to serve God and do good in the world, make the Bible your textbook. It exposes the wiles of Satan. It is the great elevator of the race, the reprover and corrector of moral evils, the detector which enables us to distinguish between the true and the false. Whatever else is taught in the home or at school, the Bible, as the great educator, should stand first. If it is given this place, God is honored, and He will work for you in the conversion of your children. There is a rich mine of truth and beauty in this holy book, and parents have themselves to blame if they do not make it intensely interesting to their children. *Testimonies for the Church,* vol. 5, p. 322.

"It is written" was the only weapon that Christ used when the tempter came with his deceptions. The teaching of Bible truth is the great and grand work which every parent should undertake. In a pleasant, happy frame of mind place the truth as spoken by God before the children. As fathers and mothers, you can be object lessons to the children in the daily life by practicing patience, kindness, and love, by attaching them to yourself. Do not let them do as they please, but show them that your work is to practice the Word of God and to bring them up in the nurture and admonition of the Lord. Manuscript 5, 1896.

Study Diligently, Systematically. Observe system in the study of the Scriptures in your families. Neglect anything of a temporal nature, . . . but be sure that the soul is fed with the bread of life. It is impossible to estimate the good results of one hour or even half an hour each day devoted in a cheerful, social manner to the Word of God. Make the Bible its own expositor, bringing together all that is said concerning a given subject at different times and under varied circumstances. Do not break up your home class for callers or visitors. If they come in during the exercise, invite them to take part in it. Let it be seen that you consider it more important to obtain a knowledge of God's Word than to secure the gains or pleasures of the world. *Review and Herald,* Oct. 9, 1883.

If we would study the Bible diligently and prayerfully every day, we should every day see some beautiful truth in a new, clear, and forcible light. *Counsels on Sabbath School Work,* p. 23.

Let All Study Sabbath School Lessons. The Sabbath school affords to parents and children an opportunity for the study of God's Word. But in order for them to gain that benefit which they should gain in the Sabbath school, both parents and children should devote time to the study of the lesson, seeking to obtain a thorough knowledge of the facts presented and also of the spiritual truths which these facts are designed to teach. We should especially impress upon the minds of the youth the importance of seeking the full significance of the scripture under consideration.

Parents, set apart a little time each day for the study of the Sabbath school lesson with your children. Give up the social visit if need be, rather than sacrifice the hour devoted to the lessons of sacred history. Parents as well as children will receive benefit from this study. Let the more important passages of Scripture connected with the lesson be committed to memory, not as a task, but as a privilege. Though at first the memory be defective, it will gain strength by exercise, so that after a time you will delight thus to treasure up the words of truth. And the habit will prove a most valuable aid to spiritual growth. *Counsels to Parents, Teachers, and Students,* pp. 137, 138.

Parents should feel it a sacred duty to instruct their children in the statutes and requirements of God as well as in the prophecies. They should educate their children at home and should themselves be interested in the Sabbath school lessons. By studying with the children they show that they attach importance to the truth brought out in the lessons, and help to create a taste for Bible knowledge. *Testimonies on Sabbath School Work,* p. 111.

Be Not Satisfied With Superficial Knowledge. The importance of seeking a thorough knowledge of the Scriptures can hardly be estimated. "Given by inspiration of God" able to make us "wise unto salvation," rendering the man of God "perfect, throughly furnished unto all good works" (2 Timothy 3:15-17), the Bible has the highest claim to our reverent attention. We should not be satisfied with a superficial knowledge, but should seek to learn the full meaning of the words of truth, to drink deep of the spirit of the Holy Oracles. *Counsels to Parents, Teachers, and Students,* p. 139.

Apply Lessons to Child's Experience. In teaching children the Bible, we may gain much by observing the bent of their minds, the things in which they are interested, and arousing their interest to see what the Bible says about these things. He who created us, with our various aptitudes, has in His Word given something for everyone. As the pupils see that the lessons of the Bible apply to their own lives, teach them to look to it as a counselor. . . .

The Bible has a fullness, a strength, a depth of meaning, that is inexhaustible. Encourage the children and youth to seek out its treasures, both of thought and of expression. *Education,* p. 188.

Each Must Study for Himself. Mothers and fathers carry a heavy responsibility in regard to their children. Those parents who believe and study the Scriptures will realize that they must obey the commandments of God, that they must not walk contrary to His holy law. Those who allow anyone, even the minister, to lead them to disregard the Word of God must at the judgment meet the result of their course. Parents are not to trust their own souls and the souls of their children to the minister, but to God, whose they are by creation and by redemption. Parents should search the Scriptures for themselves, for they have souls to save or to lose. They cannot afford to depend for salvation upon the minister. They must study the truth for themselves. Manuscript 33, 1900.

Make Bible Study Interesting to Children. Let the youth be taught to love the study of the Bible. Let the first place in our thoughts and affections be given to the Book of books, for it contains knowledge which we need above all other. *Review and Herald,* Oct. 9, 1883.

In order to do this work, parents must themselves become acquainted with the Word of God. . . . And instead of speaking vain words and telling idle tales to their children, they will talk with them upon Bible subjects. The book was not designed for scholars alone. It was written in a plain, simple style to meet the understanding of the common people; and, with proper explanations, a large portion of it can be made intensely interesting and profitable to very small children. *Signs of the Times,* Apr. 8, 1886.

Do not think that the Bible will become a tiresome book to the children. Under a wise instructor the Word will become more and more desirable. It will be to them as the bread of life; it will never grow old. There is in it a freshness and beauty that attract and charm the children and youth. It is like the sun shining upon the earth, giving its brightness and warmth, yet never exhausted. By lessons from Bible history and doctrine, the children and youth can learn that all other books are inferior to this. They can find here a fountain of mercy and love. *Counsels to Parents, Teachers, and Students,* p. 171.

Parents, let the instruction you give your children be simple, and be sure that it is clearly understood. The lessons that you learn from the Word you are to present to their young minds so plainly that they cannot fail to understand. By simple lessons drawn from the Word of God and their own experience, you may teach them how to conform their lives to the highest standard. Even in childhood and youth they may learn to live thoughtful, earnest lives that will yield a rich harvest of good. *Ibid.,* p. 109.

Give Freshest Thought; Use Best Methods. Our heavenly Father, in giving His Word, did not overlook the children. In all that men have written, where can be found anything that has such a hold upon the heart, anything so well adapted to awaken the interest of the little ones, as the stories of the Bible?

In these simple stories may be made plain the great principles of the law of God. Thus by illustrations best suited to the child's comprehension, parents and teachers may begin very early to fulfill the Lord's injunction concerning His precepts: "Thou shalt teach them diligently unto thy children, and shalt talk of them when thou sittest in thine house, and when thou walkest by the way, and when thou liest down, and when thou risest up." Deuteronomy 6:7.

The use of object lessons, blackboards, maps, and pictures will be an aid in explaining these lessons and fixing them in the memory. Parents and teachers should constantly seek for improved methods. The teaching of the Bible should have our freshest thought, our best methods, and our most earnest effort. *Education,* pp. 185, 186.

Take the Bible as the Guide. You must make the Bible your guide if you would bring up your children in the nurture and admonition of the Lord. Let the life and character of Christ be presented as the pattern for them to copy. If they err, read to them what the Lord has said concerning similar sins. There is need of constant care and diligence in this work. One wrong trait tolerated by parents, uncorrected by teachers, may cause the whole character to become deformed and unbalanced. Teach the children that they must have a new heart; that new tastes must be created, new motives inspired. They must have help from Christ; they must become acquainted with the character of God as revealed in His Word. *Signs of the Times,* May 25, 1882.

CHAPTER 78

The Power of Prayer

The Need for Family Prayer. Every family should rear its altar of prayer, realizing that the fear of the Lord is the beginning of wisdom. If any persons in the world need the strength and encouragement that religion gives, it is those who are responsible for the education and training of children. They cannot do their work in a manner acceptable to God while their daily example teaches those who look to them for guidance that they can live without God. If they educate their children to live for this life only, they will make no preparation for eternity. They will die as they have lived, without God, and parents will be called to account for the loss of their souls. Fathers, mothers, you need to seek God morning and evening at the family altar, that you may learn how to teach your children wisely, tenderly, lovingly. *Review and Herald,* June 27, 1899.

Family Worship Neglected. If ever there was a time when every house should be a house of prayer, it is now. Infidelity and skepticism prevail. Iniquity abounds. Corruption flows in the vital currents of the soul, and rebellion against God breaks out in the life. Enslaved by sin, the moral powers are under the tyranny of Satan. The soul is made the sport of his temptations; and unless some mighty arm is stretched out to rescue him, man goes where the archrebel leads the way.

And yet, in this time of fearful peril, some who profess to be Christians have no family worship. They do not honor God in the home; they do not teach their children to love and fear Him. Many have separated themselves so far from Him that they feel under condemnation in approaching Him. They cannot "come boldly unto the throne of grace," "lifting up holy hands, without wrath and doubting." Hebrews 4:16; 1 Timothy 2:8. They have not a living connection with God. Theirs is a form of godliness without the power. *Testimonies for the Church,* vol. 7, p. 42.

The idea that prayer is not essential is one of Satan's most successful devices to ruin souls. Prayer is communion with God, the Fountain of wisdom, the Source of strength, and peace, and happiness. *Ibid.*

Tragedy of a Prayerless Home. I know of nothing that causes me so great sadness as a prayerless home. I do not feel safe in such a house for a single night; and were it not for the hope of helping the parents to realize their necessity and their sad neglect, I would not remain. The children show the result of this neglect, for the fear of God is not before them. *Signs of the Times,* Aug. 7, 1884.

Formal Prayer Is Not Acceptable. In many cases the morning and evening worship is little more than a mere form, a dull, monotonous repetition of set phrases in which the spirit of gratitude or the sense of need finds no expression. The Lord accepts not such service. But the petitions of a humble heart and contrite spirit He will not despise. The opening of our hearts to our heavenly Father, the acknowledgment of our entire dependence, the expression of our wants, the homage of grateful love—this is true prayer. *Signs of the Times,* July 1, 1886.

Let There Be Households of Prayer. Like the patriarchs of old, those who profess to love God should erect an altar to the Lord wherever they pitch their tent. . . . Fathers and mothers should often lift up their hearts to God in humble supplication for themselves and their children. Let the father, as priest of the household, lay upon the altar of God the morning and evening sacrifice, while the wife and children unite in prayer and praise. In such a household Jesus will love to tarry. *Patriarchs and Prophets,* p. 144.

Let the members of every family bear in mind that they are closely allied to heaven. The Lord has a special interest in the families of His children here below. Angels offer the smoke of the fragrant incense for the praying saints. Then in every family let prayer ascend to heaven both in the morning and at the cool sunset hour, in our behalf presenting before God the Saviour's merits. Morning and evening the heavenly universe take notice of every praying household. Manuscript 19, 1900.

Angels Guard Children Dedicated to God. Before leaving the house for labor, all the family should be called together; and the father, or the mother in the father's absence, should plead fervently with God to keep them through the day. Come in humility, with a heart full of tenderness, and with a sense of the temptations and dangers before yourselves and your children; by faith bind them upon the altar, entreating for them the care of the Lord. Ministering angels will guard children who are thus dedicated to God. *Testimonies for the Church,* vol. 1, pp. 397, 398.

Prayer Makes a Hedge About Children. In the morning the Christian's first thoughts should be upon God. Worldly labor and self-interest should be secondary. Children should be taught to respect and reverence the hour of prayer. . . . It is the duty of Christian parents, morning and evening, by earnest prayer and persevering faith, to make a hedge about their children. They should patiently instruct them—kindly and untiringly teach them how to live in order to please God. *Ibid.*

Have Fixed Times for Worship. In every family there should be a fixed time for morning and evening worship. How appropriate it is for parents to gather their children about them before the fast is broken, to thank the heavenly Father for His protection during the night, and to ask Him for His help and guidance and watch care during the day! How fitting, also, when evening comes, for parents and children to gather once more before Him and thank Him for the blessings of the day that is past! *Ibid.,* vol. 7, p. 43.

Do Not Be Governed by Circumstances. Family worship should not be governed by circumstances. You are not to pray occasionally and, when you have a large day's work to do, neglect it. In thus doing you lead your children to look upon prayer as of no special consequence. Prayer means very much to the children of God, and thank offerings should come up before God morning and evening. Says the psalmist, "O come, let us sing unto the Lord: let us make a joyful noise to the rock of our salvation. Let us come before his presence with thanksgiving, and make a joyful noise unto him with psalms." Manuscript 12, 1898.

Fathers and mothers, however pressing your business, do not fail to gather your family around God's altar. Ask for the guardianship of holy angels in your home. Remember that your dear ones are exposed to temptations. *The Ministry of Healing,* p. 393.

In our efforts for the comfort and happiness of guests, let us not overlook our obligations to God. The hour of prayer should not be neglected for any consideration. Do not talk and amuse yourselves till all are too weary to enjoy the season of devotion. To do this is to present to God a lame offering. At an early hour of the evening, when we can pray unhurriedly and understandingly, we should present our supplications and raise our voices in happy, grateful praise.

Let all who visit Christians see that the hour of prayer is the most precious, the most sacred, and the happiest hour of the day. These seasons of devotion exert a refining, elevating influence upon all who participate in them. They bring a peace and rest grateful to the spirit. *Messages to Young People,* p. 342.

Children to Respect the Worship Hour. Your children should be educated to be kind, thoughtful of others, gentle, easy to be entreated, and, above everything else, to respect religious things and feel the importance of the claims of God. They should be taught to respect the hour of prayer; they should be required to rise in the morning so as to be present at family worship. *Testimonies for the Church,* vol. 5, p. 424.

Make the Worship Period Interesting. The father, who is the priest of his household, should conduct the morning and evening worship. There is no reason why this should not be the most interesting and enjoyable exercise of the home life, and God is dishonored when it is made dry and irksome. Let the seasons of family worship be short and spirited. Do not let your children or any member of your family dread them because of their tediousness or lack of interest. When a long chapter is read and explained and a long prayer offered, this precious service becomes wearisome, and it is a relief when it is over.

It should be the special object of the heads of the family to make the hour of worship intensely interesting. By a little thought and careful preparation for this season, when we come into the presence of God, family worship can be made pleasant and will be fraught with results that eternity alone will reveal. Let the father select a portion of Scripture that is interesting and easily understood; a few verses will be sufficient to furnish a lesson which may be studied and practiced through the day. Questions may be asked, a few earnest, interesting remarks made, or incident, short and to the point, may be brought in by way of illustration. At least a few verses of spirited song may be sung, and the prayer offered should be short and pointed. The one who leads in prayer should not pray about everything, but should express his needs in simple words and praise God with thanksgiving. *Signs of the Times,* Aug. 7, 1884.

In arousing and strengthening a love for Bible study, much depends on the use of the hour of worship. The hours of morning and evening worship should be the sweetest and most helpful of the day. Let it be understood that into these hours no troubled, unkind thoughts are to intrude; that parents and children assemble to meet with Jesus and to invite into the home the presence of holy angels. Let the services be brief and full of life, adapted to the occasion, and varied from time to time. Let all join in the Bible reading and learn and often repeat God's law. It will add to the interest of the children if they are sometimes permitted to select the reading. Question them upon it, and let them ask questions. Mention anything that will serve to illustrate its meaning. When the service is not thus made too lengthy, let the little ones take part in prayer, and let them join in song, if it be but a single verse. *Education,* p. 186.

Pray Clearly and Distinctly. By your own example teach your children to pray with clear, distinct voice. Teach them to lift their heads from the chair and never to cover their faces with their hands. Thus they can offer their simple prayers, repeating the Lord's prayer in concert. Manuscript 12, 1898.

The Power of Music. The history of the songs of the Bible is full of suggestion as to the uses and benefits of music and song. Music is often perverted to serve purposes of evil, and it thus becomes one of the most alluring agencies of temptation. But, rightly employed, it is a precious gift of God, designed to uplift the thoughts to high and noble themes, to inspire and elevate the soul. . . .

It is one of the most effective means of impressing the heart with spiritual truth. How often to the soul hard-pressed and ready to despair memory recalls some word of God's— the long-forgotten burden of a childhood song—and temptations lose their power, life takes on new meaning and new purpose, and courage and gladness are imparted to other souls!

The value of song as a means of education should never be lost sight of. Let there be singing in the home, of songs that are sweet and pure, and there will be fewer words of censure and more of cheerfulness and hope and joy. Let there be singing in the school; and the pupils will be drawn closer to God, to their teachers, and to one another.

As a part of religious service singing is as much an act of worship as is prayer. Indeed, many a song is prayer. If the child is taught to realize this, he will think more of the meaning of the words he sings and will be more susceptible to their power. *Education,* pp. 167, 168.

Instrumental and Vocal. Evening and morning join with your children in God's worship, reading His Word and singing His praise. Teach them to repeat God's law. Concerning the commandments the Israelites were instructed: "Thou shalt teach them diligently unto thy children, and shalt talk of them when thou sittest in thine house, and when thou walkest by the way, and when thou liest down, and when thou risest up." Accordingly Moses directed the Israelites to set the words of the law to music. While the older children played on instruments, the younger ones marched, singing in concert the song of God's commandments. In later years they retained in their minds the words of the law which they learned during childhood.

If it was essential for Moses to embody the commandments in sacred song, so that as they marched in the wilderness, the children could learn to sing the law verse by verse, how essential it is at this time to teach our children God's Word! Let us come up to the help of the Lord, instructing our children to keep the commandments to the letter. Let us do everything in our power to make music in our homes, that God may come in. *Evangelism,* pp. 499, 500.

Special Worship Period for Sabbath. At family worship [on Sabbath] let the children take a part. Let all bring their Bibles and each read a verse or two. Then let some familiar hymn be sung, followed by prayer. For this, Christ has given a model. The Lord's Prayer was not intended to be repeated merely as a form, but it is an illustration of what our prayers should be—simple, earnest, and comprehensive. In a simple petition tell the Lord your needs and express gratitude for His mercies. Thus you invite Jesus as a welcome guest into your home and heart. In the family long prayers concerning remote objects are not in place. They make the hour of prayer a weariness, when it should be regarded as a privilege and blessing. Make the season one of interest and joy. *Testimonies for the Church,* vol. 6, pp. 357, 358.

More Prayer Means Less Punishment. We should pray to God much more than we do. There is great strength and blessing in praying together in our families, with and for our children. When my children have done wrong, and I have talked with them kindly and then prayed with them, I have never found it necessary after that to punish them. Their hearts would melt in tenderness before the Holy Spirit that came in answer to prayer. Manuscript 47, 1908.

Benefits of Solitary Prayer. It was in hours of solitary prayer that Jesus in His earth-life received wisdom and power. Let the youth follow His example in finding at dawn and twilight a quiet season for communion with their Father in heaven. And throughout the day let them lift up their hearts to God. At every step of our way He says, "I the Lord thy God will hold thy right hand; . . . fear not; I will help thee." Isaiah 41:13. Could our children learn these lessons in the morning of their years, what freshness and power, what joy and sweetness, would be brought into their lives! *Education,* p. 259.

The Gates of Heaven Are Open to Every Mother. When Christ bowed on the banks of Jordan after His baptism and offered up prayer in behalf of humanity, the heavens were opened; and the Spirit of God, like a dove of burnished gold, encircled the form of the Saviour; and a voice came from heaven which said, "This is my beloved Son, in whom I am well pleased."

What significance does this have for you? It says that heaven is open to your prayers. It says that you are accepted in the Beloved. The gates are open for every mother who would lay her burden at the Saviour's feet. It says that Christ has encircled the race with His human arm, and with His divine arm He has grasped the throne of the Infinite and united man with God, and earth with heaven. *Signs of the Times,* July 22, 1889.

The prayers of Christian mothers are not disregarded by the Father of all, who sent His Son to the earth to ransom a people for Himself. He will not turn away your petitions and leave you and yours to the buffetings of Satan in the great day of final conflict. It is for you to work with simplicity and faithfulness, and God will establish the work of your hands. *Review and Herald,* Apr. 23, 1889.

CHAPTER 79

Sabbath—The Day of Delight

Prevalent Disregard for the Sabbath. I have been shown that very many of the parents who profess to believe the solemn message for this time have not trained their children for God. They have not restrained themselves and have been irritated with anyone who attempted to restrain them. They have not by living faith daily bound their children upon the altar of the Lord. Many of these youth have been allowed to transgress the Fourth Commandment, by seeking their own pleasure upon God's holy day. They have felt no compunctions of conscience in going about the streets on the Sabbath for their own amusement. Many go where they please, and do what they please; and their parents are so fearful of displeasing them that, imitating the management of Eli, they lay no commands upon them.

These youth finally lose all respect for the Sabbath and have no relish for religious meetings or for sacred and eternal things. *Testimonies for the Church,* vol. 5, pp. 36, 37.

Heed First Word of the Fourth Commandment. "Remember" is placed at the very first of the Fourth Commandment. Parents, you need to remember the Sabbath day yourselves to keep it holy. And if you do this, you are giving the proper instruction to your children; they will reverence God's holy day. . . . Christian education is needed in your homes. All through the week keep the Lord's holy Sabbath in view, for that day is to be devoted to the service of God. It is a day when the hands are to rest from worldly employment, when the soul's needs are to receive especial attention. Manuscript 57, 1897.

When the Sabbath is thus remembered, the temporal will not be allowed to encroach upon the spiritual. No duty pertaining to the six working days will be left for the Sabbath. During the week our energies will not be so exhausted in temporal labor that on the day when the Lord rested and was refreshed, we shall be too weary to engage in His service. *Testimonies for the Church,* vol. 6, p. 354.

Make Friday the Preparation Day. On Friday let the preparation for the Sabbath be completed. See that all the clothing is in readiness, and that all the cooking is done. Let the boots be blacked, and the baths be taken. It is possible to do this. If you make it a rule, you can do it. The Sabbath is not to be given to the repairing of garments, to the cooking of food, to pleasure seeking, or to any other worldly employment. Before the setting of the sun, let all secular work be laid aside, and all secular papers be put out of sight. Parents, explain your work and its purpose to your children, and let them share in your preparation to keep the Sabbath according to the commandment. *Ibid.,* pp. 356, 357.

In many families [on Sabbath] boots and shoes are blacked and brushed, and stitches are taken, all because these little odds and ends were not done on Friday. They did not "remember the Sabbath day to keep it holy." . . .

On Friday the clothing of the children is to be looked after. During the week they should be all laid out by their own hands under the direction of the mother, so that they can dress quietly, without any confusion or rushing about and hasty speeches. Manuscript 57, 1897.

There is another work that should receive attention on the preparation day. On this day all differences between brethren, whether in the family or in the church, should be put away. *Testimonies for the Church,* vol. 6, p. 356.

The Sabbath Opens With the Family at Worship. Before the setting of the sun, let the members of the family assemble to read God's Word, to sing and pray. There is need of reform here, for many have been remiss. We need to confess to God and to one another. We should begin anew to make special arrangements that every member of the family may be prepared to honor the day which God has blessed and sanctified. *Ibid.,* pp. 356, 357.

Sabbath Hours Not Ours but God's. God has given us the whole of six days in which to do our work, and has reserved only one to Himself. This should be a day of blessing to us—a day when we should lay aside all our secular matters and center our thoughts upon God and heaven. Manuscript 3, 1879.

When the Sabbath commences, we should place a guard upon ourselves, upon our acts and our words, lest we rob God by appropriating to our own use that time which is strictly the Lord's. We should not do ourselves, nor suffer our children to do, any manner of our own work for a livelihood or anything which could have been done on the six working days. Friday is the day of preparation. Time can then be devoted to making the necessary preparation for the Sabbath and to thinking and conversing about it. Nothing which will in the sight of Heaven be regarded as a violation of the holy Sabbath should be left unsaid or undone, to be said or done upon the Sabbath. God requires not only that we refrain from physical labor upon the Sabbath, but that the mind be disciplined to dwell upon sacred themes. The Fourth Commandment is virtually transgressed by conversing

upon worldly things or by engaging in light and trifling conversation. Talking upon anything or everything which may
come into the mind is speaking our own words. Every deviation from right brings us into bondage and condemnation.
Testimonies for the Church, vol. 2, pp. 702, 703.

Sabbath Time Too Precious to Sleep Away. None
should permit themselves, through the week, to become so
absorbed in their temporal interests, and so exhausted by
their efforts for worldly gain, that on the Sabbath they have
no strength or energy to give to the service of God. We are
robbing the Lord when we unfit ourselves to worship Him
upon His holy day. And we are robbing ourselves as well; for
we need the warmth and glow of association, as well as the
strength to be gained from the wisdom and experience of
other Christians. *Review and Herald,* June 13, 1882.

Let not the precious hours of the Sabbath be wasted in
bed. On Sabbath morning the family should be astir early. If
they rise late, there is confusion and bustle in preparing for
breakfast and Sabbath school. There is hurrying, jostling, and
impatience. Thus unholy feelings come into the home. The
Sabbath, thus desecrated, becomes a weariness, and its coming is dreaded rather than loved. *Testimonies for the Church,*
vol. 6, p. 357.

Attend Public Worship With Children. Fathers and
mothers should make it a rule that their children attend public
worship on the Sabbath, and should enforce the rule by their
own example. It is our duty to command our children and our
household after us, as did Abraham. By example as well as precept we should impress upon them the importance of religious
teaching. All who have taken the baptismal vow have solemnly
consecrated themselves to the service of God; they are

under covenant obligation to place themselves and their children where they may obtain all possible incentives and encouragement in the Christian life. *Review and Herald,* June 13, 1882.

But while we worship God, we are not to consider this a drudgery. The Sabbath of the Lord is to be made a blessing to us and to our children. They are to look upon the Sabbath as a day of delight, a day which God has sanctified; and they will so consider it if they are properly instructed. Manuscript 3, 1879.

Wear Comely Garments for the House of Worship. Many need instruction as to how they should appear in the assembly for worship on the Sabbath. They are not to enter the presence of God in the common clothing worn during the week. All should have a special Sabbath suit, to be worn when attending service in God's house. While we should not conform to worldly fashions, we are not to be indifferent in regard to our outward appearance. We are to be neat and trim, though without adornment. The children of God should be pure within and without. *Testimonies for the Church,* vol. 6, p. 355.

Explain Sabbath Sermon to the Children. Ministers are engaged in a sacred, solemn work, but upon those who hear rests just as sacred a responsibility. They are to hear with a determination to follow the instruction that all must practice who gain eternal life. Each hearer should strive to understand each presentation of Bible truth as God's message to him, to be received by faith and put into practice in the daily life. Parents should explain to their children the words spoken from the pulpit, that they also may understand and have that knowledge which if put into practice brings abundant grace and peace. Manuscript 41, 1903.

Provide Special Treat for Mealtime. We should not provide for the Sabbath a more liberal supply or a greater variety of food than for other days. Instead of this the food should be more simple, and less should be eaten, in order that the mind may be clear and vigorous to comprehend spiritual things. Overeating befogs the brain. The most precious words may be heard and not appreciated, because the mind is confused by an improper diet. By overeating on the Sabbath, many have done more than they think to dishonor God.

While cooking upon the Sabbath should be avoided, it is not necessary to eat cold food. In cold weather let the food prepared the day before be heated. And let the meals, though simple, be palatable and attractive. Provide something that will be regarded as a treat, something the family do not have every day. *Testimonies for the Church,* vol. 6, p. 357.

The Rest of the Day Is Precious. The Sabbath school and the meeting for worship occupy only a part of the Sabbath. The portion remaining to the family may be made the most sacred and precious season of all the Sabbath hours. Much of this time parents should spend with their children. *Ibid.,* p. 358.

Plan Suitable Reading and Conversation. The Sabbath—oh!—make it the sweetest, the most blessed day of the week. . . .

Parents can and should give attention to their children, reading to them the most attractive portions of Bible history, educating them to reverence the Sabbath day, keeping it according to the commandment. This cannot be done if the parents feel no burden to interest their children. But they can make the Sabbath a delight if they will take the proper course. The children can be interested in good reading or in conversation about the salvation of their souls. But they will have to be educated and trained. The natural heart does not love to think of God, of heaven, or of heavenly things. There must be a continual pressing back of the current of worldliness and inclination to evil and a letting in of heavenly light. *Review and Herald,* Apr. 14, 1885.

Not Indifferent to Children's Activities. I have found that on the Sabbath day many are indifferent and do not know where their children are or what they are doing. *Ibid.*

Parents, above everything take care of your children upon the Sabbath. Do not suffer them to violate God's holy day by playing in the house or out-of-doors. You may just as well break the Sabbath yourselves as to let your children do it, and when you suffer your children to wander about and suffer them to play upon the Sabbath, God looks upon you as Sabbathbreakers. *Review and Herald,* Sept. 19, 1854.

Out-of-doors With the Children. The parents may take their children outdoors to view God in nature. They can be pointed to the blooming flowers and the opening buds, the lofty trees and beautiful spires of grass, and taught that God made all these in six days and rested on the seventh day and hallowed it. Thus the parents may bind up their lessons of instruction to their children, so that when these children look upon the things of nature, they will call to mind the great Creator of them all. Their thoughts will be carried up to nature's God—back to the creation of our world, when the foundation of the Sabbath was laid, and all the sons of God shouted for joy. Such are the lessons to be impressed on the minds of our children.

We are not to teach our children that they must not

be happy on the Sabbath, that it is wrong to walk out-of-doors. Oh, no. Christ led His disciples out by the lakeside on the Sabbath day and taught them. His sermons on the Sabbath were not always preached within enclosed walls. Manuscript 3, 1879.

Other Lessons From Nature—Object Lessons. Teach the children to see Christ in nature. Take them out into the open air, under the noble trees, into the garden; and in all the wonderful works of creation teach them to see an expression of His love. Teach them that He made the laws which govern all living things, that He has made laws for us, and that these laws are for our happiness and joy. Do not weary them with long prayers and tedious exhortations, but through nature's object lessons teach them obedience to the law of God. *The Desire of Ages,* pp. 516, 517.

Give True Concept of God's Character. How can children receive a more correct knowledge of God, and their minds be better impressed, than in spending a portion of their time out-of-doors, not in play, but in company with their parents? Let their young minds be associated with God in the beautiful scenery of nature; let their attention be called to the tokens of His love to man in His created works, and they will be attracted and interested. They will not be in danger of associating the character of God with everything that is stern and severe; but as they view the beautiful things which He has created for the happiness of man, they will be led to regard Him as a tender, loving Father. They will see that His prohibitions and injunctions are not made merely to show His power and authority, but that He has the happiness of His children in view. As the character of God puts on the aspect of love, benevolence, beauty, and attraction, they are drawn to love Him. You can direct their minds to the lovely birds making the air musical with their happy songs, to the spires of grass and the gloriously tinted flowers in their perfection perfuming the air. All these proclaim the love and skill of the heavenly Artist and show forth the glory of God.

Parents, why not make use of the precious lessons which God has given us in the book of nature, to give our children a correct idea of His character? Those who sacrifice simplicity to fashion and shut themselves away from the beauties of nature cannot be spiritually minded. They cannot understand the skill and power of God as revealed in His created works; therefore their hearts do not quicken and throb with new love and interest, and they are not filled with awe and reverence as they see God in nature. *Testimonies for the Church,* vol. 2, pp. 583, 584.

A Day to Live the Life of Eden. The value of the Sabbath as a means of education is beyond estimate. Whatever of ours God claims from us, He returns again, enriched, transfigured, with His own glory. . . .

The Sabbath and the family were alike instituted in Eden, and in God's purpose they are indissolubly linked together. On this day more than on any other, it is possible for us to live the life of Eden. It was God's plan for the members of the family to be associated in work and study, in worship and recreation, the father as priest of his household, and both father and mother as teachers and companions of their children. But the results of sin, having changed the conditions of life, to a great degree prevent this association. Often the father hardly sees the faces of his children throughout the week. He is almost wholly deprived of opportunity for companionship or instruction. But God's love has set a limit to the demands of toil. Over the Sabbath He places His merciful hand. In His own day He preserves for the family opportunity for communion with Him, with nature, and with one another. *Education,* pp. 250, 251.

Make the Sabbath a Delight. All who love God should do what they can to make the Sabbath a delight, holy and honorable. They cannot do this by seeking their own pleasure in sinful, forbidden amusements. Yet they can do much to exalt the Sabbath in their families and make it the most interesting day of the week. We should devote time to interesting our children. A change will have a happy influence upon them. We can walk out with them in the open air; we can sit with them in the groves and in the bright sunshine, and give their restless minds something to feed upon by conversing with them upon the works of God, and can inspire them with love and reverence by calling their attention to the beautiful objects in nature.

The Sabbath should be made so interesting to our families that its weekly return will be hailed with joy. In no better way can parents exalt and honor the Sabbath than by devising means to impart proper instruction to their families and interesting them in spiritual things, giving them correct views of the character of God and what He requires of us in order to perfect Christian characters and attain to eternal life. Parents, make the Sabbath a delight, that your children may look forward to it and have a welcome in their hearts for it. *Testimonies for the Church,* vol. 2, pp. 584, 585.

A Fitting Climax in Prayer and Song. As the sun goes down, let the voice of prayer and the hymn of praise mark the close of the sacred hours, and invite God's presence through the cares of the week of labor.

Thus parents can make the Sabbath, as it should be, the most joyful day of the week. They can lead their children to regard it as a delight, the day of days, the holy of the Lord, honorable. *Ibid.,* vol. 6, p. 359.

CHAPTER 80

Reverence for That Which Is Holy

The Precious Grace of Reverence. Another precious grace that should be carefully cherished is reverence. *Education,* p. 242.

The education and training of the youth should be of a character that would exalt sacred things, and encourage pure devotion for God in His house. Many who profess to be children of the heavenly King have no true appreciation of the sacredness of eternal things. *Testimonies for the Church,* vol. 5, p. 496.

God Is to Be Had in Reverence. True reverence for God is inspired by a sense of His infinite greatness and a realization of His presence. With this sense of the Unseen the heart of every child should be deeply impressed. *Education,* p. 242.

"God is greatly to be feared in the assembly of the saints, and to be had in reverence of all them that are about him." Psalm 89:7.

His Name Is to Be Revered. Reverence should be shown also for the name of God. Never should that name be spoken lightly or thoughtlessly. Even in prayer its frequent or needless repetition should be avoided. "Holy and reverend is his name." Psalm 111:9. Angels, as they speak it, veil their faces. With what reverence should we, who are fallen and sinful, take it upon our lips! *Ibid.,* p. 243.

His Word Is Sacred. We should reverence God's Word. For the printed volume we should show respect, never putting it to common uses or handling it carelessly. And never should Scripture be quoted in a jest or paraphrased to point a witty saying. "Every word of God is pure"; "as silver tried in a furnace of earth, purified seven times." (Proverbs 30:5; Psalm 12:6.) *Ibid., p. 244.*

Children should be taught to respect every word that proceeds out of the mouth of God. Parents are ever to magnify the precepts of the law of the Lord before their children, by showing obedience to that law, by themselves living under the control of God. If a sense of the sacredness of the law takes possession of the parents, it will surely transform the character by converting the soul. *Review and Herald,* May 10, 1898.

The Place of Prayer—God Is There. In every Christian home God should be honored by the morning and evening sacrifices of prayer and praise. Children should be taught to respect and reverence the hour of prayer. *Counsels to Parents, Teachers, and Students,* p. 110.

The hour and place of prayer and the services of public worship the child should be taught to regard as sacred because God is there. And as reverence is manifested in attitude and demeanor, the feeling that inspires it will be deepened. *Education,* pp. 242, 243.

The House of God—His Holy Temple. Well would it be for young and old to study and ponder and often repeat those words of Holy Writ that show how the place marked by God's special presence should be regarded.

"Put off thy shoes from off thy feet," He commanded Moses at the burning bush, "for the place whereon thou standest is holy ground." Exodus 3:5.

Jacob, after beholding the vision of the angels, exclaimed, "The Lord is in this place; and I knew it not. . . . This is none other but the house of God, and this is the gate of heaven." Genesis 28:16, 17.

"The Lord is in his holy temple: let all the earth keep silence before him." Habakkuk 2:20. *Ibid.,* p. 243.

Many . . . have no true appreciation of the sacredness of eternal things. Nearly all need to be taught how to conduct themselves in the house of God. Parents should not only teach, but command, their children to enter the sanctuary with sobriety and reverence. *Testimonies for the Church,* vol. 5, p. 496.

Guard Against a Growing Carelessness. From the sacredness which was attached to the earthly sanctuary, Christians may learn how they should regard the place where the Lord meets with His people. There has been a great change, not for the better, but for the worse, in the habits and customs of the people in reference to religious worship. The precious, the sacred things which connect us with God are fast losing their hold upon our minds and hearts and are being brought down to the level of the common things. The reverence which the people had anciently for the sanctuary, where they met with God in sacred service, has largely passed away. Nevertheless God Himself gave the order of His service, exalting it high above everything of a temporal nature. *Ibid.,* p. 491.

The house of God is often desecrated, and the Sabbath violated by Sabbath-believers' children. In some cases they are even allowed to run about the house, play, talk, and manifest their evil tempers in the very meetings where the saints should worship God in the beauty of holiness. And the place that should be holy, and where a holy stillness should reign, and where there should be perfect order, neatness, and humility, is made to be a perfect Babylon, "confusion." This is enough to bring God's displeasure and shut His presence from our assemblies. *Review and Herald,* Sept. 19, 1854.

We Have More Reasons for Reverence Than the Hebrews. It is too true that reverence for the house of God has become almost extinct. Sacred things and places are not discerned; the holy and exalted are not appreciated. Is there not a cause for the want of fervent piety in our families? Is it not because the high standard of religion is left to trail in the dust? God gave rules of order, perfect and exact, to His ancient people. Has His character changed? Is He not the great and mighty God who rules in the heaven of heavens? Would it not be well for us often to read the directions given by God Himself to the Hebrews, that we who have the light of the glorious truth shining upon us may imitate their reverence for the house of God? We have abundant reason . . . even to be more thoughtful and reverential in our worship than had the Jews. But an enemy has been at work to destroy our faith in the sacredness of Christian worship. *Testimonies for the Church,* vol. 5, pp. 495, 496.

The Church—the Sanctuary of the Congregation. The house is the sanctuary for the family, and the closet or the grove the most retired place for individual worship; but the church is the sanctuary for the congregation. There should be rules in regard to the time, the place, and the manner of worshiping. *Ibid.,* p. 491.

Teach Children to Enter Reverently. Parents, elevate the standard of Christianity in the minds of your children; help them to weave Jesus into their experience; teach them to have the highest reverence for the house of God and to understand that when they enter the Lord's house, it should be with hearts that are softened and subdued by such thoughts as these: "God is here; this is His house. I must have pure thoughts and the holiest motives. I must have no pride, envy, jealousy, evil surmising, hatred, or deception in my heart; for I am coming into the presence of the holy God. This is the place where God meets with and blesses His people. The high and holy One who inhabiteth eternity looks upon me, searches my heart, and reads the most secret thoughts and acts of my life." *Ibid., p.* 494.

Remain With Their Parents. The moral taste of the worshipers in God's holy sanctuary must be elevated, refined, sanctified. This matter has been sadly neglected. Its importance has been overlooked, and as the result disorder and irreverence have become prevalent, and God has been dishonored. When the leaders in the church, ministers and people, fathers and mothers, have not had elevated views of this matter, what could be expected of the inexperienced children? They are too often found in groups, away from the parents, who should have charge of them. Notwithstanding they are in the presence of God, and His eye is looking upon them; they are light and trifling; they whisper and laugh, are careless, irreverent, and inattentive. *Ibid.,* pp. 496, 497.

To Be Sober and Quiet. Do not have so little reverence for the house and worship of God as to communicate with one another during the sermon. If those who commit this fault could see the angels of God looking upon them and marking their doings, they would be filled with shame and abhorrence of themselves. God wants attentive hearers. It was while men slept that the enemy sowed tares. *Messages to Young People,* p. 266.

Not to Act as in a Common Place. There should be a sacred spot, like the sanctuary of old, where God is to meet with His people. That place should not be used as a lunchroom or as a business room, but simply for the worship of God. When children attend day school in the same place where they assemble to worship on the Sabbath, they cannot be made to feel the sacredness of the place, and that they must enter with feelings of reverence. The sacred and common are so blended that it is difficult to distinguish them.

It is for this reason that the house or sanctuary dedicated to God should not be made a common place. Its sacredness should not be confused or mingled with the common everyday feelings or business life. There should be a solemn awe upon the worshipers as they enter the sanctuary, and they should leave behind all common worldly thoughts, for it is the place where God reveals His presence. It is as the audience chamber of the great and eternal God; therefore pride and passion, dissension and self-esteem, selfishness, and covetousness, which God pronounces idolatry, are inappropriate for such a place. Manuscript 23, 1886.

To Manifest No Spirit of Levity. Parents, it is your duty to have your children in perfect subjection, having all their passions and evil tempers subdued. And if children are taken to meeting, they should be made to know and understand where they are—that they are not at home, but where God meets with His people. And they should be kept quiet and free from all play, and God will turn His face toward you, to meet with you and bless you.

If order is observed in the assemblies of the saints, the truth will have better effect upon all that hear it. A solemnity which is so much needed will be encouraged, and there will be power in the truth to stir up the depths of the soul, and a deathlike stupor will not hang upon those who hear. Believers and unbelievers will be affected. It has seemed evident that in some places the ark of God was removed from the church, for the holy commandments have been violated and the strength of Israel has been weakened. *Review and Herald,* Sept. 19, 1854.

Take the Disturbing Child Out. Your child should be taught to obey as the children of God obey Him. If this standard is maintained, a word from you will have some weight when your child is restless in the house of God. But if the children cannot be restrained, if the parents feel that the restraint is too much of an exaction, the child should be removed from the church at once; it should not be left to divert the minds of the hearers by talking or running about. God is dishonored by the loose way in which parents manage their children while at church. Letter 1, 1877.

Irreverence Encouraged by Display of Apparel. All should be taught to be neat, clean, and orderly in their dress, but not to indulge in that external adorning which is wholly inappropriate for the sanctuary. There should be no display of the apparel, for this encourages irreverence. . . . All matters of dress should be strictly guarded, following closely the Bible rule. Fashion has been the goddess who has ruled the outside world, and she often insinuates herself into the church. The church should make the Word of God her standard, and parents should think intelligently upon this subject. *Testimonies for the Church,* vol. 5, pp. 499, 500.

Show Reverence for Ministers—God's Representatives. Reverence should be shown for God's representatives—for ministers, teachers, and parents who are called to speak and act in His stead. In the respect shown to them He is honored. *Education,* p. 244.

They [children] are seldom instructed that the minister is God's ambassador, that the message he brings is one of God's appointed agencies in the salvation of souls, and that to all who have the privilege brought within their reach, it will be a savor of life unto life or of death unto death. *Testimonies for the Church,* vol. 5, p. 497.

Nothing that is sacred, nothing that pertains to the worship of God, should be treated with carelessness and indifference. When the word of life is spoken, you should remember that you are listening to the voice of God through His delegated servant. Do not lose these words through inattention; if heeded, they may keep your feet from straying into wrong paths. *Messages to Young People,* p. 266.

Accountability of Critical Parents. Parents, be careful what example and what ideas you give your children. Their minds are plastic, and impressions are easily made. In regard to the service of the sanctuary, if the speaker has a blemish, be afraid to mention it. Talk only of the good work he is doing, of the good ideas he presented, which you should heed as coming through God's agent. It may be readily seen why children are so little impressed with the ministry of the Word, and why they have so little reverence for the house of God. Their education has been defective in this respect. *Testimonies for the Church,* vol. 5, p. 498.

The delicate and susceptible minds of the youth obtain their estimate of the labors of God's servants by the way their parents treat the matter. Many heads of families make the service a subject of criticism at home, approving a few things and condemning others. Thus the message of God to men is criticized and questioned and made a subject of levity. What impressions are thus made upon the young by these careless, irreverent remarks, the books of heaven alone will reveal. The children see and understand these things very much quicker than parents are apt to think. Their moral senses receive a wrong bias that time will never fully change. The parents mourn over the hardness of heart in their children and the difficulty in arousing their moral sensibility to answer to the claims of God. But the books of heavenly record trace with unerring pen the true cause. The parents were unconverted. They were not in harmony with Heaven or with Heaven's work. Their low, common ideas of the sacredness of the ministry and of the sanctuary of God were woven into the education of their children.

It is a question whether anyone who has for years been under this blighting influence of home instruction will ever have a sensitive reverence and high regard for God's ministry and the agencies He has appointed for the salvation of souls. These things should be spoken of with reverence, with propriety of language, and with fine susceptibility, that you may reveal to all you associate with that you regard the message from God's servants as a message to you from God Himself. *Ibid.,* pp. 497, 498.

Practice Reverence Till It Becomes Habitual. Reverence is greatly needed in the youth of this age. I am alarmed as I see children and youth of religious parents so heedless of the order and propriety that should be observed in the house of God. While God's servants are presenting the words of life to the people, some will be reading, others whispering and laughing. Their eyes are sinning by diverting the attention of those around them. This habit, if allowed to remain unchecked, will grow and influence others.

Children and youth should never feel that it is something to be proud of to be indifferent and careless in meetings where God is worshiped. God sees every irreverent thought or action, and it is registered in the books of heaven. He says, "I know thy works." Nothing is hid from His all-searching eye. If you have formed in any degree the habit of inattention and indifference in the house of God, exercise the powers you have to correct it, and show that you have self-respect. Practice reverence until it becomes a part of yourself. *Youth's Instructor,* Oct. 8, 1896.

CHAPTER 81

Coordination of Home and Church

Begin the Work of Grace in the Home. Parents, begin the work of grace in the church in your own home, so conducting yourselves that your children will see that you are cooperating with the heavenly angels. Be sure that you are converted every day. Train yourselves and your children for life eternal in the kingdom of God. Angels will be your strong helpers. Satan will tempt you, but do not yield. Do not speak one word of which the enemy can take an advantage.

Truth is pure and uncorrupted. Let it dwell in the heart. Let the determination of each member of the family be, "I will be a Christian, for in the school here below I must form a character which will give me entrance into the higher grade in heaven. I must do to others as I desire them to do to me, for only those who reveal Christ in this world can enter the courts of heaven."

Make the home life as nearly as possible like heaven. Let the members of the family forget not, as they gather round the family altar, to pray for the men in positions of responsibility in God's work. Manuscript 93, 1901.

Those who govern their families in the right way will bring into the church an influence of order and reverence. They will represent the attributes of mercy and justice as standing hand in hand. They will reveal to their children the character of Christ. The law of kindness and love upon their lips will not make their commands weak and

548

without authority, and their injunctions will not be met with disobedience. *Review and Herald,* Feb. 19, 1895.

Model Homes Make a Model Church. Every family is a church, over which the parents preside. The first consideration of the parents should be to work for the salvation of their children. When the father and mother as priest and teacher of the family take their position fully on the side of Christ, a good influence will be exerted in the home. And this sanctified influence will be felt in the church and will be recognized by every believer. Because of the great lack of piety and sanctification in the home, the work of God is greatly hindered. No man can bring into the church an influence that he does not exert in his home life and in his business relations. Manuscript 57, 1903.

Proper Church Conduct Is Learned at Home. The home is a school where all may learn how they are to act in the church. When all are members of the royal family, there will be true politeness in the home life. Each member of the family will seek to make it pleasant for every other member. The angels of God, who minister to those who shall be heirs of salvation, will help you to make your family a model of the heavenly family. Let there be peace in the home, and there will be peace in the church. This precious experience brought into the church will be the means of creating a kindly affection one for another. Quarrels will cease. True Christian courtesy will be seen among church members. The world will take knowledge of them that they have been with Jesus and have learned of Him. What an impression the church would make upon the world if all the members would live Christian lives! Manuscript 60, 1903.

Why There Is Weakness in the Church. Many seem to think that the declension in the church, the growing love of pleasure, is due to want of pastoral work. True, the church is to be provided with faithful guides and pastors. Ministers should labor earnestly for the youth who have not given themselves to Christ, and also for others who, though their names are on the church roll, are irreligious and Christless. But ministers may do their work faithfully and well, yet it will amount to very little if parents neglect their work. It is to a lack of Christianity in the home life that the lack of power in the church is due. Until parents take up their work as they should, it will be difficult to arouse the youth to a sense of their duty. If religion reigns in the home, it will be brought into the church. The parents who do their work for God are a power for good. As they restrain and encourage their children, bringing them up in the nurture and admonition of the Lord, they bless the neighborhood in which they live. And the church is strengthened by their faithful work. *Signs of the Times,* Apr. 3, 1901.

Neglectful Parents Cannot Uplift the Church. If disobedience is allowed in the home life, the hearts of the children will be filled with opposition to the government of God. The power of the Holy Spirit will prove ineffectual to soften and subdue their hearts. If in later years, under special circumstances, they yield to the gospel of Christ, they will have to fight terrible battles to bring the disloyal will into submission to the will of God. Often the church has to suffer through its members because of the wrong education received by them in childhood. When children, they were allowed to practice deception in order to gain their own way; and the spirit that was permitted to be rebellious in the home will be the last to render obedience to the requirements of God's Word. *Review and Herald,* Mar. 30, 1897.

Spirituality May Be Killed by Criticism. When you are tempted to speak cross words, pray for grace to resist the temptation. Remember that your children will speak as they hear you speaking. By your example you are educating them. Remember that if you speak cross words to fellow church members, you would speak the same kind of words in heaven, were you permitted to enter there. . . .

After the family then comes the church. The influence of the family is to be such that it will be a help and a blessing in the church. Never speak a word of complaint or faultfinding. There are churches in which the spirituality has been almost killed, because the spirit of backbiting has been allowed to enter. Why do we speak words of blame and censure? To be silent is the strongest rebuke that you can give to one who is speaking harsh, discourteous words to you. Keep perfectly silent. Often silence is eloquence. Manuscript 21, 1903.

In Care for Unfortunate Youth. Young men and women who are not under home influences need someone to look after them and to manifest some interest for them; and those who do this are supplying a great lack and are as verily doing a work for God and the salvation of souls as the minister in the pulpit. This work of disinterested benevolence in laboring for the good of the youth is no more than God requires of every one of us. How earnestly should the experienced Christian work to prevent the formation of those habits that indelibly mar the character! Let the followers of Christ make the Word of God attractive to the youth. *Fundamentals of Christian Education,* p. 51.

The Minister Has a Special Opportunity. At every suitable opportunity let the story of Jesus' love be repeated to the children. In every sermon let a little corner be left for their benefit. The servant of Christ may make lasting friends of these little ones. Then let him lose no opportunity of helping them to become more intelligent in a knowledge of the Scriptures. This will do more than we realize to bar the way against Satan's devices. If children early become familiar with the truths of God's Word, a barrier against ungodliness will be erected, and they will be able to meet the foe with the words, "It is written." *Gospel workers,* p. 208.

Be as Faithful at Home as at Worship. Parents, as teachers of your loved ones the truth should have a controlling power over your conscience and your understanding, presiding over word and deed. Be as faithful in your home life as you are in the worship of God. Give a right character to all within the home. Angels of God are present, noting how the younger members of the Lord's family are treated. The religion of the home will surely be brought into the church. Manuscript 84, 1897.

THE DAY OF RECKONING

CHAPTER 82

The Hour Is Late

Satan Is Marshaling His Host. Satan is marshaling his host, and are we individually prepared for the fearful conflict that is just before us? Are we preparing ourselves and our households to understand the position of our adversaries and their modes of warfare? Are our children forming habits of decision, that they may be firm and unyielding in every matter of principle and duty? I pray that we all may understand the signs of the times, and that we may so prepare ourselves and our children that in the time of conflict God may be our refuge and defense. *Review and Herald,* Apr. 23, 1889.

Prepare for an Overwhelming Surprise. Transgression has almost reached its limit. Confusion fills the world, and a great terror is soon to come upon human beings. The end is very near. God's people should be preparing for what is to break upon the world as an overwhelming surprise.

Our time is precious. We have but a few, a very few, days of probation in which to make ready for the future, immortal life. *Youth's Instructor,* Apr. 28, 1908.

Many Families Unprepared. On Sabbath and Sunday, in visions of the night, I seemed to be bearing my testimony before the people. On both these occasions I seemed to be in a mammoth tent which was literally packed. The Lord gave me a decided message for the people. My burden was for our families who are unprepared to meet the Lord. A special burden was upon me to point out to our people the need of seeking the Lord with close searching of heart and earnestness of purpose. . . .

Parents who are truly converted will reveal in their home life that they are bringing their lives under the discipline of the Word of God. . . . To the mother and father the right training of their children is the most important work of their life. Letter 64, 1911.

Solemn Questions for Parents. Fathers and mothers, how stands your record? Have you been faithful to your trust? As you have seen your children inclined to follow a course that you knew would result in impurity of thought and word and act, have you, first asking God for help, tried to show them their danger? Have you pointed out to them the peril of taking a path of their own choosing? Mothers, have you neglected your God-given work—the greatest work ever committed to mortals? Have you refused to bear your God-given responsibilities? In the time of trouble just before us, when the judgments of God fall upon the impure and unholy, will your children curse you because of your indulgence? *Review and Herald,* Dec. 23, 1902.

Parents New in the Message Need Instruction. Those who bear the last message of mercy to the world should feel it their duty to instruct parents in regard to home religion. Their great reformatory movement must begin in presenting to fathers and mothers and children the principles of the law of God. As the claims of the law are presented, and men and women are convicted of their duty to render obedience, show them the responsibility of their decision, not only for themselves but for their children. Show that obedience to God's Word is our only safeguard against the evils that are sweeping the world to destruction. *Testimonies for the Church,* vol. 6, p. 119.

Our Youth Need Help and Encouragement. Now is our time and opportunity to labor for the young people.

Tell them that we are now in a perilous crisis, and we want to know how to discern true godliness. Our young people need to be helped, uplifted, and encouraged, but in the right manner; not, perhaps, as they would desire it, but in a way that will help them to have sanctified minds. They need good, sanctifying religion more than anything else. *Fundamentals of Christian Education,* p. 547.

Do Not Delay. Coming events are casting their shadows upon our pathway. Fathers, mothers, I appeal to you to make most earnest efforts now for your children. Give them daily religious instruction. Teach them to love God and to be true to the principles of right. With lofty, earnest faith, directed by the divine influence of the Holy Spirit, work, work *now.* Do not put it off one day, one hour. *Review and Herald,* Apr. 23, 1889.

Do a Thorough Work. Parents, humble your hearts before God. Begin a thorough work with your children. Plead with the Lord to forgive your disregard of His Word in neglecting to train your children in the way they should go. Ask for light and guidance, for a tender conscience, and for clear discernment that you may see your mistakes and failures. God will hear such prayers from a humble and contrite heart. Manuscript 22, 1904.

Confession May Be Necessary. If you have failed in your duty to your families, confess your sins before God. Gather your children about you and acknowledge your neglect. Tell them that you desire to bring about a reformation in the home, and ask them to help you to make the home what it ought to be. Read to them the directions found in the Word of God. Pray with them; and ask God to spare their lives, and to help them to prepare for a home in His kingdom. In this way you may begin a work of reformation; and then continue to keep the way of the Lord. *Ibid.*

Give Children an Example of Strict Obedience. The special work of parents is to make the laws of God plain to their children and to urge their obedience to them, that they may see the importance of obeying God all the days of their life. This was the work of Moses. He was to enjoin upon parents their duty to give to their children an example of strict obedience. And this is the work that above everything else must be done in the home life today. It is to accompany the third angel's message. Ignorance is no excuse why parents should neglect to teach their children what it means to transgress the law of God. The light is abundant, and none need to walk in darkness, none need to be in ignorance. God is as verily our instructor today as He was the teacher of the children of Israel, and all are bound by the most sacred obligations to obey His laws. Letter 90, 1898.

Pray and Work for Their Salvation. Teach your children that the heart must be trained to self-control and self-denial. The motives of the life must be in harmony with the law of God. Never be satisfied to have your children grow up apart from Christ. Never feel at ease while they are cold and indifferent. Cry to God day and night. Pray and work for the salvation of the souls of your children. "The fear of the Lord is the beginning of wisdom." It is the mainspring, the balance wheel of character. Without the fear of the Lord, they will fail of accomplishing the great object of their creation. *Review and Herald,* Apr. 23, 1889.

Act as Character Builders. Seventh-day Adventist parents should more fully realize their responsibilities as character builders. God places before them the privilege of strengthening His cause through the consecration and labors of their children. He desires to see gathered out from the homes of our people a large company of youth who, because of the godly influences of their homes, have surrendered their hearts to Him and go forth to give Him the highest service of their lives. Directed and trained by the godly instruction of the home, the influence of the morning and evening worship, the consistent example of parents who love and fear God, they have learned to submit to God as their teacher and are prepared to render Him acceptable service as loyal sons and daughters. Such youth are prepared to represent to the world the power and grace of Christ. *Counsels to Parents, Teachers, and Students,* p. 131.

CHAPTER 83

The Rewards

A Graphic Scene of the Judgment Day. I had a dream once in which I saw a large company gathered together; and suddenly the heavens gathered blackness, the thunder rolled, the lightning flashed, and a voice louder than the heaviest peals of thunder sounded through the heavens and the earth, saying, "It is done." Part of the company, with pallid faces, sprang forward with a wail of agony, crying out, "Oh, I am not ready." The question was asked, "Why are you not ready? Why have you not improved the opportunities I graciously gave you?" I awoke with the crying ringing in my ears. "I am not ready; I am unsaved—lost! lost! eternally lost!"

In view of the solemn responsibilities that rest upon us, let us contemplate the future, that we may understand what we must do in order to meet it. In that day shall we be confronted with neglect and contempt of God and His mercy, with rejection of His truth and love? In the solemn assembly of the last day, in the hearing of the universe, will be read the reason of the condemnation of the sinner. For the first time parents will learn what has been the secret life of their children. Children will see how many wrongs they have committed against their parents. There will be a general revealing of the secrets and motives of the heart, for that which is hid will be made manifest. Those who have made sport of solemn things connected with the judgment will be sobered as they face its terrible reality.

Those who have despised the Word of God will then face the Author of the inspired oracles. We cannot afford to live with no reference to the day of judgment; for though long delayed, it is now near, even at the door, and hasteth greatly. The trumpet of the Archangel will soon startle the living and wake the dead. At that day the wicked will be separated from the just, as the shepherd divides the goats from the sheep. *Youth's Instructors,* July 21, 1892.

When God Asks, "Where Are the Children?" Parents who have neglected their God-given responsibilities must meet that neglect in the judgment. The Lord will then inquire, "Where are the children that I gave you to train for Me? Why are they not at My right hand?" Many parents will then see that unwise love blinded their eyes to their children's faults and left those children to develop deformed characters unfit for heaven. Others will see that they did not give their children time and attention, love and tenderness; their own neglect of duty made the children what they are. *Testimonies for the Church,* vol. 4, p. 424.

Parents, if you lose your opportunity, God pity you; for in the day of judgment God will say, "What have you done with My flock, My beautiful flock?". . .

Suppose you should get to heaven and none of your children be there. How could you say to God, "Here am I, Lord, and the children which Thou hast given me"? Heaven marks the neglect of parents. It is recorded in the books of heaven. Manuscript 62, 1901.

Families Will Pass in Review Before God. When parents and children meet at the final reckoning, what a scene will be presented! Thousands of children who have been slaves to appetite and debasing vice, whose lives are moral wrecks, will stand face to face with the parents who made them what they are. Who but the parents must bear this fearful responsibility? Did the Lord make these youth corrupt? Oh, no! He made them in His image, a little lower than the angels. Who, then, has done the fearful work of forming the life character? Who changed their characters so that they do not bear the impress of God and must be forever separated from His presence as too impure to have any place with the pure angels in a holy heaven? Were the sins of the parents transmitted to the children in perverted appetites and passions? And was the work completed by the pleasure-loving mother in neglecting to properly train them according to the pattern given her? All these mothers will pass in review before God just as surely as they exist. *Testimonies for the Church,* vol. 3, pp. 568, 569.

In Heaven Is a Pictorial Record. Let parents and children remember that day by day they are each forming a character, and that the features of this character are imprinted upon the books of heaven. God is taking pictures of His people, just as surely as an artist takes pictures of men and women, transferring the features of the face to the polished plate. What kind of picture do you wish to produce? Parents, answer the question! What kind of picture will the great Master Artist make of you in the records of heaven? . . . We must decide this now. Hereafter, when death shall come, there will be no time to straighten the crooked places in the character.

To us individually this should be a most important matter. Every day our likeness is being taken for time and for eternity. Let each one say, "I am having my likeness taken today." Ask yourself daily, hourly, "How will my words sound to the heavenly angels? Are they as apples of gold in pictures of silver, or are they like a blasting hail, wounding and bruising?" . . .

Not only our words and actions, but our thoughts, make up the picture of what we are. Then let every soul be good and do good. Let the picture made of you be one of which you will not be ashamed. Every feeling we cherish makes its impress upon the countenance. God help us to make our record in our families what we would wish it to be in the heavenly record. Letter 78, 1901.

Have You Been Careless? Oh, that parents would look prayerfully and carefully after their children's eternal welfare! Let them ask themselves, Have we been careless? Have we neglected this solemn work? Have we allowed our children to become the sport of Satan's temptations? Have we not a solemn account to settle with God because we have permitted our children to use their talents, their time and influence, in working against the truth, against Christ? Have we not neglected our duty as parents and increased the number of the subjects of Satan's kingdom? *Testimonies for the Church,* vol. 6, pp. 429, 430.

If mothers neglect to properly educate their children, their neglect is reflected back upon them again, making their burdens and perplexities harder than they would have been if they had devoted time and patient care in training their children to obedience and submission. It will pay in the end for mothers to make the formation of the characters of their children their first and highest consideration, that the thorns may not take root and yield an abundant harvest. *Signs of the Times,* Aug. 5, 1875.

Children Will Condemn Unfaithful Parents. The curse of God will surely rest upon unfaithful parents. Not only are they planting thorns which will wound them here, but they must meet their own unfaithfulness when the judgment shall sit. Many children will rise up in judgment and condemn their parents for not restraining them and charge upon them their destruction. The false sympathy and blind love of parents cause them to excuse the faults of their children and pass them by without correction, and their children are lost in consequence, and the blood of their souls will rest upon the unfaithful parents. *Testimonies for the Church,* vol. 1, p. 219.

Children Will Pay Tribute to Faithful Parents. When the judgment shall sit, and the books shall be opened; when the "well done" of the great Judge is pronounced, and the crown of immortal glory is placed upon the brow of the victor, many will raise their crowns in sight of the assembled universe and, pointing to their mother, say, "She made me all I am through the grace of God. Her instruction, her prayers, have been blessed to my eternal salvation." *Messages to Young People,* p. 330.

Results of Faithful Training Will Be Manifest. All who have wrought with unselfish spirit will behold the fruit of their labors. The outworking of every right principle and noble deed will be seen. Something of this we see here. But how little of the result of the world's noblest work is in this life manifest to the doer! How many toil unselfishly and unweariedly for those who pass beyond their reach and knowledge! Parents and teachers lie down in their last sleep, their lifework seeming to have been wrought in vain; they know not that their faithfulness has unsealed springs of blessing that can never cease to flow; only by faith they see the children they have trained become a benediction and an inspiration to their fellowmen, and the influence repeat itself a thousandfold. . . . Men sow the seed from which, above their graves, others reap blessed harvests. They plant trees that others may eat the fruit. They are content here to know that they have set in motion agencies for good. In the hereafter the action and reaction of all these will be seen. *Education,* pp. 305, 306.

Parents May Bring Children With Them to Promised Land. God has permitted light from His throne to shine all along the path of life. A pillar of cloud by day, a pillar of fire by night, is moving before us as before ancient Israel. It is the privilege of Christian parents today, as it was the privilege of God's people of old, to bring their children with them to the Promised Land. *Signs of the Times,* Nov. 24, 1881.

You want a household for God; you want your family for God. You want to take them up to the gates of the city and say, "Here am I, Lord, and the children that Thou hast given me." They may be men and women that have grown to manhood and womanhood, but they are your children all the same; and your educating, and your watchfulness over them have been blessed of God, till they stand as overcomers. Now you can say, "Here am I, Lord, and the children." Manuscript 49, 1894.

Broken Family Chains Will Be Relinked. Jesus is coming, coming with clouds and great glory. A multitude of shining angels will attend Him. He will come to honor those who have loved Him and kept His commandments, and to take them to Himself. He has not forgotten them or His promise. There will be a relinking of the family chain. *Review and Herald,* Nov. 22, 1906.

Comfort for a Bereaved Mother. You inquire in regard to your little one being saved. Christ's words are your answer: "Suffer little children to come unto me, and forbid them not; for of such is the kingdom of God." Remember the prophecy, "Thus saith the Lord: A voice was heard in Ramah, lamentation, and bitter weeping; Rachel weeping for her children refused to be comforted. . . . Thus saith the Lord: Refrain thy voice from weeping and thine eyes from tears; for thy work shall be rewarded, saith the Lord; and they shall come again from the land of the enemy. And there is hope in thine end, saith the Lord, that thy children shall come again to thine own border."

This promise is yours. You may be comforted and trust in the Lord. The Lord has often instructed me that many little ones are to be laid away before the time of trouble. We shall see our children again. We shall meet them and know them in the heavenly courts. Put your trust in the Lord, and be not afraid. Letter 196, 1899.

Children Will Be Borne to Mothers' Arms. Oh, wonderful redemption! long talked of, long hoped for, contemplated with eager anticipation, but never fully understood.

The living righteous are changed "in a moment, in the twinkling of an eye." At the voice of God they were glorified; now they are made immortal and with the risen saints are caught up to meet their Lord in the air. Angels "gather together His elect from the four winds, from one end of heaven to the other." Little children are borne by holy angels to their mothers' arms. Friends long separated by death are united, nevermore to part, and with songs of gladness ascend together to the City of God. *The Great Controversy,* p. 645.

The Day Long Hoped For. From the day when the first pair turned their sorrowing steps from Eden, the children of faith have waited the coming of the Promised

One to break the destroyer's power and bring them again to the lost Paradise. *Ibid., p. 299.*

Heaven will be cheap enough if we obtain it through suffering. . . . As I saw what we must be in order to inherit glory, and then saw how much Jesus had suffered to obtain for us so rich an inheritance, I prayed that we might be baptized into Christ's sufferings, that we might not shrink at trials, but bear them with patience and joy, knowing what Jesus had suffered that we through His poverty and sufferings might be made rich. *Early Writings, p. 67.*

Heaven Is Worth Everything! Heaven is worth everything to us. We must not run any risk in this matter. We must take no venture here. We must know that our steps are ordered by the Lord. May God help us in the great work of overcoming. He has crowns for those that overcome. He has white robes for the righteous. He has an eternal world of glory for those who seek for glory, honor, and immortality. Everyone who enters the City of God will enter it as a conqueror. He will not enter it as a condemned criminal, but as a son of God. And the welcome given to everyone who enters there will be, "Come, ye blessed of my Father, inherit the kingdom prepared for you from the foundation of the world." Matthew 25:34. *Christian Temperance and Bible Hygiene, p. 149.*

Partakers of Christ's Joy. We see a retinue of angels on either side of the gate; and as we pass in, Jesus speaks, "Come, ye blessed of my Father, inherit the kingdom that is prepared for you from the foundation of the world." Here He tells you to be a partaker of His joy, and what is that? It is the joy of seeing of the travail of your soul, fathers. It is the joy of seeing that your efforts, mothers, are rewarded. Here are your children; the crown of life is upon their heads, and the angels of God immortalize the names of the mothers whose efforts have won their children to Jesus Christ. Manuscript 12, 1895.

The Glorious Day of Victory. Now the church is militant. Now we are confronted with a world in darkness, almost wholly given over to idolatry. . . . But the day is coming when the battle will have been fought, the victory won. The will of God is to be done on earth as it is done in heaven. . . . All will be a happy, united family, clothed with the garments of praise and thanksgiving—the robe of Christ's righteousness. All nature, in its surpassing loveliness, will offer to God a tribute of praise and adoration. The world will be bathed in the light of heaven. The light of the moon will be as the light of the sun, and the light of the sun will be sevenfold greater than it is now. The years will move on in gladness. Over the scene the morning stars will sing together, and the sons of God will shout for joy, while God and Christ will unite in proclaiming, "There shall be no more sin, neither shall there be any more death."

These visions of future glory, scenes pictured by the hand of God, should be dear to His children. . . .

We need to keep ever before us this vision of things unseen. It is thus that we shall be able to set a right value on the things of eternity and the things of time. It is this that will give us power to influence others for the higher life. *The Ministry of Healing,* pp. 504-508.

Will God Say, "Well Done"? When you stand before the great white throne, then your work will appear as it is. The books are opened, the record of every life made known. Many in that vast company are unprepared for the revelations made. Upon the ears of some the words will fall with startling distinctness, "Weighed in the balance, and found wanting." To many parents the Judge will say in that day, "You had My Word, plainly setting forth your duty. Why have you not obeyed its teachings? Knew ye not that it was the voice of God? Did I not bid you search the Scriptures, that you might not go astray? You have not only ruined your own souls, but by your pretensions to godliness you have misled many others. You have no part with Me. Depart; depart."

Another class stand pale and trembling, trusting in Christ, and yet oppressed with a sense of their own unworthiness. They hear with tears of joy and gratitude the Master's commendation. The days of incessant toil, of burden bearing, and of fear and anguish are forgotten as that voice, sweeter than the music of angel harps, pronounces the words, "Well done, good and faithful servant, enter ye into the joy of your Lord." There stand the host of the redeemed, the palm branch of victory in their hand, the crown upon their head. These are the ones who by faithful, earnest labor have obtained a fitness for heaven. The lifework performed on earth is acknowledged in the heavenly courts as a work well done.

With joy unutterable, parents see the crown, the robe, the harp, given to their children. The days of hope and fear are ended. The seed sown with tears and prayers may have seemed to be sown in vain, but their harvest is reaped with joy at last. Their children have been redeemed. Fathers, mothers, shall the voices of your children swell the song of gladness in that day? *Signs of the Times,* July 1, 1886.

Scripture Index

Index

462
strive for natural beauty in 398, 413, 424
suited for service 420
to be, appropriate to age 414, 425
    comfortable 422, 425
    neat, attractive, clean 419, 422, 427
to, combine warmth, protection 420, 425
    fit loosely to allow free circulation 425
tight garments hinder heart and lungs 426
wearing of ribbons and bows in 422, 428
Dress, gospel requirements demand many
        to make change in 432
    love of, wrecking happiness of thousands
        435
    many are ambitious to compete with
        neighbors in 417
    of Christ's followers to be symbolic 413
    proper, blessings of 63, 64, 413–418
    self-denial in, part of Christian duty 423,
        424
    temperance in, one of grand principles
        of religious life 394
    See also Apparel
Dress question not to be made main point
        of religion 428, 429
Dressmaking, schools to teach classes in
        357, 358
Drinking, parents to teach good habits of
        187, 364, 394, 406, 407
    world's standards of, not in harmony
        with laws of health 392
Drunkenness, home not to be polluted
        with, of wayward son 241
Duties, everyday, youth to have thorough
        acquaintance with 36, 371
    little, importance of 22, 31, 37, 418
    stern, self-control valuable in grappling
        with 395
Duty, calls of, teach youth to be decided in
        following 202, 355
    neglect of, results in unhappiness, ruin
        235, 258, 332
    parents to be faithful in discharge of 289
Duty and love must be blended 258
Dyspeptics, children grow up, by being
        allowed too much food 388, 391

E

Early rising, mothers to have occasional re-
        lease from 126
Ease, parents too fond of 94
    too much, develops weaklings and

dwarfs 156, 157
Eating, between meals, evil effects of 387,
        388
    children indulged in wrong habits of 406
    God is interested in our habits of 407
    healthful, not a sacrifice, but beneficial
        385
    incorrect habits of, strengthen appetite
        and passion 403
    more danger of, too much than too little
        398
    right habits of, to be taught 187, 362,
        364
    temperance in, principle of religious life
        394
    world's standards of, not in harmony
        with laws of health 392
Eccentricity, mother not to leave mark of,
        on children 71
Economy, God's law incentive to 489
    habit of, requires persevering effort 200
    in cooking, study 376
    teach lessons of 131, 134–136, 189
Eden, loss of, caused by disobedience 79
    Sabbath and family instituted in 535
    the model school 45, 294
Education, begins in earliest years 18, 26,
        28, 32, 297
    Christian, as far as possible, all to have
        privilege of 297, 308
    erroneous, evil results of 406
    highest, that which teaches science of
        Christianity 296, 297, 497
    in early Hebrew home 19
    incomplete without teaching right prin-
        ciples in dress 419
    is religion 494
    motive in, self-seeking and rivalry 293,
        294
    physiology and hygiene basis of all 361
    street, prevented by proper home train-
        ing 115, 123
    to be obtained without sacrificing health
        340
    true, defined 293–299
    value of song in 523
    will continue through eternity 298
Educational advantages not to induce youth
        to worldly schools 328
Efficiency, result of proper concept of labor
        348

Exhaustion, results of self-abuse 444
Exhibition, of children, avoid 38
Experience, every, Bible study preparation
for 508
Extravagance, in dress, evil results of 415,
416, 434
not to be indulged 134, 135, 201
Extremes, shun in dress 414, 415
Extremities to be properly clothed 426
Eye, God's, upon all 152, 165

F

Face, See Countenance
Faculties, all, quickened by useful exercise
340, 347
to be developed, in education 154,
156, 332, 333
moral and intellectual, weakened by
stimulating food 188
teach children early to use all 120
Failure, if eternity left out of reckoning 497,
498
in afterlife, result of indulgence in youth
181
Faintness, food eaten before bedtime because of sense of 389
See also Weakness
Faith, in Christ, gives strength to character
165
teach in early years 508
parents to build fortification of, around
children 185
persevering, bring children to Jesus with
172
Faith and works to be combined 25, 66
Faithfulness and love, with firmness, happiness from 258
Faithfulness in home tasks, school to teach
320
insects teach lessons of 59
False and superficial exalted above the real
and natural 188
False balances, abomination to God 152
Falsehoods, children utter 233
how parents encourage 274
not hidden from God 153
parents should not give slightest occasion
for 150
See also Lies
Families, children in, to become educating
force 86
affection and authority places right mold

on 240
association in work, study, recreation
535
children's first duty to come into right
relation to 99
Christian, to present to world well-disciplined children 233
dressing for display 434, 435
every, a church 549
firmness, a decision, positive requirements essential in 264
happiness in, how promoted 79, 176,
276, 484
health and happiness of, depends on the
cook 371
indulgence of children brings disgrace to
178
many, unprepared to meet God 555
preparation made for visitors, but not for
386
rightly governed will influence church
548, 551
safeguarded by Bible principles 507, 508
to be channel through which virtue,
kindness, love flow 271
to eat with gladness, gratitude, cheerfulness 387
will pass in review before God 561, 562
Family altar, every family to have 517
See Family worship
Family chain, broken, will be relinked in
heaven 565-567
Family circle, love of God to be pleasant
theme in 42
place temperance on elevated platform
in 400
Family community, perplexities of a 289
Family firm, children to be made to feel a
part of 119, 126
Family happiness, three essentials to 365, 366
Family worship 520-524
Farmer, few enjoy so real an independence
as 356
requires more grace than missionary 358
Fashion considered more important than
character 162
do not sacrifice children to 181
fascinating power of 432-436
foolish, not to be followed 415
influence of, devotion to 419, 421
let children enjoy nature, not shackled to

physical and moral, of children, highest
  duty of parents 187, 188
relationship of exercise to 339-344
ruined by secret vice 446, 450-455, 458
to be first study of young 103
true pleasures do not impair 467
understanding of, philosophy, safeguard
  against evil 362
Health and morality, recklessness in one,
  leads to same in other 104
Health habits, right, insist on 364
Health principles, how to teach 103-105
Health reform, God sent light on 396, 461
  parents to know and teach 104, 409
  poor cooking makes, health deform 372
  See also Reform
Healthful living a family matter 104
Heart, converted, conforms to God's Word
  429, 430
  love the key to child's 66, 271
  natural tendencies of 202, 214, 233, 275,
    302, 416, 421, 439, 440, 533
  preparation of, for public worship 541-
    543
  purity of 27, 418, 475
  rebellion established in, by wrong disci-
    pline 237, 246, 262, 279, 281,
    282, 286
  Satan watching to sow seed of tares in
    child's 23, 31, 195
  yielding, to Christ breaks Satan's power
    260, 287, 475, 476
Hearts, of children, easily impressed 45, 149,
  498
  inspire, with noble purposes 148, 151,
    204, 243, 244, 249, 252, 265
  of, faith, to be channels of God's power 43
  parents, need to be softened by grace
    of Christ 260
Heaven, attributes of 110, 353, 354
  barred to those who indulge in self-
    abuse 444, 452
  children to be prepared for 17, 170, 190,
    311, 477, 487, 488
  entered only by, obedient 84, 224
    those of perfected character 481
  faithful training manifest in 564, 565
  home life to typify 99, 143, 548, 549
  is worth everything 567, 568
  open to mother's prayers 525, 526
  pictorial record in, of thoughts, words,

actions 562, 563
righteousness of Christ only dress admitted into 418
spirit of, is spirit of ministry 296
we shall meet and know our children in
  566, 567
will of God is law of 79
Hebrews, homes of, education in 18, 19, 32
  lessons in reverence from instruction to
    541
Heights, weakest may reach seemingly impossible 167
Helplessness, children trained in, by being
  waited on 129
Helpfulness, habits of, parents to teach 36,
  119-121, 127
  in home, learn at school 320
  lessons of, children to practice 306
  parents to be examples of 478
Heredity, laws of, parents to understand 63,
  64
Heritage, of the Lord, children are 229
  of a spoiled child 274
Holiness, achieved when appetites controlled by reason 378
  beauty of, 95, 147
  children to walk in path of 31, 417
  many parents far from 73
  practice of 396, 467
Holy Spirit, aids parents in training children
  256
  cannot, cooperate with negligent parents
    232
    soften hearts of many disobedient
      children 550
  children grieve the 41
  fruits of, are elements of character 173
  influence of, nullified by cross words
    219
  opens Bible treasures to children 495,
    496
  parents need 69, 70, 95, 215, 282, 478
  strengthens every purpose and resolution
    167
  to, be allowed to influence child 150
    depend upon, to form character 172
Holy things, hatred for, result of wrong
  discipline 87
Home, allow no selfishness in 143
  and the temperance crusade 401-409
  beauty of, noise not to spoil 97

Usefulness, life of, power lies within every
youth to live 209
of men ruined because economy unlearned 135, 136
of youth, crippled by lack of employment 350, 355
result of careful training 169

V

Vanity, children to be taught they cannot
live life of 42
in dress, frequently leads to ruin of character 416
mind that lives in pure, holy atmosphere
will not have 188
not to be fostered by praise or showy
dress 139
seeds of, sown in babyhood 140, 178
unfits youth for heaven 37
Vegetables, fresh, all to become acquainted
with value of 357
Veins contracted when limbs improperly
clad 426
Ventilation, attention to be given to 365
Vice, corrupting, prevalence of 439-443
exists in Sabbathkeeping families 440
knowledge of, cookery helps build barrier against 376
is passed from youth to youth 443
much, could be prevented if parents sustained teacher's authority 334
parents to keep children from paths of
33, 457
soul-debasing, duty to stand free from all
447
Vice, secret. See Self-abuse
Victory, early habits decide future 202
gained by mother of great value to children 217
glorious day of, coming 568
parents gain, by correct discipline 253
press on until, is gained 362
the Lord gains a, for the praying mother
212
through daily surrender 483
Vigilance, eternal, must be exercised by
parents 474
Violence, parents never to manifest 205
Virtue, family to be channel through
which, flows 271
modest a guard to 144, 417
of Joseph, result of early training 197

Virtues, diligent effort required to cherish 200
instill, from babyhood 193
Visitors, invite, to join in Bible study 511
teach children how to treat 97
Vitality, decreased, by eating between meals
388
irregularity in meals 387
Vivacity, of children, outdoor activity essential to 339
Voice, do not raise, when correcting child
246
soft tones of, influence of 93, 240
tone of, copied by children 215, 482
not changed by E. G. White in disciplining children 254
to betray no irritation 261
watch, as well as words 219
Voice culture, importance of 364, 365
Voltaire, life of, influenced by early training
196

W

Wages, high, not to induce youth to
worldly schools 328
Washing clothes, boys to understand 351
children to do own 125, 126
honor religion in 348
Waste, avoid in cooking 376
Watchfulness, faithful, children will bless
parents for 242
Weaklings, too much ease develops 156, 157
Weakness, sense of, when flesh food is dis-
continued 384
See also Faintness
Wealthy not to excuse from practical train-
ing 342, 349
Weariness, causes of 341, 365, 462
Well-doing, parents not to become weary
in 94, 242
Whims of children not to be indulged 194
Whipping, one, may be enough for lifetime
250
Whispering during sermon 542, 546
White, E. G., experience of, in administer-
ing discipline 249, 251, 253
methods used by, in protecting own sons
115
provides land for church school at
Sanitarium, Calif. 315
Wickedness traced to neglect of parents to
discipline themselves and children 276